823995
24184

3495

TRIALS
Canada 1
AND THE 1983 AMERICA'S CUP

TRIALS
Canada 1
AND THE 1983 AMERICA'S CUP

JEFF BOYD
DOUG HUNTER

Macmillan of Canada
A Division of Gage Publishing Limited
Toronto, Canada

Canadian Cataloguing in Publication Data

Boyd, Jeff, date.
  Trials: Canada 1 and the 1983 America's Cup

ISBN 0-7715-9805-X

1. Canada 1 (Yacht). 2. America's Cup races.
I. Hunter, Doug, date. II. Title.

GV830.1983.B6 1984   797.1′4   C84-099001-4

DESIGNED by William Fox/Associates

EDITED by Robin Brass

Macmillan of Canada
A Division of Gage Publishing Limited

Printed in Canada

Portions of this book have appeared in a similar form in
GAM on Yachting.

For Deb, and
for James and Joyce

table of contents

foreword

My first look at a 12-Metre was from a distance. After visiting friends on Long Island in August of 1981, I spent a day and a half in Newport, looking at the town, the mansions and, of course, the harbour. I recall standing at the end of a pier, admiring the hundreds of sailboats, pleasure cruisers, and yachts of every description. Suddenly, my eyes caught sight of two sails way across the harbour that were strikingly different from all of the others. They were taller by far, almost too tall for the length of their hulls, thrusting like huge, white knife blades from the water into the sky.

Not only did their appearance seem unusual, but their movements did as well. They were manoeuvring with unexpected precision and speed for their size – tacking one way, then the other, coming about, tacking again, back and forth, as if in a highly disciplined training exercise. I could just make out what seemed to be a crew of a dozen or so on each boat, and they appeared to be working in total unison. Upon being told that they were 12-Metre boats, I vaguely remember thinking, "Oh, that's interesting." But I placed no great significance on the classification, only on their appearance, which was impressive, to say the least.

Little did I know that I would be returning to Newport the following summer, and often again during the next, with much more than a casual interest in these "Twelves".

On May 3, 1982, I received a telephone call from a representative of a public-relations firm which was helping to organize a publicity and fund-raising campaign. Was I interested in sailing? Had I ever heard of the America's Cup? Would I be interested in creating a painting or prints to assist their cause, which was a Canadian challenge for the Cup? Could we meet? My answer was yes to all of the above, and we had a number of meetings. On July 19, I attended a press conference, where Marvin McDill announced plans for the first Canadian challenge for the America's Cup in 102 years.

However, over the course of the summer, nothing further materialized toward my being able to proceed with the project. Everything was in limbo, the result of the challenge's financial difficulties.

I was assured that it would be only a matter of time before things began moving again. Meanwhile, I felt the need to prepare for my work, if it was to materialize, through personal experience and research. I read numerous articles and books on the history of the cup and the Twelves. With permission, I visited Deep Harbour and had a first-hand look at the huge, sleek and rather mottled-looking aluminum hull of *Canada 1*, which was sitting in this vast old building awaiting completion.

Occasionally an article would appear in the press predicting that the entire enterprise was about to be abandoned. While my enthusiasm remained, the weeks dragged on with no word. I was becoming anxious to have an opportunity to see a Twelve in action before winter arrived, as I was afraid that I'd be asked to create a painting without having this chance (if and when the project got going again).

Then I was told that some of the Canadian team were about to compete in the Xerox Cup, being held off Newport in late September, and would be sailing *Clipper*, their trial horse. I decided not to wait any longer for "official whenevers" and arrived in Newport September 22, just in time to learn that the Canadians had won their first race that afternoon. Their spirits were high, but tempered with a grim determination to prove they were capable of competing against the more experienced teams.

I watched, listened, and learned. I followed the races daily aboard *Slapshot*, the Canadian tender. I met the crew and the support team, and heard the stories and the hopes and frustrations of many. While I did a large amount of observing (and a modest amount of sketching), I was becoming more and more infected with the optimism and confidence displayed by this group, while simultaneously coming to share their anxiety about their very shaky financial support.

I realized that what I was seeing was not a collection of well-heeled individuals out for a fun regatta, or a group of misfits on a lark. These were dedicated sailors – in fact, athletes, with a keen determination to represent Canada in the premier event of sailing, the America's Cup.

They came within a protest decision of winning the Xerox Cup, and certainly proved that they had the ability. What they needed desperately was support!

I felt that if the public could only be moved to understand and appreciate what this team was trying to achieve for Canada, it would respond.

Upon returning home, my enthusiasm became somewhat contagious and resulted in the first fund-raising dinner for *Canada 1*, a $50-a-plate affair held in Guelph, at the well-known restaurant Churchill's Landing, on November 13. We raised $5500, enough for a spinnaker.

Later, a series of dinners across the country repeated this example on a larger scale as the *Canada 1* syndicate worked hard to gain a response from the public.

Meanwhile, *Canada 1* was finally launched and the opportunity arrived for me to see the boat perform in Lake Ontario. She was a beautiful sight to behold – and certainly an inspiration for an artist. During the course of a few shakedown cruises, I even had the privilege of taking the helm, which was a thrill indeed!

I began a series of watercolours, one of which featured *Canada 1* racing with *Clipper* and became the official poster, and finally did a large egg-tempera portrait of *Canada 1* herself. This was unveiled in July in Toronto, along with a limited edition of reproduction prints of the painting offered for sale. The result was another $250,000 for the challenge.

Of course, my visits to Newport during the summer of 1983 culminated in race-watching, as I shared the emotions of our uphill battle to become the official challenger.

There are too many memories for me to relate here. But, as with most experiences, they can best be condensed within the framework of personal encounters and people experiences. In the end, this is what remains most vivid.

I was encouraged to share worlds with many new friends and am grateful for the opportunity. I experienced and learned a great deal and developed a strong awareness of the personal challenges and dedication involved in the world of sailing. I can't imagine a finer group of individuals to learn from than those who banded together and devoted themselves to representing Canada so admirably in the 1983 America's Cup.

This book is their story.

Ken Danby
Guelph Township
May 23, 1984

introduction

We – Jeff Boyd and Doug Hunter – first met at the Toronto International Boat Show in January 1983, where *Canada 1* was displayed to drum up support for this country's America's Cup challenge. In the midst of a 20-minute conversation, Doug mentioned that he had been approached by the syndicate in the summer of 1982 with the idea of him authoring an official account of the challenge, which he had turned down.

"Why don't you do one anyway?" Jeff suggested. "What do you need the challenge's approval for?"

By the end of this highly productive first encounter, we had decided to write together the book you now have in your hands. Over the next eight months, while Jeff sailed on *Canada 1* and her trial horse, *Clipper,* Doug paid a week-long visit to the Miami Beach training camp and made three trips to the Canadian base in Newport. Doug returned to Newport in September for the opening week of the final match between *Liberty* and *Australia II*. In the fall we divided up responsibility for interviews and then went to work shaping our raw material – interviews, documents, diaries, on-board race tapes and our own recollections – into a manuscript.

In putting the story to paper, we encountered a stylistic headache. How were we to treat Jeff, who was both a co-author and a major character? We considered periodically interrupting the story to allow Jeff to speak directly to the reader. Our publisher and our editor wisely recognized an enormous potential for clumsiness and confusion, and we followed their advice in blending the story into a single voice. This made for a seamless narrative, but it left Jeff with the queer experience of writing about himself in the third person. The reader should bear in mind that, whenever Jeff appears in the story, he is being discussed by a narrative point of view best described as Jeffdoug.

This book would not have been possible without the help of a number of people. We would like to thank our publisher, Doug Gibson, for showing enthusiasm and support for this project well before the America's Cup summer even began. Doug Hunter must also thank the Ontario Arts

Council, whose support made his visits to Miami Beach and Newport possible.

For their time and observations, we thank Terry McLaughlin, Peter Wilson, Cedric Gyles, Don Green, Bruce Kirby, Steve Killing, Sam Lazier, Tom Wroe, Hans Fogh, Richard Storer, Hugh Drake, Brook Hamilton, Jay McKinnell and Jimmy Johnston. We are particularly indebted to Sandy Andrews for the use of his journals, which were crucial to our account of training camp life, and to Doug Keary, who volunteered us his most useful desk diary. A note of appreciation goes out to Robert Martin, who provided the tape of Dennis Conner's closing speech after the final race of the historic match with *Australia II*. We must also salute Gord Crothers, who let us break his photocopier, and our editor, Robin Brass, who normally excises such an accolade but whose powers of censorship have been short-circuited in this instance. Once again, we thank you all.

Jeff Boyd
Doug Hunter

1

kingston

The world's best sailors aren't at the America's Cup. It's a fact. . . . But the America's Cup, it's something you've heard about since you were a kid. There's a mystique, an aura about it.

> – Dennis Conner, quoted in *The Grand Gesture*, by
> Roger Vaughan, 1974.

It was in the seventh grade, on the way home from school, that Jeff Boyd, who would become *Canada 1*'s tactician, was told by Peter Wilson, who would become its navigator, that if Montreal won the right to host the 1976 Olympic Games, Kingston was sure to be selected as the site of the yachting events. Wilson had acquired that intriguing nugget of speculation from one of his teachers, an avid sailor who happened to be the wife of the future president of Queen's University. The teacher was, of course, quite right: a multimillion-dollar yachting facility was built at Portsmouth Harbour, in the shadow of Kingston Penitentiary, and in 1969 the very best of racing yachtsmen from around the world began an annual summer trek to compete in the Canadian Olympic Training Regatta at Kingston, or CORK, founded to provide aspiring Canadian small-boat sailors with a first-rate competitive forum in which to hone their skills for the Games. CORK would outlive the Games to become an institution in Canadian sailing and a premier multi-class international event; the Olympics had provided the impetus to transform an already active sailing community into one of the country's most important sailing centres.

For many sailors, the America's Cup represents their loftiest ambition, but as a seventh-grader Jeff Boyd was a novice to sailing and the cup meant nothing to him. Even at the age of 26, when the opportunity to take part in an America's Cup campaign was all but upon him, his attitude toward the event was indifferent. As a boy, it was the noble heights of the Olympic Games that appealed most. Whether it was in hockey, or track and field, or some other sport, participating in the event that most exemplified noble amateurism was his ultimate ambition; sailing was a side interest at best. His first season in the Kingston Yacht Club's junior program had so terrified him that it had taken a friend the winter to persuade him to return for a second summer. All the same, the idea of the world's best at anything and the glory of the Games simultaneously descending upon the quiet city of Kingston was, a schoolboy had to admit, pretty amazing.

Dennis Conner's charge for the gold medal was over. By the start of the seventh and final race of the series, John Albrechtson and Ingvar Hansson were almost 16 points ahead of Conner and Conn Findlay. It was a triumphant series for the Swedes. At Kiel in 1972 they had finished a frustrating fourth. In any other world-class regatta a fourth-place finish would be a source of pride, but the Olympic Games honour the top three finishers far above all others. With only one entry allowed per class from each country, the competitors at the Olympics may not be as uniformly first-rate as those at a world championship, but the pressure is much higher. And in the Tempest class at the 1976 Olympic Games, there was enough talent to make the medal race a true struggle. In addition to Albrechtson and Conner, there were the 1974 and 1975 world champions, Uwe Mares of West Germany and Giuseppe Milone of Italy; Valentin Mankin of the Soviet Union, who had won the Tempest gold medal in 1972 as well as the gold medal in the one-man Finn class in 1968; and Alan Warren of Great Britain, the 1972 silver medallist in Tempests. Warren would be so disgusted with his 14th-place standing in the 16-boat fleet that he would douse his obviously outmoded boat in paint thinner and set fire to it shortly after the finish of the final race. With the gold medal, the only medal that Dennis Conner believed counted, all but assured to the Swedes, it was left to him to defend his bronze medal position against Mares, who had won the sixth race, and perhaps steal the silver from Mankin. For Conner, the final race was an exercise in salvaging the best result from an Olympic drive that had aspired to nothing short of perfection.

The road to the Games had been far from perfect, though nevertheless remarkable. The son of a commercial fisherman, Dennis Conner had grown up within a stone's throw of the San Diego Yacht Club and developed his racing skills by sailing for, with and against the best sailors in California, who also happened to be some of the best in the world. It was a tremendous environment in which to prepare oneself to become the world's best in sailing, a goal that became the focal point of Conner's life. In his autobiography, *No Excuse to Lose*, shaped into a book in 1978 by John Rousmaniere, Conner speaks of his feelings of inferiority as a child – of the other families at the San Diego Yacht Club being wealthier than his, of feeling not particularly attractive physically – which may or may not have contributed to his need to excel. Whatever his psychological motivation, he craved competition and achieved a remarkable series of successes. To the surprise of almost everyone, including himself, he won the world championship of the Maserati of one-design classes, the Star, in 1971. He conquered the prestigious invitation match racing event, the Congressional Cup, in 1973 and again in 1975. The America's Cup fell to him on his first try in 1974, when he was invited aboard the eventual defender, *Courageous*, to serve as tactician and starting helmsman after the woeful *Mariner* was eliminated from under him. And offshore fleet racing surrendered in 1975 when Conner helmed his One Tonner, *Stinger*, to victory in the Southern Ocean Racing Conference (SORC) series.

But the Olympic Games had consistently eluded him. Conner failed to make the American team in the Star class in 1968 and 1972, and when it came time to qualify for the 1976 team, the Star had been dropped from Olympic competition. After surveying the six existing Olympic classes, Conner settled on the Tempest, a two-man, trapezing keelboat. In the summer of 1975, Conner bought two Tempests, the second boat being for experts he invited to San Diego to train with him. His program was late getting off the ground, and he needed all the help he could get.

It was one of Conner's great strengths: though his tally of regatta victories gave him tremendous self-confidence and an equally tremendous ego, he was never above asking for the advice or input of lesser mortals with useful experience. Conner was a born learner. In San Diego in December of 1975, he learned much about the basics of the Tempest by pacing with Allan Leibel and his cousin, Lorne, who would represent Canada in the class at the Games.

Conner sailed in only four Tempest regattas before the Games, but he learned his lessons well. Success in one-design racing depends in part on equipment, in part on technique, in part on tactics and in part on psychology. Conner had chosen as his crew the strapping, 45-year-old Conn Findlay, who had been a winch grinder aboard *Mariner* and would sail aboard *Courageous* under Ted Turner in 1977 and serve as a spare crew with the *Defender/Courageous* syndicate in 1983. Findlay already had three Olympic medals – in rowing. Competing in coxed pairs, he had won the gold in 1956 and 1964 and a bronze in 1960. Conner understood well the nuances that separate one yacht design from another in the same manner that different airplanes or automobiles stand apart. He and Findlay came to function as a team, and technique was well taken care of. Tactics? Conner had proven he was a winner. *No excuse to lose*. If he was determined, and thorough, there was no reason why a gold medal couldn't be his. Equipment? That was a more practical matter. Find out what the Europeans were using to make them so fast, and go get it. Or copy it. He also paid careful attention to the way he tuned up and laid out his boat, and developed clever, simple adjustment systems. Then he won the American trials and moved on to Kingston.

After two races, it looked as though Conner's preparations were paying off. He had finished second twice; under the Olympic scoring system he led Albrechtson and Mankin, both with a first and a fourth, by two points. But then he began to fall off the pace, finishing third and fifth while the Swedes racked up a second and a first. The fifth race delivered Conner the opportunity to redeem himself. He performed magnificently on the opening leg. Hitting the wind shifts with great precision, he opened up a lead of well over three minutes. By the time he reached the gybe mark, though, the race had degenerated into a nightmare. The breeze had steadily deteriorated until Conner was left helpless in a flat calm. When the new breeze filled in, it came from astern, bringing with it the rest of Tempest fleet, and the Flying Dutchmans and Solings as well. The wind created a maddening traffic jam and turned the final weather leg into a spinnaker run. Conner, overrun, fell back to ninth place; the Russians finished second, the Swedes seventh.

The fiasco of the fifth race generated 24 protests from the six separate fleets, including one by Conner. It was argued that the bizarre winds had not provided a fair test of the skills that an Olympic regatta was meant to assess. The jury disagreed, and the race stood. "I had to remember losing that enormous lead," Conner would tell Rousmaniere. "It took the heart right out of me; it was the worst downer I have ever had in a sailboat."

Shortly after the start of race six, Conn Findlay's port trapeze handle broke. Conner hung in and collected a fourth. Uwe Mares of West Germany won the race, leaving him only seven-tenths of a point behind the Americans in fourth. Albrechtson finished second to solidify his position atop the standings. Mankin's third kept him in second, 7.3 points ahead of Conner. To keep his bronze medal, Conner would have to finish ahead of Mares; if he were to steal the silver from Mankin, the Russian would have to finish fifth or worse, and Conner would have to win.

The wind was 15 knots from the southwest, a good, steady lake breeze. At the weather mark, Conner held the lead. Mankin was fifth. Albrechtson, who had denied Conner his gold medal, was in second and gaining, threatening to spoil his final stab at the silver. At the gybe mark, Conner led by about 80 yards, but the Swedes continued to press, and at last went through. Conner hung on to second place. Mankin hung on to fifth, and the silver medal, leaving Conner to consider that a bronze medal was better than no medal at all.

For five months, Conner rested. He got back in the saddle by winning his second Star worlds, in 1977. Then, again, the mystique of the America's Cup beckoned, and Conner set off down a competitive path that would lead to a disappointment far deeper than that delivered in the fifth race of the Kingston Games.

In Kiel in 1972, John Bertrand had the bronze medal in the Finn class within his grasp with one race to go. That final race ended in huge disappointment, with the 26-year-old Australian slipping into fourth place. After five races in Kingston in 1976, Bertrand's position again seemed secure. Andrei Balashov of the Soviet Union headed the standings, with Bertrand in second, trailing by only three points. Two points behind Bertrand was Jochen Schumann, a 21-year-old medical student from East Germany. A relatively comfortable 13 points separated Schumann from Claudio Bierkarck of Brazil, the silver medalist at the 1976 Pan American Games.

Though he would describe himself in a North Sails newsletter after the 1980 America's Cup as "more of a tactician than a boat-speed person," in Kingston Bertrand was a self-described "speed merchant." At once affable and intense, he seemed determined, where Dennis Conner was driven. If John Bertrand wanted to win boat races, Dennis Conner simply wanted to *win*. Having captured two Australian dinghy championships by the age of 16, Bertrand was 24 when he came to the United States in 1970 as a headsail trimmer aboard the cup challenger *Gretel II*. He stayed to earn a Master's Degree in Ocean Engineering at the Massachusetts Institute of Technology. In 1975 he began training as a sailmaker under the wings of Americans Chuck Miller and Peter Barrett of the North Sails empire, an organization dedicated to research and development which operates lofts worldwide. When he wasn't training in his Finn, he was cutting very fast sails in Barrett's Wisconsin loft; his Finn sail, T3+B, was for years one of the most durable shapes of speed in the class. And after five races in Kingston, he looked like a legitimate contender for the gold medal. After six races, he looked as if he might not win a medal at all.

His undoing came in the late stages of race six. It was breezy, and the Finn, an outmoded design, is notorious for becoming more unstable the faster it goes, particularly downwind. Approaching the leeward mark that indicated the beginning of the final windward leg, Schumann of East Germany led the fleet. Bertrand, in third, capsized. Though it could have been disaster, Bertrand managed to get himself back in the race and salvaged a respectable fifth, one place behind the Russian, Balashov. Schumann finished second, which left him tied for first overall with Balashov. For Bertrand, the most damaging performance came from Bierkarck, who had passed Schumann on the final leg to win the race and hoist himself to within three points. of third place. Again, Bertrand found himself entering the final race of an Olympic regatta with a slender grip on the bronze medal.

Bertrand's strategy was simple: stay ahead of Bierkarck and the medal would be his. While Schumann and Balashov fought their own battle over the gold medal, Bertrand stuck to Bierkarck like glue, and the two rounded the weather mark about mid-fleet. Schumann finished third to Balashov's fifth to earn the gold medal. One place behind Balashov was Bertrand. Bierkarck never recovered from the opening leg, placing eleventh to end the regatta in fourth. The bronze was Bertrand's. Whereas Dennis Conner mulled over the value of his medal, Bertrand rejoiced. In time, in Newport, the Australian would be an undisputed champion.

There is a finite number of world-class yachtsmen, and a finite number of world-class events. Paths cross and intertwine, and by the time an event of the magnitude of the 1983 America's Cup comes along, many of the key players have already shared the same race course, sometimes even the same boat. (There is no better example than the fact that John Bertrand crewed for Dennis Conner during one SORC.) In Newport in 1983, the waterfront was crowded with mutually familiar faces. Many acquaintances bridged the barriers supposedly separating rival camps and, in the case of Tom Blackaller, skipper of the American 12-Metre *Defender,* and Cino Ricci, the mastermind of the Italian *Azzurra*, there existed a bond of friendship so strong that their cooperation seemed to bend the spirit of the match's nationality rules well past the breaking point.

The Kingston Olympics were a fine example of an event where the paths of the sailing elite crossed. Of the ten 12-Metres competing in 1983 to defend or challenge for the America's Cup, eight had at least one crew member with competitive roots reaching back to Kingston – six featured skippers who sailed in the Games. As we have seen, Dennis Conner and John Bertrand were there. Mauro Pelaschier, who would helm Italy's *Azzurra*, finished ninth in the Finn. *France 3*'s tactician, Patrick Haegeli, helmed a Soling; *France 3*'s skipper, Bruno Troublé, was one of his crew. John Kolius, the skipper of the defence contender *Courageous,* won a silver medal in the Soling class. Another Soling helmsman in Kingston, Iain MacDonald-Smith, became the sail coordinator for Britain's *Victory '83* challenge. One of *Victory 83*'s helmsmen, Rodney Pattisson, won a silver medal in the Flying Dutchman; another of the British challenger's helmsmen, Phil Crebbin, sailed a 470, and his 470 crew, Derek Clark, became *Victory 83*'s navigator. Mike Fletcher, the coach of the Australian Olympic sailing team, became the tactician and coach of Melbourne's *Challenge 12*. Only *Advance*, from Sydney, and Tom Blackaller's *Defender* lacked significant ties to Kingston.

There were also links at the managerial and judicial end. The Director of Sailing for the 1976 Olympics was Livius Sherwood, a provincial court justice from Ottawa whose experience in the America's Cup would lead to his appointment as Chairman of the International Jury for the 1983 match. One of the four jurors who would serve under him in 1983 was Robert Sloane of Mexico, a member of the International Jury in Kingston. All three American members of the Kingston jury held strong ties to the America's Cup. Robert Bavier, the skipper of the victorious *Constellation* in 1964, who was removed from the helm of *Courageous* during the defender's trials in 1974, was a member of the New York Yacht Club's America's Cup Committee in 1983. F. Gregg Bemis served on the 1983 Challengers' Jury. And George Hinman, who died before the 1983 match, was a past Commodore of the New York Yacht Club and a regular supporter of defence syndicates.

The Canadian 12-Metre effort of 1983, too, had links. Ignoring a myriad of managerial bonds between 1976 and 1983, there was Hans Fogh, who sailed his Flying Dutchman to fourth place in Kingston and would become one of *Canada 1*'s two sailmakers. His Olympic crew, Evert Bastet, would become a headsail trimmer of *Canada 1*. The 1976 Olympic team's spare crew, Dave Shaw, would serve as *Canada 1*'s mast man. The connections in the crew ended with Shaw though. Like *Canada 1*'s skipper, they were simply too young or inexperienced to participate in the Games at Kingston.

Terry McLaughlin came to Kingston for the last two races of the Games, watching first the 470s and Finns and then the Solings, Tempests and Flying Dutchmans. He had just turned 20, and the lake was dotted with yachtsmen whose competitor he would become in Newport in 1983.

McLaughlin was a promising young sailor who had represented Canada in the 1972 and 1974 World Youth Championships in 420s, finishing fourth and sixth. His father, Paul, was a respected small-boat sailor who had represented Canada in the 1948 and 1952 Olympics, finishing fifth in the single-handed Firefly in 1948. In 1952 Paul was eighth in the Finn, one position behind an Italian named Adelchi Pelaschier, who would again finish seventh in the class in 1956, again one position ahead of a Canadian, Bruce Kirby. Paul McLaughlin's son, oblivious to his own destiny, watched a Finn fleet in Kingston that included Adelchi Pelaschier's son, Mauro, who would continue his family's tradition of edging out Canadians by finishing one position ahead of Terry in the 1983 America's Cup challengers' trials.

There is a gentlemanliness about Paul McLaughlin that may come to Terry with age. For the time being, Terry is engaging, often hilarious and prankish – he once allowed about a dozen friends attired in jeans to infiltrate a Kingston drinking establishment with a dress code by lending them his corduroys, which they successively donned to get through the door while Terry sat at his table in his underwear. He is sure of himself; he delights in confrontations and dares, and his adversaries often lose because their threshold of self-confidence is substantially lower than his. But Terry also shares his father's capacity for silence, which can reduce communication to a simple shrug, and for icy determination, and exquisiteness at the helm. He is a winner because he has achieved that precarious balance within himself between the knowledge that he has every right to succeed and the capacity, ingrained in him by his father, to ruthlessly criticize and dissect his own mistakes.

Following in his father's footsteps, Terry prepared himself for the Olympic Games. His initial campaign was conceived with low expectations. Teaming up with Richard Zimmerman, he sailed a Flying Dutchman once owned by Hans Fogh in a few regattas before entering the 1976 Olympic trials. Fogh won the trials and advanced to the Games. McLaughlin finished fourth and headed for the spectator seats.

After the Games, Fogh moved into the Soling class. His crew, Evert Bastet, joined McLaughlin aboard a Flying Dutchman with the 1980 Olympics in mind. In their first season together they struggled, but capped it with a win at CORK, which made them the Canadian champions. The victory qualified McLaughlin for the national sailing team – Bastet was already a member.

In 1978 they travelled to Europe for the first time to sail in Kiel Week, the 1972 Olympic site's version of CORK, and placed third in the 100-boat fleet. It was the beginning of a one-boat Canadian dynasty. They became the North American champions in 1979 and qualified for the 1980 Canadian Olympic team.

Then came the western boycott of the Moscow Games, prompted by the invasion of Afghanistan. At first McLaughlin was understanding, or at least tried to be. But he began to resent the decision; he felt cheated, sensing that the athletes were being asked to sacrifice far more than the average citizen or businessman. In 1980 McLaughlin and Bastet won the Flying Dutchman world championship. It was more than apparent that in the summer of 1980 Terry McLaughlin was a favourite to win a gold medal. Politics had taken that opportunity away from him. His dissatisfaction became more public as he fell in with Larry Woods, the national team Tornado skipper, and he became a coorganizer of the team's July 19 boycott party. Though he was not without feelings for Canada, in the future McLaughlin would scoff at any suggestion that an amateur athlete went into competition for the glory of his country. That was a sorry, manipulative ruse. McLaughlin was in this game for himself.

Jeff Boyd first got to know Terry McLaughlin at the 1975 Canadian Laser Championship, sailed on Montreal's Lac St. Louis. Boyd had finished 13th in the 108-boat fleet at the first Laser Worlds, in Bermuda in 1974. (How the paths of the sailing elite intertwined. Gary Jobson, who was destined to become an America's Cup tactician, was 11th. Buried in the 30s, and not to be confused with the Australian of the same name, was an American named John Bertrand, who would win several Laser and Finn Worlds and serve as tactician on *Courageous* in 1983.) They had met for the first time in 1974 at the Ontario Youth Championships in Trenton. The youth regatta had been Boyd's second Laser event, and he finished third. McLaughlin sailed one of the worst series of his life, and Boyd saw little of the sailor whose reputation even then preceded him.

The Canadian Laser Championship served to bring them together, if only because they found themselves locked in a two-boat struggle for the same trophy. McLaughlin started the regatta well with two seconds; Boyd was courting oblivion with a 45th and a 13th. In the next race, Boyd led the fleet around the entire course. One hundred yards from the finish line, he sailed into a patch of weeds and fell back to fifth. McLaughlin made it known that he thought it was the funniest thing that had happened to anybody, ever. That gave Boyd a jolt; it made him wonder what this McLaughlin person was all about.

The next day, Boyd opened with a first and a third. He was rocketing up through the standings. McLaughlin was struggling, barely holding on to his lead. Boyd now bore watching, and before the start of the last race McLaughlin told him that he guessed he'd better start covering him.

At the weather mark of the final race, Boyd had the regatta won. He rounded third; McLaughlin was back in the 20s. But Terry fought back on the reaches, and at the finish was fifth. On the way back to harbour, each thought the other had won the regatta. The scoreboard showed that McLaughlin had prevailed, by 1.25 points.

Boyd's first impression of McLaughlin was that he was a bit of a loud-mouth. Whenever he became involved in a game of touch football, an essential part of regatta activities, the contest seemed to degenerate into the world versus the Royal Canadian Yacht Club, his prestigious home base in Toronto. At once annoying and endearing, the tendency revealed an essential part of Terry, a compulsion to escalate play to some higher plane of motivation and competitiveness. There began an intense rivalry between him and Boyd in a variety of sports. Boyd stands six feet tall and is solidly built. McLaughlin's wiry body, his angular face with sunken cheeks, conceals the 170 fit pounds distributed over his own six-foot frame. Though Boyd always pushed McLaughlin to the limit, the majority of decisions went Terry's way, and he managed to accumulate a telling psychological advantage over Boyd. When he is ahead, he is a hard man to break; when he is behind, he draws on a reserve of confidence that seems to carry him through the most difficult situations.

In the fall of 1975, following his win at the Laser Nationals, Terry McLaughlin came to Queen's to earn an Honours B.A. in Economics. There was a sailing team of sorts at the university. The appeal of the team was not tremendous. Doug Harvey, a fine sailor, had not even bothered to show up for the 1973 trials. Boyd, another freshman, picked up a friend as crew and won every trial race.

When McLaughlin arrived in 1975, the team was dramatically transformed. He is by nature a leader, happiest at the centre of attention and under pressure. He was very organized and eager to race. McLaughlin recognized the collegiate system as a terrific forum for training. More than any other type of competitive sailing, it promotes individual talent above management and money, and in the United States the top collegiate sailors almost inevitably enter directly into Olympic campaigns. McLaughlin was aggressive, making sure the team attended the important regattas in North America, and his presence pushed the other members, like Boyd and Doug Harvey, to sail their best. McLaughlin's arrival began four years of excellent Queen's sailing teams. When the team was hot, it ranked among the top ten in North America, and McLaughlin was named an Intercollegiate All American sailor in 1977 and 1979.

McLaughlin's intercollegiate career ended in time for the 1980 Olympic Games. When Canada boycotted the Games, it opened in his competitive career a nagging gap, a hole that should have been filled by an Olympic medal. Terry McLaughlin decided to plug that hole with, of all things, the America's Cup.

Jeff Boyd started sailing in 1967 at age 12. He was the first in his family to do so, his mother having enrolled him in the Kingston Yacht Club's junior program for the summer. When he decided to stick with sailing, his parents bought him and his brother a Flying Junior, a small dinghy then at the height of its popularity.

At 16, Jeff Boyd was presented by his grandmother with an International 14, a developmental two-man dinghy also riding a wave of popularity. Boyd travelled to Toronto for his first national championship in 1972, with his friend Neil Gordon as crew. They were very young, and very light, and in the fickle winds of the opening race they scored a fourth place in the 75-boat fleet.

After the race, a tall, lanky and soft-spoken fellow sailing an old green "14" came over to ask how they had done. Boyd and Gordon told him. "Good show, very good show," they were encouraged by the gentleman, who then introduced himself. He was Paul McLaughlin, whose son, Terry, was at the moment in Travemünde, West Germany, contesting the International Yacht Racing Union's World Youth Championship. It was so typical a first encounter – the elder McLaughlin, making the rounds of the competitors in a design he loved, making sure that he knew their names and they knew his; that everyone felt at home, comfortable with one another, part of the grand fraternity of competitive sailing. Boyd stuck with the class, and the fraternity.

When his career as a collegiate sailor ended, Jeff Boyd set his sights on the 1979 Pan American Games. He selected as his vehicle to a gold medal the Lightning, a 19-foot, three-man centreboarder he had never so much as set foot in. As his crew he chose two fellow Kingston natives, Peter Jones and Gord Crothers. (The thread binding the fraternity continued to weave. Jones had occasionally crewed for Rodney Pattisson, the two-time Olympic Flying Dutchman gold medallist, in 1972, and Pattisson stayed at Jones's house during the 1976 games. Jones's two former crewmates, Boyd and Pattisson, then met on the race course when Pattisson became a helmsman with the British America's Cup challenge.) A syndicate of Kingston Yacht Club members bought them a boat, which was built by Tom Allen of Buffalo. Allen, who had won his fourth Lightning world title in 1977, also provided their first suit of sails and plenty of helpful advice.

They trained well and won the Pan American team trials in 1978. But the fact that they were unknown in the class disturbed the Canadian Olympic Association, which decided not to send the Kingston crew to the Games in Puerto Rico unless they finished at least twelfth in the Lightning trials for the American team. The Americans were using the St. Petersburg, Florida, regatta in the three-leg Lightning Midwinter Championship to make their selection.

The COA decision was a tremendous letdown to the Kingston crew. But they regrouped, analyzed the situation and decided that they were only doing this because they wanted to win the gold medal. If they couldn't *win* the American trials, never mind finish in the top twelve, what were they even doing in the Lightning?

Jeff Boyd and his crew made the trip south. Not only did they win the American trial regatta; they won the Midwinter championship itself – the first Canadian entry ever to do so. The Americans were sure to be the toughest competition in Puerto Rico, and the Kingston crew's success in Florida made winning the gold medal seem only more of a certainty.

Then Jeff Boyd got sick while training in the final days before the Games. The diagnosis was mononucleosis; he was out of the picture. *Disaster*. He was replaced at the helm by the team's Laser coach, Gil Mercier. With Peter Jones and Gord Crothers still in their crew positions, Canada brought home a silver medal.

The size of the blow this untimely illness dealt to Boyd could not be exaggerated. When Terry McLaughlin had edged him out for the national Laser title in 1975, it was not the last time that Boyd would fall just short of victory; it was a lasting annoyance to him that he had never won a Canadian sailing title. He had briefly pursued a Finn program with the 1980 Olympic Games in mind, but had abandoned that in favour of the Pan American Games campaign. And for that campaign to have taken him so close to international success, only to end with such frustration, was a catastrophe he would not easily forget.

Jeff Boyd was back racing with Terry McLaughlin in the fall of 1981. They were down in Texas, at the Fort Worth Boat Club, contesting the United

States Yacht Racing Union's team racing championship in two-man dinghies. Terry McLaughlin had assembled a three-boat team consisting of five Canadians and one American. Jeff Boyd sailed one boat with his old Pan American Games crew, Peter Jones; Tam Matthews and Jay Cross, Canada's Olympic 470 team in 1980, manned the second boat; and Terry McLaughlin took charge of the third, with Carolyne Brodsky of Boston as his crew.

The team was literally unbeatable, and on their way to compiling a 10-0 winning record they were approached by Gary Jobson, who had served as Ted Turner's tactician when *Courageous* won the America's Cup in 1977. Jobson had been aboard with Turner again in 1980, but *Courageous* had done poorly against a fantastically organized Dennis Conner. Turner said to hell with the America's Cup after that ordeal, but Jobson remained interested and joined forces with Tom Blackaller, who managed the North Sails loft in San Francisco. Blackaller, a former Star world champion, had skippered the defence contender *Clipper* during the latter part of the 1980 America's Cup summer. He would assume the helm of a new 12-Metre by *Clipper*'s designer, David Pedrick. Gary Jobson would be his tactician, and Jobson's old charge, *Courageous*, would become *Defender*'s training partner.

"I hear you're doing pretty good in this thing," Jobson said, greeting McLaughlin's team, and soon digressed into a discussion of maxi boats and 12-Metres. Jobson and Blackaller were at the Fort Worth Boat Club to stir up financial support for their defence effort. Boyd found it interesting to watch them making the rounds of the club, gladhanding away, stirring up enthusiasm for the whole America's Cup scene, *their* America's Cup scene. (As it happened, Texas money would largely carry the day for the *Defender/Courageous* effort.) The sight of a couple of sailors trying to convince a group of rich people to underwrite their nautical activities, to fork over the money necessary to let Jobson and Blackaller and a crowd of other sailors and support staff partake of the hallowed Newport experience, was altogether novel and just a little bit peculiar.

Fort Worth was, in fact, a piece of fairly heavy-handed foreshadowing. Terry McLaughlin and Jeff Boyd and the rest of the team had no idea that a Canadian challenge for the America's Cup was in the works even as they watched Jobson and Blackaller make their rounds. And in less than a month the telephone would ring in the basement of Sepp's Ski Shop in Kingston. Boyd would put aside whatever bindings he happened to be mounting or edges he happened to be sharpening, and on the other end of the line would be Terry McLaughlin, who was thinking about going 12-Metre racing and wanted to know if Boyd would come along.

genesis

It is a story that now seems very old and very worn, made almost mythic by telling and retelling, mostly in the press, but quite often by Marvin McDill himself at one fund-raising appearance or another. It came to seem that the myth – the *creation myth* – had become permanently etched in McDill's mind, and that with one simple neural signal the tried and tested narrative would come tumbling forth in the steady, forceful speaking style that was his trademark.

And so, with embellishments, the myth:

It all began with the return to power in Ottawa of the Liberal Party and Pierre Trudeau in the spring of 1980. A notable election that – the Liberals had managed to form a majority government without one elected represent-ative west of Manitoba. For some the election result triggered a terrible insight into the Canadian political fabric: that what the population of the western half of the country wanted from the government *didn't matter*.

But there was another way of reacting to the election. Party allegiances aside, it had demonstrated how fractured a nation Canada had become. This was very much on the mind of a group of amateur coroners poking through the remains of the country's moral fabric while knocking back a few at Calgary's 400 Club. They were wondering what on God's green earth had happened to national unity, that sense of oneness many of them had last felt when Canada had taken on the Russians in hockey in 1972. Had Canada, as McDill would later assert, become a nation of naysayers and complainers?

It was not long before the Calgary gripe session moved on to the subject of projects that could pull the country together in a united cause. And it was Marvin McDill who uttered the fateful words: "How about the America's Cup?"

McDill had made this suggestion while standing within the borders of a province as landlocked as Tibet. The response of one of his fellow amateur coroners was not surprising.

"What the hell," the man asked, "is the America's Cup?"

What indeed? And what was Marvin McDill doing lobbing it into such a discussion? In Calgary of all places, and McDill, of all people, a native of

Winnipeg, with some experience as a Sea Cadet as a boy and a few holiday cruises in British Columbia's Gulf Islands, but not a yachtsman in even the most generous sense, a man without a fundamental grasp of what yacht racing was all about.

Mind you, he was no fool. Marvin V. McDill – tall and trim for a man of 50-odd years, with a shock of white hair, a face that assumed a look of perpetual exhaustion, and eyes that were forced to put in too many hours by the imagination behind them – Marvin V. McDill was a major force in Alberta's oil and business community. A respected and successful litigation lawyer, he had once been a law partner of Premier Peter Lougheed and was now a member of the firm of Ballem, McDill, MacInnes. (The "Ballem" was John Bishop Ballem, Q.C., novelist and dabbler in television programs, former solicitor for Imperial Oil, vice-president of the Canadian Bar Association in 1966, and a director of Sulpetro Oil and Scotia Oil.)

And he had learned, somehow, somewhere, of the America's Cup. He explained to his fellow 400 Club members what it was all about, or at least as much as he understood. It was this yachting trophy that the Americans held. The rest of the world had been challenging them for it since the last century and the Americans had yet to lose. It represented the longest winning streak in sport.

People listened, some of them close enough to get hooked. The men and women who would eventually become involved with McDill in mounting a Canadian challenge were as naive about yacht racing as he. But they understood and appreciated sports, specifically amateur sports. It was something almost all of Calgary seemed to understand, the relation between exploits on the playing field and community pride. The city had fought hard for the right to host the 1988 Winter Olympics, and it had also given birth to the Canadian assault on Mount Everest. The Everest climb might not have involved a playing field, but it was certainly athletic, and, most important, it represented one of those almost impossible dreams that are a bit pointless in the larger scheme of things but that allow people's hearts and spirits and hopes to soar above the mundane.

Robert Muir, the general counsel of Dome Petroleum, who became the challenge's vice-chairman, was bullish on community sporting activities; so was the challenge's director of finance, J. Crawford-Smith, a senior partner with Clarkson Gordon in Calgary. Leslie Fryers, a Calgary lawyer who became the challenge's director of law, was a member of the YMCA's Women's Health Club and the Royal Montreal Golf and Country Club; another director, Ted Grisdale, a sales manager with Wellhead International of Calgary, was a long-time hockey coach. The lone yachting authority was John Morgan, the vice-chairman of the Montreal investment firm of Walwyn Stodgell Cochran Murray. Morgan, who had been a race course vice-chairman at the sailing events of the 1976 Olympic Games, had held executive positions with the Canadian Yachting Association and the International Yacht Racing Union. Most important, he was race committee chairman for the challengers' trials of the 1980 America's Cup. It was because of this experience that McDill made him the director responsible for rules and procedures. Together, under the leadership of McDill, these men and women resolved to be the first to remove the America's Cup from the table it was bolted to in the New York Yacht Club. And it was all for the cause of Confederation.

The first hint that something strange and wonderful was afoot in the oil- and wheat-rich expanses of Alberta came in the form of a telephone message. It said, "Call Bob Nowack. Urgent." It was handed to George Cuthbertson, the co-founder and then-president of C&C Yachts, in the midst of an intense company meeting in the fall of 1980.

Bob Nowack was a Calgary yachtsman (a seemingly incongruous label, given the expanses of water in that Prairie province) whose *Alberta Bound,* a C&C design, would serve as alternate on the 1981 Canadian Admiral's Cup team. The two men knew each other fairly well, and Cuthbertson – a big man, tall and sturdily built, with horn-rim glasses and close-cropped hair the colour of an overcast sky – had to wonder what Nowack could want that was so urgent. At the first opportunity, he returned the call.

Bob Nowack asked him to "come out here and talk 12-Metres."

Nowack's invitation startled him, as it would anybody. "If you're thinking of 12-Metres," Cuthbertson replied, "you can be thinking of only one thing."

"That's right," said Nowack, "We are."

There had been a time when George Cuthbertson had shown an interest in the America's Cup. A person with the rare opportunity to browse through the scrapbooks of C&C Yachts will find himself, while viewing page after page of newspaper clippings, magazine articles and promotional material dating to the early 1960s, stumbling upon stories and photographs from the 1964 America's Cup – *Constellation* and *Sovereign,* head to toe in one of the most lopsided matches ever. They appear in the scrapbooks, unexplained, then vanish, taking the America's Cup forever with them from the pages, and evidently from the ambitions of George Cuthbertson.

Cuthbertson was one of the few Canadians with experience in Metre-class yacht design, perhaps the only one alive. As a young man, he had modified the 8-Metre *Venture* for the Royal Canadian Yacht Club's successful 1954 challenge for the Canada's Cup, the Great Lakes match racing trophy. But, however much he may have admired the grace and elegance of the Metre-class yachts, he could not admire their outmoded status in yacht design; in 1968 Cuthbertson was a member of the RCYC committee that modified the rules governing the Canada's Cup to move competition out of 8-Metres and into the realm of modern offshore designs.

There was another reason for Cuthbertson to say no to an America's Cup project. Something as monstrous and awe-inspiring as an America's Cup challenge, tempting as it might seem to the layman, was simply not in the plans of C&C. Although the company and its widely admired design office still regularly turned out custom designs, it was primarily concerned with the production of a line of stock racer-cruisers. Custom projects on the scale of an America's Cup assignment have a habit of consuming and undermining the company involved, and Cuthbertson did not seriously entertain the thought of becoming involved in one.

As for Bob Nowack, he wasn't interested in becoming involved in the challenge bid either; he was making enquiries as a favour to McDill, who was looking for some friendly advice on how to get the ball rolling. So Cuthbertson passed on some friendly advice. It wasn't "Drop the notion" or "See a psychiatrist." It was "Call Bruce Kirby."

And so, Marvin McDill and Bruce Kirby came together. As George Cuthbertson had guessed, Kirby, one of Canada's few independent yacht designers, was very interested in creating a 12-Metre, which would tentatively be named *Crusader.* But Kirby felt he could contribute a lot more to a challenge than just the design. He had seen a lot of America's Cups and was a pretty good sailor himself. When it came time to draw up a contract, Kirby decided to give the Calgary lawyer two options. The challenge could contract him just to design the boat; such a contract would probably have been worth about $100,000 to Kirby. Or the challenge could contract him to be a *designer/consultant,* thereby allowing them to take advantage of his expertise in all aspects of the campaign; *that* contract was worth about $300,000 to Kirby. A budget published by the challenge's fundraisers listed Canada 1's design fees at $375,000. The figure included the work of consultants like Killing, but the bulk still went to Kirby.

The designer/consultant contract sounded like a good idea, and McDill accepted it. The fee was generous, probably one of the best financial returns Bruce Kirby had ever experienced, and it raised an interesting point about Marvin McDill. The lawyer had developed a reputation for cleverly constructed contracts concerning supplies and services to the Canadian challenge, but when it came to paying key personnel, he never nickel-and-dimed them. He adopted a philosophy of paying top money for top people, and as a result the fees dispensed were generous – managerial salaries of about $5000 per month were not unusual.

Which brings us to another designer, a fellow named Alexander Cuthbert who came to regrettably dubious distinction with the *Countess of Dufferin,* a design commissioned by Major Charles Gifford and his RCYC syndicate for the America's Cup match of 1876. The America's Cup was still in its infancy – the schooner *America* had only won the famed race around the Isle of Wight that brought her the pitcher destined to bear her name in 1851. Challenges from foreign yacht clubs had not begun until 1870, and the one from the Royal Canadian Yacht Club was the third. Any attempt at a post-mortem of the Cuthbert design is frustrated by the fact that she was poorly finished and rigged, a mortal fault brought upon by the Achilles' heel of cup challenges: insufficient funding.

Having seen the *Countess of Dufferin* thrashed by the New York Yacht Club's *Madeleine,* the RCYC backed off from any further forays into this financially terrifying nook of competitive yachting. Alexander Cuthbert, on the other hand, was still game and found the Bay of Quinte Yacht Club of Belleville, Ontario, eager to become involved. Cuthbert was back in New York in 1881 with another competently designed, badly under-funded and poorly finished challenger, the *Atalanta.* She was nautically roundhoused by another crack American yacht, the *Mischief.*

But Cuthbert still got up off the mat. In fact he was prepared to bring the *Atalanta* back for another try, and it took all the Machiavellian cunning of the New York Yacht Club's legal minds to stop him. The matches with the *Countess of Dufferin* and the *Atalanta* had been embarrassingly lopsided, and the legal wizards had the sanctity and prestige of the trophy in mind when they conspired to prevent Alexander Cuthbert, or anyone else like him, from ever appearing again. The rule they devised seems to have been motivated by a snobbish lack of respect for Canadian yachtsmen from the Great Lakes, for it specified that the challenging club must lie on the sea, or on an arm of the sea with more or less direct access to it. The likes of Cuthbert need no longer apply.

Although the America's Cup is traditionally viewed as a contest between nations, it is technically between yacht clubs. The New York Yacht Club, as the longstanding bearer of the trophy, would yet again be its defender in 1983. Other yacht clubs from around the world were free to submit challenges; those clubs would have to decide among themselves, in a series of trials over the summer of 1983, which would advance to meet the NYYC's defender, also selected through a series of trials.

The summer of 1983 would be the most crowded in the history of the America's Cup. No fewer than seven challenges were received by the NYYC. Three alone came from Australia – the Royal Yacht Club of Victoria in Melbourne, the Royal Sydney Yacht Squadron (which became the challenger of record, and thus responsible for overseeing the selection trials) and the Royal Perth Yacht Club (a fourth Australian challenge, from the Royal Queensland Yacht Squadron, was issued, then withdrawn). Two challenges were forwarded from England, from the Royal London Yacht Club and the Royal Burnham Yacht Club. The Royal London Yacht Club withdrew its challenge, as did the Royal Gothenburg Yacht Club of Sweden. The French challenge would be represented by the Yacht Club de France. And 1983 would see the first challenge from Italy, forwarded by the Yacht Club Costa Smeralda of Sardinia.

Canada too was prepared to challenge, but Marvin McDill couldn't figure out from where. He needed a yacht club, but he didn't belong to one. Moreover, he was afraid that a challenge meant to serve as a rallying point for the aspirations of the general public might fall prey to the destructive forces of political chicanery. McDill was adamant, for example, that no government funding be involved. But the greatest danger he saw was in selecting a particular established yacht club; it would identify the challenge too strongly with one place and could alienate the rest of the yachting community and the public, defeating the whole purpose of the venture.

It then occurred, rather brilliantly, to McDill that he didn't *have* to associate his challenge with an established yacht club. If the rules said the challenge had to come from a yacht club, then by God he'd invent a yacht club of his own.

In December of 1980 the Secret Cove Yacht Club was born. It was located at the Jolly Roger Inn on Half Moon Bay, some 40 miles north of Vancouver. McDill knew the location from his vacation cruises; the facilities for the club were next to nonexistent, and the Jolly Roger's proprietor, Donald Mac-Donald, was named its commodore.

McDill submitted the Secret Cove challenge to the NYYC on March 31, 1981. Its flag officers did not find the instant yacht club as amusing as some Canadians did. First of all, they wanted to know whom and what they were dealing with. It had been 100 years since a Canadian yacht club had contested the America's Cup, and it appeared that the NYYC's wariness of its country's northern neighbour had not completely subsided.

Marvin McDill would look back on his meetings with the NYYC with a fondness that displayed an appreciation of the absurd. According to McDill, the club representatives politely asked him how many members this Secret Cove Yacht Club had. McDill was wide open to suggestions. What do *you* think is a good figure? he replied. When they asked him how much the club charged for dues, McDill came right back, genial and accommodating as ever: What do *you* think is fair?

The NYYC had to think about this. In the end, they came to appreciate the philosophy behind McDill's challenge. On August 17, 1981, the Secret Cove

Yacht Club challenge was accepted, subject to the conditions that the club produce 100 members and hold an annual regatta. McDill complied; he was in business.

But the delays surrounding the forwarding and acceptance of the challenge hurt McDill's plans. He had originally hoped to have a crew training aboard a boat in the summer of 1981. At the end of that summer, all he had was a piece of paper from the NYYC recognizing his challenge. The delays also meant that virtually nothing had happened on the fund-raising front.

But fund-raising had been delayed not only by the NYYC's time-consuming deliberations over the legitimacy of the Canadian challenge, but by a lack of charitable status which would make contributions to the campaign tax-deductible. In the United States, the People-to-People Sports Committee had been established as an entity of the federal government during the Eisenhower administration as a means by which athletic organizations could issue tax receipts to their supporters. It had been regularly used by America's Cup defence syndicates and was processing the funds underwriting the *Defender/Courageous* effort for 1983. (Dennis Conner's campaigns employed the tax-deductible framework of the Fort Schuyler Maritime College.) But Canada had no bureaucratic equivalent, and McDill struggled unsuccessfully to have Canada's America's Cup Challenge, Inc. registered as a charitable organization.

Instead, the mandarins of Ottawa suggested that the challenge channel its funds through the appropriate federal sports body, the Canadian Yachting Association. The CYA agreed to act as the challenge's charitable front, on the condition that it receive 5 per cent of all donations; over time, the share would be reduced to 2.5 per cent. The CYA stated that the money was required to cover the the administrative costs of processing the donations and issuing tax receipts. Word also spread that the money would assist the national sailing team, which was preparing for the 1983 Pan American Games and the 1984 Olympics.

But the team saw little of the CYA's own share of the ultimately small amount of money raised for *Canada 1* —the team's operating expenses were only part of the larger CYA pie through which the available *Canada 1* funds were distributed. With little actual financial gain from the CYA-CACC arrange-ment, the chronically cash-short national team's own fundraising efforts were damaged by the public impression that any donation to the America's Cup challenge would also be of measurable assistance to national team members.

Securing a charitable framework had been an important step for McDill's challenge. It was the lack of such a framework that had contributed significantly to the short existence of a Vancouver challenge in 1971. McDill was then given the chance to improve the financial status of the challenge immeasurably in September 1981 when he was invited to speak at a gentlemen's smoker at the Royal Canadian Yacht Club. The club is an important centre of both nautical and financial power in Canada, and its members were curious to find out who Marvin McDill was and what he had in mind.

McDill told them…about national unity, about pulling the country together with this project. The evening did not go well. McDill felt that the crowd scoffed at his ideas, and he was undoubtedly right. Such a reaction was, after all, almost inevitable. He was an outsider, an oil field lawyer with about as much sea sense as an armadillo, who had popped out of nowhere, charging pell-mell for the America's Cup, the most famous prize in yachting, chattering away as if he expected to show up and *win*. It all made the yachting establishment look like a bunch of do-nothing paperweights, armchair anchors. Didn't he think the yachting establishment ever considered challenging for the trophy? All the time! There was all that talk and planning in Vancouver in 1971, for example. True, the schemes never got anywhere, but that was because wiser heads prevailed; they realized what a waste of time and money and resources the America's Cup was.

The attitude of many was summed up by Gordon Fisher, a former Commodore of the RCYC who also happened to be the president of Southam Communications. A powerful man with powerful friends, with a word he could make or break the challenge's chances for substantial corporate backing in the east. The day before the gentlemen's smoker, McDill had sat down to lunch with Fisher and another prominent RCYC member, Gord Norton, who had been a member of Canada's fifth-place Dragon crew at the 1960 Olympic Games. After much soul searching, Fisher wrote a kindly letter to McDill explaining why the America's Cup was such a bad idea.

Fisher was negative, but in what was meant to be a helpful way – he intended to save McDill and anyone else who joined him from a hopeless and worthless cause. Fisher explained how the match did not attract, in his opinion, the most accomplished sailors. Twelve-Metres were obsolete pieces of machinery, and besides, he agreed with Ted Turner, the 1977 America's Cup winner who had also spoken at the gentlemen's smoker: Bruce Kirby's background did not justify anyone spending millions of dollars to campaign one of these obsolete machines from his drawing board.

Fisher was also afraid that McDill's challenge would steal the country's best young sailors out of the boats in which they could be winners and deposit them in a 12-Metre in which they would be pointlessly thrashed.

"When you get right down to it," Fisher decided, "I believe it is more in the national interest to concentrate our talents on the things we do best, rather than by letting ourselves be distracted by the meaningless and frivolous publicity that surrounds the America's Cup, the greatest aberration in the world's greatest sport."

Marvin McDill replied to Gordon Fisher on December 13, 1981. While keeping the door open for Fisher to contribute expertise, should he change his mind, McDill informed him that "we do not propose to 'steal' any sailors but only wish to offer Canada's sailors an opportunity to compete against the world's best. We shall never win if we do not try and surely there must be something we can do as Canadians to demonstrate that we have the technology, ability and desire to compete with the world, otherwise we shall continue to suffer from a national inferiority complex. . . . We intend to pursue this project as vigorously as possible. We now have the basic financing in place and are moving ahead with our plans for training, design and construction."

McDill's challenge was a reality. In one year's time Gordon Fisher would change his mind and join him.

The "basic financing" Marvin McDill referred to in his letter to Gordon Fisher was a $2 million, interest-free loan from a wealthy western Canadian, Vern Lyons, of Ocelot Drilling. But Marvin McDill had also found sympathy with an important member of the eastern yachting and business establishment. Paul Phelan, 64 years of age, is a prominent member of the RCYC who had contested the right to challenge for the Canada's Cup in 1978 with *Mia VI*. A strong supporter of Olympic sailing, Phelan had been an avid Dragon sailor. Terry McLaughlin often refers to Paul Phelan as his uncle, although the two men are, in fact, cousins. Phelan is enormously wealthy, overseeing the operations of the Victoria Hotel on Toronto's Yonge Street, the Cara empire, which, among other things, is a supplier of airline food, operates the Cara Inn near Toronto International Airport and owns the restaurant chains of Harvey's and Swiss Chalet. Phelan's wife, Helen, is the sister of George Gardiner, the chairman of Gardiner Group Stockbrokers, Ryerson Oil and Gas, and Scott's Hospitality (whose holdings include the Scott's Kentucky Fried Chicken chain and the Commonwealth Holiday Inns).

Phelan is a romantic when it comes to the sea. He is in love with the idea of the "proper yacht" and the Corinthian (amateur, always gentlemanly) pursuit of yacht racing. David Lees of *Toronto Life* magazine would recognize in him a childlike public persona, which encourages those around him to shower him with flattery. He is a shrewd man, although when it comes to boats and the sea he sometimes lets his sentimental impulses take charge. At least on a nautical level, Phelan could appreciate the daring of McDill's dream, its visionary quality. Paul Phelan liked to dream too. He purchased *Intrepid,* the last great wooden 12-Metre, which defended the America's Cup in 1967 and 1970, from Baron Bich of France, and leased it to Marvin McDill's syndicate for one dollar.

Paul Phelan's single gesture of generosity was a substantial one. It helped overcome the cool reaction Marvin McDill and his challenge had received in the east and in the yachting establishment in particular. Paul Phelan, although he was not an intimate of McDill and his directors, would do more than any other individual to ensure that the challenge survived. He was on the sidelines, a silent force, watching.

In the basement of Sepp's Ski Shop in Kingston, Jeff Boyd answered the telephone. The familiar voice of Terry McLaughlin was on the line.

"Want to sail 12-Metres with me?" Terry asked him.

"Yeah, right," Boyd managed.

"No, no, no," McLaughlin assured him, "I think I'm serious. There's this guy, George Wilkins, in town. He's here to recruit a crew to sail on a Canadian 12-Metre." McLaughlin then filled him in on the challenge, and on McDill – a smart lawyer, a guy accustomed to seeing things go the right way.

"I guess they want you to be skipper, right?" Boyd wondered.

"Yeah," said Terry, "and you can be my tactician." At least, that's what they'd aim for. No guarantees – it all depended on who else they had lined up.

McLaughlin then got in touch with George Wilkins, who didn't really know who Jeff Boyd was, and persuaded him to give Boyd a call. George Wilkins was a friend of Bruce Kirby. A health problem had forced him to give up dentistry, but his practice had been insured, and now he was occupying himself with the task of assembling a crew training program for the Canadian America's Cup challenge. He rang up Boyd and told him there was no chance of his being considered for the program unless he came to Toronto for an interview – something which was not demanded of everyone, but Boyd did it anyway. Borrowing his father's car, he headed down Highway 401.

Jeff Boyd was in a state of limbo. Twenty-six years of age, he had just returned from the USYRU team racing championship and was toying with the idea of getting a serious job as he put in his hours at the ski shop. He had gone so far as to check out a few possibilities in Toronto. And then Terry McLaughlin's voice had come over the telephone line. Terry the Leader, the Motivator – he was like a gravitational anomaly positioned over the America's Cup, and he was dragging Boyd in. The America's Cup had never posed any particular attraction to Boyd. Without Terry McLaughlin's presence, he would never have considered participating in the campaign. Terry was game, and that made it interesting; Boyd was willing to follow, if only to explore this strange avenue of yacht racing with him, to see what it was all about. It wasn't until two years later, when the 1983 America's Cup was over, that he would learn that McLaughlin had not committed himself to the program until *after* Boyd. That would give Boyd the most paralyzing feeling – the feeling of a near miss, that he had, without even knowing, narrowly avoided being hit by a truck.

Boyd met with George Wilkins for over two hours, during which time Wilkins explained that the crew would be subsidized for expenses. In a short time, Wilkins got back to him and invited him on board. The schedule Wilkins had drawn up went more or less as follows:

1) Go to Florida on February 1, 1982, to be introduced to 12-Metre sailing. Return home for a break at the end of May.
2) Move to Newport, Rhode Island, on June 20 for continued training and initial sail testing. End training on September 20.
3) Go to Florida again for more training on November 1. Stay there until March 31, 1983. By this time, the challenge's second generation of sails would be tested.
4) Move to Newport on May 1 for the final push. The boat works perfectly and sail development is on schedule. The tight, crack crew is ready to race.
5) June 20: Their first race after a year and a half of training. Also their first win.
6) September 20: Take the America's Cup home.

To prepare the crew candidates for the long grind ahead, Wilkins suggested a list of inspiring reading. In addition to advising every book about the America's Cup they could get their hands on, he included *The Inner Game of Tennis* and *Golden Girl*. Drawing on his dental background, he also decided that all crew candidates should have their wisdom teeth removed before joining the training program. Some dutifully complied.

The chase for the America's Cup was on.

strength in numbers

On January 7, 1982, Steve Killing, a tallish, youngish Canadian yacht designer, travelled to Barrington, Rhode Island, to have a good look at *Clipper*, an American 12-Metre the fledgling Canadian challenge had just got its hands on through a complicated lease/purchase agreement. Killing would be joined in Barrington by Bruce Kirby, the newspaper journalist cum magazine editor cum Olympic/offshore helmsman and yacht designer who had been selected to pen Canada's first challenger for the infamous trophy in 102 years. Kirby, a Canadian citizen living and working about two hours from Barrington in Rowayton, Connecticut, had selected Killing to be his assistant.

The pair were preparing construction drawings for their own 12-Metre and had come to Barrington to figure out how *Clipper* was put together. Foremost in their minds were the intricacies of the scantling rules determining 12-Metre construction. The rules, at first glance, are very detailed and no-nonsense. Set down by Lloyd's of London, they specify, among other things, that an aluminum 12-Metre must have 43 ribs, that every fourth rib must be a large one, and that the weight-saving holes in the ribs must be of a specific dimension. It is because of the Lloyd's pronouncements on scantlings that aluminum 12-Metres look almost identical below deck. Almost – but not quite. Aluminum had only become an approved construction material with the America's Cup of 1974, and if anyone had figured out the loopholes of the scantling rules in the eight short years and three America's Cups since then, it was the Americans. Kirby and Killing were determined to familiarize themselves with these loopholes by examining *Clipper*. At the same time, they wanted to find out, through *Clipper*, what the Americans knew about excellence in 12-Metre design.

The two men had known each other for about ten years, having first sailed together aboard Gerhard Moog's *C-Mirage* in the 1973 Miami-Montego Bay Race, Killing's first big offshore event. After graduation from the University of Western Ontario with awards for scholastic achievement and a degree in civil engineering in 1972, Killing had begun seven years in the design office of C&C Yachts. Because Kirby was a friend of George Cuth-

Steve Killing and Bruce Kirby

bertson, Killing ran into him from time to time over the years. They did not sail together again until early 1981, when Killing joined Kirby aboard the 40-footer *Runaway* for half of that season's SORC. Kirby was *Runaway*'s designer, co-owner and skipper, and had his eyes on a spot on the three-boat Canadian team for the Admiral's Cup, the unofficial world ocean racing championship, which was using SORC as a qualifying event. *Runaway* made the cut and went on to finish as top boat on the sixth-place Canadian team in the Solent-based series.

While *Runaway* raced in the south of England, Killing stayed home in Midland, Ontario, with his wife, who was expecting their first child. But Killing felt that Kirby had invited him to sail in SORC partly with sizing him up for an America's Cup project in mind. By the first race of the 1981 SORC, Kirby had already been conversing with Marvin McDill over a possible Canadian challenge. And, when the time came, Kirby recommended that his *Runaway* crew member, who had already notified the challenge of his interest after learning of their plans through an article in the Toronto *Globe and Mail*, be hired as an assistant designer. Kirby would perform the actual design work; Killing was along to assess the theoretical potential of Kirby's creation.

Killing had been a casual observer of the America's Cup. Back in his design office was a file full of related clippings, the sort of file he is sure almost every yacht designer keeps, with *If Ever* written across the tab. But Killing had never watched an America's Cup race; although he had inspected the odd 12-Metre on dry land, he had never seen one sailing.

Thus, strolling into the second of three warehouse-like buildings at the Cove Haven Marina in Barrington came as a new experience. Cove Haven, about 20 miles north of Newport, was where many 12-Metres, American and foreign alike, came for modifications. It was also where they came to be stored, either between campaigns or, in the case of the less successful designs, presumably until some marine museum was willing to take them in. *Clipper* was definitely there to kill time between campaigns. Although her hull was designed by David Pedrick, her deck and keel (duly modified), came from *Independence*, designed and skippered unsuccessfully by the 1974 winner, Ted Hood, in 1977. Russell Long, a young member of an establishment New England family, had mounted and skippered the *Clipper* campaign in 1980; Pan American Airlines had paid her bills, thereby creating the first defence candidate backed exclusively by a corporation. *Clipper* had been late entering the defence fray. Hampered by limited funds and inexperience, *Clipper* was ultimately no match for Dennis Conner's ruthlessly efficient *Freedom* campaign. But those-in-the-know knew a good 12-Metre when they saw one, and McDill's acquisition of *Clipper*, overcoming the best efforts of the New York Yacht Club to prevent her from falling into foreign hands, was a considerable coup.

Killing entered the Cove Haven warehouse, his eyes searching among the many large yachts crammed into the building for the telltale blue bow. He suddenly adjusted to the strange reality of Cove Haven. *Every one of these yachts was a 12-Metre*. They were straight out of his file back home, their decks draped in protective tarps of various patriotic designs. In one corner sat *Intrepid*, the wooden 1967 and 1970 winner which would shortly join *Clipper* as a trial horse in the Canadian camp. The hard-chinned *France 1*, a casualty of the summer of 1970, sat forlornly off by herself, her neglected wooden hull visibly separating from her keel. *Australia*, the 1977 and 1980 finalist, was also there. And flanking *Clipper* were the 1974 and 1977 winner, *Courageous*, and the 1980 British contender, *Lionheart*.

This did not make sense to Killing. He had thought that the foreign yachts would be back in their home countries, having something done to them or use made of them. At the very least, they should have been locked up in their own compartments. It was as though vital design secrets were in danger of leaking from one rival camp to another through the physical proximity of their competing yachts. It seemed incongruous to him that the same yachts that had been attacking each other with such ferocity on the race course were now nestled topside to topside at this Newport outpost.

While the yachts posed no security threat to each other, their owners certainly did. The proprietor of the marina was well aware of the potential for espionage under this single, remarkable roof. A few hours in the company of these yachts with a tape measure would have been a very enlightening experience. Originally it was the plan of Kirby and Killing to spend the night in the building, examining *Clipper's* scantlings, but the security personnel had other ideas. "They were keeping an eye on us," Killing remembered, "making sure we didn't go wild and start cutting holes in *Courageous*."

They settled into a careful inspection of *Clipper*. Crawling around inside her, measuring plate thicknesses, they confirmed one loophole in the apparently rigid scantling rules: you could lessen the risk of hobby-horsing by eliminating heavy plating near the ends of the hull, providing you compensated by using heavier plating in the centre of the hull's bottom. And, while there was no time or opportunity for surreptitious measurements in this collection of America's Cup victors and pretenders, they did take a long, hard look at *Clipper* and her stable mates. One factor in particular interested Killing and Kirby – namely, how the many designers represented by their work in this Newport outpost had tackled the crucial area where hull meets keel, where the International Rule comes down hard and heavy.

Bruce Kirby was born in Ottawa in 1929, the same year as George Cuthbertson, generally regarded as the dean of modern yacht design in Canada. While Cuthbertson graduated in engineering from the University of Toronto and moved within a few years into the design and brokerage business, Kirby took a far more circuitous route. An eight-foot dinghy aside, Cuthbertson began his career as a keelboat designer – his first commission was, amazingly enough, an ocean racer over 50 feet long. Kirby was a small-boat enthusiast and newspaperman with a side interest in dinghy design. He is one of the few Canadians to have sailed in three Olympic Games. As a Finn sailor, he placed eighth in 1956 and 11th in 1964. He competed in the Star class in 1968: his performance, he says, without being specific about statistics, was "awful." When his crew, his brother, became seriously ill before the Games, Kirby replaced him with a 140-pound cousin, a disastrous size for a Star sailor, but Kirby had understood that the Acapulco breeze would be light and he took a chance. The conditions could not have been less suitable. Kirby, 39, parted with Olympic competition and found himself on the verge of becoming a full-time yacht designer.

Bruce Kirby is a large man, as most former Finn sailors are. His curly hair and beard are speckled with grey; his hands are broad and sturdy, his face creased with age and from much standing in the way of sun and wind and ocean. He has a writer's affection for telling stories, and he is never short of reminiscences or explanations of his craft. He has many admirers. Scott Graham of the Chicago design team of Graham and Schlageter, which has produced many offshore champions, holds him in considerable esteem. There are people who only half-jokingly refer to him as "Olin," a most complimentary reference to the yacht design giant, Olin Stephens. "I think he may be something of a genius," an old acquaintance and critical admirer observes, with a wonder in his voice that says, *Wouldn't it be something if it were true*.

A model carver as a boy, Kirby designed his first boat in 1958 at 29. It was a version of the International 14, a developmental dinghy class active in England, Canada and the United States. He called it the Kirby Mark I; the Mark II followed in 1962, and over the years his dabbling in the class led clear to a Mark V. He had no formal training, picking up the necessary science along the way. "Bruce is really seat-of-the-pants, chock full of amazing ideas," Killing noted when *Canada 1* was completed. "Most of them are very good. His intuition is superb."

It is tempting to draw parallels between Kirby and Ben Lexcen, the designer of *Australia II*, who also has no formal training and got his start dabbling in his country's radical philosophical equivalent of the International 14 – the Australian 18. Both men, while far from ignoring the value of such scientific aids as tank testing and computerized performance prediction, draw essentially by instinct. Arguments aside as to their relative skills, the major difference between Lexcen and Kirby is that Kirby is a comparative latecomer to America's Cup design. When Kirby became the first Canadian to design a 12-Metre, Lexcen had just tucked his third under his belt.

Kirby's first popular design triumph was the Laser, a singlehanded, rigid one-design whose basic shape he arrived at literally while handling the telephone call that commissioned it. The design, completed in 1969, went into production in 1971 with Performance Sailcraft of Montreal. It was as much of an overnight success as a yacht design will ever be. There are now well over 100,000 sailing around the world, and competition in the class is of the highest calibre.

The popularity of the Laser is such that the little dinghy is sure to intrude into any passing reference to its designer; it has practically become Kirby's calling card. It was a calling card that could produce puzzled reactions whenever a *Canada 1* supporter or public relations type offered it up as the designer's sole credential: what was the designer of a cartoppable daysailer doing creating a 63-footer weighing in at over 25 tons?

But the Laser was Kirby's ticket to fame and helped give him the freedom to leave his career as a journalist and pursue yacht design full time. He had been a reporter with the *Ottawa Journal* from 1950 to 1956 and a copy editor with the *Montreal Star* from 1956 to 1964, when he moved to the United States to become the editor of *One Design and Offshore Yachtsman*, the forerunner of *Yacht Racing/Cruising* magazine.

It was journalism that introduced him to the America's Cup. While at the *Star*, he pieced together his coverage of the 1958 series, which marked the beginning of the modern era of cup competition in 12-Metres, from wire service reports. When the 1962 match came along, he persuaded the newspaper's publisher, who happened to be a sailor, to send him to Newport to see the action firsthand. He has not missed a match since.

The 1962 match was a classic, with the Americans winning by sailing smarter. The defender, *Weatherly*, was slower than *Gretel*, the Australian challenger, but the cup was saved by Bus Mosbacher, the father of modern match racing tactics. Though he may not have had the background of a Dennis Conner, he was an accomplished one-design sailor, the first to assume the helm of a 12-Metre. Mosbacher had very nearly won the 1958 defence trials with *Vim*, a 12-Metre built before the Second World War, and Kirby recognized an aura about Mosbacher of rightness and infallibility, a psychological edge he could use to make a competitor with superior boat-speed sail a race his way, and lose to him in the process. Many things changed over the years following Mosbacher's masterful defence – the length of preparation, high-tech developments of hull and sail design – but the level of sailing skill and crew work did not. And neither did the fact that must have been obvious to Kirby – that it was possible to outdesign the Americans. Outsailing them was another matter.

Kirby's first keelboat design commission came in 1971. Clark, the Seattle boat builder, wanted a winning Quarter Tonner (the name pertains to the rating formula, not the actual weight of the boat) that also happened to be eight feet wide and draw four feet of water. Kirby came up with the San Juan 24. After winning a number of Quarter Ton regattas soon after it appeared, it went on to be the second most economically rewarding design in Kirby's career, behind the Laser. About 1500 are now sailing worldwide, and it was the best-selling 24-footer until the J-24 came along. The fact that it was Kirby's first keelboat design had raised problems for him. Unsure how to calculate righting moment, he called George Cuthbertson. Cuthbertson read out of his blue book of statistics and ratios the righting moments of a number of designs close to the San Juan 24 so that when Kirby did calculate its stability he would know whether he was in the ball park. It was a generous move by Cuthbertson; the San Juan 24 probably cut deeply into the sales of his own designs.

Kirby's next design was a 30-footer, which he hoped Clark would put into production, but the Seattle builder balked at the idea. Kirby had some excess cash from Laser royalties and decided to launch the prototype himself. The boat was built by the Gougeon brothers of Michigan, and Kirby sailed it with encouraging results in the 1975 Half Ton Worlds in Chicago. The regatta was another case of first-class sailors crossing paths at a first-class regatta. The event was won by an Australian boat, *Foxy Lady*, with *Australia II* tactician Hugh Treharne on board; Tom Blackaller of the *Defender/Courageous* group sailed *Checkered Demon* to second. Fourth was Hans Fogh at the helm of the C&C design, *Landed Immigrant*. After the Worlds, Clark reconsidered their initial resistance to the design, and the San Juan 30 was born.

Still more keelboat designs followed, including the popular Kirby 25 and Kirby 30. Finally there was *Runaway*, at 40 feet the largest boat Kirby had created. From there he made an astounding leap in scale – to *Canada 1*, the very antithesis of *Runaway* at almost 63 feet in overall length and more than 50,000 pounds in displacement.

It was in 1967 that 12-Metre design took a great leap forward and then froze again into a discernible lineage which, until the breakthrough by Ben Lexcen in 1983, triumphed over all efforts to move the shape of America's Cup yachts in a new direction. The boat was *Intrepid*, and her designer, Olin Stephens of the firm of Sparkman & Stephens, revolutionized the class by separating the rudder from the keel. In doing so, the keel was made smaller and more efficient, and the rudder, further distanced from the boat's turning axis, was made more effective. To assist the rudder in controlling the impulses of this heavy-displacement design, a second, smaller rudder, called the trim tab, was added to the trailing edge of the keel. And to maintain the enormous hull volume a 12-Metre requires to achieve its displacement, some of which had been lost in reducing the size of the keel, Stephens created a bustle, a swelling of the hull extending from the keel to the rudder. The bustle also gave the design directional stability and, through manipulation of water flow and stern wave, artificially increased *Intrepid*'s waterline length, the major factor in determining a design's hull speed.

Intrepid was never seriously threatened during either the 1967 defence trials or the finals against Australia's *Dame Pattie*, a design by Warwick Hood made obsolete the moment Olin Stephens' new defender hit the water. *Intrepid* was the progenitor of the modern 12-Metre, and her lineage can be traced through *Courageous*, the 1974 and 1977 defender; *Enterprise*, the 1977 contender; and *Freedom*, the 1980 defender. This lineage, however, fails to illustrate the serious mistake made in 1970, when all of the American defence candidates took a secondary trend in 12-Metre design, of maximiz-

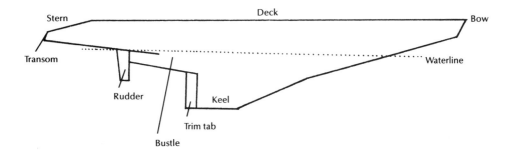

ing displacement and waterline length at the expense of sail area, to a detrimental extreme. The American yachts that year were all too long and heavy (including the new Sparkman & Stephens contender, *Valiant*) and in the finals *Intrepid*, herself redesigned to be longer and heavier, nearly lost to the Australian challenger, *Gretel II*. The designer of the Australian boat, Alan Payne, had given the Americans their last significant scare in 1962 with *Gretel*; he alone in 1970 refined the *Intrepid* concept in the proper direction. After *Gretel II*, the faster boat, lost 4-1 in 1970 through inferior sailing, the design community, Olin Stephens included, fell back onto the proven path.

Stephens returned *Intrepid* close to her original lines and produced a more refined and slightly lighter offspring of his 1967 breakthrough. The offspring was *Courageous*; after a titanic struggle with *Intrepid* over the summer of 1974, *Courageous* was selected for the defence on the basis of the final trial race, and went on to defend the trophy that September, and again in 1977.

With *Courageous*, the nature of a winning 12-Metre became clear, and all successful conventional contenders simply refined her concept even further, until in 1980 it seemed the design process could go no further. It was a frightening thought to the Americans – that they had come to the end of the road in design superiority, and that it was only a matter of time until the foreign challenge camps came up with a contender in every aspect equal or superior to their own. "The next America's Cup is going to be the most competitive series we have had in a long time," William Langan, Sparkman & Stephens' project designer on the 1980 defender, *Freedom*, prophetically wrote in *Yachting* in 1981. "The design process used for *Freedom* in 1980 will not be sufficient for 1983. The designer of the defender must beat the challenger to the next innovation if there is one to be found. To do less than this will mean a much greater risk of losing the Cup."

With *Freedom*, the *Intrepid* lineage had come to the end of a very narrow road, for the yachts had become terminally inbred. A modern, developmental rating formula like the International Offshore Rule dictates the dimensions of hundreds of new designs each year, but the IOR has stayed fresh because of the variety of designers employing the formula and the variety of sailing conditions, yacht sizes and competitive needs to which it is applied. A 12-Metre is but one level-rating class controlled by the International Rule, a very old, simple and, today, unpopular formula created in 1906 with strong prejudices against developments in design which have since become staple characteristics of modern sailing craft. The 12-Metre could not be more atypical of today's racing designs and continues to exist only because of its association with the America's Cup. It is long, narrow and, above all, heavy. The 12-Metre is a "floating lead mine," a 55,000-pound hole in the water. About 40,000 pounds or nearly 80 per cent of its displacement is composed of lead ballast, an astronomical amount when measured against the 2000 pounds of ballast carried by a fleet-footed trimaran of comparable size.

If there were no restrictions on America's Cup designs other than overall length, the trophy would be contested by multihulls, as is the Little America's Cup, a much less known series which has produced mind-boggling advances in aerodynamic design, particularly in complicated, fixed-wing sail configurations. The Little America's Cup is about advancement at the outer reaches of sea-going high technology. From a technological standpoint, the America's Cup (sailmaking and mechanical gear aside) has concentrated on advances in hull shape which begin and end within the microscopic realm of metre class design.

Of the eight 12-Metres launched in the United States from the 1970 to the 1980 matches, the majority were a part of the *Intrepid* family tree. That is because a finite number of things are expected of a 12-Metre. The 12-Metre is designed only for the America's Cup, which means keeping in mind the idiosyncrasies of match racing and the sailing conditions on Rhode Island Sound. Until *Australia II* moved competition to Perth, all important 12-Metre sailing has occurred in a limited environmental framework. A contender is not expected to perform in less than 5 knots of breeze, because the America's Cup course, in those conditions, cannot be completed within the 5 hour 15 minute time limit. And a contender rarely sails in more than 30 knots because, for safety reasons, a race is almost never started in more than

25 knots. There is often a slight chop during the final series. Competitors must also contend with the confused slop thrown up by the wash of the huge spectator fleet, and boats are designed with this not insignificant factor in mind.

It is easier to design a 12-Metre that excels at either extreme of the 5- to 25-knot wind range, and the Australians, until *Australia II*, consistently appeared in Newport with challengers happiest in lighter winds. But by doing so a contender places all its eggs in one basket, and its chances for victory are more at the whim of the weather than is desirable. Performance ranges tend to cross over at 11 or 12 knots, and this has been the targeted peak of excellence for most designs commissioned by conservative backers.

Conservatism has generally characterized America's Cup efforts – don't mess with what works. There were two active theories on mounting a winning effort. Theory #1 held that success lay in executing an end run around the establishment with a boat at least slightly out of the ordinary. Theory #2 advised designing a boat in the *Intrepid* lineage and playing either superior sails or sailing skills as one's trump card.

Americans strongly favoured Theory #2. There was too much at stake – the possession of the cup, the millions of dollars spent – to justify abandoning the *Intrepid* lineage in favour of experimentation. It would have been rash, irresponsible. Besides, the lineage had just begun, and there was plenty of time, it seemed, for fine-tuning the basic concept. The conservative approach was sustained by Sparkman & Stephens' domination of the design process. Except for *Weatherly*, Olin Stephens created every defender from 1958 to 1980; his design office was also at the forefront of modern offshore racing during the 1960s and early 1970s. Stephens' background in metre class design is awesome. As a young man he designed the 8-Metre *Conewago*, which defended the Canada's Cup for the Rochester Yacht Club in 1932 and 1934. After developing the breakthrough *Intrepid*, Stephens allowed himself to falter only once, with *Valiant* in 1970, before picking up the thread and continuing with his explorations of the basic shape of the 1967 defender.

If 12-Metres were going to be launched in the United States that challenged the *Intrepid* lineage, they would likely have to come from outside the Sparkman & Stephens office. But the community of designers of 12-Metres, or of any metre class, is small. It is also populated by former Sparkman & Stephens employees. David Pedrick was project engineer for the design group on *Courageous* and the 1977 contender, *Enterprise*, and when he left the company, he designed *Clipper* for 1980 and *Defender* for 1983 – both of conventional dimensions which left no doubt as to their ancestry. The Dutchman Johan Valentijn, another former Sparkman & Stephens

employee, has played a head-spinning game of multiple nationalities, allowing him to meet nationality rule requirements and design contenders for
Australia (*Australia*, with Ben Lexcen, for the 1977 match), France (*France 3*,
1980) and the United States (*Magic*, *Liberty*, 1983). Still another Olin
Stephens protégé, Andrea Vallicelli, created one more *Intrepid* sibling –
Azzurra, for the 1983 Italian challenge. (That *Azzurra* belongs to the lineage
there is no question: when the Italian syndicate acquired *Enterprise* as a trial
horse for its yet-to-be-designed challenger, it also received Sparkman &
Stephens' working drawings for the boat.)

Of these three Sparkman & Stephens graduates, only one, Johan Valentijn, has gone out on a limb. His *France 3*, an otherwise essential post-
Intrepid design, sported a double articulated trim tab. The trim tab, in
addition to assisting the rudder in steering, also generates additional lift from
the keel, at a slight expense in drag, when turned about two degrees to
leeward. To increase the effect, Valentijn developed a larger trim tab which
hinged twice, but mechanical difficulties led to its being scrapped in favour
of a single trim tab.

Beyond the ranks of current and former Sparkman & Stephens employ-
ees, American 12-Metre designers are few and far between. Only three such
Americans have designed a 12-Metre since *Intrepid*'s debut. Boat-builder
Charles Morgan poured his heart and savings into his wooden design,
Heritage, for the 1970 trials. The multi-talented sailmaker Ted Hood had
designed the 1962 contender *Nefertiti*. When he returned to the America's
Cup in 1977 after his 1974 victory at the helm of the Sparkman & Stephens
design *Courageous*, it was in command of *Independence*, which he had
created with a significantly reduced bustle. But *Independence* was eliminated in the 1977 trials, and it was left to Ben Lexcen to resume the task of
eliminating the bustle, at the benefit of manoeuvrability, when he shocked
the sailing world with *Australia II* six years later.

The other American to design a 12-Metre since *Intrepid* is Britton Chance.
Chance had assisted Hood in the design of *Nefertiti*, and from 1964 to 1965
studied 12-Metre design with the aid of a $10,000 grant from the 12-Metre
Development Fund, which had been established to encourage young
American designers to familiarize themselves with America's Cup yachts,
thereby helping to avoid in the future the sort of rude shock *Gretel* had
given the New York Yacht Club in 1962. Chance was, and still is, a brilliant
designer who has contributed many clever innovations to offshore yachting,
particularly the introduction of the centreboard and daggerboard to the
modern ocean racer in the early and mid-1970s.

Chance was responsible for the redesign of *Intrepid* for the 1970 match,
which brought on that other rude shock from Alan Payne, *Gretel II*. It was
subsequently believed, with good reason, that Chance's changes had made

Intrepid slower, and he received more than his share of criticism. But Chance deserves no more abuse than the other American designers who had erred in the pursuit of displacement and sailing length. (It has been argued that the error lay not in pursuing this design trend, but in the fact that *all* the American designers did, thereby leaving no alternatives for the defence selection.)

Still, if the 1970 series made some observers harbour doubts about Chance's abilities as a 12-Metre designer, the 1974 defence trials ensured that no one would offer him an America's Cup assignment again. A firm believer in the power of the test tank as an analytical tool, Chance was done in by the scale distortions later recognized as inherent in testing a design for a hull over 60 feet long with a model only three feet long. The tank approved of his idea of equipping his contender with a sawn-off "fastback" bustle that had to be seen to be believed. Christened *Mariner*, the Chance design was one of the worst 12-Metres ever launched. The design community was alerted to the siren call of an inadequate tank test program, at the expense of the reputation of Britton Chance.

Mariner did more than simply go slow; she probably singlehandedly turned campaign backers, particularly in the United States, sour on the idea of spending millions on a contender that didn't fall faithfully into the *Intrepid* lineage, and this reticence no doubt placed pressure on designers – Sparkman & Stephens – not to be too visionary. "Radical" came to equal "failure." Sticking to the *Intrepid* lineage offered a better chance of short-term success, but the lack of experimentation would mean trouble further down the road in America's Cup history.

The Australian challenges, however, were consistently willing to take chances, if only at times within the confines of the *Intrepid* lineage. A possible area for improvement was the amount of freeboard carried by a 12-Metre. If the amount of hull exposed above the waterline could be reduced, the centre of gravity would be lowered, resulting in a stiffer boat by transforming hull weight into ballast. Chopping off a few inches of topside meant not simply lowering the location of the weight of the deck: it also meant lowering the position of the weight represented by all of the winches, the crew and the rigging. It would also reduce the windage, and a few inches less exposed hull is nothing to sneeze at in a yacht over 60 feet long. In 1974, *Courageous* made a tentative effort to lower freeboard. Her sheer was peculiarly straight, and her freeboard at the bow, according to Bruce Kirby, was about five inches lower than at the stern.

Ben Lexcen and Johan Valentijn carried the freeboard issue further in 1977: their *Australia* was all-around lower to the water, and its transom was dramatically raked to reduce weight in the stern, to lessen hobby-horsing. After *Australia*, raked transoms, an idea explored on *Valiant* and *Gretel II* in

1970, became *de rigueur*, and the race for lower freeboards was on. It became a prime area of concern for Olin Stephens in the design of *Freedom* for 1980; by reducing freeboard six inches below the norm, he saved about 800 pounds in effective ballast.

The design of *Freedom* was carried out by a four-man team headed by Stephens. The boat was meant to be an improvement on *Enterprise*, which had probably been an improvement on *Courageous*, which had been an improvement on *Intrepid*. Stephens never bothered to tank-test *Freedom*. It was a largely intuitive process. The design of *Enterprise*, regarded as the fastest straight-line 12-Metre of her time, had been exhaustively tested and prodded in its development. For *Freedom*, Stephens dusted off a one-third scale model of *Enterprise* and towed it down the test tank at Hydronautics in Maryland for old times' sake. After the tests, he decided to round out the leading edge of the hull to reduce the chance of stalling when coming out of a tack, and smoothed the lines of the underbody at the termination of the bustle to improve the flow of water and increase the effective sailing length. *Freedom* became the 12-Metre best suited to winning match races on Rhode Island Sound in September while surrounded by a spectator fleet which produced, as John Bertrand observed in 1983, sea conditions like those in a washing machine.

Freedom underwent the most intense fine-tuning ever experienced by a 12-Metre. Her trial horse was *Enterprise*, which, after corrections to its 1977 rig, was fully capable of defending the cup. But Conner kept *Enterprise* to himself, employing her to hone his own boat and keeping her out of the defence trials. *Freedom* won 48 races against her American rivals – *Courageous* (with her winning 1977 crew, including Ted Turner, almost intact) and *Clipper*. She lost only six.

The 1980 challenger was *Australia*, the Lexcen-Valentijn design modified for a second try by Lexcen. It was an interim challenge by Alan Bond, the brash real estate developer who had bankrolled *Southern Cross* in 1974 and *Australia* in 1977. With 1980 an Olympic year, Bond figured he would not be able to attract the sailing talent necessary to win the cup and decided to go ahead with a minimal effort to maintain momentum until a more serious challenge could be made in 1983.

But Bond had not counted on the wonderful innovation that would inadvertently come his way from England. The British were back for the first time since the disastrous performance of *Sovereign* in 1964. Their boat was *Lionheart*, designed by 26-year-old Ian Howlett, who had investigated the tank testing of 12-Metres while attending Southampton University. Howlett produced probably the largest 12-Metre since the overkill by the Americans of 1970. It is estimated that she topped 60,000 pounds, and her hull lines were appropriately swollen, particularly around the bustle.

Lionheart was reasonably fast in a straight line but not particularly manoeuvrable, and she was eliminated by *France 3*. The French yacht was defeated in the challengers' finals by *Australia*, which had already sidelined Sweden's *Sverige*. What interested the Australians about her was her unusual rig. Tony Marchaj, a faculty member of Southampton University, had topped an otherwise conventional spar with an extraordinarily bendy section, which allowed *Lionheart* to support a huge mainsail roach and thus a sizable amount of unmeasured sail area. The Australians quietly noted the benefits of the rig and went out and designed one of their own. The new mast meant new sails, and the Australians kept the whole package under wraps until they had eliminated the final challenge candidate, *France 3*. Then they sprang it on the Americans, leaving the defender no time to build one for herself.

When the wind was light, *Australia* was untouchable. She won one race and was leading in another when the time limit ran out. "If we were able to get the right sail combination," John Bertrand would recall, "there was a chance of winning the America's Cup. If you look at all the other areas, in every one-for-one situation – tactics, crew work, basic sail handling, number of races sailed – *Freedom* had a strong advantage in each one of these." The one-for-one situations ultimately prevailed and Conner won 4-1. But it was obvious the Australians had come close by daring to go out on a limb.

"We learned a lot over the summer from watching the races," wrote Langan in 1981, "but one lesson was exceedingly clear. The Australians showed that through innovation and a little gambling, the U.S. can be beaten. Given more time to work the bugs out of their rig, the Australians could have made the cup races even more interesting. Some day the U.S. will lose the cup because the challenger will be as thoroughly prepared and will have taken calculated risks, gambling on the chance of developing a superior boat."

For the 1983 match, Johan Valentijn, having added American national status to his collection, was asked by Dennis Conner's defence organization to pursue an unorthodox avenue of design of his selection, in the hope that the breakthrough – or rather the break with the *Intrepid* lineage – Langan had warned was necessary would emerge. Valentijn produced *Magic*, which, like France 3, sported a double articulating keel; several feet shorter than the average 12-Metre, this exploration of the extremes of the International Rule proved inferior to that exquisite benchmark of normalcy, the 1980 defender *Freedom*. The same fate befell *Spirit*, the somewhat radical design created for Conner by Sparkman & Stephens.

The reigning defence syndicate then returned to Valentijn for *Liberty*, designed with instructive input from Conner and his navigator, Halsey Herreshoff. Halsey, 47, was the grandson of Nat Herreshoff, the designer whose genius, like that of Olin Stephens, had almost singlehandedly kept the America's Cup in the trophy room of the New York Yacht Club. A crew member of *Columbia* in 1958, *Courageous* in 1974 and *Freedom* in 1980, Halsey Herreshoff had taught naval architecture at the Massachusetts Institute of Technology. The combined input of the three men resulted in a committee decision so firmly rooted in the *Intrepid* family tree as to be devoid of any of the intuitive leaps called for by Langan.

The Australians would not get the chance to improve on their bendy mast – it was outlawed by the International Yacht Racing Union. But they returned in 1983 with another innovation, this time of their own inspiration, and the Americans would confirm their own worst fears by having nothing with which to counter it. The warnings of Langan, and no doubt others, had come to nothing.

Bruce Kirby's first opportunity to design a 12-Metre came in 1974. A Montreal group had expressed interest in launching a challenge, and Kirby got as far as researching the International Rule and doing some preliminary sketches. As a sailor, journalist and designer, Kirby had come to know the key 12-Metre designers over the years, and his multiple occupations made it easier for him to pick up the meatier statistics and design principles than if he had simply been a yacht designer. Alan Payne was very open, and even Olin Stephens would drop the odd vital number. By the time the Montreal group appeared on the scene, Kirby had accumulated a lot of information on 12s, and when the group fell apart the numbers and photos and drawings were stored in a filing cabinet drawer devoted to the America's Cup. When the 1983 challenge was over, the collection of numbers and photos and drawings had expanded to six drawers.

What Kirby discovered while familiarizing himself with the International Rule was a simple formula that dictates quite specifically what a yacht should look like. His assistant, Steve Killing, put it best: "When you go into an America's Cup effort for the first time, you've got this head full of phenomenal ideas. You're ready to revolutionize the class. 'Let's get these things modernized, none of these old wishy-washy-looking 12-Metres,' you say, because we've developed things a lot further under the IOR. You don't see any IOR boats with keels that look like 12-Metre keels. 'Tuck up the bottom, put on a nice keel, and away we go.' Then you find out that if you do that you'll be allowed *half* the sail area that you would otherwise have."

The International Rule places clear restrictions on certain dimensions – draught (maximum 15 per cent of waterline length), beam (minimum 11.8 feet), mast height (maximum 82 feet) and jib hoist (75 per cent of mast height). There are but a few key components in the formula. There is the girth measurement, which controls the shape of the underbody of the hull amidships and prevents the sort of tucking Killing spoke of. To discourage overhangs which are too flat and long, the rule takes its waterline measurement not from the actual waterline (known as the "floating" or "load" waterline) but along a plane 180 mm higher. The lower the boat's freeboard, the more costly it measures, and the freeboard component was made more penalizing after the 1980 series, although a "grandfather" provision allows *Freedom*, the 12-Metre to reduce freeboard most significantly, to continue sailing under the old penalty.

All that is left is sail area, plugged into the formula in square-root form. Ultimately, the key relationships in a 12-Metre design are sail area, waterline length and displacement. Although displacement does not appear in the formula, it is still a crucial measurement. The regulations pertaining to the formula prescribe a certain displacement for a certain load waterline length, and if displacement is lighter than that permitted by an applicable calculation, a heavy rating penalty is assessed on the calculated waterline length. Because no designer is willing to invite this penalty, the waterline length and displacement are closely tied, and if one measurement is determined, the other is immediately known. Additionally, waterline length and displacement are inversely proportional to sail area. One cannot go too far in one direction without sacrificing advantages in the other. More sail area, for example, means more horsepower, but it also means less displacement, making the boat more tender, and less waterline length, giving the boat a lower potential hull speed.

Designers, when working under the International Rule or any other rating formula, attempt to get around these relationships so that the pluses in their design outnumber the minuses. When a design is heeled, for example, its long overhangs lengthen the waterline length far beyond that of the load length, a common design strategy restricted somewhat by the practice of measuring the waterline length higher on the hull. And, as we have discussed, the bustle artificially increases the waterline length by moving the stern wave further aft. (It is the distance between bow and stern wave, and the relative resistance therein, which determine a yacht's effective waterline, or sailing, length, and thus its potential hull speed.) We have also seen that reducing a yacht's freeboard makes it "stiffer," more resistant to heeling, without actually adding ballast and thus increasing both displacement and waterline length.

All these design considerations are important, but the essential challenge is striking that perfect balance among sail area, waterline length and displacement. This balance of factors, Kirby would come to reflect when the 1983 series ended, may well be more crucial to the success of a 12-Metre than any subtle manipulations of hull shape. With *Courageous* and *Australia* in 1977, the three key figures began to settle into fairly narrow ranges. The major step with *Freedom* had been to increase stability at no expense in displacement by significantly lowering freeboard. The next step seemed to be to decrease displacement at no expense in stability. Kirby, and Sparkman & Stephens, would attempt to make a noticeable advance in stability without touching the boat's conventional displacement. Only Lexcen, with *Australia II* and *Challenge 12*, would tackle lowering displacement too, and only Lexcen would succeed.

In the almost paranoid world of secrecy that the 12-Metre designer inhabits, the key dimensions are treated as state secrets. The most closely guarded is the load waterline length, and it is *never* revealed in the yacht's paint job. The simplest of the three key dimensions to ascertain, from it displacement can be easily determined, and soon the essence of a design is laid bare. In an America's Cup summer, there are plenty of figures in circulation – in press statements, newspapers and magazines – and they are usually, when wisdom prevails, annotated with the caution "approximate." They are always meaningless, fodder for the unsuspecting press and public. Stated displacements are, almost without exception, high. In the press kit prepared for the 1983 match, *Canada 1* is listed at 60,000 pounds, about 6000 pounds above its more likely displacement. *Australia II* weighs in at 54,000 pounds – most experts agree that it tips the scales at about 51,000. Designers of 12-Metres, Kirby included, are happy to offer dimensions of their yachts, but they may change them from day to day, never sticking with one set of figures long enough for the learned to take them seriously.

During the *Canada 1* campaign, Kirby was unyielding about figures. One day at the Canadian training camp in Miami, several crew members casually asked him how much shorter the newly arrived *Canada 1* was than *Clipper*. Kirby refused to tell them. Miffed, the crew went to the repair trailer for a tape measure and determined for themselves that *Clipper*, at 64 feet, was longer by 18 inches.

Taken at its extreme, Kirby's tight-lipped stance could be seen as a vote of nonconfidence in the crew's ability to keep its collective mouth shut. At the end of the challenge effort, Jeff Boyd had only a ball-park idea of *Canada 1*'s displacement; at one point Terry McLaughlin reacted to a display of reticence on the part of Steve Killing by asking him if he thought Dennis Conner was going to rush out and copy them. Kirby was probably right in not handing out dimensions that might fall on the ears of people with no business knowing them. ("The only reason people want to know the numbers," he once observed, "is so they can tell somebody.") There are some things in this world best kept to oneself. The numbers were his—he had shaped them to satisfy an archaic, demanding rating formula. If he had to, he would take them to the grave.

the machine that lies

The test tank is an apparatus with a dark, dangerous past, and Bruce Kirby eyed it with some suspicion. It was a necessary tool in this project, but Kirby had never had one of his designs clamped in its analytical jaws, and he knew that designers before him had been fooled by data of the most misleading nature. The test tank had put its seal of approval on *Mariner*, and the woefully slow Britton Chance design was only one such experience. To be fair, the scientific community had learned its lessons well. Scale distortion was recognized as the horror it was, and instrumentation was far more accurate. All the same, the test tank was a new experience to Kirby, and he was afraid that either it or the technicians would somehow pull the wool over his eyes. His assistant, Steve Killing, was a bright guy, but he had helped design the tank, and that might put him too close to the issue to be non-partisan. Kirby needed a third party, someone whose opinions he could trust without question. He called Sam Lazier, a friend who had sailed *Torch*, his very first Mark I International 14. Lazier, a professor of mechanical engineering at Queen's, had been chief measurer for the Kingston Olympics. Kirby had already discussed the project with him and now asked him to visit the tank and make sure he wasn't snowed by a lot of fuzzy mathematics. Lazier was happy, as he would describe it, to hold Bruce's hand.

In 1975 Steve Killing, a junior member of C&C Yachts' design staff, was sent to Ottawa to spend a year turning the test tank of the National Research Council into a world-class facility. The NRC tank was unsuitable for testing sailboat designs; the test hulls, or "plugs," could be towed down the tank only in an upright position, a feature betraying its purpose for freighter designs and the like.

Suitability of the NRC tank aside, there were many things wrong with tank testing at the time. To casual observers, tank testing seemed about as cold and analytical, and thus as certain, as yacht design could become. But that was far from true, and the greatest problem was scale distortion. Water does not act on a full-size hull the way it does on a model a fraction of the size.

The three-foot hulls the Stevens Institute of New Jersey favoured were far too small to draw conclusions from. They rarely told much of significance about the after third of a hull, and in the case of Britton Chance and *Mariner* had led the designer to disastrous conclusions. Tank testing was only as good as the eyes that attempted to make sense of the tufts that flowed along the plug's contours. For all the appeal the test tank may have had, it was still largely an aid to intuitive design.

Many problems could be solved by simply making the models larger. An increase in scale would make subtle changes in hull shape easier to assess and would reduce the reliance on hyper-sensitive measuring devices. In the new NRC tank, plugs were increased to a relatively enormous 14 feet in length; with new instrumentation, the tank was used in 1976 by Killing to help design the 1978 Canada's Cup challenger, *Evergreen*, which he sailed on as foredeckman.

There were many good things about the new NRC tank. For example, it was the first in the world to tow the plug from its imaginary sail plan's centre of effort – the plug "sails" down the tank, rather than simply being pushed. But there was room for upgrading in instrumentation and analysis. A problem during the *Evergreen* project had been scattered data. When testing at a certain angle of heel at various speeds, for example, one aims to produce a nice curve out of the data. "Scatter," readings that fall outside the desired range due to any number of anomalies, made arriving at a best-fit curve far less scientific than one would have preferred. Computerized analytical methods introduced after the *Evergreen* project made fairing data into pleasing curves much simpler and, most important, much more accurate.

Accuracy was the greatest worry when it came time to drop a 12-Metre hull model into the NRC tank. Bruce Kirby was obliged to produce a reasonably conventional 12-Metre, and performance differences among conventional 12-Metres are extremely small. One per cent is considered significant. In a straight upwind drag race to the lay line, a one per cent speed advantage would mean that the leeward yacht could tack and cross; it could mean a victory margin of over two minutes at the finish line. But a one per cent advantage is not easy to find under the International Rule. It is even less easy to detect in the test tank, particularly in a tank with a margin of error three times the margin of performance being researched. Before Kirby's design plugs could enter the tank, the NRC was informed, the margin of error would have to be reduced from three per cent to one per cent. Only then would they have a chance of drawing any worthwhile conclusions. The NRC complied.

Even with these improvements, the angst of tank testing was far from resolved. Since the *Evergreen* project, Killing had become more objective about the test tank's purpose. Ideally, a designer wants the tank to say, "Yes, your intuition is right. Go ahead and build it." But what happens when the tank tells the designer he is *wrong*? The designer and test tank might sit in a stalemate. Whatever the reputation and accuracy of a certain tank, the ideas in a designer's head still carry a lot of weight, and there is the danger of the designer concluding that the tank doesn't know what the hell it's talking about and building the boat anyway.

To avoid this kind of stalemate, another analytical tool was needed to cast the deciding vote. That tool was the computer. As with the test tank, the computer was a familiar analytical tool to Killing when Canada's 12-Metre program began. Following the *Evergreen* project in 1978, Killing saw the future, and the future was the desk-top computer. He went down to his local Radio Shack and bought one of his own, the TRS-80 Model II, for home use. His enthusiasm for the machine so outstripped that of his employer that he left C&C in 1979 to set up his own design office in Midland, Ontario.

The computer would serve as a measuring stick of a 12-Metre design's theoretical potential through performance prediction, which calculates a yacht's speed in various winds and on various headings through the computer's weighing of a hefty number of relevant statistics. For the America's Cup project, Killing employed the Measurement Handicap System program developed at MIT by Professor Jerry Milgram, a program described by Killing as "a cheap and fast way to test out wild ideas."

Killing and Kirby examined only one wild idea, and it wasn't even their own. The design was the V-06, a very short 12-Metre with a deep "V" IOR-type bow designed by an Englishman named Chris Freer who was convinced, as Killing had once been, that 12-Metres were wishy-washy old things in drastic need of modernizing. Freer had been successful in having his design, which had been drawn for the aborted Royal London Yacht Club challenge of 1983, appear in an issue of *Canadian Yachting*. Killing lifted the hull lines and statistics from the pages of the magazine and fed them into the MHS program. The V-06, Killing decided, would be okay in very light air, which, in America's Cup terms, is five or six knots. Once it ran into typical America's Cup breezes of 11 or 12 knots, it also ran into a lot of problems. So much for wild ideas.

On February 19, Steve Killing loaded a 14-foot model of a 12-Metre onto a truck and headed for Ottawa. The wooden plug had been built at the boatyard of Bill Goman, another C&C Yachts alumnus, who was turning out a line of keelboats designed by Killing. The plug was called *Springboard*; it was, he understood, a state-of-the-art American 12-Metre design that would serve as a point of reference for a second model, which would more closely represent Kirby's design for the Canadian challenger.

To outsiders, Killing would describe *Springboard* as a conceptual amalgamation of *Clipper* and *Freedom;* Sam Lazier would call it "basically *Clipper.*" In truth, *Springboard* was neither. Bruce Kirby was holding his cards so close to his body that not even his associates knew precisely what *Springboard* represented. It was enough that they knew it to be something proven which could provide a sound base of comparison for Kirby's own concepts. Kirby asserts that *Springboard* represented a specific 12-Metre. He also asserts that it wasn't *Clipper.* The designer refuses to reveal the true nature of *Springboard,* although by his own admission he is very familiar with the lines and figures of *Courageous* and *Australia.* It would not be too daring, then, to assume that what Steve Killing drove to Ottawa was a 1:5 model of *Courageous.*

Tank testing proceeded at breakneck speed. Time and money were binding issues: to the point, money was limited and a final drawing of the design had to be completed by April. By February 26 the testing of *Springboard* was complete. On March 21 Killing was again loading a truck in Midland, this time with a 14-foot plug called *Take Off, Eh* named in homage to those two famous hosers, Bob and Doug McKenzie, and to the fact that the second model was something of a take-off on the first.

The testing of *Take Off, Eh* took only five days. The tank had been well tuned before the arrival of the Kirby project, and little time was wasted in mechanical adjustments during the testing of either model. All the same, data collection was complicated by the way the plug "sailed" down the tank by being towed from its centre of effort. A host of sailing dynamics arose; with subtly changing water conditions, these dynamics would cause a plug to wander in its path down the tank, and great concentration was required from the technicians to accumulate accurate data.

The coordinator of the tank testing program was David Murdey, an engineer who had worked alongside Killing in the development of the NRC tank in 1975. Murdey was an Albacore sailor in Ottawa, Kirby's home town, and the engineer's obvious competence won the trust of the designer. All the same, Sam Lazier still paid a visit to the tank, and what he saw did not impress him.

The skill of personnel did not concern him, nor did the soundness of the tank's analytical ability. The whole program was too brief. There was no time, for example, to do separate wind tunnel tests on keel and rudder configurations. (Lazier had also hoped that there would have been more room in the design program for investigating the technology of the rig and its components. He had planned to install load cells in the shrouds of the completed boat to keep track of forces in the mast, but when it came time for the experiment the $50,000 budget was more urgently needed for the sail inventory.)

Lazier was also disappointed in the size of the models they had to use.

Ideally one would like to tank-test full-scale hull models. That had been tried, in a way, at sea with actual boats. Dragons had been instrumented with pressure transducers, and shortly before his death, C&C Yachts co-founder George Cassian had done the same to a stock keelboat design in cooperation with the University of Toronto. Even Olympic gold medalist Rodney Pattisson, who would serve as one of *Victory 83*'s helmsmen, had once wired up his Flying Dutchman. In tank testing, the bigger the model the better. With more money, Lazier felt that the Canadians could have gotten a 1:4 model into the NRC tank; Ben Lexcen was laying the groundwork for the designs of *Australia II* and *Challenge 12* with massive 1:3 plugs.

Having been put in charge of analyzing Bruce Kirby's design ideas, Steve Killing felt the same frustrations. The time restraints were more annoying than those imposed by money. If he could do it all over again, Killing would handle 80 per cent of design analysis through a computer performance prediction program based on an earlier systematic set of tank tests. Such a program could evaluate sail area, stability and hull dimension changes, including changes to draught and the prismatic coefficient, a scientific term which describes the mathematical formula used to calculate a hull's volume. Keel and rudder design could be handled separately in a test tank. The NRC did have a small water tunnel, which followed the principles of a wind tunnel with high-speed water. But, for the *Canada 1* program, Killing would have had to develop an analytical technique before actually going ahead with the tests. And there was never any time for that.

Money restraints meant that the tank was never used to its full potential. Even with all the time in the world, a proper tank test program could not be carried out with only two models. A minimum of three to five models, says Killing, are needed to recognize beneficial design trends. Two models can only confirm an idea a designer has. You really want to use the tank to start learning new things, and find out, as Lexcen did through the use of many model configurations, what can pay off under the International Rule.

Most of all, it would have been nice to have had time to try something really off-the-wall. "Even if we'd found *Australia II* and she proved two per cent faster," Killing would lament, "it would have been a pretty risky move building *that* boat, it being our first one and not having another one to fall back on."

At one point, Kirby was planning a third model. Keel shape aside, *Take Off, Eh* was a fairly conservative variation on *Springboard*. Had a third model been possible (there was even speculation at one time of building a second boat if the money poured in, of Kirby locking himself in a room for a month or so and churning out another design), Kirby would not have been satisfied to make simply another small step. He would have gone shorter and lighter, a major step pursued by Valentijn with *Magic*. But *Magic* proved a failure and Kirby feels almost relieved that he was shackled by time restraints. With a program of unlimited length, brainstorming could have led him *anywhere*, down unimaginable *cul de sacs*. The austerity of the program might have saved him, he muses. With more time, he could have gone for a break-through, listened to the machine that lies, and made a huge, sorry mistake.

Bruce Kirby had an understandable prejudice for the merits of *Take Off, Eh*, which was his very private vision of how to improve *Courageous* or what-ever *Springboard* happened to represent. At first there was a question of whether the tank was even capable of turning up any merits. Scaling laws meant that the rudder and keel couldn't be analyzed with tremendous precision, and when David Murdey examined the differences in shape between the two models, he told Kirby that he doubted the tank could reveal significant differences. But Kirby pointed out that what might not be significant in Murdey's experiences was extremely significant in the realm of the 12-Metre. All Kirby wanted was one per cent, a margin of difference that verged on the tank's margin of error.

After two days of sailing *Take Off, Eh* down the tank, graphs of perform-ance differences between the two models were displayed on giant televi-sion screens. *Take Off, Eh* was proving faster – barely. In seven to ten knots of wind, the Kirby design's velocity made good to windward (VMG) appeared to be about one per cent superior, but as the wind increased, the performances of the two models came back together. Conversely, when sailing downwind *Take Off, Eh* showed itself to be increasingly superior as the wind increased, partly because it was a lighter design. Lazier felt that Kirby was disappointed in the results, that he had hoped *Take Off, Eh* would prove to be some quantum leap in the tank. Kirby denies this: only he knew, he says, what design *Springboard* represented, and therefore only he knew how much of an improvement would satisfy him. Normally in the tank one tries to flush out an improvement by going too far in a design change and in the process turning up more measurable differences. But restraints in the Canadian program meant that the tested model had to be quite close to the actual design. It was a miracle at all that a design as conservative as *Take Off, Eh* exhibited any measurable improvement at the scale at which it was tested.

Kirby had learned nothing new from the tank. If the apparatus wasn't throwing him a curve ball, he might even have an improvement on a known winner on his hands. Before the tank testing of *Take Off, Eh* was even completed, construction of *Canada 1* began.

What set *Canada 1* apart from other conventional 12-Metres was its keel. The keel serves several functions. By countering side-slipping, it determines how well a yacht tracks to windward. By housing ballast, it determines how stiff a yacht is. And by assuming a certain lateral plane, or side profile, it determines how well a yacht manoeuvres. The keel, obviously, is of major importance in any yacht design, and it became the focal point of Bruce Kirby's efforts to improve the *Intrepid* lineage.

There are only two measurements in the International Rule which have any bearing on the shape of a 12-Metre keel. One is the limitation on draught; the other is the girth measurement factor. The girth measurement is plugged into the formula as a factor designed to penalize and therefore discourage a rounder cross-sectional hull shape and a more separate keel. The penalizing figure is determined by the difference between what is known as chain girth and skin girth. At a point 55 per cent along the measurement waterline from its forward end, the length of the skin girth is determined by measuring along the surface of the hull from the floating or load waterline to a point on the hull 1500 mm lower. This point is usually about halfway down the keel. Chain girth is determined by measuring the straight-line distance between the point on the hull 1500 mm down from the load waterline and the point where this straight line meets with the hull as a tangent. The difference between the two measurements is entered into the formula. Thus, the shorter the skin girth, the less the penalty.

In some ways, a short skin girth is not a bad idea. It means a lower penalty and consequently room for measurement gains elsewhere in the formula. And it means a less rounded hull, which means less drag-producing wetted surface. But a short skin girth means that the keel is less well delineated from the hull, and potentially less efficient. At Cove Haven, Kirby and Killing had the opportunity to examine *Lionheart*, the British maxi-dimension contender by Ian Howlett. *Lionheart's* displacement meant that plenty of fullness was called for, and Howlett used it to his rating advantage. Where the girth measurements are determined, *Lionheart* was incredibly full, taking virtually no penalty at all. Aft of that point, Howlett attempted to salvage some performance characteristics by strongly delineating the keel, from where the hull flowed back into the full lines of the bustle.

Kirby was not going to attempt a zero penalty in girth – he was too committed to delineating the keel to do that, and *Canada 1* didn't have the massive displacement to justify it. Instead, Kirby opted for a fairly standard girth measurement penalty, so that at the point where the penalty is determined the hull cross-section took on a very conventional wineglass shape. Fore and aft of that point, however, the hull was tucked up significantly, so that there was a line where hull and keel met.

A key concern of Kirby's was increasing a conventional design's stiffness without having to load on more ballast. *Freedom* had been the most successful in 1980 by reducing freeboard and thus lowering the standard 12-Metre's centre of gravity. But that had led the authorities to create the stiffer freeboard penalty, partly to prevent future designs from becoming so low to the water that they became unseaworthy. But Kirby, and many other designers for the 1983 series, decided that the penalty was outweighed by the performance gains. He turned Steve Killing and his computer performance prediction program to the task of determining a suitable balance between loss in rating penalty and gain in stiffness. Killing first investigated the relationship with an exaggerated reduction in freeboard of nine inches. While the resulting sacrifice of sail area hurt boat-speed in lower wind velocities, the lower freeboard began to pay off in the 11 knot range. While theoretically sailing with 20 degrees of heel, the design gained 2000 pounds of effective righting moment without any increase in ballast. Lower freeboard was evidently worth pursuing, and Kirby eventually settled upon a 3½-inch penalty with a resulting increase in righting moment of about 800 pounds. Ben Lexcen would take even greater penalties for his two new designs, *Australia II* and *Challenge 12*.

Lowering freeboard wasn't enough. Kirby also wanted to get the ballast lower in the boat. All modern conventional 12-Metres carried some amount of sweep in the leading edge of their keels. In yachts like David Pedrick's *Clipper* and *Defender*, and Ian Howlett's *Victory 83*, the sweep was so pronounced that the line from the bow, along the forward underbody and to the tip of the keel was almost an unbroken curve. Pronounced sweep meant that there was very limited room at the keel's short tip for ballast, and often it was difficult to get all of a design's ballast into the keel. In the case of *Clipper*, several thousand pounds were positioned in the bilge.

The higher in the boat the ballast is placed, the more problems it causes. Ideally, ballast is placed as deep in the boat as possible and over as short a longitudinal area as possible. Ballast that won't fit in the keel has to be kept as low as possible in the bilges; but the bilges are relatively shallow and cover a wide area of the boat, and when ballast is moved into them it naturally starts spreading fore and aft. This makes the ends heavier and the boat more susceptible to pitching in a sea.

Consequently, the best way to get as much ballast as low as possible in the boat at the benefit of stiffness is to find an accommodating keel shape. Designs like *Clipper, Defender* and *Victory 83* are prime examples of the "lifting body" concept of design. With a boat so long and narrow, lateral resistance is provided not only by the keel, but by the keel and the deep, narrow hull shape together. The hull and keel combine to form, in effect, the same basic profile as one half of a delta-wing aircraft. The alternative to the "lifting body" is the "fuselage-wing," in which the hull is basically the main body of the boat and the keel concentrates on providing lift and stiffness. This concept is typical of the modern IOR design, with its smaller, deeper and very efficient high-aspect keel.

The International Rule discourages high-aspect (i.e. deep and narrow) keels: the draught limitation effectively makes them impossible. It does not rule out the possibility of a keel with a steeper leading edge, which can do away with the acres of wetted surface in the forebody of the lifting body shape and consequently improve manoeuvrability. Some of this removed wetted surface reappears in more efficient form in the now-much-longer keel tip. A longer keel tip means a lot more room deep down for ballast, and Kirby was able to pack virtually all of *Canada 1*'s lead into the keel.

But a long keel tip is not without drawbacks. The longer a keel tip, the more turbulence is created. Unless one could think of a way of controlling the turbulence, there was a limit to the practical length of the tip. Kirby was mainly concerned with making a conventional 12-Metre as stiff and manoeuvrable as possible without going too far into left field. As it was, he had already gone too far with his keel configuration for some backers and supporters, who had expected something a little more bland and a little less risky. Kirby thought his keel was revolutionary enough to warrant its concealment until the day of the boat's launching but was not being kept awake at night by the sort of dream that Ben Lexcen had. Lexcen, too, was after a long keel tip, but he wanted one so long that turbulence would be a serious problem. And because the problem was so serious, he had been driven to come up with a solution that had occurred neither to Kirby nor to virtually any other 12-Metre designer: *wings*.

in the land of the manatee

Remember that a cup campaign is very much like the formation of a new business. There is the Syndicate, which we will call the Organizers and Directors, and they provide the venture capital. They appoint a president, who is the skipper, and as chief executive officer he surrounds himself with other key personnel and the operational personnel as well. We might consider the operational personnel as the remainder of the crew. The skipper must answer to the Chairman of the Board, who is probably the Syndicate representative. The proforma is developed over a period of about 6 months and indicates that progress will be made and it shows a profit by the 1st September. The profit that the Syndicate anticipates is winning of the trials.

> – "Notes – 12 metre – America's Cup Campaign,"
> acquired by the Canadian challenge and attributed
> to Bill Ficker, skipper of the defender *Intrepid* in 1970.

It has been estimated that there are only about 1000 manatees left in the wild in Florida's waters, and they are being killed off faster than they can reproduce. They are strange, ungainly-looking animals, something of a cross between a tuskless walrus and a small whale, that laze just below the surface of the state's rivers, which makes them easy and unfortunate prey for the propellers of careless powerboaters. As in many places in Florida, there are signs posted under the huge bridge and causeway that span the mouth of Tampa Bay, warning boat operators of the animals' presence. The crusade to save the poor creature has even infiltrated Florida's living rooms; from time to time the laid-back recording star Jimmy Buffet has appeared on television, imploring people to handle their boats more carefully in manatee-infested waters.

Manatees may be hard to spot in Florida, but 12-Metres are even harder, and in early 1982 two began sailing out of a marina near the town of Palmetto. Palmetto is located in Manatee County, and the marina rests on the final, broad expanse of the Manatee River. The two 12-Metres were rare even as 12-Metres go. *Intrepid* was the best wooden 12 ever built, and

Clipper was considered by some to be the best aluminum design of its breed. The pair formed the heart of the Canadian challenge's crew-training program.

The site of the training base was to the west of downtown Palmetto, near the end of 10th Street West on the grounds of the Snead Island Boat Works. The Ringling Bros. and Barnum & Bailey Circus show train is just down the road and so is the Bradenton Yacht Club; Bradenton, where Carling Bassett developed her court skills, lies opposite Palmetto on the south side of the Manatee River. To the east of Palmetto are grapefruit groves and colonies of mobile homes. Palm trees mix freely with deciduous varieties in the sandy soil, and the landscape is dotted with one-storey cottages raised above the ground on cinder blocks. The land is mainly flat and sparse; as in much of Florida, one gets the feeling that there are never enough buildings and trees to fill up the empty space. The town is uninspiring, dotted with such basic enterprises as Varnadore Auto Sales, the Alvarez Mexican Restaurant and a spate of fast-food joints.

The Canadian training base was as unassuming as the town. A plain, hand-made wooden sign at the marina's entrance was the sole warning that ambitious things were afoot only a matter of yards away. The west side of the small yacht basin featured a row of protected slips. On the grassy area to the north, several tractor-trailers were parked, chock-full of equipment and gear for the Canadian challenge. A small, pretty cottage to the east served as the training camp's headquarters. Moored in the basin was a houseboat that served as a combination office/residence for one of the challenge officials, and a 54-foot Hatteras motor yacht that acted as the training vessels' tender. Above all else there were the two training vessels moored nose-to along the basin's north face, their sterns pointing to the basin's gap – a gap so narrow that *Intrepid* and *Clipper* had to be manoeuvred carefully into the more roomy stretches of the Manatee River, where manatee were indeed sighted and Tampa Bay was but a short sail away.

Eric Jespersen and Don Campbell were the first crew candidates to arrive in Palmetto; both showed up in late January to help set up the camp and prepare *Clipper* for the arrival of the rest of the sailors. Eric "Dispenser" Jespersen, 20 years of age, was a big strong lad, six feet two inches in overall length and displacing 200 pounds. When it came time to drape him in a team uniform, he would require a size 46 jacket. A member of a boat-building family in Sidney, B.C., he brought useful construction and rigging skills to the program. He started sailing very young and had amassed a wealth of experience in boats large and small, including building and sailing his own Star. He became one of the campaign's most versatile crew members, but ultimately was not to survive the 1983 cup summer as part of

Fred Schueddekopp and Rob Muru

the *Canada 1* crew because of a clash of wills and personalities with Terry McLaughlin. Don "Campbelloni" Campbell was a chunky 21-year-old from West Vancouver with strictly big-boat ocean racing experience. Young and keen, he was a good winch mechanic and would primarily be used as a back-up crewman. Back-up or not, Campbell developed a calculating eye for the camera and at times would seem almost singlehandedly to represent the crew in the visual media.

Early in the first week of February, a wave of recruits, Terry McLaughlin included, arrived in camp. Bob "Not to Worry" Vaughan-Jones, 22, from Delta, B.C., had crewed aboard the winning boat at the 1976 Canadian Youth Sailing Championship. His crew duties saw him finish seventh that year at the World Youth Sailing Championships, and in 1979 he and his

Robin Wynne-Edwards and Eric Jespersen

skipper won the North American Fireball titles. The bearer of a Class 9 commercial pilot's licence, Jones had left his job as a bush pilot for the opportunity to sail in the America's Cup. Sheer determination and hard work would earn him the foxhole position on *Canada 1*.

Rob Muru, 22, of Toronto was an excellent Laser sailor who had finished 28th in a field of 380 at the 1980 Worlds. Muru was also a fine Soling crew and had won a gold medal in Lightnings at the 1981 Canada Games. Arriving in Palmetto, he had never crewed on a keelboat, but he learned quickly and emerged from the long selection process as *Canada 1*'s mainsail trimmer. Being the occupant of the "hot seat" on a 12-Metre, Muru would take a great deal of heat and criticism from many sources, but survived the flak to do a very creditable job.

Fred Schueddekopp, 26, of Vancouver had spent six years as a sailmaker with the North organization. A former Wayfarer and Star sailor, his keelboat experience had been highlighted by his place on the 1980 Pan Am Clipper Cup team. Schueddekopp was a nonstop worker who joined the program as a mainsail trimmer, and when that role aboard *Canada 1* fell to Muru, he assumed the role of tune-up helmsman aboard *Clipper*.

Paul Phillips, 24, of Barrie, Ont., was a sailmaker who would never settle into any one crew position. In the fall of 1982 he would be asked to become an in-house sailmaker for the program and, after taking the training course

Brent Foxall: would you buy a used brush from this man?

necessary for running an industrial sewing machine, found himself with the skills that allowed him to spent many hours and nights mending and altering the often battered sail inventory.

Ed "Fast Eddy" Gyles, 25, of Toronto raced regularly aboard 8-Metres and IOR keelboats. He was one of the few candidates with match racing experience, having sailed in the 1978 Canada's Cup trials and been a member of the Royal Canadian Yacht Club's Pacific Challenge teams from 1975 to 1981. Gyles, who had once been granted a tryout with the Winnipeg

Blue Bombers, soon staked out the foxhole as his territory. When Bob Jones earned the foxhole position aboard *Canada 1*, Gyles moved to *Clipper* and eventually to the maintenance crew.

Rob Kidd, 20, of Brantford, Ont., had completed two years of a degree in mechanical engineering when the America's Cup came along. Another veteran of the 1978 Canada's Cup trials, Kidd brought a mix of keelboat and dinghy experience to the camp and was employed in any role in the foredeck area. He settled in as a back-up crew on *Clipper* and finally moved to the maintenance crew.

Bob Whitehouse, 40, of Islington, Ont., also arrived at this time. Married with a young son, Whitehouse was a native Australian who was in the process of obtaining Canadian citizenship. He had been made the campaign's salaried head of maintenance, although he actually had limited experience in maintaining keelboats. Whitehouse held a B.A. in industrial design and had established his own boat-building business in Toronto, turning out Albacores and Flying Dutchmans. He was long associated with Terry McLaughlin, having been a Flying Dutchman coach for the Canadian Yachting Association, and had lit the flame at the 1980 Olympic boycott party.

In mid-February another wave of recruits arrived. Greg Tawaststjerna, 23, of Toronto, had been recruited by Terry McLaughlin to serve as back-up helmsman. A good instinctive sailor, "Twister" had finished 13th at the 1980 Laser Worlds and would finish sixth in 1982. A runner-up to McLaughlin in the 1980 Olympic team trials in Flying Dutchman, Tawaststjerna had no previous keelboat or match racing experience, but when he finally left the campaign to pursue a Finn program for the 1984 Olympics, his loss was felt deeply. But his departure would also help normalize life in the camp; Twister was a determined partier.

Rob Webb, 31, of North Vancouver, better known simply as "Omar," was the only married crew recruit. A diesel mechanic with a private school education, Omar had 15 years of ocean racing and sailing experience. He would fall into the role of mast man; the job's requirement of heaving huge bundles of sails above and below deck made it the most physically demanding, and the strain would be telling.

Robin Wynne-Edwards, 24, of Kingston, Ont., arrived in Palmetto at the wheel of Jeff Boyd's van, which was filled with his boardsailing equipment and that of Boyd and others. Wynne-Edwards was a boardsailer through and through, and had competed in the Windsurfer Worlds in Japan in 1981. He would become a grinder and reliable back-up crew, as well as a versatile maintenance man familiar with all of the working gear on board a 12-Metre.

Paul Hansen, another young Vancouverite, brought a background in one-designs to the campaign. He had crewed on 505s as well as Stars, and also carried on his family's tradition in competitive cycling. During the campaign, Hansen would add running to his athletic résumé. Alongside Phil Gow, he would become one of *Canada 1*'s two full-time grinders. Gow, 20, was a Halifax native whose six-foot four-inch frame had seen service in university swimming and water polo competition. An accomplished Laser and Finn sailor, he was quiet and fit – in short, the ideal grinder. He was also an avid and competitive runner, and it was he who introduced Hansen to the pastime. Gow and Hansen were tireless workers, dedicated to keeping in top shape. They would become almost inseparable in training and socializing – and eating, something at which they were prodigious.

In addition to Gow, six other crew candidates arrived around the third week in February. Brent Foxall, 25, of Vancouver held a B.A. in geography and made his living as a mast builder. An excellent Laser sailor and superb dinghy crew, "Fox" was the 1980 Fireball North American champion. He became the team comedian, a master at nicknaming people and imitating such well-known sailors as Dennis Conner, Tom Blackaller and Carl Buchan. (There are girls in Newport who to this day think Foxall is an Australian.) His strange, Joycean way with the English language led to his dictionary of "Favourite Foxallisms." On the sailing front, his all-around skills would allow him to fill in at any position, and eventually he became a valuable back-up bow man.

The man who would become *Canada 1*'s bow man was Donald Alexander "Sandy" Andrews, 25, of Toronto. Andrews started sailing in dinghies like the 505 and 470, but moved into keelboats, where he gained most of his competitive experience. Closely associated with Gerhard Moog of the Royal Canadian Yacht Club and *Dynamo*, Andrews sailed in four SORCs, the 1980 Sardinia Cup, and was a member of the 1975 Canadian Admiral's Cup team. At five feet ten inches and 165 pounds, he was a relatively small member of the crew, and his role would demand of him many muscle-wrenching moments atop *Canada 1*'s spar at sea, attending to one gear failure or another. His fine mechanical skills, combined with his steadily improving tactical abilities, would assure him his key position on *Canada 1*.

It would be an understatement to call Daniel Palardy, 25, of St-Hyacinthe, Que., a quick learner. When he arrived in Palmetto, he had been sailing for only three years, but he had invested those three years extremely well. A civil engineering degree, combined with two years as a "boat nigger" (the title by which all persons who make their living maintaining and delivering other people's yachts refer to themselves), had made him a knowledgeable boat technician. All of his sailing experience had come aboard IOR ocean racers based in Europe. He had raced French and British boats in locales as diverse as the Virgin Islands and the Solent. Among many other assignments, he had crewed aboard the Peterson 45 *Marionnette VIII* in the 1982 SORC, the Frers 51 *Blizzard* during Cowes Week, and the Frers 77 *Helisara VI* during the 1981 Maxi World Cup in Sardinia. A man who pulled more than his own weight, Palardy would serve as a sail trimmer on *Clipper* and eventually as the back-up navigator.

Eric Martin, 21, from Laval, Que., was a Laser and Finn sailor who had won the Quebec Youth Championship in 1980. His brother, Eddie, who finished fourth in Lasers at the 1979 Pan American Games (at which an automobile accident broke both his legs), also joined him in the training camp. Both would leave the program after the breakup of the Newport training camp in August of 1982 to become regularly employed citizens. Two Torontonians with extensive keelboat experience became temporary members of the program. Bryan Gooderham left after the Easter break in Palmetto to rejoin the crew of the C&C 45 *Amazing Grace VI* in its drive for a spot on the 1983 Canadian Admiral's Cup team; David Ross, a well-travelled ocean sailor and navigator, was short on experience in around-the-buoys racing, and his lack of size (six feet tall and less than 150 pounds) led to his departure from the program after the summer of 1982.

The last crew candidate to join the Palmetto camp was Peter Wilson, who arrived March 10. A childhood friend of Jeff Boyd, Wilson went by the nickname of "Two Ton" – the origin is obscure, although as a boy he had been on the chubby side, and there exists a treasured photo of the young Wilson cycling across a bridge, with a road sign before him reading "Two Ton Limit." Wilson's sailing background was strictly dinghies: he had sailed with Boyd in International 14s in the mid-1970s before moving to Toronto and serving as Terry McLaughlin's "14" crew for the 1981 and 1982 seasons. Wilson was destined to become *Canada 1*'s navigator. Although his navigational experience was nil, Two Ton was an electrical engineer, a valuable asset in coming to terms with the new wave of on-board instrumentation. But before he could become navigator he had to get into the camp, and it took an inordinate amount of persuasion on the part of Boyd and McLaughlin to convince George Wilkins to offer him a tryout. Once on board, he would become infamous for his absentmindedness. He often missed *Canada 1*'s morning departure and was usually ferried out aboard a rubber dinghy.

All in all, there were some very good sailors in Palmetto. Even so, despite the prestige of the America's Cup, they did not represent the cream of Canadian yachtsmen. A deciding factor for many potential candidates was the commitment the program required – at the very least, a year and a half of one's life. For those with families and careers, the commitment was prohibitive. Terry McLaughlin was the only national team member to sign on. After hearing of the challenge in the fall of 1981, he had discussed it with other team members, who were even more sceptical than he at first was. Ultimately their decision not to participate was dictated by the fact that the last Olympics were only a year or so in the past, and to qualify for the boycotted Games they had taken a lot of time off work and in some cases had delayed careers. There was an understandable reluctance to remove themselves from the marketplace for another year and a half. And those who weren't concerned about removing themselves from the marketplace opted to invest their time in a shot at the 1984 Olympics. With a year separating the 1983 America's Cup and the 1984 Olympic Games, only Terry McLaughlin seemed confident that there would be enough time to prepare for the Games when the cup challenge was over.

Thus, it was a very young and eager roster of crew candidates that arrived in Palmetto to learn how to sail 12-Metres. But enthusiasm in the end could not make up for skill, and before *Canada 1* entered the 1983 challenge trials, three of her eleven crew positions would be filled by sailors who had not been present at the Palmetto camp.

Jeff Boyd flew to Florida on February 8. With him was John Millen, 21, of Toronto, an excellent high-performance trapeze crew who was working his way through the McLaughlin family. He had crewed first for Terry's father, Paul; with Terry's brother, Frank, he won the 1981 International 14 World Championship. And he was now in Palmetto to sail with Terry. Millen exhibited a healthy interest in sports and girls, and would succeed in keeping the training program loose with his own brand of hockey-related humour.

When Boyd and Millen arrived at the boatyard, everyone had left for the day, having put in long hours of work on *Clipper*. After checking out the 12-Metre, they at last met up with the rest of the crew and a game of touch football ensued. Since their university days, Jeff Boyd and Terry McLaughlin had regularly run a particular play which, for murky reasons, Bob Vaughan-Jones dubbed the "Kingston 35" in Palmetto. Boyd would run a straight down-and-out pattern; after a pump-fake from McLaughlin, he would go for the long bomb. Not an altogether unusual play, except that they liked to use it the first time they got their hands on the ball. The first time they got their hands on the ball on that day, they ran the play with customary success. For Boyd, the 12-Metre training camp was formally open.

At the crew house, Boyd and Millen were told they would be roommates. The building sat off on its own in Palmetto, about three and a half miles from the boatyard, and almost everyone in the crew would make a habit of running back to the crew house every other day. It was known as the Crusaders Club, less formally as Cockroach City; the ramshackle three-storey hotel had been renovated for the Canadians, but by the time they left

Starting practice aboard the two J/24s

in May it was beginning to fall apart again. It was an immense place, with double bedrooms, two recreation and sitting rooms, a laundry room, a dining room, and a tactical room with video playback equipment.

Millen and Boyd were also told that dinner was at 6:30. Everyone else was seated by 6:20, and the two arrived to find all but themselves wearing jackets and ties. Boyd wondered what the hell was going on, having heard nothing of any formal dining regulations.

"Sure you know," he was chided. "Wilkins told you in your first interview."

That, upon reflection, was probably true. But it had been a long day, and he didn't feel like going back to his room to change. "You'd better hope the Admiral doesn't show up," he was warned. "The Admiral" was Rear Admiral Jeffry V. Brock, ret'd., the challenge base's director of operations.

Boyd started eating. The rest of the crew implored him to go put on a jacket and tie, but he refused to budge. Millen decided otherwise.

As soon as Millen left, McLaughlin gave the signal and Boyd recognized the con. When Millen returned, fashionably attired, he found the rest of the crew shovelling back their dinner in their underwear.

For the first three days, Boyd could not relax. What distressed him most was the dynamics of the crew candidates. Individually, he enjoyed their company. As a group, he found them oppressive. Egos were on the line; the first few days were a hazing session, with the sailors warily circling each other, sizing each other up. A lot of bragging going on, aggression the favourite tool for carving out safe psychological niches. *I do what I want, don't worry about other things*, Jeff Boyd wrote to himself. *I've got a feeling we can go all the way, so I put up and push Terry.*

Terry was a concern. Like everyone else at the time, he was high-strung, and with McLaughlin the tension produced a kind of aggravated singlemindedness. Boyd prayed that McLaughlin would mellow, and waited for Peter Wilson to arrive, knowing that Two Ton would be a calming influence. That afternoon Boyd and McLaughlin had gone at it in a pair of J-24s arranged for their use by Bud Larson, commodore of the Bradenton Yacht Club, so that they could practise starting manoeuvres while the 12-Metres were being prepared. The boats were a bit too jumpy for their purposes but kept them occupied. McLaughlin, running on his own high-voltage energy source, fought for and gained the high ground. *Tomorrow I'll be a little more aggressive*, Boyd decided. *We had some close calls and, yes, when Terry screams at me I'm a little intimidated. Tomorrow when he screams, I'll scream right back.*

The next day, he forced himself to be more keen and aggressive. Back in the J-24 again, he fared better, but fell into several disagreements over right-of-way; one serious argument arose when McLaughlin adamantly refused to admit fault when reviewing one incident. That argument dogged him. Was Terry so forceful in the support of his own case because he was absolutely sure he was right, or was it because he was incapable of admitting he was wrong?

And there was another facet to Boyd's concerns about the dynamics of the crew candidates. He was a dinghy sailor who had come to Palmetto to call the shots aboard a heavy-displacement 64-footer as the tactician for another dinghy sailor. How would the dinghy and keelboat elements in the crew mix? Whose territory was a 12-Metre? Was it truly a glorified daysailer racing on an overgrown dinghy course? Or did the size of the America's Cup design place it more firmly within the realm of the offshore racer? *I am not the stereotype big-boater*, he wrote. *However, I'm starting to lose some of my negative thoughts about the scene. I think I feel more comfortable today vs. yesterday. Time will tell. Just remember: Puerto Rico was hell. This has got to get better.*

Nothing could be worse than Puerto Rico. He and his crew had arrived there in 1979 two weeks early, had seen the tremendous breeze and had become only more confident that they could win the gold medal. Then Boyd came down with what he thought was a sore throat. But it got worse, and when the team doctor showed up, he told him he had mononucleosis. He didn't get out of bed for three days.

He was sure that when the racing started they could just load him onto the boat in a wheelchair; he could sail for three hours, then get loaded back into bed again. But it didn't work out that way. He was totally drained of strength, and in the end Gil Mercier had to step in as skipper. Boyd was left with nothing but a sense of half-finished business.

Patience, more confidence, he noted to himself in Palmetto. *Get psyched*.

When Jeff Boyd's concern about his relationship to the rest of the sailors in the camp relaxed, it served only to strip bare his concerns about the way the camp was being run. He craved a disciplined routine; without it the camp seemed to lack direction. At an early meeting, Boyd had asked George Wilkins of his crew training plans. Did he intend to divide them into two distinct crews, or would he be moving everyone around? Wilkins was not particularly forthcoming in either answers or ideas, and the disorganization it suggested rattled Boyd. At the prompting of McLaughlin, who didn't want to become known as the principal troublemaker, Boyd began asking other questions, about guest experts, about the sail program. It was the beginning of the confidence gap between the crew candidates and those charged with shaping them into a winning America's Cup crew.

the admiral

The Admiral could best be described as seaworn. Though not especially tall, he was barrel-chested, and his hair was white and his face deeply cragged. There was a grizzled roughness to him, an overall finish that suggested he had spent his life wrestling with forces of nature considerably more powerful than himself. He was born in Vancouver in 1913 and had begun his naval career on loan to the Royal Navy, serving with it throughout the Second World War in locations as diverse as the North Atlantic, West and North Africa, and the Mediterranean. After the war, he was named commander of Canada's Pacific destroyer fleet and saw action in Korea. He reached the peak of his naval career as Vice Chief of Naval Staff, then served as Senior Officer-in-Chief of Command and Marine Commander. A respected career officer with the Royal Canadian Navy, he actively and unsuccessfully lobbied against the merging of the branches of the Canadian military into the Canadian Armed Forces. Having earned a hefty list of orders and decorations, he retired in 1964 to live with his wife, Patricia, in Westport, Ontario, and spend his winters in Florida. In 1981, McClelland and Stewart published the first volume of his memoirs, *The Dark, Broad Seas*. Over his long career, Rear Admiral Jeffry V. Brock, DSO, DSC, CD, RCN(Rtd), had commanded thousands of men in the most harrowing of situations. He came to Palmetto to oversee the training of two dozen civilian sailors for an assault on the America's Cup. He demanded respect and utter loyalty, and he received neither.

The Admiral's first deputy director of operations was Captain William Stuart, another former navy officer. He served in both the Second World War and the Korean War, and left the Royal Canadian Navy in 1969 to join the Canadian Coast Guard, of which he became Director in 1973. Since leaving the Coast Guard, Captain Stuart had become a marine consultant to oil companies working in the Arctic, and his business interests prevented him from serving with the challenge any later than March 12, 1982.

The Admiral brought in Captain Ray Creery as his replacement. Captain

Creery had served in the Mediterranean and on Russian convoys. He saw anti-submarine duties aboard HMCS *Kootenay* and took part in the Allied invasion of Western Europe. In 1944 he underwent pilot training and went on to command both the 833 Squadron and the 19th Carrier Air Group. After holding several senior staff and diplomatic appointments, he retired with captain's rank and turned his attention to the government of the Northwest Territories, in which he held several key positions. In assuming his new assignment in Palmetto, he left the staff of a wooden-boat-building firm in Maine.

The challenge's support services manager, Roger Sweeny, had commanded two destroyers as an anti-submarine specialist, as well as the sail trainer HMCS *Oriole*. He had held senior appointments in the Arctic and in Denmark, and after retiring from the navy in 1980 had earned his master's certificate and returned to sea in the merchant navy. To the crew candidates Sweeny and Creery were known as the Admiral's Men.

The two other senior staff positions in Palmetto were far removed from this naval background. The personnel manager was Harry Roman, a 54-year-old native of Estonia with a Swedish/Canadian education and a background in 5.5-Metre competition. A member of Canada's sailing team at the 1968 Olympic Games, Roman had served as a national team coach from 1977 to 1980 and had a soft spot for iceboat racing. The administration manager was Kevin Singleton, a tall, sturdy, bearded native of England who emigrated to Canada in 1973. Singleton was a chartered accountant with over 30 years' experience in boating and held a British Department of Trade and Industry Ocean Yacht Master Certificate.

Despite the fact that the training camp was very much the Admiral's show, he chose to keep a low profile with the crew. He joined them at dinner only occasionally. In one of the first such encounters, he gave a fairly stirring speech about how Canada was going to win the America's Cup. He was, without a doubt, a well-spoken man. As the speech went on, he began to allude to how, when the 12-Metres were ready, they would begin training by doing "Chinese fire drills," as they became known, practising bringing a 12-Metre alongside the tender, raising and lowering the mainsail, and other such things.

Terry McLaughlin was seated next to the Admiral, and during the speech he began to screw his face into expressions both puzzled and miffed. When the Admiral was finished, he asked, "Do you mean that, the first time we go out, we don't get to *sail*?" The Admiral assured him that they just wanted to be sure they were seamanlike, that they got the basics down pat, that they didn't rush into anything.

Soon after the Admiral's dinner speech, the trouble began. The first casualty was George Wilkins, who had been in Newport arranging for the transport of *Clipper* to Palmetto. Once at the base, he and the Admiral fell into irreconcilable differences, and in less than two weeks he was gone. The vacuum of responsibility for on-the-water crew training would be filled by Steve Tupper of Vancouver, who had only recently left his position as coach of the national sailing team. Tupper, who had placed fourth in the Dragon class at the 1968 Olympics, was a welcome addition to the camp – as a coach he was well respected and highly organized – but his presence could do little to offset the complete consolidation of power with the Admiral after Wilkins' departure.

The problem the crew candidates had with the Admiral was not, as some outsiders imagined, a back-breaking militaristic routine. On the contrary, there were scheduled days off, and plenty of leisure time for tennis, football, and other pursuits. Nor was it that the Admiral was incompetent. He was, in fact, a superb organizer; when his expertise was called for, he could move mountains. He had established the facilities in Palmetto for the Canadians, and he would do the same, with impeccable attention to detail, with the base of operations planned for Newport for the summer of 1982. The essential problem with the Admiral was that he knew next to nothing about yacht racing and consequently about how to deal with competitive sailors.

The dilemma struck home with Jeff Boyd on February 21. *Time is cruising along faster than I could imagine*, he wrote. *As far as routine goes, I'd say my appetite is back and I'm sleeping well. There are still many problems with this syndicate. Of course, from my point of view it is all middle-management problems. They aren't sailors! They don't understand sailors and have plenty to learn. It is frustrating. Unless some management attitudes change, I doubt I'll be here much longer. If any Americans could see us now, they would have some real chuckles.*

The most serious mistake the Admiral made with the crew candidates was to isolate them from the world at large and the plans of the challenge syndicate. At one meeting, Fred Schueddekopp casually asked what was happening back home with the sail development program, an understandable question from any sailor, never mind one with a sailmaking background. The Admiral replied by asking Schueddekopp if he had enough money to buy sails. Schueddekopp replied that, no, he didn't. The Admiral then informed him that he was a guest of the challenge, that they were all lucky to have been invited, and a guest doesn't ask his host how much money he is spending on what kind of sails.

"Palmetto was like a boot camp," McLaughlin recalled. "You weren't allowed to ask questions about aspects of the program, especially sails. You weren't allowed to phone people or talk to the press. You were almost cut

12-Metre Deck Layout

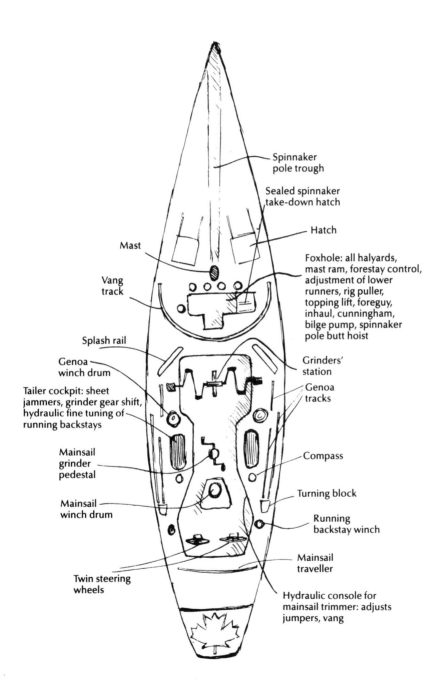

Spinnaker pole trough

Sealed spinnaker take-down hatch

Hatch

Mast

Foxhole: all halyards, mast ram, forestay control, adjustment of lower runners, rig puller, topping lift, foreguy, inhaul, cunningham, bilge pump, spinnaker pole butt hoist

Vang track

Splash rail

Grinders' station

Genoa winch drum

Genoa tracks

Tailer cockpit: sheet jammers, grinder gear shift, hydraulic fine tuning of running backstays

Mainsail grinder pedestal

Compass

Turning block

Mainsail winch drum

Running backstay winch

Twin steering wheels

Mainsail traveller

Hydraulic console for mainsail trimmer: adjusts jumpers, vang off from reality back in Canada. But, being immersed in that system, you started to think that maybe this is the way America's Cup campaigns are. Back in the old dinghy days, you and the crew would make all the decisions about equipment and sails, the state of your program." Whenever McLaughlin did leave Palmetto to attend some regatta, he'd view the camp from a fresh perspective and think, *This is crazy*.

In fairness to Rear Admiral Brock, his conduct was entirely consistent with his naval background, which was supposedly the reason command of the camp was assigned him. There were the officers – his management appointees – and there were the men. A good naval officer, like Brock, treats his men well, and is solicitous about their welfare to get the best from them in return. But essentially "the men" to him are faceless, replaceable bodies. The commanding officer reinforces the dignity of his position by keeping aloof from the crew, except to grace the odd occasion with a stirring, onward-and-upward speech. The last thing he would do is invite or tolerate the input of the crew in his planning.

McLaughlin and Boyd were sorely tempted to leave, but they didn't. One of the reasons they stayed was that they had invested so much time convincing Peter Wilson to quit his job and attend the camp and George Wilkins to let him attend. Now that they'd gotten Two Ton involved, they couldn't pack their bags before he'd even arrived. So they stayed put, and McLaughlin, not surprisingly, became the ringleader of dissent. At mealtimes he and Schueddekopp passed subversive notes back and forth, and ultimately it became the Admiral's aim to remove McLaughlin from the pro-

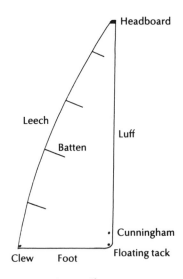

Mainsail

gram. McLaughlin and Brock were both strong leaders accustomed to being the focal point of attention. With neither harbouring much respect for the other, one of them would have to go.

Their first opportunity to sail a 12-Metre came on February 20. *Clipper* was at last seaworthy and in the water. The Admiral was all for leaving dock, but only for running through his Chinese fire drills, which he hoped to continue for any number of days. The Admiral's ideas, by and large, had merit, but he was dealing with an impatient young crew who had been waiting weeks at the base for the opportunity to learn how to sail a 12-Metre.

It would be very much a case of the blind leading the blind. They had only one expert in camp – Kim Roberts, the crew's "professor of 12-Metres," an employee of the Newport Offshore boatyard who had sailed aboard *Clipper* at the beginning of the 1980 defence trials. Much of Roberts' sailing experience revolved around yacht deliveries and, although he was no expert on a tactical level, he provided a wealth of information about the mechanics of sailing a 12-Metre. He went out of his way to be helpful to the sailors at the Palmetto base and was regularly on board *Clipper* during the early stages of the program. Jeff Boyd and Terry McLaughlin made a habit of taping his talks in an attempt to have them transcribed into a manual similar to Gerry Driscoll's infamous "book." (According to North sailmaker Jim Allsopp, when you were invited aboard the *Enterprise* program, in 1977, Driscoll sent you a copy of his manual, which outlined in detail the role of every crew member of a 12-Metre. The theory went that if you read the

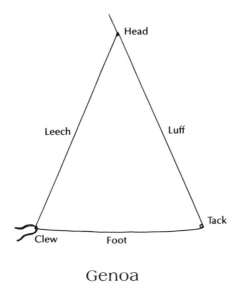

Genoa

book before showing up, you'd know your exact duties without ever having stepped on board the boat. It was the yacht-racing equivalent of the football playbook.)

Against the Admiral's wishes, they decided to take *Clipper* for a sail. Kim Roberts would be skipper, McLaughlin would helm the boat, Muru would be navigator and Boyd would be tactician. The excursion did not start well; McLaughlin fell into a veritable screaming match with personnel manager Harry Roman over whether the crew could take their lunch with them on *Clipper* rather than eating on shore. Then, with McLaughlin at the wheel, *Clipper* was towed toward the narrow gap of the marina basin.

Clipper, however, was not cooperating. Despite McLaughlin's best efforts, the boat was crabbing toward the pier wall; even with the helm hard over, it refused to respond. Like most modern 12-Metres, *Clipper* is equipped with twin wheels, set side by side to allow the skipper to see more by positioning himself further outboard. Inside each of these wheels is a smaller wheel, which controls the trim tab. Kim Roberts noticed that the trim tab was cocked out of position. He corrected its wheel, and *Clipper* obediently responded to McLaughlin's helm. The first seagoing crisis of the training program had been narrowly averted.

Once out of the marina, they began to raise the mainsail. As tactician, Boyd had the responsibility of helping to hold up the boom so that it cleared the helmsman's wheels. The sail seemed to take forever to go up, and its size struck Boyd as overwhelming. When the head of the mainsail reached the jumper struts, there was a snap, followed by a loud crash as the sail collapsed to the deck.

Boyd and Muru looked at each other in embarrassment. It was they who had nico-pressed the halyard to the headboard car, the device which guides the sail luff up the slot in the mast and locks it in position at the very top. Boyd and Muru had attempted to attach the halyard with a nico sleeve and wire configuration of their own improvising. The failure was a sound lesson learned. Fred Schueddekopp promptly went aloft in the bosun's chair and re-swaged the halyard.

Clipper was soon cruising along Tampa Bay on a close reach in eight knots of wind. Although there was no instrumentation on board, they seemed to be churning along at a healthy nine knots. Boyd looked out across *Clipper's* deck to see a powerboat planing to keep up. The sails were in ragged shape, but sails meant nothing to Boyd. *Nothing* meant anything; there was no time to think deeply about what was happening.

They nosed about for some marks to round, then sailed upwind for a while. They performed a few clumsy tacks, complete novices when it came to the intricate task of turning a 12-Metre through the wind. Boyd, using a hand-bearing compass for the first time, practised calling lay-lines. The crew was keen and, for the most part, very quiet. McLaughlin peppered Roberts with a barrage of questions. *Clipper* pressed on, displaying the awesome power and speed of a 12-Metre.

Twelve-Metres are big boats, with plenty of things along their 60-odd-foot length waiting to break, rip, chafe and collapse. The loads involved in setting and trimming their sails are tremendous, measured in the tens of thousands of pounds. When their huge genoa jibs are eased while under sail, the wire-rope sheets groan in their blocks like the buckling bulkheads of a mortally wounded submarine; the sound travels clearly across the water, striking fear and respect into the hearts of unsuspecting observers. Every now and then the boat will make *one of those sounds* . . . an eerie squeal or short, whip-like crack that could be something serious, or something minor, or nothing more than the vessel making its own engineering adjustments to accommodate the godawful stresses threatening to wring life itself out of the cavernous aluminum hull.

After about an hour and a half of sailing, they decided to hoist a spinnaker. It went up in an unsightly mess; they had forgotten to disengage the tacking line which attaches to the foot of the jib and helps to tow it past the mast when coming about. Another lesson learned.

Soon after, a powerboat pulled alongside. It was from the training base; the Admiral wanted them to come in. They did.

battle lines

I would keep crew meetings well organized and not let them become "gripe" sessions. Particularly, I would limit them only to the crew and perhaps with one Syndicate member present, perhaps the Syndicate manager. I don't feel wives or anyone else should be in a crew meeting.

– "Notes – 12 metre – America's Cup Campaign"

That first sail aboard *Clipper*, unapproved and ultimately terminated by Rear Admiral Brock, set the tone for the rest of the Palmetto training camp: the Admiral was by and large on one side, the crew candidates on the other.

After returning to dock from the initial sail, the crew decided they should take *Clipper* out the next day, while they still had the benefit of learning from Kim Roberts, who was due to leave camp soon. But the Admiral decided that Terry McLaughlin, instead of sailing on *Clipper*, should go to the airport to pick up the sails for the Catalina 38 that had been chartered for practice for the Congressional Cup, the match racing series based in Long Beach, California. To the sailors, removing McLaughlin from *Clipper* for a simple errand made no sense at all, except as a clumsy effort by the Admiral to get him off the 12-Metre and on his way out of the program. The sailors consequently boycotted the sail. "Sailidarity" was born.

That evening, Fred Schueddekopp, Bob Vaughan-Jones, Rob Muru and Jeff Boyd went to Harry Roman's room at the Crusaders Club to meet with Roman, Roger Sweeny and Bill Stuart. They entered the room at 10:00 p.m. and didn't emerge until after midnight. It was a long and largely unproductive evening, with both sides arguing in circles. The crew candidates' position was that management's method of dealing with McLaughlin was threatening the success of the challenge. Management wasn't so sure; they viewed the Flying Dutchman skipper as a replaceable subordinate.

Boyd didn't get much sleep that night.

On February 24, *Intrepid* was hoisted from the water so that her outfitting might begin. *Clipper* was out for her third sail; the Catalina 38 was on the water as well. Those crew candidates rotated to shore duties walked about the hull of the wooden 12-Metre, assessing the magnitude of the task before them. The underbody required some filling and fairing, but most of the work was confined to the deck and interior – the boat had been completely stripped of fittings and hardware. Optimistically, they hoped to have it sailing by March 14.

The next day, while waiting for a morning fog to burn away so they could go out in *Clipper*, the sailors tackled *Intrepid*'s sail trailer, removing all the sail bags and dumping out their contents. *Intrepid*'s inventory was then inspected and categorized: of the 62 sails, only 16 were still serviceable.

Maintaining a working sail inventory for both 12-Metres was a problem. A few days later, sailing *Clipper* on February 28, they ripped the "Brick," a two-ply, five-ounce headsail left over from the 1980 America's Cup, when it caught on a spreader tip during a fouled-up tack. It was the only decent heavy-air sail they had, and the crew decided to eat lunch while figuring out what do do next. By the time lunch was over, the wind had died enough for them to hoist a single-ply headsail and continue their practice session.

At the end of that day, nine of the sailors walked to a field up the road from the Crusaders Club to play touch football. *I was on the same team as McLaughlin and Boyd*, Sandy Andrews would write in his journal. *Those two guys are amazing. I thought that it was to be a fun game but those two took it very seriously. It seemed as if they were at times behaving like poor sports, but then you realized that they were just taking the game so seriously. If a play didn't go right they would analyze it, and explain mistakes made by the rest of us so we wouldn't do it again. Both of them started to get quite agitated whenever we fell behind. I didn't even know or care what the score was. Those two are extremely intense competitors with a very strong will to win. I guess that's what makes good skippers.*

March 1 was a grim day; there was rain in the morning, and for the rest of the day an overcast sky kept temperatures unseasonably cool. While one group of sailors trained on *Clipper*, another stayed ashore to work on *Intrepid*. Without the necessary parts available, there was little for the *Intrepid* group to do, and they spent their time learning how to do rope-wire splices and mastering other rigging skills.

The crew on *Clipper* devoted their day to tacking and spinnaker handling. Because class rules limit the crew to only 11 men, they must work as a highly coordinated unit during any sailing manoeuvre. Tacking a 12-Metre is an act of great complexity. To begin with, it is not the easiest boat in the world to steer. It is long and heavy, and not particularly well behaved. If you let go of the wheel, it is likely to lurch off in one direction or another, but, because of its considerable length and narrow width, it takes a while to do so. This quality allows a helmsman plenty of time to respond to the design's digressions in heading, but it also makes it difficult to steer because news of its intended meandering is late to reach the helmsman. The feel of the wheel is heavy and mushy, and you may not realize as soon as you would like that the boat is determined to put its nose into the wind.

Intentionally putting the boat's nose into the wind is another matter. The first part of a basic "open field" tack, getting the boat from close-hauled to head-to-wind, takes six to eight seconds, depending on the boat and the skipper. It is a slow process and there is a lot going on. Ideally the skipper would like to initiate his tack in a flat section of water, but in reality this is hard to do. Exactly when a 12-Metre tacks is dictated more by the tactical situation it finds itself in, because in match racing tacking involves maintaining a synchronized cover of the trailing opposition or trying to break that synchronized cover if you happen to be behind.

Tacks can be panicked affairs – especially sneak tacks, in which many of the crew are lounging, bored and nonchalant, on the weather rail, lulling the opposition into a false sense of security. When the sneak tack is initiated, these rail-lounging crew members dive into the cockpit and begin to churn horizontally mounted handles that drive the two primary winches. A sneak tack can give you a three- or four-second jump on the opposition, and can help you eventually get their tacks out of phase with yours, thus breaking their cover. The Canadians would be able effectively to avoid being caught by a sneak tack by having Jeff Boyd watch the opposing skipper's hands. Should he cross one hand over the other on the wheel, it was a sure indication that he was about to change course.

If a skipper cannot pick a spot of flat water to tack in, he can at least delay his tack until his opposition is encountering water considerably less horizontal than his. Tacking when the opposition has just had the misfortune to slam into several successive waves is always a good idea; handling a few such waves badly can reduce boat-speed by as much as half a knot, and this reduced speed will invariably produce a poor tack when he attempts to stay in phase.

Initiating a tack requires coordination between the skipper and the mainsail trimmer. The 12-Metre has a rather small rudder for its size, to reduce turbulence, and the boat's balance is greatly controlled by sail trim. We begin our tack from starboard to port. At the tactician's signal, the skipper announces, "Ready about." The mainsail trimmer fixes his eyes on the rudder and trim tab wheels. Seconds before the helm moves, the mainsail trimmer cranks in his sheet, which is engaged in the self-tailer on

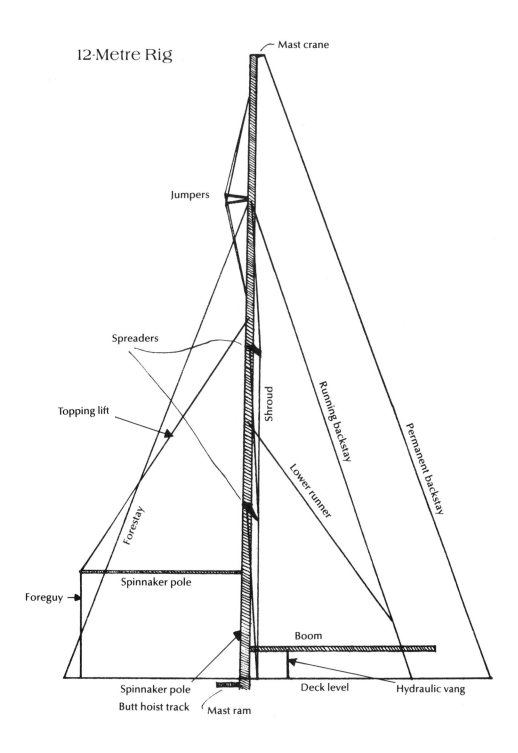

12·Metre Rig

Mast crane

Jumpers

Spreaders

Topping lift

Shroud

Running backstay

Permanent backstay

Lower runner

Forestay

Spinnaker pole

Foreguy

Boom

Spinnaker pole

Butt hoist track

Mast ram

Deck level

Hydraulic vang

the mainsail winch drum. The trimmer drives the drum, which is mounted on a pedestal forward of the twin wheels, with his own set of coffee-grinder winch handles. By cranking in the sheet, he closes up the leech of the mainsail, thereby increasing the weather helm. In other words the boat is now balanced to steer itself into the tack, relying less on the drag-inducing rudder.

While the mainsail trimmer cranks in his sheet, the skipper centres the trim tab and puts half a turn on the rudder wheel, just enough to get the boat head-to-wind in the six to eight seconds. The tactician cross-hauls the mainsheet traveller, which runs on a track on the transom, to windward, bringing the boom across the centreline of the boat to further load the helm and initiate the tack.

And then, for a few glorious seconds, the 12-Metre's velocity made good to windward (VMG) actually increases as it carries its considerable momentum into the eye of the wind. From that point on, however, its speed begins to plummet. The second half of the tack takes less time than the first as the crew strives to bring their boat back up to speed.

As the boat goes head-to-wind, the port tailer or sail trimmer sneaks wraps off his drum until it is down to wire. Just as the jib luffs, he eases out eight feet of the rope-wire sheet; when there is a significant luff, he lets the sheet fly, allowing it to smoke through his sailing gloves while leaving half a wrap on the drum. (Not everyone uses gloves. Once, after seeing the narrow-diameter spinnaker sheets on Terry McLaughlin's Flying Dutchman, Jeff Boyd asked Terry's crew, Evert Bastet, who would become a tailer in the summer of 1983, if he ever wore them. "Gloves?" he replied. "Oh yeah, sometimes. In the winter.")

While the port tailer lets his sheet fly, the starboard tailer hauls in his as fast as possible. The forward-facing grinder on the starboard side watches the clew of the genoa. When it clears the shrouds he yells, "Go crazy!" and he and three other grinders begin spinning their coffee-grinder handles at a velocity that would wrench the arms off ordinary citizens. The grinders aim to get the clew of the jib into the lead block so that the sail helps pull the bow over onto the new tack; as the bow falls off, the sheet is eased about a foot. There is also a lead puller that has been shifted forward about 12 to 18 inches before the tack, which, by changing the sheeting angle, "powers up" the jib for acceleration. Once the boat has built up speed, the jib is sheeted closer and the lead puller eased back.

Throughout the tack, the mainsail remains sheeted in, but as the boat lays off onto the new tack, the sheet is eased to the point where the helm is balanced. Excellent coordination between trimming and steering is needed here; if the mainsail is improperly eased, lee helm can develop when the jib fills. If lee helm forces the boat to come out of the tack pointing too low, distance to windward is lost; if, however, the boat comes out pointing too high, there is insufficient power in the sails to build back speed properly.

Recapturing speed is the essential task when falling onto the new tack. The mainsail trimmer eases the permanent backstay to straighten the mast and power up the top of the sail. The shape of the top third of the enormous mainsail is affected by the cunningham. The inhaul, a floating tack, adjusts the middle third of the sail; the sail's bottom third and overall draft is controlled by the outhaul, which hydraulically jacks the boom away from the mast – in 1983 the American 12-Metres regularly adjusted the outhaul during tacks, because from the clew to the terminal point of the lower section of the running rigging, where it overlaps with the genoa, the mainsail is normally quite flat. The mainsail, in short, is large and complicated, and perfect trim is essential to the speed of the boat. By oversheeting it, the mainsail trimmer could actually force the boat to tack against the wishes of the skipper.

Throughout the tack, the tactician and the navigator keep their heads down. Once past head-to-wind, the tactician eases his running backstay – enough that it doesn't interfere with the mainsail leech, but not so much that it whacks the starboard tailer on the head. Once onto the new tack, the tactician pulls the traveller to windward to centre the boom and the navigator grinds on his running backstay.

Whether or not a tack is a success is determined by The Numbers. The Numbers are a particular boat's performance blueprint, the result of long hours of on-the-water data collection and computer performance prediction. The Numbers provide the afterguard with target figures for boat-speed – when straight-line sailing in a given wind range, for example. The Numbers also provide an optimum heading – how close to sail to the wind, and how far off the wind to steer to get from the windward to the leeward mark on the run in the shortest space of time. For the 12-Metre sailor, The Numbers outweigh the arguments and theories of yacht designers. If a boat won't produce Numbers as impressive as the opposition's, the design simply doesn't cut it; the worst thing that can be said about a 12-Metre is that "it steers lower Numbers."

During a tack, everyone on board is tuned in to The Numbers. They are flashing away in digital readout; once the port tailer in our tack has released his sheet, he begins to call out the boat-speed readout. The rest of the crew listen carefully through the racket of the manoeuvre, knowing as they perform their duties whether the tack was a success by how low the announced figures sink and how quickly they climb again.

If the tack is poor, it could well be the fault of the person calling out the figures, for the key to a good tack is the break by the tailer, the point at which he lets his sheet fly. If he lets it go too soon, the foxhole man, who occupies a small cockpit of his own just astern of the mast, will find himself in a herculean struggle to assist the genoa through the foretriangle with the tacking line, which attaches to the foot of the sail slightly forward of the shrouds (a position that would be determined by the Canadians through surveillance of Dennis Conner's defence operation).

If the port tailer lets the sheet go too late, the starboard tailer cannot keep up with the yards of heavy rope-wire sheet thrashing dangerously in the air. It was a common error when the Canadians began training, and during the practice session on March 1 an unruly sheet lashed four people on *Clipper*. Three were unhurt. Bob Vaughan-Jones, the unfortunate tailer, was left with scrapes on his face and silver streaks of galvanizing across his freshly chipped teeth. He was loaded onto the *Mako*, the camp's twin-engined runabout, and ferried to the hospital and a dentist.

With the day's practice over and Bob Vaughan-Jones patched up, the sailors in camp held a crew-only meeting. There was a meeting scheduled with the Admiral the next day, and they wanted to review subjects and strategies for the encounter. In the hour and a half they were together, they discussed air fare home, free time, medical and dental insurance (apropos of the day's misfortune), income tax, house rules at the Crusaders Club, and stirring up gear and equipment donations. Most of the meeting, however, was concerned with the sail development program. It was decided that Fred Schueddekopp and Jeff Boyd would ask the questions on behalf of the group in order to relieve as much as possible the suspicions the Admiral had focused on Terry McLaughlin.

The meeting could not have gone worse. The Admiral was furious that they had held an unsupervised meeting the previous night and forbade any others without a management representative. Laying down the law, he stressed that the training camp was not a democratic one, that the crew candidates were to have no input in the greater decision-making process. This the sailors found deeply disturbing. If management, who didn't know much about yacht racing, didn't want the input of the crew candidates in establishing the sail program, for example, whose opinions were they relying on, if any? The Admiral had at one time indicated that the sail program could be handled by placing responsibility for it with a specially appointed director. There was nothing particularly wrong with that from an organization point of view, but why was management seemingly so determined to short-circuit the crew candidates out of any input or authority? This was the most upsetting thing about the Palmetto camp – that the sailors were repeatedly reminded, by either action or direct words, that they were simply *candidates*, and as such were entirely subordinate, and replaceable, with no need to be kept informed of other aspects of the challenge. The Admiral wanted a military mental discipline, "a good attitude and willingness to follow orders," as Sandy Andrews wrote to himself. The Admiral refused to tell the meeting who the people involved in the decision-making process were; he would not even tell them who was insuring them, even though almost everyone in the crew knew that it was Ed Gyles's father, Cedric, the president of Reed Stenhouse.

Certainly the program required a figure of authority, one the crew could look up to for direction and reassurance – someone who had been through the America's Cup before. The program needed, in short, a Dennis Conner, a sailor-patriarch who could infuse the ranks with confidence. If the Canadians were allowed to do the 1983 America's Cup all over again, they would probably start by going outside the country to hire such a sailor-patriarch. But there was no such person in the first Canadian challenge, and in Palmetto the crew instinctively turned to an authority figure in their own ranks. Not surprisingly, it was Terry McLaughlin. But the Admiral's behaviour seemed to indicate that McLaughlin and his circle were on their way out.

Leroy the cook on the steps of the Crusaders Club

March 3, the day after the tumultuous meeting with the Admiral, was scheduled for sail training, but Steve Tupper wisely made it a maintenance day so that the sailors could mull over what had been said to them.

The issue of authority was far from resolved. Before dinner, the Admiral held a meeting with the Congressional Cup crew, composed of Terry McLaughlin, Jeff Boyd, John Millen, Fred Schueddekopp, Eric Jespersen, Bob Vaughan-Jones and Rob Kidd. In January, McLaughlin, with financial backing arranged through George Wilkins, had put a crew together to attend the Pacific Coast Match Racing Championship. With Carl Buchan of Seattle as tactician, they had won the event and thus qualified for the prestigious Congressional Cup series. In addition to a strong group of American sailors, the event would be attended by a number of 12-Metre skippers.

The Admiral was having second thoughts about them attending the Congressional Cup. He was now discussing it as not a bad idea, but not a necessary idea either. As for the Congressional Cup crew themselves, he met with them individually and required them to fill out a form stating their reasons for being in Palmetto. It was a veritable pledge of allegiance; Boyd felt that, in the Admiral's mind, they, as the core of troublemakers in camp, had been kicked out, and by filling out the form they could re-enlist.

And the Admiral had come up with a novel way of getting rid of Terry McLaughlin. He informed McLaughlin that the campaign was not in the market for skippers at that time. He could stay and train in camp until his March 11 departure for the Congressional Cup. When the series was over, he would not rejoin the program until specifically invited to do so – that is, when they decided to hold helmsman's trials.

There is no one in the crew who can accept this, Sandy Andrews wrote in anger, *but accept it we must. There is nothing else to do. If we try to do anything then we are shipped back home too but without any hope of being asked back later*.

The Congressional Cup crew filled out the forms. It was an unfortunate experience for Rob Kidd – he was the crew's spare, and his innocent relationship with the rest of the crew led to his being treated like a first-class rabble-rouser. Jeff Boyd took a long weekend off and, with Greg Tawaststjerna, attended the Laser Midwinters. Terry McLaughlin decided to sail in the Snipe Midwinters. Boyd and Tawaststjerna were second and fifth respectively when bad weather made the regatta a non-event. McLaughlin finished terribly. The winter was not living up to its potential.

While Boyd, Tawaststjerna and McLaughlin were racing dinghies, Rudy, the camp's cook, was flying off the handle. He was an odd fellow, always full of stories he could never quite live up to (his best were that he used to cook for the Kennedys, and that he and a trained troupe of chimpanzees had regularly appeared on the *Tonight Show* and *The Ed Sullivan Show*). Shortly before dinner on March 7, he began berating the crew for getting him fired by constantly complaining about him. He reported to the police that his car keys had been stolen. When the police arrived and began looking for his keys, Rudy jumped in his car and headed for the hills, with the police shortly thereafter in hot pursuit.

The next day Leroy Jones, his replacement, arrived. He seemed to be screwed together straight, bearing no tales of preparing the meals of presidential families. His first chore at the Crusaders Club was cleaning up the pie that Rudy had thrown at the tender driver, Jimmy Johnston, which had splattered on the kitchen floor.

congressional cup

My goal is to win, and I want to win. I originally came here to sail with Terry. The management, I believe, is here to help. I'm upset by some of the management's opinions of us. I feel at present a little helpless over my own destiny.

– diary of Jeff Boyd

On March 10, the Admiral hosted a press conference and an ambitious reception attended by the mayor of Palmetto, the commodore of the Bradenton Yacht Club, the owners of the Snead Island Boat Works and the Lieutenant-Governors of Manitoba and Nova Scotia. In a customarily eloquent speech, he thanked the local dignitaries for their support and informed one and all that the Canadians intended to win both the America's Cup and the Congressional Cup (to ensure success in the latter event, the Admiral had ordered the crew to bring back the trophy).

The crew candidates, who had spent the morning working in the boatyard, had been issued polyester shirts bearing the Secret Cove Yacht Club logo and the following insignia:

$$\frac{12}{KC\ 1}$$

Pinned to their shirts were military-style tags bearing their last names. After the press was given a tour of the boats and facilities by the crew, the entourage headed for the Crusaders Club for a hot buffet lunch. The Admiral then shed the crew candidates and took the press upstairs to the tactical room to introduce his management team.

Armed with glossy black-and-white portraits, the Admiral revealed not the Canadian sailors, but the *system* behind them. There was himself, and Roger Sweeny, and Ray Creery, and Harry Roman, and Kevin Singleton. Admiral Brock also introduced Steve Tupper, but that was as close as he got to identifying individuals in the crew candidates' ranks. The Admiral's press conference was a far cry from the one that would occur in January 1983 with the christening of *Canada 1*, where each of the two dozen sailors hoping to secure a position aboard *Canada 1* would be introduced to the gathered throng – first and last name, and home town too.

The only crew candidate at the press conference was Terry McLaughlin, who had sneaked into the room and seated himself with the reporters. There was little representation from the yachting press, although *Sail*, the largest-circulation boating magazine in the United States, had sent a representative. The fellow in town from Warwick-Bradshaw, the Toronto public relations firm contracted to promote the Canadian challenge, allowed to the crew candidates later that he thought the press conference went well. Terry McLaughlin reported that anyone who knew anything about sailing would have been a little embarrassed: the Admiral was clearly unqualified to handle questions dealing with the intricacies of yacht racing. One of the highlights of the press conference came when the *Sail* representative asked the Admiral, while staring directly at Terry McLaughlin, who would be named the Canadian entry's skipper. In handling that hot potato the Admiral managed to avoid mentioning the existence of Terry McLaughlin, never mind acknowledging that he was in the room.

The farewell party for the Congressional Cup crew was scheduled for the evening following the reception and press conference. For over a week, the crew candidates had been inviting just about everyone they ran into, including employees of the boatyard and the Nautilus fitness centre the camp frequented. In all, over 100 people attended, eating barbecued hot dogs and hamburgers and dancing to music provided by a lethal 200-watt stereo system the sailors had rented. A few neighbours who came by to investigate the noise ended up joining in. Paul Phelan, who was in town, cut a fine figure on the dance floor with one of the elderly noise investigators.

The Admiral donated two kegs of beer. The gift prompted the sailors to invite him to attend, which he did. His presence was subdued, and brief.

While the Congressional Cup crew was winging its way to Long Beach, the rest of the sailors were out for the day on *Clipper*. The winds were light and restricted practice to the morning. That didn't stop problems from arising, though. While sheeting the spinnaker clew to the end of the pole in preparation for a hoist, it got away from the bow man, Sandy Andrews, and very nearly towed him into Tampa Bay. Andrews managed to gather up most of the sail, but in the meantime it had twisted itself around the retrieval line. The spinnaker went up in a knot, then fell into the water, where it ripped in two. It was an old sail and the crew concluded that it probably wasn't worth repairing. The whole sorry sequence was captured by a pair of Canadian newspaper photographers.

For the Congressional Cup series, the Canadians drew *.38 Calibre*, the same Catalina 38 they had chartered for the Pacific Coast Match Racing Championship, also held in Long Beach. The Catalina 38 was a cruising-oriented design with a crowded cockpit, and their boat came with fairly flat sails, which would give it an edge in heavy air but make it something of a lame duck in light winds. Terry McLaughlin and Jeff Boyd were skipper and tactician; Ed Gyles handled the bow; John Millen was mast man; Boyd added the mainsail to his responsibilities; Fred Schueddekopp and Eric Jespersen were grinders; and Bob Vaughan-Jones tailed. They were also joined on board by an owner's representative.

Their first race in the round-robin series, held on a windward-leeward course, came against Scott Perry, who had been Ted Hood's tactician aboard *Independence* in 1977. It was an uneventful match which the Canadians won.

The second race was more interesting. The boat representing the Secret Cove Yacht Club fouled Harold Cudmore of the British America's Cup program during the pre-start manoeuvres. In the America's Cup such an incident would lead to disqualification, but the Congressional Cup featured the unusual provision of allowing a competitor to exonerate himself by sailing around one end of the starting line. A competitor was required to acknowledge committing a foul by raising a white flag, and this Terry McLaughlin, true to form, at first refused to do. He then relented; after winning the start, the Canadians quickly spun around the pin end of the starting line.

It was a frustrating race. On the second windward leg, the Canadians ground down Cudmore in a tremendous tacking duel to take the lead, but at the end of the next leeward leg the British skipper gained an inside overlap and held his lead to the finish, delivering McLaughlin his first defeat of the series.

The third race of the day for the Canadians came against John Bertrand, the Olympic bronze medalist at Kingston and skipper of *Australia II*. Bertrand took the start, but McLaughlin sailed off on port tack, picked up a favourable wind shift and took the lead. On the second beat, Bertrand forced McLaughlin into a close coverage situation by initiating a tacking duel. At first Bertrand closed ground, but McLaughlin soon fell in phase with his tacks, locked him in a windward blanket and scored his second win of the day.

The day concluded with a race against Russell Long. Long fouled them before the start, and the Canadians went on to build a huge lead at the weather mark, only to have a squall terminate the race and leave them with a 2-1 record.

The second day of the event did not go well. The air was light, and the Canadians started off by losing their resail against Long when a shift turned the race into a dull parade. After beating Pelle Petterson, the skipper of the Swedish 12-Metre *Sverige* in 1977 and 1980, they met up with Dennis Durgan, Dennis Conner's tactician aboard *Freedom* in the 1980 America's Cup. While chasing each other around the committee boat before the start, Terry McLaughlin called for room, pointing to the nearby judge's boat as an obstruction. Though the Canadians won the race by over three minutes, Durgan protested them over the starting incident and, to the shock of McLaughlin and his crew, won. The day concluded at a disappointing 3-3.

On the final day, the Canadians were up against Dick Deaver and Rod Davis, two Californians who had previously won the Congressional Cup, and another British 12-Metre helmsman candidate, Phil Crebbin. They lost to Deaver in much the same fashion that they had fallen to Russell Long. During their race against Davis, *.38 Calibre* suffered a breakdown to her starboard primary winch. They lost the race, and were faced with the possibility of having to sail their final race, against Phil Crebbin, without the vital winch. Bruce Brown, the vice-chairman of the regatta, came on board to help fix it; he was still on board when the ten-minute gun for the race against Crebbin sounded. McLaughlin sailed back and forth before the committee boat, working himself into a froth. "I didn't come 3000 miles to race with no winch!" he screamed at the officials, pointing to an empty winch base; Brown had removed the winch completely. "How do you expect me to race like this?"

(McLaughlin would apologize for his behaviour at the awards ceremony that evening. "In the ten-minute sequence," he told the crowd, "I spent two minutes trying to get the vice-chairman of the Congressional Cup off the boat, three minutes circling the committee boat trying not to get invited back next year, and five minutes not letting the British know we were racing.")

Because of the broken winch, *.38 Calibre* was hopeless in a tacking duel. The Canadians decided they would simply sail straight for the lay-line at the first opportunity, where they could sail directly to the weather mark. After starting to windward of Crebbin and covering him for two tacks, they did just that. Despite a snarl on a smaller winch they were using as a substitute for the broken primary, they went on to win.

Scott Perry, whom the Canadians had beaten on the first day, won the event. Rod Davis was second; Dick Deaver, third. With a 4-5 record, Terry McLaughlin found himself in a four-way tie for fourth place with Phil Crebbin, Russell Long and Dennis Durgan. John Bertrand and Harold Cudmore tied with three wins apiece. Pelle Petterson, by winning only one race, received a sailing primer traditionally given out to the last-place finisher. Although the Canadians finished with a losing record, they could console themselves with the fact that they had finished ahead of all the other non-American crews.

At the Congressional Cup, Fred Schueddekopp arranged a dinner meeting to be attended by himself, Terry McLaughlin, Jeff Boyd, John Bertrand and Tom Schnackenberg. The Canadians did nothing but ask questions. Some were embarrassing, they knew so little. The Canadians felt they could sail with the Australians – the Congressional Cup had proved that. They just had to figure out how to sail 12-Metres.

The Australians were helpful. They unloaded reams of information without stopping to think that they should hide anything, although they weren't saying anything about *Australia II*. They were coolly sure of their effort. Their self-confidence was amazing, Boyd would think; the reason others so freely offered knowledge was that they didn't take the Canadians seriously as a 12-Metre threat – not like the British, with their formidable organization and sacks of money. The Canadians were pretty cocky thinking they could take the Australians on in Newport; the thought that they might not be taken seriously fuelled their desire.

John Bertrand was a new face to the Canadians; Tom Schnackenberg was not. A New Zealander by birth, Schnackenberg was a small, balding man who possessed a trademark floppy white sun hat and a moustache that rivalled Bertrand's Fu Manchu. One of the bright lights of the North Sails organization, Schnackenberg was a computer man, most at home running offsets and percentages and broadseams through a computer all day, which is what he had done with his time as one of four sailmakers with *Australia* in 1980. During the early 1970s he had worked in the North loft in Toronto for Dave Miller, the Canadian who won a bronze medal in Solings at the 1972 Olympics. Terry McLaughlin at one time had actually worked under Schnackenberg in the Toronto loft; Schnackenberg, in turn, had crewed for McLaughlin in 470s. He was friendly, unpretentious, a great one for remembering a face, and something of a genius. McLaughlin had once claimed that Schnackenberg was so bright he developed migraines outsmarting himself.

John Bertrand was also a sailmaker, and also, it turned out, an exceptionally nice person – almost too nice, it seemed, to have the killer instinct necessary to win the America's Cup. Regardless, his credentials were impeccable. The manager of the North loft in Melbourne, the 36-year-old Bertrand had already sailed aboard the 1970 and 1974 Australian America's Cup challengers when he won his bronze medal in Kingston. While learning the sailmaking trade in the United States, he had scored his first major match-racing success. He served as tactician aboard *Golden Dazy*, which defended the Bayview Yacht Club of Detroit's hold on the Canada's Cup in 1975. The losing Royal Canadian Yacht Club was so impressed by Bertrand that when the match was over its flag officers quietly debriefed him to find out where they had gone wrong.

Bertrand skipped the 1977 Australian challenge, and might well have turned his back on the America's Cup indefinitely were it not for the western boycott of the 1980 Olympic Games in Moscow. Bertrand, who had been selected as Australia's representative in the Soling class, joined his country's cup challenge at the last minute as team coach and headsail trimmer. At the end of the series, Alan Bond, the Perth real estate magnate who had backed every Australian challenger – and finalist – since 1974, elected to return to Newport in 1983 with a fourth and possibly final challenge. Ben Lexcen would design the new 12-Metre, christened *Australia II*. And John Bertrand, Bond had decided, would skipper her.

Over dinner, Schnackenberg and Bertrand told their Canadian hosts, with great emphasis, that the sail program was the key to a successful 12-Metre campaign. It was not what the Canadians needed to hear to set their minds at ease, having just left Palmetto and the battle with the Admiral over the state of their sail program.

It was, at the very least, a peculiar dinner. Here they were, thought Boyd, with the people their fund-raisers were proclaiming they were going to beat, and these very people were supplying them with the necessary ammunition. And the more the Canadians learned at dinner, the more they realized how far out of the picture they were. They were too deep into the campaign to believe the rhetoric back home. The magnitude of the task now appeared frightening; the whole challenge was beginning to feel like a very bad dream.

Marvin McDill had come to Long Beach to see some of the Congressional Cup. Despite the disappointments of the second day, McDill showed himself to be a patient and understanding man, and the crew went into the final day with the feeling that they ought to win a few races for Marvin – something that became a regular objective. The Canadian sailors invited Bertrand and Schnackenberg out again, this time to lunch with McDill. The Australians gave him an earful of what 12-Metre sailing was all about and what it took to win. It was the beginning of the turnaround.

arrivals, departures

The Congressional Cup crew, minus Terry McLaughlin, arrived back in Palmetto on March 22. Rob Webb had fallen overboard on *Clipper* earlier in the day, and while on the way to the airport in one of the camp's vans to pick up the returning crew, Bryan Gooderham was forced off the road and into the ditch, ruining the steering and flattening a tire.

In the crew's absence, Steve Killing and Bruce Kirby had paid a visit, sailing on *Clipper* and chatting with the sailors in camp as they developed the deck layout for *Canada 1*. Kirby seemed to believe that the camp was desperately short of people who knew about sails and emphasized that the sail trimmers should be the best sailors on board. Kirby also provided the first information regarding the sail program, saying that an order had been placed with the North loft in Toronto about six weeks previous.

That revelation produced further resentment toward the Admiral – only a few weeks before he had told the sailors that no decisions about sails had been made. Whether or not the Admiral was aware of the sail order, the belief strengthened that he was deliberately leaving the crew candidates out in the cold on crucial details of the challenge. When the Congressional Cup crew was back in Palmetto, they learned of another rumour – that the Admiral had tried to resign but had been talked into staying by Marvin McDill. Whatever Rear Admiral Brock's status, he was almost invisible in the day-to-day lives of the candidates. Steve Tupper was now firmly in charge of training activities at the base.

The day before the Congressional Cup crew's return, *Intrepid* had at last been launched. The completion of her outfitting had been assisted by Jean Castenet, the manager of the French challenge. On March 25 *Intrepid* and *Clipper* sailed together for the first time, although much of the day was devoted to tuning up. The next evening the first crop of guest experts arrived. Dave Vietor, the president of Horizon Sails, had been the mainsail trimmer on *Clipper* in 1980 and had since bought *Courageous*, which would train with Tom Blackaller's new contender, *Defender*. Argyle Campbell had contested the U.S. Olympic team trials in Tempests against Dennis Conner in 1976. A Congressional Cup winner, Campbell was a candidate for the helm of *Courageous*. Terry McLaughlin also appeared in camp; having just won the Flying Dutchman Can-Am series, he stopped in at the Crusaders Club for breakfast. None of the visitors stayed long. McLaughlin visited his brother, who was sailing in the 470 Midwinters in St. Petersburg, before heading back to Toronto.

At the managerial end of things, much was afoot. Steve Tupper flew to New York on March 30 for a meeting with representatives of Hood Sails (Tupper had left the Hood loft in Vancouver to join the camp), with the sailors in camp logically guessing that they would be discussing new sails for the challenge. The next day, Marvin McDill and several directors arrived for a meeting with the training camp staff. Again the rumours ran rampant: Harry Roman and Roger Sweeny were on the way out, the Admiral was about to be replaced. At the morning crew meeting, Steve Tupper, having rushed back from New York, informed the crew that a policy decision had been reached regarding sails that would take care of a program at least until July 1. Tupper had not been given permission to reveal the policy, though he assured the sailors that they would be told that day.

The policy waited until the next day, April 2. Marvin McDill revealed at the morning crew meeting that the syndicate intended to go with one principal sailmaker without excluding the contributions of any others. That sailmaker would be North, although the syndicate also hoped to have two jibs and several spinnakers from Hood by the time the camp moved to Newport.

McDill also told the crew that the new 12-Metre would be built by July 15. He would not reveal the name of the builder, explaining that a deal had not yet been struck. That came as curious news to the crew candidates. When Kirby and Killing had been in camp, they had reported without hesitation that the builder would be Fred McConnell of Parry Sound, Ontario. Despite that lapse in consistency, the sailors were impressed with McDill; for many it was the first time they had properly met him. *He seems to be a pretty straightforward guy with his head screwed on right*, Sandy Andrews concluded.

With the camp about to be blessed with a week off, the rumours of the past few days began to solidify into reportable fact. While Bob Vaughan-Jones was driving Steve Tupper to the airport, Tupper informed him that the Admiral had resigned. But, at dinner that night, the news of resignation proved to be premature. Ray Creery told the sailors that the high-echelon meeting of April 1 had been a stormy one, the result being that the Admiral's powers had been significantly reduced. Rear Admiral Brock would be taking on a lower profile, spending more of his time at his winter home in Fort Myers, Florida, completing the second volume of his memoirs. It appeared that Creery would be assuming more responsibility. The wheels of change were in motion.

The Palmetto camp resumed training on April 13. Eric Martin's brother,

Eddie, joined the program, as did Brook Hamilton, significantly increasing the challenge's Quebec contingent. Hamilton, a young, bilingual Montrealer, was a nonstop worker with a fount of practical knowledge who joined the small pool of tender drivers.

Rob Muru returned at the wheel of his van, which was loaded with a pair of goalie nets and over two dozen hockey sticks. That evening Palmetto witnessed its first road hockey game. It didn't like what it saw. The sport paralyzed the town's residents with bewilderment and fear, and a neighbour had the police move in and break the game up.

And Terry McLaughlin was back, officially for a two-week tryout. It was time to get serious again. Aboard *Intrepid*, McLaughlin and Boyd ran the crew through a series of starting-line manoeuvres: "ragtime" (luff the sails), "poofters" (slow the boat to a crawl), "drop trou" (back the boat up) and "schmeeblies" (get the boat up to speed). The next set of guest experts was due in two days, and the fine-tuning of the Canadians' greatest weapon was about to begin.

In the ten minutes of pre-start manoeuvres in a match race, a competing yacht has two objectives only: cross the starting line not necessarily when the gun goes, but ahead of, or with better speed and position than, its opponent; and force an incident. An "incident" is yacht racing's sanitized term for an infraction of the racing rules.

As a development of the basic laws of the sea, the racing rules were designed to establish order and right-of-way in a sport that employs no referees. Competitors are expected to conduct themselves in a gentlemanly manner. If two or more parties differ on the race course as to who is right or wrong, protests ensue, and back on land they present their cases and call their witnesses before a hopefully impartial jury. It is all very rigid and legalistic and, as in life itself, an unsatisfied party can appeal his case to a higher authority. Appeal rulings establish precedents much the same way as in common law. Accomplished racing yachtsmen know their rule book and appeals inside out. Those who do not are sitting ducks in a match-racing start.

The many rules and interpretations conspire to produce a strange *pas de deux* between two yachts determined to gain the upper hand. Because a rule infraction leads to disqualification, it is possible to win a match race before even crossing the starting line. Some skippers are not content to leave the occurrence of an "incident" to chance, but go actively looking for one. The intricate manoeuvres of a match-racing start have evolved as a means of controlling the movement of the opposition, but these manoeuvres can also be used to force the other boat into committing a foul. Winning a race on the basis of a pre-start foul is not something most sailors

Starting Area

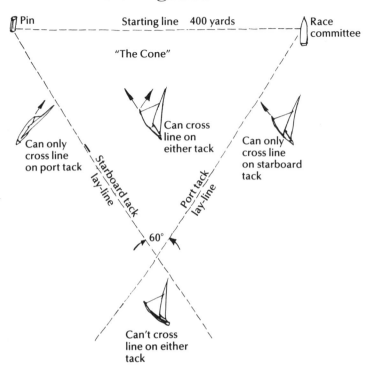

are proud of, but forcing an incident is often crucial to winning, particularly for a slower boat. An incident is an ace up the sleeve; should one lose at the finish line, there is always the possibility of reversing the result in the protest room. Some skippers are more aggressive about collecting incidents than others; in 1983, Bruno Troublé of *France 3* was notorious for his pursuit of rule infractions.

Most of a start involves circling or luffing head-to-wind. Circling is the activity most characteristic of match racing. Carl Buchan, the tactician for the Canadians at the Pacific Coast Match Racing Championship, once observed that circling was simply a way of killing time. There is certainly a large amount of truth to this; pre-start manoeuvres do not usually heat up until the final two minutes, as it is difficult to control, or "pin," the opposition for the previous eight minutes. In theory, though, two-boats engage in circling to pursue a tactical advantage. If you are good and perform your circles by the textbook, you can close on the opposition on each circle, and after five circles (or about 4½ minutes for a 12-Metre) can gain a two-boat-length advantage. Then you are no longer circling with someone – you are on his tail and able to control his movements and drive him away from the starting area.

Mosts pre-start jousting takes place in the "cone," an area bordered by the starting line and the lay-lines to the starting mark and the committee boat; in 12-Metre racing, the lay-lines meet approximately at a 75-degree angle, depending on wind strength, waves and boat-speed, well below the starting line. If you can stay inside the cone, you are reasonably safe. On either side of the cone, you can lay the starting line only on one tack; below the peak of the cone, you can't lay the starting line at all. A good starter can control the circling so that the circles work their way out to either extreme of the cone's sides so that the opposition can only lay the starting line on one tack. Having forced the opposition into that situation, the trick is to prevent him from getting on that tack. Conversely, a good competitor who finds himself outside the cone can control the circles so that they gradually work back into the cone.

Circling isn't the only way to herd the opposition outside the cone. In light air, it can be effective to circle for a time and then sit on the opposition's wind. Twelve-Metres don't generate a tremendous amount of speed in light air, and if one is blanketed it has no opportunity to build up its apparent wind. Apparent wind is what you feel when you stick your hand out the window of a moving car; it is the wind felt and in part generated by an object in motion. In 12-Metre racing, the apparent wind can be as much as 50 per cent stronger than the true wind. The yacht draws extra power from the wind it generates, and 12-Metres have been called apparent wind machines, capable of clocking six and a half knots of boat-speed into six knots of true wind. If a 12-Metre is unable to build its apparent wind, it has neither speed nor pointing ability (defined as the closest angle a yacht can sail to the true wind). Changing pointing ability also changes the shape of the cone, and it becomes easier to pin the opposition outside of the lay-lines.

There are a limited number of circumstances in which a competitor can force an incident. When circling, port-starboard disputes and tacking too close are the basic rule infractions. The opportunity for a port-starboard incident, for example, presents itself in the opening moments of the pre-start manoeuvres. The yachts are assigned to opposite ends of the starting line; at the ten-minute gun, they approach each other like a pair of prize-fighters, albeit prizefighters steaming along on a beam reach. The boat on starboard tack (with the wind striking on its starboard, or right, side) has right of way, and it usually approaches the opposition weaving all over the damn place. But at some point (accepted interpretations of the rules hold this to be one boat-length) the starboard-tack boat must hold its course so that the other boat can properly avoid it. This "freezes" the course of the starboard-tack boat just before and as they cross, and for a moment gives the port-tack boat an advantage. Usually the boat on port will try to cross to windward, and then do whatever the other boat does. If the starboard-tack boat bears away and gybes, it does too; if the starboard boat hardens up and tacks, it

Intrepid *paces with* Clipper.

follows suit. The result? The starboard-tack boat is now on port, with the port-tack boat now charging at it on starboard, with right-of-way. Instant incident.

Luffing head-to-wind kills time, slows down the pace, and can give a yacht with the opposition pinned on its tail a breather and a chance to regroup. The only real incident available from a luffing situation is one involving windward-leeward rights. When moving at less than three knots, 12-Metres tend to lose steerage. That is a frightening circumstance with a boat of such size and tonnage, and in a luffing situation a 12-Metre does not need much encouragement to start going sideways. Windward-leeward rights prescribe that a windward yacht must keep clear. A yacht that loses steerage while head-to-wind and drifts down onto a yacht beside it has disqualified itself.

The definition of tacking can also enter into luffing situations. When a boat is moving from its course to head-to-wind, it is luffing. If, however, a boat that has luffed head-to-wind falls even slightly past head-to-wind, or does so and tries to come back head-to-wind, it is by definition in the process of tacking. A boat in the process of tacking has no rights; the opposition could theoretically sail right over it, sink it, and disqualify it. But this type of protest situation gets talked about more than it is actually contested. It is difficult to prove that another boat went past head-to-wind. To prove any sort of protest beyond the mundane port-starboard and windward-leeward, you need an impeccable witness, like a stationed jury boat. Or the persuasiveness of a video replay. There would be plenty of video cameras in Newport in 1983, and jurors would be treated to the novel sight of yachtsmen dragging wiring and monitors and videotape and other electronic equipment into a crowded protest room in their efforts to prove that they had indeed come up with an incident – or that they were being unfairly railroaded out of a victory by one.

On the evening of April 15, Dave Miller arrived in camp. The lanky sailmaker for whom Tom Schnackenberg had once worked was now running the North loft in Vancouver. Miller was a three-time Olympian; he had helmed a Star to seventh place in 1964, and in 1968 had crewed for Steve Tupper in Dragons. When Miller steered a Soling to a bronze in 1972, he became the first Canadian to win an Olympic yachting medal since 1932. Miller would be joined shortly in camp by Don Martin, a multiple winner of the Pacific Challenge match-racing series regularly held between Canadian yacht clubs in Vancouver. The two were down as guest experts, but rumour had it that Miller was after the helmsman's position and Martin the tactician's role.

Miller assumed the helm of *Intrepid* the next day. His knowledge and general tinkering with rigging impressed the crew, but he did not fare well in the four starts he sailed against Terry McLaughlin and *Clipper*; McLaughlin won three cleanly, and the fourth was a draw. Miller displayed no shortage of tactical knowledge. It was the boat that handcuffed him – he was not accustomed to the large heavy-displacement design, and could not manoeuvre it with the finesse McLaughlin had developed. The following day, McLaughlin again prevailed in the practice starts.

When Don Martin arrived the day after, the action began to heat up. In the first start, Terry McLaughlin, steering *Clipper*, wanted to protest *Intrepid* for tacking too close. No, no protest, Steve Tupper ruled. It was just a practice start. "Practice protest," McLaughlin suggested.

McLaughlin won the first three practice starts and the race that followed. He dominated the next series of starts that day as well, but during the second start Miller ran *Intrepid* into *Clipper*'s transom when he allowed McLaughlin no time to respond to a luff. The collision crushed *Intrepid*'s wooden bow, leaving an eight-inch-long dent about three feet aft. Miller and *Intrepid* sailed one more race, lost narrowly and headed in for repairs.

That evening Ellen Pomer of the campaign's public relations firm dropped by the Crusaders Club to explain their plans to the crew. Rob Muru asked her to arrange a Noxzema commercial for him.

"Why Noxzema?" she asked.

"Because I wash with it," Muru deadpanned.

Dave Miller and Don Martin sailed against Terry McLaughlin and Jeff Boyd until April 24. Martin steered the odd start, and although the Vancouver duo won a number of races, they were never able to dominate McLaughlin, even though they regularly switched boats. But Miller had impressed the crew, and he was far from through with 12-Metres.

His stay ended on a sour note. A final race was held on an Olympic triangle in breezy conditions. Miller, at the wheel of *Intrepid*, drove over a poor lee-bow cover from *Clipper* to round the weather mark first. After *Clipper* parted one of her Kevlar spinnaker guys, *Intrepid* moved into a greater lead. At the leeward mark, however, a conservatively timed spinnaker drop backfired on *Intrepid* when the starboard winch broke and the guy was released prematurely. The sail fell in the water, was dragged out of the hands of the crew stuffing it below and did unmentionable things to *Intrepid*'s speed. McLaughlin cruised by to windward in *Clipper*, *laughing his head off*. It was pure slapstick to him, on a par with Jeff Boyd losing his lead at the 1975 Laser Nationals by sailing into a tangle of weeds. But some of the crew of *Intrepid* failed to see McLaughlin laughing at the situation; they thought he was laughing at *them*, and found it difficult to forgive him.

Greg Tawaststjerna returned to Palmetto on April 25, having just sailed in the 1982 Laser Worlds in Sardinia. The Canadian contingent had done exceptionally well: Terry Neilson of Toronto had won the event; his training partner, Andy Roy of Ottawa, had finished second. Tawaststjerna was sixth, and Steve Fleckenstein of Saint John tenth.

A fresh recruit arrived the same day. Tom Corness was a Thunder Bay native who possessed a degree in chemistry he had never used and had played professional hockey in Europe. He was an excellent big-boat mechanic who understood well the stresses and strains on fittings and hardware. He had quit his job as the paid captain on Huey Long's *Ondine* to join the Canadian challenge and had gained a degree of 12-Metre experience through Long's son, Russell, and *Clipper* in 1980. Although he would see occasional service as a mast man, Corness's main task became keeping Canada's 12-Metres in one piece under the supervision of Bob Whitehouse.

And there were visitors. On April 27 two employees of the Fitness Institute arrived to conduct tests on the crew candidates and prepare individual workout programs. The institute's representatives were taken for a sail on *Clipper* so that they could better understand the physical demands placed on different crew members. The sailors were poked and prodded and timed and wired to determine endurance, body fat percentage, strength, flexibility, reaction time and lung capacity. The studies concluded that Eric Martin, scoring 78 out of a possible 100 points, was the fittest member of the camp. John Millen rated a 72 and Eric Jespersen a 70. Phil Gow and Sandy Andrews came in at 68.

On May 2 the latest guest expert arrived. Chuck Bentley was a Canadian offshore racer who had sailed in the 1975 and 1981 Canada's Cup trials and the 1979 Admiral's Cup, in addition to several SORCs. Though Bentley had never actually made it to the Canada's Cup finals, he had accumulated a more-than-average amount of match-racing experience along the way. He was not, however, a strong match-racing starter, and the unfamiliarity of the 12-Metre made him only more cautious. On the water, McLaughlin and Boyd dominated his every move, and not even the presence of Greg Tawaststjerna could make him competitive. Though scheduled to stay in camp for two weeks, at breakfast on May 7 Bentley announced that he was going home. The crew candidates never saw him again.

On May 4, the Canadians made a valiant attempt to demolish their pair of 12-Metres. Terry McLaughlin and Jeff Boyd were sailing *Intrepid*: Greg Tawaststjerna and Chuck Bentley had *Clipper*. The program called for Tawaststjerna to steer two practice starts before handing the helm over to Bentley for a race. During the first start Tawaststjerna gybed *Clipper* close alongside *Intrepid*. McLaughlin didn't think *Clipper* had enough room to complete the manoeuvre and headed up. *Intrepid* headed up too. Then both bore off, only to head up together again in a confused effort to avoid each other. The two boats were now dangerously close. With visions of both being sunk and one dismasted, Sandy Andrews left the bow of *Clipper* to find safety. He started to run for the leeward rail, but then he figured that if the mast fell that would be the prime place to get flattened. He didn't want to go to the windward rail because there wasn't going to be much of that left when the boats collided.

Then, when it seemed that one boat could not avoid ramming the other, the pair altered course enough to only graze topsides and ensnarl their rigs. Incredibly, *Intrepid* and *Clipper* were still in one piece and no one was hurt.

The day began on May 5 with Terry McLaughlin perched atop one of *Clipper*'s primary headsail winches at dockside. Don Campbell took hold of the handles and began grinding away in third gear, thereby creating a slowly revolving, music-box McLaughlin. Campbell asked John Millen to shift him into second. Millen, in the tailer's cockpit, duly hit the clutch pedal; when he shifted Campbell into first, McLaughlin was hurled off the winch top and into the water.

So began a day of odd events. On the way down the channel, McLaughlin abandoned the wheel to Peter Wilson. Two Ton, who was standing forward of the wheel, agreeably began steering *Clipper* while facing the transom. That gave McLaughlin a bolt of inspiration, and they ran through a gybe with the entire crew facing the wrong way. It went surprisingly well.

There was a good breeze, and Chuck Bentley had the wheel of *Intrepid* for the day. During the first practice start, he lost steerage while luffing head-

Greg Tawaststjerna

to-wind and collided with *Clipper*. McLaughlin spent the day in complete control. After a healthy victory in the day's race, almost the entire crew of *Clipper* were trapezing or hiking with the aid of spinnaker sheets as they charged home on a tight reach.

That evening they headed over to the Bradenton Yacht Club to watch two films. On the way back in a packed van, an anonymously uttered "Milkshake" set off a temporary revolt against the diets prescribed by the Fitness Institute. Many milkshakes and sundaes later, they felt guilty but satisfied.

The morning of May 6 brought an important meeting between the crew candidates and Rear Admiral Brock, who was accompanied by Captain Sweeny and Commander Creery. The Admiral proceeded to remind everyone how they were at war, and how war demanded dedication and secrecy. The war was a psychological one, and he stressed how important it was for the move to Newport to be smooth and faultless. All the while he returned to a favourite topic – just how much everything cost.

But the move to Newport was the key topic. They were going to roll into that town, details were going to fall into place like this – a smack on the palm – and they were going to look and act smart.

After the meeting, Terry McLaughlin looked at Jeff Boyd. Jeff looked at Terry. McLaughlin summed up what he was thinking exactly: "This guy just said we're going to win the America's Cup because we're going to move from Palmetto, Florida, to Newport, Rhode Island, without any hitches."

With the departure of Chuck Bentley, the camp turned its attention to a series of races between Terry McLaughlin and Greg Tawaststjerna that would be used to determine the principal helmsman. Twister was not happy with the arrangement: McLaughlin had an established afterguard in Jeff Boyd and Peter Wilson, while Twister was using Dave Ross as navigator and Rob Kidd as tactician. Tawaststjerna did not feel that it was the right time for holding trials, and many crew candidates agreed with him. They felt that they should wait to give others a chance to prove themselves. Holding the trials now would only make McLaughlin look good. But there was also the feeling that it might not be a bad idea to get on with the trials. Selecting a skipper might promote more cooperation between him and the designated back-up helmsman. The holding of trials may simply have been a way of saving face for the Admiral, who had, after all, banished McLaughlin from camp until helmsman's trials were held. Now McLaughlin was back, and he had to sail trials against somebody, even if that meant elevating Greg Tawaststjerna, who had been invited down as a back-up helmsman, to the role of full-fledged helmsman candidate.

Whatever the circumstances, Terry McLaughlin further strengthened his position as the frontrunner for the job. Twister was steadily improving as a starter. He was very good at shaking off the opposition during the pre-start manoeuvres, but hadn't got the knack of completely turning the tables. His performance was also hampered by the fact that his knowledge of the rules at that time was less sophisticated than that of McLaughlin and Boyd (who would spend much of their spare time the next two years reading and rereading rules and appeals). In situations where right-of-way was hazy, McLaughlin could often talk (or shout) Twister out of having things his way. But this also made Twister a bit unpredictable – he would sometimes turn aggressive, but for the wrong reasons. And once across the starting line, he was not yet a consistent threat to McLaughlin.

Tawaststjerna needed time, but the back-up helmsman's role was a thankless job, probably the toughest in camp. It required an exceptional mental attitude for a person to stick with it, and in the end Tawaststjerna would decide that he had better things to do with his sailing career than tune up Terry McLaughlin, Jeff Boyd and Peter Wilson.

On May 14, it was made known that the wheels of change had turned further. After the day's sail, Steve Tupper gathered the crew candidates to tell them that he would have an announcement of the utmost importance in the Crusaders Club's tactical room. When the crew showed up, Tupper was nowhere to be seen. Harry Roman instead revealed that the announcement of utmost importance would be delivered two days later.

On the 16th, Ray Creery appeared at the morning meeting to drop the bomb. The Admiral had been asked by the challenge directors to resign. This news produced a strangely mixed reaction among the sailors. Though they had long been at odds with the Admiral, he had been a less domineering force lately. Nobody, however, was sorry to see him go. What was upsetting was Creery's announcement that he had decided to resign too. Despite his close association with Rear Admiral Brock, Creery had been well liked by the sailors, who felt he had carried out his administrative duties well.

The resignation of Roger Sweeny, which followed, meant a complete housecleaning of naval personnel from the campaign. The Admiral would be replaced by Lynn Watters of Montreal. Watters, a member of Canada's fifth-place Dragon crew at the 1960 Olympics, had been a back-up juror at the America's Cup.

The Palmetto camp disbanded on May 19. When the sailors regrouped in Newport in June, they would be training under a much-changed administration. That administration, however, was doomed to an even shorter-lived tenure than that of the Admiral. Money was draining away. The challenge was dying.

10

suiting up

Don Green was preparing to compete in Florida's Southern Ocean Racing Conference (SORC) series in January 1982 when the call came from Marvin McDill. While the Calgary lawyer wouldn't go so far as to make Green a director of the Canadian America's Cup challenge, he did want Green to assume responsibility for the construction of the new 12-Metre and the establishment of her sail program. That was quite a plateful; Green didn't know if he really needed all that responsibility. So McDill gave him the option of picking one area. Sails, thought Green. He'd take on the sails. Then he packed his bags and went yacht racing for a month.

Green had made his sailing reputation almost overnight, with *Evergreen*, the radical 41-footer he sailed to victory in the 1978 Canada's Cup. He was an outsider when he set his sights on the Canada's Cup, the 46-year-old president of Tridon, an auto-parts manufacturer with plants and warehouses spread around the globe. Tridon had begun as the Hamilton Clamp Company, a small family business Green had transformed into a multi-million-dollar operation. *Evergreen* was his first custom yacht, but Green had a knack for surrounding himself with the most qualified people imaginable. He was by nature an organizer, someone who got the right people to do the right things, who hated loose ends. With *Evergreen* he managed to attract none other than Lowell North, founder of the North Sails empire, and Tim Stearn, an American mast builder and first-rate offshore sailor. With North and Stearn on board and Green at the helm, *Evergreen* won the 1978 match against Detroit's Bayview Yacht Club, but not before Green and crew had engaged in battles both political and nautical with the Royal Canadian Yacht Club over *Evergreen*'s and the Royal Hamilton Yacht Club's right to represent Canada in the Canada's Cup. In addition to his victories around the buoys, Green won his fair share of the political frays and emerged with the respect and grudging admiration of the yachting establishment. He garnered many institutional honours and responsibilities – Commodore of the Royal Hamilton Yacht Club, the Order of Canada, a director of the Canadian National Sportsmen's Shows – but he remained essentially apart from the establishment, and this aloofness was probably why Green was one of the few hard-core racing yachtsmen from the eastern heartland that Marvin McDill turned to for advice and assistance after the initial snub he received at the Royal Canadian Yacht Club.

Outsiders McDill and Green might have been, but hardly of the same quality. Green had fought with the yachting establishment, yet had made his peace; the establishment accepted him because they respected him – he was probably the most successful offshore racer the country had produced. He had achieved success largely by working outside the Canadian competitive mainstream, instead tapping a motherlode of expertise in the United States through the North Sails organization. His latest *Evergreen*, a radically constructed 45-foot ocean racer, would never be seen in Canada. She had been built in San Diego to a design commissioned from a South American, German Frers, and had consequently been registered in the United States; had Green taken delivery of the boat in Canada, the duties and charges would have been assessed at about half its value.

Green's connections with the high-tech yachting fraternity were phenomenal. At the 1982 SORC, where the new *Evergreen* made her debut (rushed to completion on the front dock of the St. Petersburg Yacht Club – how that depressed him; it was not the way he liked to do things at all), his crew included Tim Stearn and Lowell North; Peter Barrett, the North Sails executive who had trained John Bertrand and won silver and gold Olympic medals (the gold with North in 1968); Iain MacDonald-Smith, Olympic gold medallist in 1968, who ran North's English loft and was sail coordinator for the British America's Cup challenge; Tom Schnackenberg, the North designer in charge of the sails for *Australia II*; Hans Fogh, head of the North loft in Toronto; Steve Calder, one of Fogh's employees; and Chris Boome, the vice-president of Barient Winches.

Green had once been involved in discussions with a Montreal group about a possible America's Cup challenge. The group had gone so far as to approach the New York Yacht Club and obtain a tentative agreement that the rules could be stretched to consider a challenging club in a place like Montreal or Kingston as resting on the requisite arm of the sea. But Green had been discouraged by the group's plans for a one-shot challenge. He saw the cup as unwinnable on a first try and envisioned an operation prepared to make several successive challenges, as the Australian Alan Bond had. He withdrew from the Montreal group, which subsequently collapsed.

He held greater hope for the efforts of McDill, whose legal skills he greatly admired. "I hope that the syndicate's not going to be disappointed," he reflected after returning home from SORC. "I get the feeling that they think they're going to win this thing hands down. I have not talked to enough of the group to understand their effort, their philosophy. I'm really hoping that it's, 'We're going into this thing, we're going to try to make this a Canadian effort. We're going to give it our damnedest. And, yes, we'd like to win. If we don't, well, it was a crack at it and hopefully we or somebody else will do it again the next time and learn from our experience.' What will blow the thing apart very quickly will be if they *expect* to win." Don Green thought of the first excursion to Newport as training camp. They would learn what they could and win it another time.

In the beginning, Bruce Kirby and George Wilkins assumed responsibility for the sail inventory. At their request, John Marshall, the president of North Sails, forwarded a sail program proposal to Kirby on January 21, 1982. Marshall had established North's east coast loft in 1969 and had won a bronze medal in the Dragon class at the 1972 Olympic Games. His experience in 12-Metres was extensive; the Harvard graduate had been aboard *Intrepid* with Jerry Driscoll in 1974 and sailed with Lowell North aboard *Enterprise* in 1977. He made it to the America's Cup finals with Dennis Conner and *Freedom* in 1980 and would race with Conner again in 1983 as *Liberty*'s mainsail trimmer.

Marshall emphasized that "if you do select North as your sailmaker for the project, the full assistance and facilities of the firm worldwide will be drawn upon to support you. The rules of the event, of course, put certain limits on specific questions of sail design." A very good point: after March of that year, sailmakers involved in America's Cup campaigns were forbidden to look beyond their borders for design input. It was intended that a competitor's sails be designed by a citizen of its country. "But, on the other hand," Marshall went on, "*all* cloth technology presently under development for the U.S. boats would be committed to you as well as our full battery of 12-Metre rig and sail plan computer flow studies, all our sail shape test results, and all the necessary computer designs and cutting programs which the U.S. 12s will be using." Marshall also explained, "While the new rule interpretation requires the sail *designs* to be independent after March 1, 1982, it is my explicit understanding that the computer programs and systems of the North group are the common tools of all our designers. As these programs are improved and updated the Canadian designers will be kept fully up to date."

According to Marshall, the key person in a sail program is the sailor/sailmaker, "the experienced expert sailor...who can evaluate sail test results, review sail shape measurements and then come aboard the boat and integrate these inputs with his own feel for the boat and sails to produce a logical next step or a new direction for the sail program. Only after the expert sailor/sailmaker has drawn his conclusions does the sail designer get his instructions and go to work. With all due deference to our designers, let's realize that John Bertrand gave the direction to Tom Schnackenberg and Rob Antil on *Australia*, that I defined for Dave Hirsch the designs he should execute for *Freedom*."

Marshall had Hans Fogh of North's Toronto loft in mind for the Canadian sailor/sailmaker role, with assistance from Dave Miller of the Vancouver loft. Fogh would oversee the Canadian sail program and answer to Marshall on its progress. For sail designers, the Canadians could employ Paul Davis of the Toronto loft and Sven Donaldsen of the Vancouver loft.

Next the campaign would require an on-board liaison man, someone in the crew to maintain sail test records, photograph the sails and serve as a coordinator between the North staff and on-the-water activities. Marshall considered it fortuitous that Fred Schueddekopp of the Vancouver loft was in the crew training program; should he make the final cut, he would be an ideal liaison man. The campaign would also require a paid sailmaker on the team roster to carry out daily sail maintenance and on-site recutting.

As for the sail program itself, Marshall divided it into four phases. Phase 1, which would cover February to June of 1982, involved accumulating a standard inventory modelled on that of *Freedom* in 1980 which would be used as the basis for future development. The inventory consisted of two mainsails, five genoas and six spinnakers. Total cost: $100,600 American.

Phase 2, June to September, 1982: Install the racing mast meant for the new Canadian 12-Metre in her trial horse and fit the luff curves of the mainsails to its specific characteristics. Then build, test and fine-tune a second-generation light-air mainsail during July and August. When September brings heavier winds to Newport, develop a "bullet-proof" heavy-air mainsail. The creation of a second-generation medium/heavy-air mainsail would follow in September and October and continue in Florida if necessary.

With genoas, the main goal would be developing leech-cut sails equal or superior in straight-line performance and markedly superior in tacking ability to *Freedom*'s sails. In leech-cut genoas, which were used with success by *Australia* in 1980, the cloth panels run vertically rather than horizontally, taking advantage of the directional strength of Mylar sailcloth (a layer of Dacron bonded to a layer of stretch-resistant plastic Mylar film) with significant savings in weight. The lighter a sail the better, and for the *Australia II* effort in 1983 Tom Schnackenberg would devote his efforts to reducing weight aloft while increasing the shape-holding strength of the sail. Marshall noted to Kirby in his proposal that his company expected weight savings in a #2 genoa to be as high as 36 per cent.

During Phase 2 the spinnakers of the Phase 1 inventory would be used to establish ideal downwind sailing angles. A second generation of the key spinnaker types would also be developed. The cost of the Phase 2 program for three mainsails, five genoas and four spinnakers: $102,500 American, not including a contingency budget of $30,000.

Phase 3 would cover winter training in Florida. The focus of this phase would be experimentation with Kevlar, a Du Pont fibre with a tensile strength greater than stainless steel. Kevlar had made its America's Cup debut in a *Mariner* mainsail in 1974, but the fibre was not employed successfully until the 1980 match, when a Kevlar/Dacron weave was bonded to Mylar. Marshall believed that the use of Kevlar in headsails would be necessary to keep pace with the rest of the cup syndicates in 1983. Once the leech- or vertical-cut headsails had been perfected in Phase 2, Phase 3 should be turned over to having a crack at developing one or two Kevlar headsails. If development succeeded, it would be pursued further; if it didn't pan out, the syndicate could return to further fine-tuning the vertical-cut Mylar inventory. While all this was going on, the syndicate might find that it needed some duplicate sails for comparing the new boat with its trial horse. A tentative budget for Phase 3: $100,000 American.

Phase 4 would involve sail development and duplication throughout the Newport summer. Cost: anybody's guess.

Despite the considerable planning and detail, there was a significant problem with John Marshall's proposal; it was clear that he expected North Sails to be the exclusive sailmaker for the Canadian program, and the Canadians were not sure one sailmaker was such a great idea. Marshall emphasized that for the program to begin on schedule a decision should be made by February 1. On February 9 an order was confirmed at the Toronto loft from Bruce Kirby for four sails – one mainsail and three genoas. The order was worth $46,814 Canadian, and a $23,500 deposit was sent to the loft on March 22. A week later, the Canadians were meeting with representatives of Hood Sails in New York.

At the 1982 SORC, while *Evergreen* chased Dennis Conner and *Retaliation* for division honours in Class B, Don Green tried to drum up enthusiasm for the Canadian America's Cup effort amongst the North personnel, especially Lowell North and, when he ran into him, John Marshall, who had already discussed the challenge with Bruce Kirby. But he was most interested in the personal plans of Tom Schnackenberg. As it turned out, Schnackenberg was still a Canadian citizen, which would have made him eligible to design sails for the challenge. But Schnackenberg was committed to the *Australia II* effort and was afraid of spreading himself too thin. He did agree, however, to share the information he had on 12-Metre sail design at that time, and Hans Fogh's loft duly despatched Paul Davis to New Zealand to meet with him.

Despite the initial sail order by Kirby, Green hadn't made his mind up on what sort of sail program the Canadians should pursue. "You can lock yourself in with one sailmaker, and demand that you get certain types of services," he reflected at the time. "You can get it all down in writing so that you know the whole program. That's one way. The pluses are commitment of one or two people plus a world organization, like North, and they're going to be behind you and they're really going to push. The disadvantage is that you're ruling out experimenting with anybody else's sails. You're limiting yourself. The disadvantage of bringing in many sailmakers is that you don't get the full commitment of any one sail company, although in some ways you do." Whichever way the syndicate went, it would not be Green's decision. Although his word carried weight, he was concerned simply with finding out which sailmakers and lofts were interested in the Canadian program, and what they were capable of contributing. He would leave the ultimate decision to others.

Green had an understandable personal bent toward North. He was a long-time customer and knew the higher personnel the way few yachtsmen ever do – he sailed with them. Green had also played a key role in bringing Hans Fogh's independent sailmaking operation, Fogh Sails, under the North umbrella. When Dave Miller had gone west to operate the North loft in Vancouver, the North organization had been unable to maintain a strong loft in Toronto. A silver medallist for Denmark at the 1960 Olympic Games, Fogh had established an Elvström loft in the city in 1969, and soon went into business under his own name. Following the 1979 Admiral's Cup, in which Fogh had sailed aboard the original *Evergreen*, Fogh Sails and North Sails made a share trade; Don Green came in as director and minority share-holder, and the Toronto operation was rechristened North Sails Fogh.

Green was well aware of his obvious ties to the North organization and made a conscious effort to be as impartial as possible. During the SORC, he sought out Robbie Doyle of Hood Sails to see what his employers had to offer, and travelled to New York at the end of March to meet with Marvin McDill and representatives of Hood. The next day, McDill and several directors flew to Palmetto to deal with the Admiral, where McDill made his announcement to the crew that the syndicate intended to go with North as the principal sailmaker, at the same time leaving the door open for the future participation of other firms, such as Hood.

The news of the talks with Hood did not sit well with North. Jay Hansen, the manager of the North-Fogh loft, wrote Don Green on April 7, outlining the basic sail program suggested by John Marshall to Bruce Kirby. Hansen also touched on the envisioned exclusive relationship between North Sails and the Canadian challenge. "More than one sailmaker," Hansen suggested, "simply results in less being achieved with more time spent." After pointing out the necessity in Phase 1 of equipping *Clipper* with a *Freedom*-type inventory, Hansen noted, "If the syndicate were to decide to have a 'mini sail battle' between North and Hood sails, then this first stage of development would be delayed and probably forgotten through time restraints. If Hood is asked to build their latest development sails, North would be forced to do the same. There is no doubt that this contradicts the goal of building the fastest 12-Metre sails in the world, as we'll never know for sure how fast *Clipper* would be in comparison to *Freedom*."

Jay Hansen concluded, "It is obvious, Don, from the above that much time of three of our company's key personnel, Hans Fogh, Paul Davis and myself, will be taken up by this project. It is a costly and potentially dangerous venture (both from a marketing and business standpoint) for us. Therefore, unless we are allowed to have the control and the ability to make the fundamental decisions to succeed in the stated goals, we simply cannot accept the responsibilities as outlined above. If the syndicate insists on having another sailmaker involved, then we would say we would be happy to make sails and ensure that the dimensions and shape are correct just as we would for any custom boat, but only that. Having two sailmakers involved will only waste our time and that of the syndicate, and compromise the goal of winning." Hansen pledged that his loft was willing to have another sailmaker build any type of sail as a means of ensuring that North's sail development direction was correct.

"It is an argument that going to one sailmaker compromises the effort and therefore the end result. Unfortunately for the committee the issue of sail development is so complex and time consuming that they have no choice but to have one sailmaker, and to put one hundred per cent confidence and funding behind them."

Confidence was a key word in the reasoning of Hansen's superior, Hans Fogh. He was confident of his own skills as a sailmaker and he expected a customer to be equally confident. Bringing another sailmaker's product in was fine for comparison, not for competition. It was, ultimately, a matter of pride.

On June 3 Don Green, John Marshall, Hans Fogh, Jay Hansen and Steve Tupper met to settle once and for all the issue of the sail development program. It was resolved to being the North program, as proposed, with an inventory of *Freedom*-type sails. John Marshall advised that in testing subsequent second-generation sails, the program should aim for an improvement of distance made good by the 12-Metre of four to ten feet for every minute sailed.

The next day, Fogh wrote Green and outlined a proposed inventory for Phase 1 of the program. Of the 12 sails suggested, four were already on order through Kirby. On June 15 Lynn Watters wrote Fogh from Newport to approve the inventory, ordering the eight remaining sails. The cost of all 12 sails was $107,189. The Canadian challenge had bought itself a sail program.

A month later, the crew candidates decided otherwise.

11

assembly

Three boat builders were sufficiently intrigued by the thought of welding together Canada's first 12-Metre to tender bids. Andy Wiggers of Oshawa, Ontario, was the first to become involved, voicing his interest in August of 1981. Fred McConnell of Parry Sound, Ontario, and Tom Wroe, head of Kingston Aluminum Yachts of Kingston, soon followed. At one point the three were discussing tackling the boat as a joint project, but each wanted the actual construction to take place on his home turf. Eventually they agreed that Wiggers' operation was the best site. Then Wiggers was swamped with work on IOR designs and wisely decided to withdraw from the America's Cup project.

That left Fred McConnell and Tom Wroe. The two men did not particularly get along with one another; with Andy Wiggers gone, a joint effort was out of the question. Each tendered his own bid and McConnell won. McConnell was an old ocean-racing colleague of Bruce Kirby who had built aluminum boats before, but never one with round bilges. He elected to subcontract part of the job to Kingston Aluminum Yachts, which was experienced in round bilge construction; Tom Wroe would become the project foreman, and from his own operation he brought seven men. McConnell was sensitive about this association and discouraged any mention in the press of Kingston Aluminum Yachts' involvement in the project.

But the key figure in the construction of *Canada 1* was not Fred McConnell or Tom Wroe; even they would admit that the successful completion of the 12-Metre lay on the shoulders of Brian Riley, a 31-year-old construction specialist from New Zealand. Riley, who had once been in charge of boat building at the renowned New Zealand yard of McMullen & Wing, had supervised the construction of *Australia*, the 1977 America's Cup finalist, and *France 3*, built for the 1980 series. Riley's projects verged on works of art, and many considered *France 3* the best-built 12-Metre in Newport in 1980. Not only was he a master at building in aluminum on a large scale; he was also an expert at such skills as welding and cutting, which made him an excellent teacher.

Riley's services had been arranged by Bruce Kirby and formed the heart of McConnell's bid. Wroe has since indicated that he too was prepared to use

Riley, but the New Zealander was not among the management and construction people named in his bid, and it was the proposed employment of
Riley as construction supervisor that no doubt carried the day for McConnell.

Construction took place in an abandoned fertilizer factory McConnell had
leased for the job, on an Indian reservation outside Parry Sound. To reach
the site one had to cross a very old and narrow bridge; engineer Sam Lazier
would be consulted before the completed hull was trucked across it. The
site had been selected in part with secrecy in mind, and it was difficult to
imagine a place more off the beaten track of 12-Metre aficionados.

The first task was the lofting. This involved reproducing the designer's line
drawing full-size on the shop floor and, as is customary, refairing the lines in
the process to increase resolution and accuracy. This task was taken care of
by Brian Riley. The boat would be built upside-down. By the end of the third
week in April, Riley had completed the lofting of the deck, and the work
crew was building the male plug for the keel out of three-quarter-inch
plywood. The keel would be cast in lead at Canada Metal in Toronto from a
mould formed by packing the plug in sand mixed with resin. But before the
keel could be completed, Bruce Kirby stepped in. He had changed his mind
about its shape.

Sam Lazier understood that, in the third test-tank model sailing around in
Bruce Kirby's head, the designer wanted to explore further the shape of his
yacht's keel. When the construction and testing of a third model proved
impossible, Kirby decided to make an intuitive change to the basic keel
shape he had investigated with the second model. He called Lazier to tell
him about it.

Kirby wanted to get rid of the rounds where the hull turned into the
leading edge of the keel and where the leading edge turned into the keel's
bottom at the "toe." The changes were a matter of inches and could not
have been measured in the tank. Nor would they invalidate anything already
determined by the tank. The slightly shorter chord length where the keel
met the hull would reduce interference drag the tiniest amount and also
allow the boat to turn the slightest fraction more easily. But the changes
were to a great degree cosmetic. The hard notches and angles made the
keel look that much more distinct from the hull; the new profile would score
psyche points as much as anything else.

Lazier listened to Kirby's intentions, then told him that he couldn't see
what improvements the changes could bring about. Well, at least they
weren't a step backwards. "Trust your instincts," Bruce Kirby remembers
Sam Lazier emphasizing throughout the design process. Kirby made up his

mind to go ahead with the changes, and the plywood plug was duly rebuilt.

Despite their earlier differences, Fred McConnell and Tom Wroe got along well during the project, regularly putting in 10- to 12-hour days together. McConnell's personal resources were stretched to the limit; he had jobs under way at four other sites and would usually arrive at the fertilizer factory at ten in the morning after first checking up on the other projects. Wroe and his men were keen when the project began; they knew more about round-bilge construction than McConnell's men and were learning more all the time from Brian Riley.

Construction of the boat was greatly assisted by the use of an Eckold press, a marvellous invention used for curving plating. Steve Killing located the machine through his brother, Andy, who worked for Russell Brothers, a tugboat builder. The company agreed to lease the Eckold press to the project for one dollar. The press has a head shaped like a cloven hoof. When the head stomps down on a section of plating, the two sides of the hoof spread apart to stretch the plating's surface, forcing it to take on a convex shape. A substitute head would push its cloven sides together, shrinking the plate surface and creating a concave curve.

Welding the aluminum would be a challenge, as the work force already knew. Preparation had to be immaculate: all surfaces had to be absolutely clean, as dust would cause porous welds. The surfaces to be welded could not be ground, as resin in the grinding discs would create dirt. Once during construction the roof of the old factory leaked overnight, washing dirt off the deck and onto the seams that were to be welded, causing a delay in construction while the seams were recleaned.

In addition to learning a lot, Wroe and his men were well paid – $16 an hour. They spent six weeks in Parry Sound, working on the plywood forms for the frames, the frames themselves, the deck, the cockpit, the transom and a number of fittings. As the project progressed and more of McConnell's own men became available from other duties, the ranks swelled to an unmanageable size and he let go every one of Wroe's team but Peter Mitchell, his best welder. When the Kingston workers left Parry Sound, the deck was complete and the frames were standing.

As for McConnell, what many thought the most lucrative yacht construction project in the country steadily drained his resources. He concentrated on the 12-Metre almost exclusively, neglecting contracts for several fibreglass boats. When the Canadian challenge suddenly could no longer pay its bills, Tom Wroe and his men were back running Kingston Aluminum Yachts. Andy Wiggers was busy in Oshawa building his custom IOR yachts. Fred McConnell, in Parry Sound, was bankrupt.

12

newport

Where to begin? There are, first of all, the bars and restaurants – the Black Pearl, the Raw Bar, the Candy Store, for example, on trendy and lively Bannister's Wharf, or the Moorings, or Salas', or the Rhumb Line, or the Boathouse, or the Corner Store. There is the Ark, and there is also the Victory Club, and Christie's, and the Southern Cross. The waterfront of Newport, Rhode Island, teams with cozy abodes dispensing food and beverage. It is not much of a place to dance – in Newport you eat and drink and, although the seafood is wonderful, mostly you drink. It is a place to knock back a few and see who's out and around. Twelve-Metre crew jerseys work like magnets, attracting comments and hangers-on, "racer chasers" and free rounds.

Newport is a tourist town, albeit one that has managed, just managed, to develop its waterfront without pandering to the lowest common denominator of sightseer. The attraction is the distinctive hum of the waterfront, and that hum has been amplified immeasurably by the presence of the America's Cup. At first the cup boats arrived only once every three years or so, but the level of preparation escalated to the point where competitors began training and fine-tuning a year before the actual summer of selection trials. The America's Cup, with its attendant yachts and support staff and personalities, made a more permanent home for itself in Newport, and that made the town a more consistent tourist attraction. The 12s gave the port its special feeling, and in the seasons, the months, the days leading to the America's Cup itself, a sightseer could walk the waterfront, stare at the 12-Metres in their compounds, brush past crew members on the street, and frequent the watering holes to absorb the chatter – to speculate on the fortunes of the various contenders and perhaps buy a drink for and catch the ear of some large individual in a challenge or defence jersey. In Newport, an outsider could feel as though he were backstage at the launching of an extravagant Broadway production. Once the races for the America's Cup were under way, the spectators were bridled and broken, crammed aboard charter boats that were herded outside the race area by the Coast Guard, the competing yachts mere specks in the distance. But, back on land, the world was their beach ball – it was the competitors who were captive. The town was small; there were only so many places in the limited footage of Thames Street and America's Cup Avenue where the competitors could hide in their efforts to unwind.

And not all of them wanted to hide – some were out in full plumage to be stroked, seduced, what have you . . . the sailor's ultimate fantasy! Only in the America's Cup could a sailor hope to be treated like a splendid young god, and for some the temptations of the waterfront were just a little too stimulating. There were lithe youthful creatures in town with their own fantasies to be sated, and they were enough to make any number of yachtsmen forget their goal – to win the America's Cup – and instead build their daily routine around a more immediate satisfaction – putting on their crew togs at the end of the day and plunging into the waterfront carnival to meet the racer chasers.

It is de rigueur when discussing Newport to mention the very rich. They are most certainly there, as the evidence is everywhere – the private beach clubs, the motor yachts the size of restaurants, the breathtaking houses south of downtown on Harrison Avenue and Ocean Drive, the grass tennis courts of the establishment known as the Casino at Memorial Boulevard and Bellevue Avenue. The rich themselves are not easy to spot, or at least to distinguish from the rest of us. But people don't come to Newport to gawk at the very rich. They come, instead, to gawk at the monuments they have left. Hop in a car, cab or tour bus and in no time one is wheeling along Bellevue Avenue, neighbourhood of historical excess.

The people who built these awesome estates, patterned on European models, did not live in Newport. They only summered there, on the outskirts of town. Newport was founded in the seventeenth century by Protestants fleeing persecution from fellow Protestants in Massachusetts, who had originally fled persecution on the other side of the Atlantic. The lifeblood of the town was provided by fishermen. The cream of eastern society were late arrivals, taking their cue from southern plantation owners who found the summer climate of seaside Newport to their liking. By the late nineteenth century, the summer residents had created for their own amusement a social whirl of dress balls, dinners for 400, blacklists and rich men's wives who had nothing better to do than orchestrate the whole thing.

History has a way of catching up with the well-to-do, and soon there were wars and depressions to contend with. Genetics didn't help much either. Family trees branched into new generations, the fortunes were spread around in smaller lumps. Too many heirs with dangerous habits and not enough common sense. Most of the old mansions are museums now. Or dormitories for 12-Metre crews.

The Canadians took over Sherman House, a large estate on Shephard Avenue, a narrow road which runs east off Bellevue Avenue in the heart of Newport's grandiosity. The house contained about 25 bedrooms and was owned by Salve Regina College, which was renting another property to the *Australia II* challenge; it had been previously converted into a nursing home and thus was equipped with a full institutional kitchen and three dining areas. The college intended to use the estate as a dormitory, but there were problems with applicable fire regulations, and until the college was ready to make corrective renovations it was happy to rent the estate to the Canadian America's Cup team.

The first crew candidates arrived in Newport at the end of the first week in June. The move was not as smooth as the Admiral had hoped, as the arrivals learned that neither *Clipper* nor *Intrepid*, which had been delivered to the Cove Haven Marina, would be available in Newport for outfitting for almost two weeks. To alleviate thumb-twiddling, Bruce Kirby recruited some of the sailors as crew for his 40-footer, *Runaway*, which he was sailing as an independent entry in the Onion Patch series, Long Island Sound's version of the Admiral's Cup. (Kirby would announce his second in class in the Astor Cup race of the series by walking into Sherman House in the wee hours of the morning and pulling the fire alarm.)

Despite the efforts of management, there wasn't enough to occupy the minds of the sailors and prevent them from complaining amongst them-selves. They complained mostly about the training base at the Newport Shipyard. The shipyard was a dusty-grey-gravelly pier, largely devoid of structures, frequented by lobster fishermen with their boats and equipment. It formed the extreme north side of Newport's mooring-dotted harbour, far from the hub of Newport life along the east side, where the rest of the America's Cup syndicates would establish camp. The Admiral had explained in Palmetto that one of the reasons for choosing the isolated site was to preserve the Canadian challenge's secrets. Some felt that, if anything, the Canadians should be close to the other cup efforts so they could do some secret-stealing of their own – they were the last challenge that needed to worry about keeping aces up the sleeve, as whatever cards they held had been well thumbed by other challenge efforts.

In the end, it was probably good for the challenge that the Admiral had brought them to the shipyard, away from the downtown distractions. But for the time being the crew candidates found plenty to carp about: the decks installed for them at the shipyard were too rickety; it was difficult to get on and off boats in the slip; the challenge would not have its own Travelift (a mobile sling hoist used to remove the 12-Metres from the harbour) within the fenced-in compound and would have to rely on the lift of the shipyard in maintaining the boats (which had to be scrubbed down regularly because, for the sake of a racing finish, 12-Metres are not coated with antifoulant); the base was not located at Newport Offshore alongside all the other challenges. They complained about the skimpiness of their clothing issue and, above all, the disorganization they felt was crippling the challenge.

Bruce Kirby sensed the mood of the sailors and asked Don Green to drop by and deliver a bit of a pep talk. Green was sailing *Evergreen* in the Onion Patch as part of the three-boat Ontario team. He decided to decline Kirby's request; he was fully occupied with the task of winning the series – *Evergreen* would finish top boat and Ontario top team. He didn't know how McDill's syndicate would feel about him taking it upon himself to fire up the camp. The syndicate, he decided, would have to look after its own problems.

Clipper went for its first Newport sail in the hands of Canadians on June 23. Neither Jeff Boyd nor Terry McLaughlin was yet in camp; Greg Tawaststjerna would handle the helming duties. The day began oddly with Tom Blackaller of the *Defender/Courageous* effort parking himself at a table with two other people on the dock next to the Canadian camp. Blackaller never said hello; occasionally he would leave the table to look over the fence at the Canadian operation.

They set sail along what would become a familiar route – past Goat Island, then Fort Adams, and down the neck and past Castle Hill to the open stretches of Rhode Island Sound. They sailed well out, beyond Brenton Reef Tower, into 18-knot winds and a heavy sea, a big change from the calmer waters of Tampa Bay.

Once hard on the wind, they inspected the rig, only to discover that the tip of the mast was deflecting about 18 inches to leeward. Rather then risk losing the rig, Steve Tupper decided they should sail back "inside," on Narragansett Bay. As they sailed in, the Canadians were passed by the British hopeful, *Victory*, and her trial horse, *Australia*, the 1977 and 1980 finalist. The British waved and welcomed them to Newport.

Once back on Narragansett Bay, *Clipper* acquired a shadow, an enormous motor launch displaying a New York Yacht Club burgee. The people on board busied themselves with firing cameras at the Canadians.

"We must look like a real bunch of kids," said Don Campbell.

Greg Tawaststjerna smiled. "We *are*."

With Jeff Boyd and Terry McLaughlin not due in camp for a few days, Peter Hall, a Soling sailor from Montreal, arrived with his crew of Phil Kerrigan and Dennis Toews to sail *Clipper*. The three men had no aspiration to join the challenge; they were there to help the crew candidates in any way they

Steve Tupper

could, and their assistance was appreciated. They would stay for a few days, then return in a week to sail a mini-round-robin series with Greg Tawaststjerna and Terry McLaughlin.

On their first day out on *Clipper* under Hall, June 24, the crew tore a number of old headsails and discovered that two new genoas from the North-Fogh loft were equipped with improper luff tapes. On the 26th, the Canadians crossed paths with the British. *Victory* and *Australia* had just begun a short race when *Clipper* doused her spinnaker and decided to join in. Hall held with a wind shift for a moment, then tacked and crossed the bows of both British 12s; an annoyed Harold Cudmore advised them to beat it.

John Bertrand had been sailing with the British that day and showed up the next morning for a sail aboard *Clipper*. It was difficult to tell who got more out of the day. Bertrand ran them through a novel drill, twice around a triangle without anyone uttering a word, and satisfied his curiosity by poring over every inch of the boat, asking for explanations of many pieces of gear.

After a number of practice starts and short windward-leeward courses with Hall at the helm, the Canadians returned to harbour to watch the start of a tall-ships race to Portugal. *It is only today that the magnitude of America's Cup involvement became apparent to me*, wrote Sandy Andrews. *There were probably almost as many pictures taken of us as of the tall ships. People were yelling and waving to us, they were blowing horns, ringing bells, yelling "Good Luck" and even singing "O Canada." I think I could get used to this high-profile living.*

June 28. The antagonism between the crew candidates and management which had so plagued the Palmetto camp was threatening to return. At the morning crew meeting, Steve Tupper laid down the rules for Sherman House, stressing in particular that no guests were allowed in a candidate's room after 9:00 p.m. or in any part of the house after 11:00 p.m. This was not received well, and Tupper would not elaborate on the reasons for the different hours applying to different locations; it seemed clear that he was attempting to put a damper on the sort of activities encouraged by those carnival temptations of the waterfront.

At 2:00 a.m., Tupper struck, catching Eric Jespersen and Eric Martin with girls in their rooms. Their defence was that they had only been handing out telephone numbers – no explicit stroking or seducing of young gods going on here, good lord – but the curfew had been broken and both sailors were docked their expenses for the week.

The incident disappointed the crew candidates. In Palmetto they had considered Tupper a friendly voice in management. Now, in Newport, he was tougher, more distant. His new power – although Lynn Watters, a syndicate director, was in Newport, Tupper was pretty well in charge of the operation – changed him, as it must. Having entered the program as a coach, he used his new authority to instil some discipline. The crew resented the curfews; there was a feeling that there should be no house rules except those of common courtesy. But, at the same time, there were worries among the crew candidates about the conduct of a few in their ranks.

It wasn't the sort of activity that Martin and Jespersen had been caught in that worried them – it was the ruffling of the plumage, the donning of gear emblazoned with the logo of the challenge, to follow the buzz of the waterfront and knock back a few, sometimes more than a few, and troll for young things...all of this in the team colours, night after night, until an image of the challenge had begun to form in the minds of others. Rowdy, boozy, no self-control, no commitment to the cause. A challenge not to be taken seriously. Those crew members who succumbed to the routine illustrated the ever-present danger that a sailor could lose his perspective on the undertaking – that winning or losing couldn't change the thrill of wearing the uniform, the duds that drove people crazy. The team colours, the maple leaf with the sail plan imposed on it, could earn you a friend for life, or for one night of drinking, or adulation, or stroking and seduction or what have you. As far as most of the crew were concerned, it was one thing to feel proud of the team, of the colours, and it was certainly okay to meet girls, but it was another thing altogether to allow the plumage-ruffling to become your entire *raison d'être*. The reported comment by a *Victory* syndicate member – "The Canadians are the least of our problems. They drink and party too much" – rankled in some people's minds. Though the curfew may have been a clumsy attempt at dealing with this larger problem, Steve Tupper concluded the case of Martin and Jespersen with some imagination. The subsidy the two were docked was invested in a splendid feast at Sherman House for the entire crew. The meal was well received.

July 5 was the fourth day in the mini-round-robin series between Terry McLaughlin, Peter Hall and Greg Tawaststjerna. McLaughlin, who won both his races, was on his way to capturing the series.

But the progress of the series was not the foremost concern of the sailors. That night they held a subversive meeting; as was customary, McLaughlin chaired the session and Fred Schueddekopp took down the minutes. The general feeling was that the challenge was going nowhere; the departure of the Admiral had not brought the sense of direction the sailors had hoped for. The sail program was barely alive; they would be getting only one new mast. In the meantime, *Clipper* was forced to test sails without the proper racing mast that would provide the ideal luff curve. When the mast did arrive, there would be no back-up of the same design should a breakdown occur. And the sail orders from North-Fogh were being held up by the scarcity of Mylar/Kevlar material, brought about in part by the collapse of the cloth manufacturer, Windmaster. Some of the crew felt they were wasting their time in Newport; they feared that the campaign was in danger of falling hopelessly behind and that it would be better in the long run if they simply abandoned the challenge.

The crew presented their list of grievances to Steve Tupper on July 6. He seemed unfazed, admitting that the same problems were on his mind and that he hoped to have them resolved soon. The headaches were mounting; Hans Fogh's arrival with new sails for testing would be delayed a week. The next day, *Clipper*'s mainsail grinder pedestal broke, bringing sailing exercises to a halt after less than an hour. On the way back to base, *Intrepid*'s boom snapped in two. The boom and pedestal were repaired, and on July 9 the Canadians again attempted to put in a full day of training. Upwind practice was brought to a halt when *Clipper* tore the clew patch of her genoa after a 70-tack drill; downwind practice with *Clipper* ended when a spinnaker guy snapped. The boats and their weathered sail inventories were steadily deteriorating.

On July 12 Terry McLaughlin decided to do something about the sail development program. He was not a fan of the one-sailmaker concept. Like many of the crew candidates, he instinctively looked beyond his own challenge for clues to mounting a successful campaign, and more often than not his eyes settled on the efforts of Dennis Conner. In 1980 Conner broke with America's Cup tradition by abandoning the practice of committing to one principal sailmaker. Instead, he invited the rival sail companies to pit their latest designs against each other, using *Enterprise* and *Freedom* as test platforms. With an inventory primarily supplied by North Sails and Sobstad Sails, and the on-board expertise of John Marshall and Dave Hirsch of North and Tom Whidden, the president of Sobstad, *Freedom* lost only six of 51 races over the summer of 1980.

The two-sailmaker program appealed to McLaughlin, partly because *Freedom* had been so phenomenally fast in 1980, partly because he was a great believer in the adversarial system – competition bringing out the best in people. And although it was fine to talk about ordering a few sails from Hood as a measuring stick for Hans Fogh's efforts, Hood's star had been fading rapidly on the America's Cup scene; the battle, at least on the American front, was between North and Sobstad. And in 1980, aboard *Freedom*, Sobstad had been especially strong in the headsail department, dominating the defender's spinnaker inventory. John Marshall suggested in his January 21 letter to Bruce Kirby that this bias in the inventory was due more to politics than to sail testing data: ". . . our North medium ½ oz. #25 was by far our fastest chute in its [wind range]. Since Dennis's deal with Tom Whidden called for him to make most of the chutes we weren't able to bring all our designs up to the level of the #25. We equalled but didn't beat out the Sobstad ¾ and 1.5 sails." In his letter to Don Green of June 4, Hans Fogh emphasized, "For years we have made the fastest spinnakers and I do not see why we cannot improve those built for *Freedom*."

Assurances from North Sails aside, it seemed possible that, by ignoring Sobstad, the Canadian challenge might be weakening its headsail inventory. But the regulations governing the America's Cup dictated that a competing syndicate could only race with sails designed by a citizen of its country. North was established in Canada; so was Hood. Sobstad was not – at least not for the moment. As early as January of 1982 there had been rumours that Storer Sails of Barrie, Ontario, was considering a share exchange similar to the one that brought Fogh Sails into the North fold. Its founder, Richard Storer, was an accomplished small-boat racer who, in much the same manner as Hans Fogh, had left his native England to set up shop in Canada.

Terry McLaughlin used Storer's sails on his Flying Dutchman and during the summer of 1980 had been employed in customer services by the Barrie loft. Although Richard Storer would not advertise his operation as Sobstad Storer until 1983, by the summer of 1982 it was clear to insiders that the merger would go through. Storer, in fact, had been considering the merger for four years, and had joined forces with Sobstad with the America's Cup specifically in mind. And so, on July 12, Terry McLaughlin rang up Tom Whidden at the Sobstad loft in Old Saybrook, Connecticut, to see what his company could do for the Canadian challenge.

Sobstad, it turned out, was willing to do a lot. Whidden wrote McLaughlin the next day, outlining a basic start-up inventory with an accompanying price list. The Connecticut loft, he explained, was only about 70 miles from Newport; he could deliver the inventory in the next two to six weeks and would personally check the sails to ensure that they were to McLaughlin's liking. While Whidden didn't say so in his letter, the inventory, because it was designed and constructed in the United States, could not be used by the Canadians in Newport in 1983. It could, however, provide a base to build on; these sails would probably all be worn out before the next summer anyway.

"Sobstad is the only American sailmaker to date to have built sails for Dennis Conner's 12-Metre effort," Whidden casually revealed. "Dennis has sailed approximately 50 days so far, so naturally, we have a lot of testing hours, input and pictures to draw from on what will now be our 2nd generation 1982 12-Metre sails. I believe that we can help you immensely to immediately have a competitive yet simple 12-Metre sail inventory."

Tom Whidden seemed prepared to make available to the Canadian challenge a tap into American 12-Metre sail technology. McLaughlin, as the leading choice for the skipper of Canada 1, would do whatever possible to arrange the participation of Sobstad.

Steve Killing was in camp on July 13 to oversee the establishment of a proper sail-testing technique. Attempting to determine whether one sail is faster than another is a grim exercise. Arriving at meaningful conclusions is not easy when one is attempting to detect an improvement of four to ten feet extra distance covered per minute.

The key is reducing the variables. Ideally one would like to start with two identical boats with identical rigs sailed by identical crews. This combination being impossible, one strives to undertake the task with boats of comparable speed and identical rigs. Steve Killing found himself testing sails with two boats that displayed divergent capabilities according to the breeze, and that were not yet, and never would be, equipped with identical rigs.

But, even had these variables been eliminated, the campaign still would have had to contend with changing wind and weather; with the fact that one

Hans Fogh, standing at the stern, joins Clipper *for a practice sail, with Greg Tawaststjerna at the wheel.*

sail can be faster than another on a given day; and the fact that it is a boring exercise, which brings up the human factor. Is one crew concentrating as hard as it should? How much of a difference in the final computations can the attentiveness of the sailors make when the difference to be detected is so small – so well within the variation of a crew's performance on a given day, in a given boat, over a given hour?

The only answer was to test the sails to death, chew up great chunks of training time amassing great chunks of data that could be used to bludgeon the variables into submission. In the end it became a statistical game – test one sail against another, collect as much as 30 hours of data, and hope that the sails hadn't changed shape (which they probably had) by the end of the procedure, thereby making the entire exercise irrelevant . . . then stare at the damn numbers, push them around a bit and make an educated guess.

Steve Killing got *Clipper* and *Intrepid* on the water, flying their standard inventory. As they sailed parallel courses, hand-bearing compasses and optical range finders were employed to determine which boat was doing better by how many feet. Then *Intrepid* hoisted a new North heavy-air headsail dubbed the "brick," and the data collecting began all over again.

The two boats sailed upwind together for what seemed an interminable time; the foredeck crew on *Clipper* fell into playing hangman. Terry McLaughlin soon discovered that straight-line sail testing, though necessary, wasn't the most stimulating nautical experience. *It really isn't very exciting,* Sandy Andrews wrote, having observed McLaughlin in action, *and the lack of competitiveness seems to bother him. You can tell that he is just itching to throw a luff or tack to cover instead of being forced to just sail parallel.*

McLaughlin got his chance to mix it up when *Clipper* and *Intrepid* chanced to cross paths with *Victory* and *Australia*. The British yachts crossed the Canadians, carried on a few hundred yards, then fell onto the same tack. *Victory* was closest to *Intrepid*; after a few tacks, it appeared that the British challenger was pointing higher than Canada's wooden trial horse. McLaughlin hailed *Victory*, hoping to interest the British in a team race – *no more sailing in a straight line*. But they failed to respond and sailed off on their own.

As for the new headsail? The parallel sailing indicated it pointed much higher, but at the same time seemed to go a lot slower. It had not been a fair test though; the wind had turned out to be below its designed range. The results of the day: inconclusive.

July 14: More sail testing, more hangman, more inconclusive results. Bruce Kirby, who spent the day on *Intrepid* with Terry McLaughlin, revealed that a mast for *Canada 1*, as the new boat had finally been named, was on its way from Proctor in England. McLaughlin wanted to know why they didn't have two identical spars, for *Clipper* and *Canada 1*. Kirby replied that that was the plan, but he wanted to check one Proctor out first before committing himself to two. Then McLaughlin wanted to know why they hadn't gone with a firm like Le Fiel, which supplied the spars for Dennis Conner. The news that the British were replacing their Proctor spar with one from Stearn Sailing Systems only seemed to make the choice of Proctor less wise.

Hans Fogh arrived that night, sooner than expected, bringing with him two genoas and a spinnaker. The genoas were Mylar leech-cut; the following day, testing proved the medium-air one to be a significant improvement over the comparable sail in *Clipper*'s inventory. Fogh took the wheel of *Clipper* and managed to out-tack Tawaststjerna, who had lately been showing an edge over McLaughlin in this department.

Returning to dock, the Canadians went hunting boardsailors on Narragansett Bay, chasing them down with the 12-Metres, blanketing them to windward in sneak attacks that sent the unsuspecting sprawling into the water. It was an activity that became habit-forming. Their efforts were alternately cheered and booed by the occupants of nearby moored boats.

That night, the Canadians went head-to-head with the *Victory* camp in a

The "bee suits": members of Britain's Victory *syndicate confer with Peter de Savary, right foreground.*

volleyball tournament, and for once they were more organized and spit-and-polish than the British. Each side sent a team to the other's crew house. At the British house, the Canadians found a sadly drooping net with meandering boundary lines; at Sherman House, the British encountered a playing court out of the Boy Scout Handbook – straight chalk lines and a taut net strung on Kevlar line between aluminum poles, held aloft by nico-pressed guy wires. The Canadians, who had been practising for the encounter, won the matches at both locations, three games straight.

The Canadians invited the British to return later in the evening to watch a video of *Animal House*. None showed up.

On the evening of July 16, the British challenge threw a party to mark the opening of the Victory Club, a bar/disco established by its syndicate head, Peter de Savary. It was a jacket-and-tie affair; free champagne flowed and the club was filled to capacity. The British had officially arrived in Newport.

Other challenges who moved into Newport established their presence with marketing promotions for the corporations backing them. The Swedes initiated the practice, bringing a new angle to the America's Cup game, namely that not only the yachting industry could get a lot of mileage out of the contest: corporate sponsors of foreign challengers could bring their products along with the boat and crew to make a promotional dent in the American market. When a 35-year-old real-estate tycoon named Alan Bond challenged the Americans for the first time in 1974, there were some, Dennis Conner included, who viewed the boisterous Australian's presence as some sort of media stunt. Bond was not in Newport to sell real estate, but when he made his fourth trip to the harbour in 1983, he made sure that Australia knew about it by putting a photograph of *Australia II* on cans of Swan Lager, produced by the brewery he owned. And Australia, like the Swedes, established a monstrous trade show called Aussie Expo on two floors of the Newport Bay Club, at which American distributors could secure the rights to everything from sheepskin jackets to aboriginal chant cassettes. The Italians also followed the Swedish lead, establishing a more modest pavilion to the west of Bannister's Wharf.

And the British? They came to Newport with a product of their own. The product was *style* – not a style everyone appreciated perhaps, but a style nonetheless. It was a campaign based firmly on the idea of doing things right; image was of the essence. The blue-and-gold of the challenge was everywhere – in the uniforms, the yachts, the support craft – and the radios at sea crackled with such code names as "Longbow" and "King Arthur." Under the guidance of Peter de Savary, the British radiated the very American belief that money was the root of success in such undertakings, and if Peter de Savary did not outspend the defence effort of Dennis Conner, he surely came very close.

The velocity of money in de Savary's hands meant that the British developed a knack for excess. So many 12-Metres – three (*Lionheart,* left over from 1980, *Australia* and *Victory*) during the summer of 1982, and a fourth on the way that fall when the British decided the Ed Dubois-designed *Victory* wasn't fast enough and commissioned Ian Howlett of *Lionheart* fame to produce *Victory 83*. And so many support staff; Newport was infested with British sailors whizzing about on motor scooters in their striped "bee suit" jerseys and waving team credit cards in Newport establishments.

The British were almost immediately resented by those on the sidelines, the armchair enthusiasts with a soft spot for the underdog who despise any effort that looks a little too cocksure. And the British image wasn't helped by the reprimand that came from the New York Yacht Club in 1982 when British surveillance of Dennis Conner's training efforts proved a tad too persistent and led to ugly incidents on the water.

The knack for excess took hold early. At the 1981 Admiral's Cup, de Savary's Dubois 45, *Victory*, led the three-boat British team to triumph over the defending team from Australia, which included *Apollo*, a Ben Lexcen design owned by Alan Bond. At the end of the series, de Savary challenged Bond to a match race. The stakes: $10,000 in gold coins, carried on board both *Victory* and *Apollo* during the race. The wind died before a winner could be decided and de Savary turned his ante over to charity.

Charity allowed de Savary to win this first round in showmanship, but there was never really a second round, because nobody wanted to win quite as badly as the British merchant banker. In the battle to attract attention through spectacle, the *Victory* challenge won by acclamation. Other syndicates put on their little shows, but nobody else displayed de Savary's single-minded determination to dominate the social scene. It wasn't enough simply to come out ahead of the other syndicates: the British intended to eclipse the traditional efforts of those descendants of Newport society. In opening the Victory Club, the British made known their intent to dominate the night life of the town. Tackling the dress ball crowd would come later, and to win that battle de Savary would call in the ultimate shock troops – British royalty.

July 18 was yet another in a series of foggy days. There were enough clear patches for the Canadians to join up with the British for a long session of upwind sail testing. *Clipper* appeared to be the fastest boat; by Peter Wilson's calculations, the Canadian trial horse was outperforming *Victory* by about one metre per minute. *Intrepid* could keep pace with *Victory* on starboard tack, but not on port; *Australia* proved the slowest.

The crews of *Intrepid* and *Clipper* were beginning to take shape. In the past, Steve Tupper had made up the crews arbitrarily; now, with skills developing, the camp began to fall into two crews whose ranks were, nonetheless, flexible. It was possible to see who had desire and potential, and Terry McLaughlin bargained and traded with Greg Tawaststjerna to put together the roster he wanted. At the start of the day's sail on July 20, McLaughlin tried to psyche his crew. He wanted them to consider themselves a team, the best team, better than Tawaststjerna's on the water, at the base camp, back at Sherman House. The all-round great guys, who wanted to win more than anyone and anything else.

There would be a few days of intense crew training in preparation for a series between McLaughlin and Tawaststjerna. That night Gil Mercier arrived in camp to serve as Greg's tactician. It was Mercier who had replaced Boyd at the helm of the Lightning at the 1979 Pan American Games. His appearance at the base, like some ghost from the past, inspired McLaughlin nudgingly to suggest to Boyd that maybe he was again on his way into the outbasket.

Outbasket. Now that was a fine word, a popular Darwinesque term coined in Palmetto by Bob Vaughan-Jones and enthusiastically adopted by Terry McLaughlin to describe the fate of any person or thing in the program that didn't cut the mustard. The training program was in the outbasket business, weeding out the less than perfect from the ranks of the all-round great. With the picking of crews and trials between McLaughlin and Tawaststjerna looming, the serious task of outbasketing had begun.

On July 21, Fred Schueddekopp, secretary of subversive meetings, decided to make his views (and, naturally, those of Terry McLaughlin) known on the challenge's sail program. He drafted a proposal on purchase and delivery, and ten copies were circulated among the directors and administration of Canada's America's Cup Challenge.

"As Canadians," Schueddekopp opined, "we enjoy a unique position in terms of being able to work close at hand with the big American sailmaking firms. Our best results will be obtained by trying hard to come close to the sail programs being undertaken by the American defenders as opposed to trying a lot of our own ideas. We simply don't have the full-time personnel to undertake a program like the Australians who have, as their key people, two excellent sailmakers in John Bertrand and Tom Schnackenberg. Although the idea of copying is not an original or perhaps ethical approach, it is the one which will get the best results in our case."

Schueddekopp argued for a two-sailmaker program, as opposed to the exclusive program lobbied for by North Sails. "If John Marshall really believed in his approach, then he wouldn't be getting involved with Conner again," Schueddekopp argued, "who up to this point has worked exclusively with Sobstad. . . . We have so much to learn in the area of sails (having had absolutely no background, even within our domestic sailmaking industry) that it can't hurt to learn as much as possible from all interested firms.

"The gap in sail technology," he went on, "is smaller than ever with everyone using virtually the same materials. The same goes for design now that computers help take the place of endless recutting and reshaping. With the right approach and timely purchasing, there is every reason to believe that we can have sails almost identical to those of the defender. Given that the boats are similar enough, this leaves the contest to tactics and boat handling, as it should be. Let's not make the same mistakes as previous challengers by overlooking the importance of sails in this program."

Under Schueddekopp's plan, North would continue to be the principal sail supplier to the challenge, but sails would also be purchased from other major firms, specifically Sobstad and possibly Hood. In Phase 1, for example, the delivery date of which was set at September 1, five of the six spinnakers ordered would come from Sobstad. The proposal's three phases involved a minimum of 50 sails and a tentative budget of $462,000. "It should be noted," wrote Schueddekopp, "that in 1980 Dennis Conner selected his final inventory from about 70 new sails purchased during his campaign."

Marvin McDill appeared in camp the next day. He attended the morning crew meeting and gave the impression the campaign was going ahead like clockwork. The only real news was that the challenge might switch its winter training base from Palmetto to Charleston, South Carolina. Charleston, it would turn out, was the site preferred by Bruce Kirby, because sea conditions there would be closer to those of Newport.

Before the day was out, McDill had met privately with Fred Schueddekopp to discuss the sail program. It was a turning point in the challenge, the first time the advice of the sailors had been given serious consideration. With the meeting between McDill and Schueddekopp, the idea of a one-sailmaker program effectively died.

But the meeting was not without a snag. No longer attempting to project a sunny picture, in private with Schueddekopp the Calgary lawyer admitted that the challenge was running out of money. Of the two million dollars of seed money, about three-quarters had been spent, and the public fund-raising campaign was not yet under way.

Around noon the breeze died out and was later replaced by the sea breeze. During the calm period we had lunch and drifted around by the British boats. We saw that the crew on Victory *all had on white uniforms and ties. So we all made up ties from sail ties and duct tape and then sailed past them, singing. They weren't too amused. The only thing that they responded to was our question of whether Rosco, their bow man, had fallen in yet today. We knew that he has already fallen in twice this week.*

– Diary of Sandy Andrews, July 24.

Monday, July 26, was the start of the helmsmen's trials between Terry McLaughlin and Greg Tawaststjerna. The night before, Jeff Boyd and Terry McLaughlin had gone to dinner with Rod Davis, the 1981 Congressional Cup winner and mainsail trimmer on *Defender*, to discuss the trials, and concluded that if he and McLaughlin could dominate Tawaststjerna and Gil Mercier during the pre-start manoeuvres, they could likewise dominate the races.

Before the first race could get under way, Tawaststjerna had the tack ring pulled out of the genoa on *Intrepid*. He took his time making a sail change, delaying the re-start so that the wind could build, to *Intrepid*'s advantage. He got what he wanted. *Clipper* and McLaughlin narrowly won the start, but Tawaststjerna hit a favourable shift and took the lead. McLaughlin didn't get it back until three legs later. Sharp tactics gave him an inside overlap at the leeward mark, and he parked *Clipper* on *Intrepid*'s wind for the final leg to take the first race of the series.

In the second race of the day, *Clipper* again got off to a good start, only to have the head tear out of the genoa. Tawaststjerna managed to force McLaughlin over the line early in the re-start, but shortly thereafter *Intrepid*'s genoa and its clew parted ways, bringing the day's racing to an end with one race completed and three sail blow-outs. The following day brought light winds, and Tawaststjerna, at the wheel of *Clipper*, took both races.

On July 28, there was rain, and wind – almost 30 knots of it, out of the southeast. *Clipper* and *Intrepid* were towed out of Narragansett Bay for the third day of the series. Once past Castle Hill, the Canadians could see the mountainous waves carving across Rhode Island Sound. The afterguards of the pair of 12-Metres looked at each other and came to a sad understanding. There was no point in hoisting their battered inventories – the sails would only disintegrate. They turned back for the base.

The crew candidates assembled in the sail trailer for another subversive meeting. Their situation was not good. There were strong rumours circulating that the syndicate was broke. Without money, there was no program for sail testing, there were no guest experts – there was, in short, no purpose to being in Newport. In the little more than a month that the camp had been truly operating, the sailors had learned little more than that Newport had waves and Palmetto didn't. Maybe they should just go home and stop spending money the challenge didn't have and wasting their own time in the process.

They approached Steve Tupper with their thoughts. Again, Tupper wasn't surprised by the verdict reached at a subversive meeting. He was just as worried as they were and promised to take up the issue of breaking camp with McDill, who would be meeting shortly with potential corporate sponsors.

The next day, Terry McLaughlin won all three races to take the series, 4-2. Tawaststjerna had been enjoying an enormous lead in the second race of the day when a disastrous leeward mark rounding allowed McLaughlin to cruise by. That misfortune seemed to take the heart out of Greg; he never threatened in the final race.

At the end of racing, the crews returned home to don formal attire and head over to Fort Adams for the dedication of a new wooden-boat museum. An armada of American defence hopefuls – *Courageous*, *Defender*, *Freedom*, and *Spirit* – attended with their crews. The Canadians showed up, as requested, with *Intrepid*, the last great wooden 12-Metre. The sketches for the proposed layout featured *Intrepid* as a prime display. It was a strange feeling, seeing the boat you were using to prepare for the America's Cup treated by others as a venerable antique.

Four consecutive days off for the crew followed. Terry McLaughlin left camp to attend the Pre-Olympic Regatta in Long Beach, California, and when sailing resumed on August 3, with more sail testing under the direction of Steve Killing, Jeff Boyd assumed the helm of *Clipper*.

On August 4 Steve Tupper reported to the sailors that Marvin McDill had not been in favour of breaking camp – it would not impress potential backers or the general public. Late that night Bruce Kirby dropped by Sherman House with the rumour that the challenge had landed itself a fantastic chunk of money. The next morning, Steve Killing reported that he'd heard they had just received about a quarter of a million dollars. Steve Tupper then got in on the act, announcing the next morning that there would be an important meeting after dinner. Sandy Andrews, who had spoken with Kirby about money the night before, assumed that it would be good news, and said so to the rest of the crew. They left dock in a cheery mood.

While *Clipper* was changing mainsails during the day's sail testing, Greg Tawaststjerna went cavorting off in *Intrepid* and caught up with *Defender* and *Courageous*. Tawaststjerna parked *Intrepid* in their lee and began sailing along with them, but the Americans did not want to play and despatched their tender to herd *Intrepid* away. Tawaststjerna would not cooperate, initiating a tacking duel with the power boat. Finally the tender swept around *Intrepid*'s stern and filled the 12-Metre's cockpit with water. With the mainsail change on *Clipper* complete, Tawaststjerna reluctantly returned to the routine of sail testing.

The challenge, Steve Tupper told them at that evening's meeting, was broke. Everyone was going home. If fund-raising went well, they would be back in business on September 8. It was a Thursday night. Everyone was to be out of Sherman House by noon, Saturday.

Rumours abound, Sandy Andrews wrote later in August. *There are corporate sponsors jumping out of the woodwork trying to bail us out; there is no corporate money available at all anywhere in Canada; the program is ready to start up again; the whole campaign is called off permanently. . . . It eventually became clear to everyone that we wouldn't be starting up again on the scheduled date. The papers are full of how we are totally broke, of how McConnell may be forced to sell off* Canada 1 *if he doesn't get some money soon, of how McConnell has had to halt construction as there is not enough money to continue. Among the crew there is growing frustration over the lack of progress, and the lack of news. It is very difficult being kept in the dark. There is, however, still a basic core of optimism. Not many of the crew seem to believe that the campaign will fold up permanently.*

13

xerox

To me, the big surprise of the Xerox series was the strong showing of the Canadians.... it was a shock to see Terry McLaughlin and his mates put up such a good fight.

– Tom Blackaller, *Yacht Racing/Cruising,* January 1983

The 1982 Xerox 12-Metre regatta was an undefinable event. No doubt the sponsoring corporation hoped it would be a 12-Metre world championship. The New York Yacht Club effectively discouraged that possibility, however. Determined that no American 12-Metre should reveal its strengths or weaknesses against foreign competition before the actual America's Cup match in September of 1983, the club warned that any defence aspirant participating in the Xerox regatta would automatically disqualify itself from contention. David Vietor consequently decided against entering *Courageous*, and it was left to the foreign challengers to contest the trophy. And not all of them appeared on the starting line for this unique series of fleet races. Neither the Italians nor the Australians had their challengers in Newport; the British, with their stable of *Lionheart*, *Australia* and *Victory*, would contest the trophy against *France 3* and *Clipper*, the Canadian entry shoved into the ring at the last minute in an effort to resuscitate a dying challenge.

It was Terry McLaughlin who recognized the regatta's possibilities. It was, above all else, an opportunity to maintain momentum in the Canadian program while also learning a few things. And if a Canadian crew fared well, it could only mean a shot in the arm for the fund-raisers. McLaughlin lobbied hard and convinced Marvin McDill to scrape up a few thousand dollars, primarily so that *Clipper*, which was being held on the Newport Shipyard property until outstanding bills were met, could be put back in the water. And after he had rounded up the necessary money, McLaughlin rounded up the necessary crew.

Jeff Boyd and Robin Wynne-Edwards left Kingston around noon on September 16 in Boyd's van. They talked nonstop to Newport, speculating on the future of the Canadian challenge and making alternative plans should it go bust. Neither wanted the challenge to end, but the summer's turn of events had left them in limbo. Despite a general sense of unease, the commitment of the crew was tremendous. Bob Whitehouse had taken Daniel Palardy, Don Campbell, Rob Webb, Eric Jespersen and Brent Foxall to Parry Sound to complete work on *Canada 1*. And when Boyd and Wynne-Edwards arrived in Newport around 9 p.m., they met up with just enough able and willing hands to race a 12-Metre. Sandy Andrews would be bow man; Tom Corness, mast man; Ed Gyles, foxhole; Phil Gow, a grinder alongside Wynne-Edwards; John Millen and Bob Vaughan-Jones (who had somehow reached Newport from Vancouver without the assistance of either money or a plane ticket), tailers; Rob Muru, mainsheet man; Peter Wilson, navigator; and Terry McLaughlin and Jeff Boyd, skipper and tactician. The support staff – Shep Higley, Jimmy Johnston and Brook Hamilton – reappeared in Newport intact. Sharon Mooney, the challenge's meteorologist, also showed up. The cook, Leroy Jones, was still in town. The entourage moved back into Sherman House, took up a collection so that Jones could buy groceries and cook a few meals, and prepared to make *Clipper* seaworthy again.

Friday, September 17, was an extremely busy day. The first race of the regatta was on the 21st and they hoped to be on the water for a sail by four o'clock. Leroy served up breakfast at seven o'clock, and Tom Corness arranged with Newport Shipyard to have *Clipper* in the water early; the boat was launched and had its mast stepped by noon. Wynne-Edwards, Gow and Gyles tore down and greased the winches; Two Ton organized the electronics; Andrews and Corness tended to the rig; Vaughan-Jones straightened out the running rigging; and Millen, Muru, Boyd and McLaughlin attacked the sail inventory.

Kevin Singleton, who was running the challenge's office, was the only member of management still in Newport. He instructed the crew not to go near *Intrepid*, because Paul Phelan, who would be down later in the week, was planning to sell it. With that fact in mind, McLaughlin, Boyd and Muru rescued *Intrepid*'s good two-ply, five-ounce Dacron mainsail and headed for the Newport sail loft of Bill Shore in hope of changing to a smaller-diameter luff tape compatible with the mast grooves of both *Intrepid* and *Clipper*. The sail was their saviour – it was their only heavy-air mainsail, and they would have to have it when the wind was above 15 knots.

The Canadians were a regular customer of Shore Sails. They had been so regular over the summer, in fact, that their repair bills amounted to an outstanding debt of $1800. McLaughlin, Boyd and Muru left the sail in Boyd's van, electing first to test the atmosphere of the establishment.

France 3, *with her distinctive red-white-blue hull*

The moment they walked in, one of the seamstresses headed straight for Bill Shore to tell him there were some Canadians in the loft.

Shore came out of his office. "You've got an outstanding bill," he informed them, adding that his brother, who managed his Newport loft for him, was quite upset about it.

Then Shore recognized Boyd. They hadn't seen each other in over two years. Shore, a former Lightning world champion, had been very helpful in getting Boyd's Lightning program for the Pan American Games going. Boyd asked Shore if the loft would do the work if the crew first removed the old luff tape and cleaned up all the threads. Shore relented and invited them into his office. With the Canadians stressing that they could pay for this particular job, Shore gave the go-ahead. While several Canadian sailors picked away at threads on the loft floor, their prime adversaries in the Xerox regatta comfortably carried on with business one level below. The British had rented the basement of the loft and had installed a computer and three sailmakers of their own.

When the work at Shore Sails was done, the Canadians went for a sail. *Slingshot*, their 54-foot Hatteras, running roughly and low on fuel, was capable only of towing *Clipper* long enough for the crew to hoist the mainsail. There was just enough breeze to check the rig, and Corness noted a few necessary minor adjustments. The whole process of tuning a 12-Metre rig was still a mystery to Boyd. To adjust a particular shroud, the mast first had to be raised by two 50-ton jacks at its base so that spacing plates could be removed and the mast lowered. After a shroud was adjusted, the mast had to be jacked up once again and the spacers reinserted beneath it.

The next morning, Terry McLaughlin bumped into his sometime 470 crew, Tom Schnackenberg. Schnackenberg, the principal sail designer for *Australia II*, had popped up at Xerox as a consultant for Peter de Savary and the British *Victory* effort. The New Zealander would serve as mainsail trimmer on *Australia*, which would be co-skippered by Kip Hobday, the British challenge's assistant director, and de Savary. McLaughlin invited him out for a sail on *Clipper*.

Saturday was a bright, sunny day, with a wisp of wind out of the northeast. With Schnackenberg on board, the Canadian crew carried on like an assortment of house league players who suddenly found themselves on the ice with Wayne Gretzky – they were petrified of somehow screwing up in front of this genius. *Clipper* was flying Aggie, her 1980 light Mylar/Kevlar mainsail. Schnackenberg pronounced it "Okay," and proceeded to dictate notes on how to recut it and every other sail they hoisted for his viewing benefit. The Canadians by then had received two #1, two #2 and a #3 headsail from the North loft in Toronto. Schnackenberg would look at a sail, and if he liked what he saw, would conclude, "Yes, this looks *testable*," meaning that the sail looked all right on its first hoist and might be worth checking out against another sail. The Canadians decided that they still had much to learn about 12-Metre sail shape.

As the day passed, *France 3* appeared and joined in some side-by-side upwind pacing. Schnackenberg told his hosts not to take the pacing seriously. The wind was light and flukey, and he assured them that Dennis Conner never attempted to do any sail testing in less than 12 knots of apparent wind. When the sea breeze filled in to a pleasant ten knots true, *Clipper* settled into a series of long upwind beats. They practised sail changes, and Schnackenberg transferred to *Slingshot* for a more objective view of things. His lectures continued. He explained the best method for taking photographs of sails in conjunction with their sail development program, and McLaughlin volunteered his own camera so that Schnackenberg could snap a few sample frames.

Nearing the Block Island bell buoy, *Clipper* and *France 3* turned back and hoisted spinnakers. While the Canadians felt that *Clipper* had shown an advantage upwind, *France 3* seemed to be markedly superior when running. When the French sailed away from them, the Canadians elected to practise their gybes. Schnackenberg had to get back to his computer in the basement of the Shore loft, so *Slingshot* ferried him back to port. As Ed Gyles had amassed a lengthy list of repairs to be performed on *Clipper* before the day was out, Bob Vaughan-Jones was transferred aboard *France 3*'s tender, *Nanny*, where he convinced the French in the nicest possible manner that they should tow *Clipper* into dock, which they did, while *France 3* sailed the 20 miles. Once ashore, the Canadians fell into what was becoming a familiar routine: work on *Clipper*, fold the sails, find some food and hold an end-of-day meeting.

Sunday brought plenty of wind out of the northeast, but they were determined to examine the rest of their sail inventory. The *Intrepid* mainsail held a satisfying shape, and from there they inspected their #3, #4, and #5 headsails; once past #2, everything was Dacron. Terry McLaughlin and Rob Muru had unearthed an old #5 mitre-cut, a rather small headsail with a lot of hollow in the leech and not much length along the foot and hoist. If it ever blew the shingles off, the #5 would definitely be a secret weapon. The rest of the day was devoted to ironing out crew work.

On Monday, it again blew strongly from the northeast. In 15 to 18 knots of wind, *Clipper* left dock at 10 o'clock to practise downwind routines and tacking. For the tacks, the crew changed stations; McLaughlin wanted the tailers and the mainsheet man to experience steering a 12-Metre through a tack. During one tack, while Jeff Boyd was tailing, Phil Gow was hit in the arm by flailing wire, an experience similar to being struck by a baseball bat –

you hurt like hell, then go numb. Boyd said he was sorry, McLaughlin said Vaughan-Jones turned the boat too fast, Vaughan-Jones said Boyd's tailing was shabby, and Gow didn't say anything at all, continuing to grind as he tried to shake off the beating.

Around noon, *France 3* cruised by in search of some pacing. McLaughlin suggested a race, windward-leeward with a match-race start. Over the radio came the French reply: "*France 3* acknowledges the race, but *France 3* will be not very aggressive." It would be the first 12-Metre match-racing start for the Canadians outside their own camp. After some circling and various other manoeuvres, *Clipper* started on starboard, to windward of *France 3*. With the yachts exhibiting equal speed over the short beat, *Clipper* pinned *France 3* with a close windward cover and ran it past the lay-line. *Clipper* rounded the windward mark with an excellent spinnaker set; *France 3* struggled. Just before the finish, a fresh puff of wind tore a clew out of *Clipper*'s ¾ NB, the Canadians' only decent spinnaker. The day was over. There was work to be done on the boat, Rob Muru had to repair the spinnaker, and Terry McLaughlin and Jeff Boyd were due at a skippers' meeting for the regatta at four o'clock.

The skippers' meeting was in the main cabin of a sail training vessel at the Newport Yachting Center. Boyd and McLaughlin were surprised to see Lynn Watters and Kevin Singleton. The British presence was intimidating. It was the first time they had encountered Peter de Savary and his cigar in the flesh, and everyone in the crowded cabin seemed to be attired in the trademark yellow and blue of the *Victory* effort. Boyd and McLaughlin, unimpressively adorned in street clothes, were awash in British bee suits, more than aware of the strength and panache of the organization they were intending to take on the next day. Xerox would be a showcase for aspiring British 12-Metre helmsmen. The main battle was between Phil Crebbin and Harold Cudmore, aboard *Victory*, and Rodney Pattisson and Lawrie Smith, who were sailing *Lionheart* as a means of getting themselves back into the British cup program.

At the end of the skippers' meeting, Bruno Troublé and Terry McLaughlin autographed a few hundred regatta posters. That evening, McLaughlin and Boyd described the meeting to the rest of the crew and finished off with a pep talk before heading for bed. How well the Canadians could expect, or deserved, to finish the next day was a question that plagued everyone. Shortly before lights out, Jeff Boyd and Peter Wilson reviewed the Loran navigation coordinates for the course marks inside Narragansett Bay and made a careful study of the tide charts. If the Canadians would learn anything from Xerox, it was the importance of navigation in winning and losing races.

On Tuesday, they were at Newport Shipyard at 7:30 and on the water by 9:00. Kevin Singleton had managed to loosen up a few dollars, and the support crew were at last able to put a full tank of fuel in *Slingshot*, whose foredeck was buried in back-up sails Terry McLaughlin and Rob Muru had organized. Gliding past Fort Adams in a 10-knot northeasterly, they hoisted Aggie, their light-air Mylar/Kevlar mainsail. After dropping *Slingshot*'s tow, *Clipper* ran down the channel, past Castle Hill, for the open stretches of Rhode Island Sound.

Ed Gyles ground down the inhaul, and the entire tack patch pulled out of Aggie. Scratch the only good light-air mainsail.

The mainsail was dropped, bundled and transferred to *Slingshot*. While the old *Intrepid* mainsail was rigged, Two Ton arranged for repairs to Aggie with the Canadian shore base, code-named Forum. Rob Muru had spent the previous evening mending the ¾ NB spinnaker in the British loft in the basement of Shore Sails, paying their sailmakers off with beer as they taught him how to put the sail back together. Because of their debts, the Canadians could not return to the Shore loft, and relying on the charity of the British sailmakers again was out of the question. Singleton telephoned the local Horizon loft, the idea being to try to do business with someone who wasn't familiar with the Canadian financial situation. Money was so tight that Singleton continually radioed back to *Clipper* for estimates of the damage to determine if they could afford to pay for repairs. Meanwhile the airwaves crackled with the voice of Peter de Savary, instructing that funds in the hundreds of thousands of dollars be transferred from one Swiss bank account to another.

In no time *Clipper* was among the rest of the Xerox fleet and into a start sequence. The race committee had signalled a windward-leeward course, twice around. The Canadians decided to start at the pin end of the line, which was completely uncontested. But McLaughlin was late hitting the line, having taken a conservative dip before steering onto the race course.

The wind was shifty for the first beat. *Lionheart*, which had sailed far to the left side on the opening leg, rounded the weather mark first, followed by *Victory* and *Clipper*. *Australia* was far behind; *France 3* retired. On the run, the order remained the same, with *Victory* moving out on *Clipper* and closing on *Lionheart*. *Clipper* hung on to finish third, paying dearly in the process. On the second windward leg the Canadians had ripped their N22, their best #2 headsail.

There was no time to clean up between races, the race committee having allowed only enough of a break to wolf down lunch. The second race would be a windward-leeward, twice around with a finish to windward. Crew work on *Clipper* had been poor in the opening race, and they were keen to show some improvement. In a freshening breeze, the weather end of the starting line was heavily favoured, and *Clipper* undisputedly won the start.

Clipper rounded the weather mark first, with Peter de Savary and *Australia* close behind. Beginning the second windward leg, the Canadians were still ahead, but the wind was dropping. Caught with the heavy *Intrepid* mainsail and N13, their Dacron #3 headsail, they seemed to be all but going backwards. *Australia* cruised through *Clipper*'s lee and opened up an enormous lead.

McLaughlin called for a headsail change, opting for the N12, a #2 two-ply Mylar cross-cut. With the new sail, *Clipper* held on to second place at the windward mark, with *Victory* steadily closing. On the final run, *Victory* continued to press, but *Clipper* held it off long enough to wrap it in a tight windward cover for the final leg. Upwind, the poor condition of *Clipper*'s sail inventory became obvious, and *Victory* drove through. *Lionheart*, which had begun the last leg in fourth, sailed far to the right and passed both *Clipper* and *Victory*. With *Australia* claiming a comfortable first, the British swept the top three places. *Clipper*, collecting fourth, returned to dock to organize sail repairs and general maintenance.

Following the race there was a press conference and reception at the Newport Yachting Center. Terry McLaughlin and Jeff Boyd arrived together, frustrated by their day's results, knowing that to attract financial backers they would have to improve. After a few drinks, their worries didn't seem so insurmountable. The rest of the crew, with the exception of Rob Muru and John Millen, who were repairing sails, finished up at the shipyard and headed over to the yachting center for the free food and drink.

Gary Jobson of *Defender* was the press conference's moderator. Lined up across the head table with him were Peter de Savary (complete with cigar), Lawrie Smith, Harold Cudmore, Phil Crebbin, Terry McLaughlin and Bruno Troublé. The British were tight-lipped and smug, exuding confidence. Bruno Troublé relied on one pat explanation for his performance: "New mast, new crew, no time." For 15 minutes Terry McLaughlin sat completely disregarded. The drought of questions was finally broken by George Wilkins, who had taken to writing about the Canadian challenge after being removed from the campaign.

Wilkins wanted to know the age of the mainsail that *Clipper* had been flying that day. McLaughlin leaned over to confer with Bruno Troublé. "Bruno says about 1979," the Canadian skipper dutifully reported, explaining how the sail had been carefully aged in the challenge's trailer.

He was off and running. More questions followed, some planted, most naturally rising to the call of McLaughlin's irreverence. He was cutting, sarcastic, self-deprecating and, above all, entertaining. The press loved it.

The next day a local newspaper reporter referred to McLaughlin as the new Ted Turner.

At the end of the press conference, it was back downstairs for more free food and drink. *Clipper*'s crew, which had packed the auditorium, dug into the hors d'oeuvres and generally got a little happy. McLaughlin was congratulated for "winning the press conference," if not the races. Jeff Boyd chatted with Tom Schnackenberg to try to figure out why *Australia* had been so fast upwind and was introduced to Dave Hirsch, a North sailmaker who was part of Dennis Conner's defence effort. The America's Cup fraternity had grown one crew larger.

September 22 was overcast and raining. It was also foggy and blowing like crazy – the most godawful day, not one on which you wanted to leave the house, never mind go sail a 12-Metre you didn't want to be caught aboard in more than 12 knots of wind. It was the kind of day you donned your foul-weather gear and sea boots right after breakfast and didn't take them off until the sun went down. The wind was piping in excess of 30 knots when the Canadians reached Brenton Tower, where they learned that the start had been postponed until 1:30 and that the race would be held on Narragansett Bay. The conditions left the *Clipper* crew ill at ease, but Terry the Leader suggested some practice sailing to loosen them up.

After an aborted sail transfer from *Slingshot* off Fort Adams, they hoisted the *Intrepid* mainsail and their secret weapon, the #5 mitre-cut. Sailing upwind, they acclimatized themselves to what were colloquially known as "Cape Horn" conditions; soon their initial nervousness passed, and they were running through spinnaker hoists and gybes. McLaughlin had them primed and ready.

They decided to keep Brook Hamilton on board as the 12th man (the extra crew member had been permitted for the Xerox regatta, at the suggestion of the French) and keep him at the grinder handles full time to pump the bilges. McLaughlin, always searching for good press, brought Robert Martin of the *Globe and Mail* temporarily aboard for a spell at the helm.

With the wind down to 25 knots, the rest of the Xerox fleet appeared. The race committee signalled the course: around Prudence Island to port, a distance of about 25 miles.

Clipper started late, at the race committee end of the line, then tacked and headed for the shore and what Wilson and Boyd hoped was a favourable current. It paid off. *Clipper* came off the shore on starboard, in the lead, but with *Victory* closing on every tack.

"Why are they gaining?" an agitated McLaughlin yelled at Boyd over the wind.

"I don't know!" an equally distraught Boyd yelled back.

Victory, on port, crossing with feet to spare, executed a "slam-dunk," tacking directly to windward on *Clipper*. The Canadians felt the manoeuvre was a little too close and decided to raise a protest flag. Boyd, too terrified to climb onto the sloping transom in this weather to attach the red flag to the backstay, instead tied it to the running backstay.

Clipper tacked away onto starboard; *Victory* continued on port. A clocking breeze allowed the Canadians to lay the mark at the top of Prudence Island. The *Victory* crew, badly overstanding, rounded two minutes behind. It was all downhill to the finish; *Victory* closed, but not enough. A win for the Canadians, and an important one, for Paul Phelan had watched the entire race from *Slingshot*. Crew spirits were high. A press conference again followed – no drinks this time, and far fewer laughs. On the way home Boyd and McLaughlin picked up some no-name beer for the rest of the crew. Leroy cooked up a fine meal. Everyone went to bed.

Navigation had won the race for them on Wednesday; it would lose it for them today. The sky was sunny, and there was a breeze of about 12 knots from the east, which the Canadians expected to veer and build. After winning the start, *Clipper* sailed to the left in anticipation, and in the process overstood the weather mark. The only excitement on the beat came when Sandy Andrews, the bow man, was swept overboard by a wave and retrieved by John Millen at the jib clew.

Clipper rounded the mark fourth with a good spinnaker hoist. A luffing duel between *Australia* and *Lionheart* allowed the Canadians to slip through to second place, behind *Victory*, which they held to the finish.

The day's second race never happened. The breeze had built to over 30 knots from the southwest, and the race committee cancelled competition for the rest of the day. The crew of *Clipper* had just gone through a difficult mainsail change, all for nothing. They noticed that most of the people aboard *Slingshot* were seasick. The boat was crowded with *Clipper*'s support crew, a television crew led by *Clipper*'s young owner, Russell Long, members of the Canadian press, and Ken Danby, the Canadian realist painter who was preparing sketches for an official poster and a commemorative painting. (Danby was a real trouper. During the day he could be seen on the bow of *Slingshot* helping with the sail transfers, having himself a hell of a time.)

On the way in, Terry McLaughlin called for a spinnaker hoist; the Canadians tore past the rest of the Xerox fleet. McLaughlin turned the helm over to Rob Muru, who strived to keep *Clipper* under control. The boat buried her bow several times and they were taking on a considerable amount of water. Ed Gyles closed up the foxhole hatch and two people started bailing. Jimmy Johnston, the team photographer/tender driver who was the 12th man in the crew for the day, annoyedly emptied water out of his camera. The crew to a man enjoyed the ride, feeling proud of their efforts, perhaps a little naive about the limits to which they were pushing *Clipper*. But it was important to make an impression on the people aboard *Slingshot* if money were to be raised, and this they most certainly seemed to be doing.

Back at the house, Leroy gave the crew hell for not winning. After the revelry of the first press reception, he lectured, they had gone out and won a race. Last night they were deadly serious, and today they finished second. "We now know," he declared, "what we must do." Producing a $20 bill, he offered to buy the first round of drinks at the Candy Store, one of the trendier bars on Bannister's Wharf. The entire crew headed downtown.

Friday was sunny, with a dying 12 knot breeze out of the northwest. The crew was loose; on the way out to the start area Terry McLaughlin suggested a spelling bee, which Two Ton won hands down.

The fading air caught *Clipper* upwind of the starting line, and the Canadians barely made it back to the pin to start to leeward of the fleet. They would sail a full America's Cup course: once around a right-angle triangle, finishing with a windward-leeward-windward, a total of 24.3 miles. In conditions that left the yachts close to drifting, *Clipper* sailed far to the left on the first beat. Everyone else went right. When the sea breeze slowly filled in, *Clipper* was the first to catch it, but the wind angle was poor and they were forced to reach to the first mark. They rounded second, behind *Lionheart*.

The breeze built on the reach. It was too tight a leg to fly a spinnaker, and during the resultant genoa change (in which the old genoa had to be carefully lowered and retrieved outboard off the new genoa) it seemed that every member of the crew was on the foredeck. It had been customary for the Canadians to have the navigator participate in such tasks, but as the Xerox regatta had progressed, they began to keep Peter Wilson back at his station, concentrating on his main role. Approaching the gybe mark behind *Lionheart*, Wilson spied through binoculars that the race committee, because of the wind shifting left, had decided to change the course of the next reaching leg. Rather than executing a planned bearaway set (that is, a spinnaker hoist while bearing off for the gybe mark) with a ¾-ounce spinnaker, the Canadians re-rigged for a gybe set, hoisting a 1.5-ounce spinnaker just as they made their gybe at the mark. Boyd went forward for the hoist. It worked perfectly. He returned to his station to see *Lionheart* dead to leeward, struggling to head up. *Clipper* steamed into first place in a typical Newport breeze of 12 to 15 knots. The Canadians hung on to win; *Victory* passed *Lionheart* on the last leg to take second place.

McLaughlin turned to Boyd. "That win," he said, "might be worth $100,000."

McLaughlin, always eager to have VIPs steer a 12-Metre, brought Ken

Danby aboard on the way in to try his hand at the helm. Back at Newport Shipyard, there was a small crowd awaiting their arrival. With one drop race allowed in the scoring system, the rag-tag Canadians were only one point behind *Victory* heading into the final race. Lining the docks were a television crew, a film crew compiling the official Xerox movie (who wanted to be on board *Clipper* for the deciding race) and a slightly crazy Frenchman with three bottles of Mumm's champagne for the crew to sample. And the Canadian crew appeared to be generating interest back home. All week, Robert Martin of the *Globe and Mail*, Kevin Scanlon of the *Toronto Star* and Keith Beaty, a photographer for the *Star*, had been with the Canadian effort, learning what the challenge program was all about. Not only was there media interest: that day Marvin McDill arrived, with two of the challenge's board members.

While drinking the champagne and celebrating the win, Terry McLaughlin instructed Rob Muru to change the name of *Slingshot* to *Slapshot*. Later that evening, while the rest of the crew were downtown celebrating, Muru and John Millen headed for the shipyard. The next morning, the Hatteras's transom indeed read *Slapshot*, with a crossed hockey sticks logo. The name change confused the hell out of the race committee, which gave the support staff no end of amusement.

The final race would be around Conanicut Island on Narragansett Bay. The day began sunny and hot, the water a flat calm. In the lightest zephyr, the Canadians took the president of Xerox Canada for a spin in *Clipper*. Also on board were a sound man and a cameraman from the Xerox film crew.

When the start was postponed, a swimming race was organized, a relay between *Australia* and the race committee launch. The winning team would receive free champagne at the Victory Club, courtesy Peter de Savary. The Canadians were represented by John Millen, Ed Gyles and Phil Gow. When *Australia* swung in the wind, leaving Gow, who was waiting his turn, further away from the race committee launch, Terry the Swimming Coach went crazy – a sort of happy crazy, thought Boyd. The *Australia* crew won. It would be the only bright spot in the day for the British yacht.

When the sea breeze filled in, a starting line was set just south of Newport Bridge. The first mark was to the south, off Fort Adams. After rounding the mark to starboard, the fleet was to proceed around Conanicut Island. The opening leg was only about one mile long; with an eight-knot wind, there would be little time for the fleet to spread out before reaching the mark. The yachts were destined to arrive at the mark in a jam; even worse, the buoys-to-starboard course meant that a competitor approaching on the lay-line that would carry him around the mark would be on port tack and would not have right-of-way, as is the case in a traditional buoys-to-port course.

Clipper crossed the starting line on port tack; the rest of the fleet

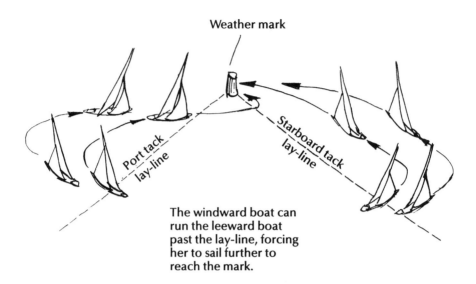

Weather mark

Port tack lay-line

Starboard tack lay-line

The windward boat can
run the leeward boat
past the lay-line, forcing
her to sail further to
reach the mark.

approached the Canadians on starboard. *Clipper* ducked the transoms of *Victory* and *Lionheart*, then crossed the bow of *Australia* before dipping below *France 3*. The water was like glass and every sound carried with exceptional clarity. Because it was a Saturday, the bay was dotted with spectator craft, which crowded the Xerox fleet from astern. The hullabaloo of the spectators was proving to be an enormous distraction to *Clipper*. It made Boyd wonder how he and the rest of the crew would fare if transfixed in the sights of an America's Cup audience.

France 3, furthest to the right on starboard tack, had been forcing the three British boats to the left, into a stronger flood tide. All four boats then joined the Canadians on port tack, with *Clipper* the furthest to the right. Boyd aimed the hand-bearing compass – they were in a dead heat with the rest of the fleet. And then, all at once, *Clipper* shot ahead. Better wind, less tide, luck, skill, call it what you will, but the Canadians had moved into the lead, and *Clipper*'s afterguard elected to tack back and consolidate their position. *Clipper*, on starboard, crossed every bow; unbelievably, to the crew, the spectator fleet let out a lusty cheer.

They tacked onto port on the hip of the fleet and promptly fell down into the opposition. Terry the Philosopher assessed the situation. "Well," he decided, "we sure blew that."

Lionheart squeezed out from the pack into the lead. *Australia* and *France 3* tacked onto starboard, forcing *Clipper* to duck their transoms. The Canadians had *Victory* pinned to their right on port tack, and they ran the British yacht past the starboard lay-line before they tacked onto starboard for the mark.

While *Clipper* was busy sailing *Victory* past the starboard lay-line, Peter de Savary was inexplicably flipping *Australia* onto a port tack collision course with *France 3*. The impact ripped off *Australia*'s bow forward of the headstay; a holed *France 3* was hammered over onto port tack, into the path of *Clipper*. Bruno Troublé bore *France 3* off, and the tricoloured 12-Metre slid down the port side of *Clipper* with paper's-width clearance, leaving a streak of red paint along *Clipper*'s genoa.

Clipper beat *Victory* around the mark and began to chase *Lionheart* to the head of the island. Jeff Boyd looked back to see *Australia* motionless, her amputated bow dangling by a section of mangled aluminum. *Australia* had retired, but the French took down their genoa, which had been torn in the collision, hoisted a new sail, sealed the hole in their port side with duct tape and continued to race. (The incident had cost de Savary an estimated $40,000 for repairs to the two boats; part of *Australia*'s bow now hangs in the Raw Bar on Bannister's Wharf.)

The run began in consistently light wind, and *Clipper*'s ¾ NB spinnaker looked heavy. *Victory* closed, overlapping to windward. The Canadians luffed but the British refused to respond, claiming they needed water to navigate safely with the island to windward. Amid much noise and shouting, *Victory*'s spinnaker billowed into *Clipper*'s rigging. Both sides displayed protest flags and *Victory* sailed into second place. *France 3* closed, but *Clipper* held her off and sailed back up the east side of the island to a third-place finish.

A large crowd again greeted *Clipper* at the shipyard. The French crew invited the Canadians over to their house for dinner. McLaughlin, Boyd and Wilson disappeared to fill out a protest form. At the hearing, their case was thrown out and *Clipper* was disqualified, making *Victory* the overall regatta winner and the Canadians third, behind *Lionheart*.

By the time *Clipper*'s afterguard arrived at the French crew house, all the food was gone. The Canadians and French headed for Le Club and the Victory Club, where they took part in drinking contests with the British, whom the Canadians suspected of cheating, and where the Canadian efforts were seriously undermined when their anchor man, Ed Gyles, wandered off in the haze of alcohol and could not be found.

The following day, the crew was back at Newport Shipyard to pull *Clipper* out of the water, remove her rig and strip her deck of hardware. Marvin McDill dropped by to congratulate them on their effort and stayed for a meeting at which the crew, pulling no punches, aired their views on the Canadian program. McDill seemed to listen.

After dinner McLaughlin, Boyd and Two Ton treated themselves to a whirlpool bath at the Playoff, a Newport racquet club and Nautilus fitness centre, then headed downtown for a quiet beer. The bartender at the Raw Bar bought them a round, telling them what a great job they did considering the lack of money and practice. What would become the afterguard of *Canada 1* was beginning to sense that Newport liked the Canadians, or, more accurately, liked the underdog.

On Monday, September 27, Robin Wynne-Edwards and Jeff Boyd drove the van to Boston for a spot of rest and relaxation. Everyone else went back from whence they came. It was over; it was successful.

14

the post-xerox blues

The crew of *Clipper* returned home from the Xerox regatta buoyant and optimistic. In part the high came from the novel experience of racing against other challenge syndicates, but it was largely fuelled by pride in their underdog performance, the feeling that they were truly a grass-roots campaign, and the sense that they had pumped some life into a dying enterprise. They were confident they would soon be back training.

Jeff Boyd returned to Kingston. He moved into his parents' home and went back to his old job at Sepp's Ski Shop with the understanding that when he left it would be in a hurry. Days and weeks passed with no news, and every week brought another rumour. Labatt's was about to hand over $1.2 million; a Mr. X was going to come through with $3 million. And on and on – other faces, other figures. But nothing concrete.

Bill Cox and Paul Henderson. Both are short, stocky men. Cox is completely bald and proud of it; Henderson still has some hair left on the sides. Cox is the vice-president of Glen Warren Productions, an operation affiliated with CFTO, the CTV network's flagship station in Toronto. Henderson is a plumber who sailed for Canada in the 1964 and 1968 Olympic Games and is a vice-president of the International Yacht Racing Union. Cox was the chef de mission of the Canadian sailing team at the 1968 and 1972 Games. Both men are members of the Royal Canadian Yacht Club, and in early 1982 both wanted to get involved in the America's Cup challenge in the worst way.

The two men were a team. Henderson was the idea man, Cox the expeditor. Fascinated by the fledgling *Canada 1* campaign, Henderson decided to see if he couldn't provide a little input into the challenge process. The crew was training in Palmetto, and the problems with the Admiral were approaching the crisis point. Having been in touch with John Morgan, the first eastern director in Marvin McDill's organization, Henderson picked up the telephone and called Doug Keary.

Keary's reputation as a yachting bureaucrat was impeccable. He played a key role in establishing the multi-class CORK event in Kingston in 1969, and from 1973 to 1975 was head of the Canadian Yachting Association's instruc-

141

tor development program. Keary had chaired the CYA committee that oversaw the development of the Portsmouth Harbour Olympic sailing site in Kingston for the 1976 Games. He had helped establish the Ontario Sailing Centre on Lake Couchiching and from 1976 to 1978 served as its director. Keary was also an enthusiastic sailor, having raced Snipes, a two-man dinghy, out of the Oakville Yacht Squadron for years.

Keary's great strength was as a mediator. He was likable man, who had time and again displayed a talent for bringing opposed forces together and orchestrating a unified effort. He had enjoyed a long and successful career in the construction business, in the end selling his company to his employees. With his financial man as partner, he had then established Northsted and carried on as a real estate investor and landlord. But that did not require much of his time, and he was getting a little restless. He felt, as he puts it, a psychological need to chase some fire trucks, get out in the world to mediate and organize again, to see if he could still do it, if he still had it. Paul Henderson saw him as a replacement for Rear Admiral Brock, and Doug Keary was willing to listen.

Keary had always thought that the America's Cup was an overblown, nothing event. He sailed in club races that were more interesting, he used to think. The Snipe sailors in Oakville were deadly serious on the race course, and the brilliance of their tactics was wondrous to behold. It seemed to Keary that winning the America's Cup could not be as difficult as an individual winning an Olympic medal or a world title, which entailed fighting up through the ranks of your own country's best sailors before bashing it out with the elite of two dozen other countries. At the America's Cup, you were just sailing against one guy who might have been up drinking the night before.

But Keary came to consider that what makes the America's Cup a true world series is that there are no barriers to success. There are financial limitations on Olympic campaigns, but in the America's Cup everyone is theoretically prepared to spend the last available dollar to win. The problem, of course, is finding the money, but the contestants' willingness to go to the limit can only produce perfection. In the words of Dennis Conner, *No excuse to lose*. "That's crazy, a killer," Keary would think whenever he stopped to consider the America's Cup. Perhaps, but it was also something he hadn't done before – something that looked impossible to tackle, and that only made it something he was interested in butting his head against.

When Paul Henderson rang up Doug Keary, he wanted to know how healthy he was. Keary felt fine. Henderson then arranged a meeting with Keary to discuss the replacement of the Admiral. During the meeting Henderson was on the phone with John Morgan in Montreal, assessing the problem. Each man had his replacement candidate sitting with him, something that neither knew. Henderson had Keary, Morgan had Lynn Watters. When Morgan wondered what Henderson thought of Watters, Keary listened as Henderson, unaware that Watters was also listening in, observed that Watters was a terrific rules man, no doubt about it, but that he couldn't see Watters in charge of some unwieldy organization. After a little more discussion, John Morgan decided to go with Watters as the Admiral's replacement for the summer of 1982. Keary was content with the decision and stepped back from the brink.

At the end of the summer, with the training camp disbanded and the challenge in disarray, Bill Cox met with Marvin McDill to discuss its future and what Cox and the eastern yachting establishment – namely the Royal Canadian Yacht Club – could do about it. Out of that meeting came the participation of Bob Grant, a past commodore of the Royal Canadian Yacht Club. Cox kept plugging, organizing a workshop in Toronto for early October, an entire weekend of brainstorming by interested parties. He mailed out invitations, one of them to Doug Keary. Keary called Cox to find out who was going to be there. Cox rang off about 100 names; Keary said forget it, the thing would be a circus. He didn't have time for that sort of free-for-all and instructed Cox to get back to him when the various parties had figured out what they wanted to do.

The workshop was held at the Carlton Club, the Royal Canadian Yacht Club's city station near Bloor and Yonge streets. Before the meeting, Terry McLaughlin, Peter Wilson and Jeff Boyd met at McLaughlin's cottage on the Toronto Islands to draft a reorganization structure. Among the people they would confer with at the Carlton Club were Marvin McDill, John Morgan, Don Green, Bob Whitehouse, Lynn Watters, Steve Tupper and Kevin Singleton, and any number of heavyweights who drifted in and out during the two days. Representatives of the press (Robert Martin of the *Globe and Mail*, John Bleasby of *Canadian Yachting*) were invited to a preliminary meeting, in hope that they would be instilled with fresh enthusiasm for the crippled challenge.

For the three crew representatives, it was a frustrating weekend. There was no formal agenda, and as they regrouped into one think tank after another the number of uninformed people became alarming. Two Ton found it frightening to discover how disorganized some of the challenge's own people were. The quote of the weekend belonged to Lynn Watters who, as acting director of operations, was the man who had signed the cheques at the training bases. When it was revealed that the undertaking was some $250,000 in debt, Watters snapped impatiently, "And what the devil are we going to do about it!"

Don Green, for one, resigned. He saw the situation as hopeless in light of its stated goal – to win the America's Cup. He also now disagreed with the two-sailmaker program, feeling it would waste valuable time and money. Knowing that Terry McLaughlin was interested in assuming responsibility for the sail program, he stepped down. But before he left the challenge, he urged McDill to name Terry McLaughlin *Canada 1*'s skipper. Before the weekend was out, Marvin McDill did.

Separate from the rest of the workshop, Steve Tupper, Bob Whitehouse, Lynn Watters, Peter Wilson, Terry McLaughlin and Jeff Boyd met to draw up a provisional training schedule with an accompanying budget that called for *Canada 1* to start sailing in Toronto in mid-November.

With the workshop over, Terry McLaughlin began laying plans for the Canadians to travel to New Orleans at the end of October to defend their USYRU team racing title. Terry McLaughlin and his Flying Dutchman crew, Evert Bastet, would sail one boat; Jeff Boyd would helm the second, with Bob Vaughan-Jones as his crew. Greg Tawaststjerna would be the third helmsman, and Rob Muru his crew.

The entire team would make the trip to New Orleans in Boyd's van. Boyd drove to Toronto on October 26 and met McLaughlin at the Carlton Club. Concerned about the lack of information after the Cox workshop, Boyd wondered, "What's going on with the 12? It sure would be nice to know."

McLaughlin exploded, tearing into Boyd. Didn't he think *everyone* wanted to know? He wasn't anybody special. Boyd thought he had just been airing what was on his mind, and for that he had been thoroughly lambasted. *Great*, he thought to himself, *it's going to be a fun weekend in New Orleans.*

The dressing down had been an emotional spillover by McLaughlin, who had been following developments with the same concern and frustration. He relaxed and told Boyd that the problem was a dispute between the western group of directors, led by Marvin McDill, and the eastern establishment, whom the sailors had excited with their performance at Xerox. Nothing more was said. They headed south.

The team racing championship was a disappointment. At the awards ceremony following the regatta, Terry McLaughlin was called forward. Terry the Philosopher addressed the gathered crowd. "Well," he reflected, "last year we were 10-0 and won. This year we were 5-5 and tied for third." He paused. "I guess we fucked up."

Mid-November: the date the provisional schedule had pinpointed for *Canada 1* to begin sailing in Toronto arrived. *Canada 1* was not yet sailing, and there was little word on progress at the organizational level. In the meantime, Terry McLaughlin was making plans for a round-the-world excursion with his girlfriend, Mickey Jeltes. Mickey was Dutch; Terry had met her while racing his Flying Dutchman in Europe – her uncle was a class measurer who had been in Kingston for the 1976 Olympics (how the thread of the

Canada 1 *near completion in Port Credit, Ontario*

fraternity continued to weave). John Bleasby, writing in the RCYC's newsletter, mischievously referred to the trip as a practice honeymoon. McLaughlin would combine the trip with the Flying Dutchman world championship in Australia, in which he would finish third.

Before November was out, Terry McLaughlin invited Jeff Boyd to the Carlton Club to meet Gord Norton of the RCYC. Norton asked questions of the two sailors for three hours and wrote a stream of notes. McLaughlin wanted Boyd to be the challenge's crew contact, the acting skipper, while he was gone, and filled him in on sail orders and the plans for winter training. Gord Norton, he was informed, was to be operations coordinator, and they were trying to get Doug Keary as site director for the winter training base. Jeff Boyd knew Keary through the Ontario Sailing Association and was pleased to hear that he might become part of the management.

Since Xerox, *Canada 1* had been moved from the McConnell operation in Parry Sound to Harbour Marine Services in Port Credit for the fairing and painting of the hull and the final bolting on of hardware. In addition to HMS employees, the work was being performed by Eric Jespersen, Don Campbell, Daniel Palardy and Sandy Andrews under the direction of Bob Whitehouse.

During this final finishing, *Canada 1* was surrounded by a tall plywood screen. Bruce Kirby was being especially secretive about the shape of his 12-Metre, particularly its keel. The reasoning went that because Sparkman & Stephens' modifications of the keel of *Spirit*, its design for the Conner campaign, had brought it closer to the shape of the keel of *Canada 1*, Bruce Kirby might be sitting on a breakthrough worth concealing for a while. But the plywood screen also created an aura of mystery that the world would come to know far better when Alan Bond similarly hoisted a "modesty skirt" about the hull of *Australia II* during the summer of 1983. Things that are hidden are sure to score psyche points, and when the American yacht designer Roger Marshall sneaked a peek at the keel (supposedly at the request of David Vietor, the owner of *Courageous*) while passing through town, the breach of security was treated so seriously that an enraged Don Campbell came close to dumping Marshall in Lake Ontario.

Canada 1 was in Port Credit because of Paul Phelan. Rather than simply giving the challenge the money necessary to finish the yacht, Phelan, for about $200,000, had acquired *Canada 1*'s first mortgage, thereby technically making himself her owner. The mortgage gave Phelan, and the eastern establishment, effective leverage in the reorganization of the challenge effort. And although Phelan seldom appeared at meetings, he was known and felt as a force to be reckoned with; Marvin McDill would honour Phelan by naming him the challenge's Honorary Commodore-at-Sea.

The eastern and western factions were locked in a stalemate that November. Marvin McDill represented the authority of the challenge; he had legal title to *Canada 1*, and his contrivance, the Secret Cove Yacht Club, was the challenger of record. But McDill was broke. The eastern faction could provide money and expertise but wanted some measure of power in return. How much power the easterners wanted and how much power McDill would grant had yet to be determined.

Bob Grant decided to contact a fellow Royal Canadian Yacht Club member, Cedric Gyles, in the hope that he could bring about a resolution. Gyles, whose son Ed was a member of the crew candidates ranks, was a westerner who over his career had worked his way eastward. He was raised in Vancouver, where his grandfather had been commodore of the Royal Vancouver Yacht Club. From 1948 to 1951 he was a member of the Calgary Stampeders, playing in the 1948 and 1949 Grey Cups and earning a victor's ring in 1948. It was a time in the Canadian Football League when players still played both ways, Gyles as a halfback. He also ran back punts, in an era when no blocking was allowed on punt returns. This sort of punishment made Gyles aware of the dangers the game posed to his mind and body, and he retired early, embarking on a successful business career.

He spent about 35 years on the Prairies, part of it as president of the Winnipeg Blue Bombers. His sailing skills got a bit rusty, but when he came to Toronto he made a point of getting his hands back on a helm and bought an 8-Metre, *Norseman*, in 1973.

Cedric Gyles had followed the America's Cup as a boy and was well read on the contest. He had always wanted to see Canada enter a challenger again, and when the opportunity arose to become involved in the 1983 challenge, he readily accepted. Although Gyles did not know Marvin McDill well, he knew *of* him. During his Calgary years, Gyles had been a founding member of the 400 Club, of which McDill later served as president. He met McDill when the Calgary lawyer returned to speak at the RCYC in February of 1982, and at that time offered him whatever assistance he needed. McDill, as it turned out, did need help; Gyles, as president of Reed Stenhouse, arranged the insurance on *Clipper* and *Intrepid* and gave McDill the "family price" for health and accident coverage.

Bob Grant already had a committee lined up before Gyles even agreed to lead them. They were RCYC bigwigs all – Paul Henderson, Bill Cox, Bob Grant, Tony Griffin, John Lockwood, Basil Rodomar, Paul Phelan and Gordon Fisher (who had reconsidered his scepticism of the previous year). The group was under the impression that it had an operating agreement with the western organization. Gyles telephoned McDill to review what he understood was their agreement. McDill's reply was negative in the extreme. Gyles clearly had some fences to mend.

The eastern establishment was growing impatient, and there was talk of a new non-profit corporation being formed to carry on the challenge, and to hell with Marvin. But Gyles recognized a naïveté in the ranks of his operating group. Although they knew far more about sailing than did McDill, they knew nothing about the America's Cup. Gyles recognized that McDill was the most astute of them all. He understood the scope of the project; he also had the experience of Palmetto, Newport and the Xerox regatta behind him. And McDill had made a succession of smart moves. The pan-Canadian concept was a sound one, and he had managed to secure *Clipper* as a trial horse. Having *Canada 1* completed and using her as a showpiece for fundraising was a good idea. A depressed economy had pulled the rug out from under him before he could finish the construction of *Canada 1* and put the fund-raising machine into gear. Now McDill found the boat in the hands of an easterner, whose fellow easterners (some of whom had scoffed at his notion of a challenge in the first place) were eager to take his national dream and run with it. In the fall of 1982 Marvin McDill was justifiably paranoid about losing control of the ambitious project he had almost singlehandedly launched.

McDill hadn't done everything perfectly – there had been the Admiral

Canada 1 *being launched in Port Credit, Ontario*

episode, for one – but he had done amazingly well. Cedric Gyles had great respect for him. Although McDill received support from Don MacDonald and Crawford Smith, Gyles felt that the westerners on his board of directors were weak, and that McDill should have expanded its membership more ambitiously once the challenge got off the ground. All the same, there was nothing McDill had done that would suggest incompetence. Gyles was compelled to tell his committee that, had they launched the challenge, they might not have made the mistakes McDill did, but they would have made a whole lot of different ones. Whether they liked it or not, the only person in the country who knew anything about organizing an America's Cup challenge was a yachting neophyte from Alberta.

The essential problem dividing the east and west was the concept of "new" debt and "old" debt. The "old" debt was anything incurred by McDill before the collapse of the challenge in August. The "new" debt was whatever had mounted up since. There were parties in the east who would just as soon ignore the old debt, let McDill sink with it and start off with a clean slate. To Gyles the distinction between the debts was nonsense. Debt was debt, and he persuaded McDill to try to isolate it through a reorganization of management. Thus the Toronto operations committee was approved. It was directly responsible to McDill in Calgary and would endeavour to raise money in eastern Canada and also oversee the running of *Canada 1* and its base. The agreement worked, Gyles felt, because he made sure he always kept McDill informed of their actions. Even if it was something minor, Gyles stuck to the courtesy of soliciting the advice and approval of McDill. He generally talked to McDill every other day. Back in Toronto, he devoted much of his energy to reminding others that the challenge was still McDill's show, not theirs.

Canada 1's launching in Port Credit on November 23 was accompanied by much publicity. It was also accompanied by a telephone call to Kingston by Terry McLaughlin, who told Boyd, "We're sailing for a while. Why don't you, Two Ton and Robin come to Toronto?"

On November 26, Boyd, Wilson and Wynne-Edwards crowded into Wilson's Volkswagen Rabbit and drove to Port Credit. Snow fell in large wet flakes, and Boyd had trouble concentrating on the idea of sailing. There was a reunion of crew members in the parking lot of Harbour Marine Services, which produced the decision not to take the boat out after all. Boyd had barely got out of the car before the HMS office handed him telephone messages from Bill Cox and Terry McLaughlin.

He called Terry, who told him to be in the Reed Stenhouse offices in the Royal Trust Tower at 5:30 p.m. History was going to be made. In a symbolic reconciliation between west and east, Marvin McDill and Paul Phelan were going to shake hands.

At 5:30 it happened. McDill, Phelan, Gyles, Cox, Rodomar, McLaughlin and Boyd were sipping cocktails, wearing smiles, and toasting the challenge Plans for winter training were discussed, as well as the sail program and fund-raising. It was decided that there should be a press conference to announce the new organization, and Phelan offered the Victoria Hotel as the site.

Marvin McDill then allowed how he thought he could persuade James Richardson, the former defence minister whose family controls Richardson Securities, to come through with some financial assistance. "Call him right now," Phelan veritably ordered him, and he headed into Gyles's office to do so (Richardson couldn't be reached).

Bill Cox filled Jeff Boyd in on a taping planned for Sunday, the 28th. The CTV show "Thrill of a Lifetime" had a candidate lined up who wanted to steer *Canada 1*, and Cox had been happy to comply. Boyd told Cox that "Bobo" Whitehouse would not allow cameras on board; Cox replied that he'd have to. McLaughlin then informed the gathering that, in his absence, Jeff Boyd would be in charge as acting skipper. His round-the-world excursion was due to start the next evening. With Cox emphasizing the importance of the television show, the weight of responsibility seemed a lot heavier than Boyd had been prepared for.

Saturday, November 27, could not have been more perfect. Jeff Boyd's first sail on *Canada 1* took place on a beautiful day, sunny and crisp, and the temperature would warm to five degrees Celsius. The only real drawback was the ice on the cockpit floor, which would make for slippery footing whenever the boat was heeled. *Canada 1* was towed out of Port Credit Harbour by "my little *Pleiades*," a smart power launch modelled on the lines of a Nova Scotia fishing boat that Paul Phelan had had built for the 1976 Olympic Games.

Sails were hoisted just outside the Port Credit breakwater. A fair number of spectator craft were on hand. Terry McLaughlin, at the wheel, was wired for sound. Filming was being conducted by Dale Hartleben, who had been chosen to produce the official documentary on the Canadian challenge. As a partner of Ottawa's Budge Crawley, Hartleben had won an Oscar for best documentary with *The Man Who Skied Down Everest* (a film known to some wags as *The Man Who* Fell *Down Everest*).

Canada 1 cruised around, hoisted a spinnaker, took it down, did a few circles and shook off the spectator fleet. All of which left Terry McLaughlin a bit bored. His interest perked when he spotted another sailboat in the distance, a cruiser about as graceful as a Winnebago when compared to *Canada 1*. McLaughlin aimed the 12-Metre at the seagoing Winnebago, and when he caught up, proceeded to carve tight circles around it. This soon became tiresome and *Canada 1* returned to Port Credit, coasting back into her slip. The crew cracked open beers in the parking lot and stood around in their Mustang foul-weather gear, renewing acquaintances. It would have made a great beer commercial, but at the time there wasn't a brewery in sight willing to associate itself with a limping America's Cup challenge.

Sunday, November 28, was Grey Cup day, and the day was appropriately grey – overcast, cold and threatening rain. The crew intended to spend the outing in further shaking down the Bruce Kirby design, but they also planned to conjure some publicity in the process. There were two additions to the crew. Jay "Bond" McKinnell was a friend of Jeff Boyd through Laser and Finn competition. As his nickname suggested, he would become responsible for Canadian espionage activities (the nickname was modified to "Bondo" when McKinnell became coated in fairing compound during alterations to *Canada 1* in the summer of 1983). Al Megarry was a student at Queen's who had crewed on board the winning Canada's Cup yachts in 1978 and 1981. Still in his early twenties, he came to the program with a high recommendation as a sail trimmer from Hans Fogh.

The first task of the day was to deal with the "Thrill of a Lifetime" taping. The crew treated the undertaking as something of a joke, although they considered that someone whose thrill of a lifetime was to sail a 12-Metre couldn't be all bad. As skipper for the day, Boyd rehearsed a prearranged script with the show's producer. Then their thrillee, Michael Green, strolled down the dock, beaming. Boyd invited him aboard and asked him if he wanted to go for a sail.

"*Do I?*" Green exclaimed. Cut. Perfect. Print it.

Michael Green turned out to be a pleasant person. He had grown up in Kingston and knew Boyd's sister, and he happened to steer the boat quite well.

With the taping session out of the way, *Canada 1* turned to its next publicity venture of the day – sailing past Exhibition Stadium while the Grey Cup was under way. With a southeast wind of 15-18 knots, the crew headed east with its small armada of spectator boats. They were told to watch for a CBC representative with a walkie-talkie on the Ontario Place breakwall. No CBC representative. They were told to watch for a small plane that would fly over the stadium towing a sign that read "Look toward the water and see our challenger for the America's Cup, *Canada 1*," or perhaps something shorter. The plane never got off the ground. It was iced up in St. Catharines.

Its bid for nationwide television exposure a bust, *Canada 1* short-tacked up the Western Gap into Toronto Harbour. When they reached the opposite end of the harbour, they hoisted their one and only spinnaker and gybed back and forth, returning to the Western Gap. With Bruce Kirby at the helm, *Canada 1* swung breathtakingly close to the Toronto waterfront. Ed Gyles's brother and a few of his friends yelled the football game score to them from the balcony of the family's condominium at the Harbour Castle.

The crew was becoming cold and wet and hungry. There was no food on board – at the last minute before leaving dock Daniel Palardy had borrowed some money from Bob Whitehouse, who seemed to be privately bankroll-ing the sailing excursions, to buy a case of Diet Coke. Rain was falling and it was getting dark. The crew, deciding they had done more than enough in the cause of public relations, opted to return to port. Paul Phelan fed them soup aboard *Pleiades*, and they headed home to watch what was left of the Grey Cup, a game only slightly better suited to the brooding season.

On November 29, *Canada 1* was again sailing on Lake Ontario. Bruce Kirby, keen to debug the boat as much as possible before winter closed in, was angered by Terry McLaughlin's departure on a world tour. He felt that his presence was vital at such a critical time, with the boat newly launched and the syndicate undergoing a traumatic reorganization.

Kirby was constantly interested in the crew's opinions of the boat. *What does it feel like?* Jeff Boyd allowed that, while he hadn't steered 12-Metres long enough to be an expert, he thought that *Canada 1* seemed lighter on the helm, laid off easier after resting head-to-wind in a semi-stalled situation, and appeared to have a quiet, undisturbed quarter wake.

Terry McLaughlin had not said much after his first sails that fall, not wanting to express an unfounded opinion. He had been rightly tight-lipped. Compared to other challenges, they hadn't spent much time on *Canada 1*, or any 12-Metre for that matter. They were still learning, and a lack of instrumentation aboard *Canada 1* didn't help in reaching conclusions about the boat. It was all guesswork, wishful thinking. The crew yearned for a Dennis Conner to take the design for a spin and give it the thumbs up or thumbs down.

While they may not have had Dennis Conner, they did have Hans Fogh and Greg Tawaststjerna, both of whom came for a sail on November 29. It was another overcast day, very cold, with a stiff breeze out of the northwest. Once again *Pleiades* towed *Canada 1* out of Port Credit Harbour. At *Pleiades'* helm was Ben Colenbrander, Paul Phelan's right-hand man and chauffeur, who tended to Phelan's farm, yachts and other gentlemanly possessions.

Canada 1 hoisted her spinnaker and embarked on a tremendous ride eastward with Twister at the wheel. Realizing that they could end up in Rochester if the boat suffered a breakdown, the crew decided to douse the chute and head upwind. The smooth downwind slide had proved deceptive; once on the wind they realized they had as much as 30 knots across the deck.

The main was ragging, deafening. The crew was uneasy. Bob White-house, in the foxhole, watched the mast bend and shake as much as 30 inches off the centreline and quickly told Bruce Kirby that they'd better ease off before they lost the rig.

Seconds later, the boom glanced off the head of Robin Wynne-Edwards and crashed onto the after deck.

The crew acted as dazed as Wynne-Edwards, at last realizing that the mainsail halyard car had disintegrated. The main was completely lowered and *Canada 1* returned to port under genoa only. It was not the last time the mishap would occur; it would return to haunt them in a critical race in the summer of 1983.

Jeff Boyd returned to Kingston for a few days. While he was away, *Canada 1* continued to sail, each day with a different television crew, a different media representative tagging along. Boyd returned to Toronto on December 3; Bill Cox had lined up a select and formidable group of Canada's financial elite. Cox thought it only proper that these potential backers be taken for a sail on the yacht they were being asked to underwrite. Among them were Gordon Fisher (Southam Inc.), Galen Weston (head of George Weston Ltd., proprietor of such enterprises as the Loblaws chain), Fred Eaton (of the Eaton family retail empire), Michael Davies (an avid sailor and publisher of the Kingston *Whig-Standard*), Irving Gerstein (Peoples Jewellers) and such heavyweight RCYC members as Jim Crang and Tony Griffin.

Ben Colenbrander fired up *Pleiades*, and *Canada 1*, with a crew of 18, once again headed out of Port Credit Harbour. The water was glassy and there was only about six knots of wind, not enough for a 12-Metre to pull out the stops, but it made for an enjoyable sail all the same. It struck Jeff Boyd that this handful of multimillionaires, who on their own were capable of saving the Canadian challenge, were actually having *fun*. He made sure that each took a spell at the wheel and that each had an opportunity to spin the grinder handles (the handles were always guaranteed to mesmerize the uninitiated – people couldn't resist the urge to take them in hand and whale away).

Later in the day, Bill Cox, Cedric Gyles and Gord Norton came alongside aboard *Pleiades*. With them was Doug Keary, who had been persuaded to join the challenge. The multimillionaires transferred to *Pleiades* and the eastern committee members boarded *Canada 1*. Cox would tell the sailors that they had done a reasonable sales job on the business moguls. Although some later came through with personal donations, the companies they represented did not come on board as major corporate sponsors, as had been hoped. The sailors were deeply disappointed.

Saturday, December 4, was sunny and warm. Ken Danby accompanied *Canada 1* aboard *Pleiades*, shooting off rolls of film. Danby had organized a fund-raising dinner for the challenge in Guelph on November 13; limited-edition photographs taken by the artist at the Xerox regatta were auctioned, and the evening had netted the challenge about $6000. (The objective of the evening had been to raise enough money to purchase a spinnaker, and many of the attendants were hoping that the city of Guelph's logo could be embossed on the sail. Terry McLaughlin was ready to agree to anything, but later convinced the fund-raisers that the spinnakers all had to be identical, to keep the opposition guessing on their sail selection during the race.)

Cameras were everywhere that Saturday. The Canadian sailing photographer, Franz Rosenbaum, was buzzing about in a small powerboat, and Dale Hartleben was aboard *Canada 1* with camera and sound men. Jeff Boyd had never actually met Hartleben before, and he watched with curiosity as the filmmaker strolled about the boat, doing this damned trick with his hands – palms out, thumbs pointed toward each other, with Hartleben staring between his hands, framing his subject matter and panning this way and that. He fretted about the quality of light as the film rolled, but mostly he fretted about continuity – Terry McLaughlin wasn't even on the continent, and Jeff Boyd was steering. Hartleben apologized to Boyd: his face would have to stay out of the shots. The cameras zoomed in on Boyd's gloved hands clutching the wheel. Back in the editing room, Boyd's hands could be transformed into Terry's.

Once rid of the film crew, the sailors drifted about, shirtless. The December air had climbed to about 12 degrees Celsius, and some of the crew were determined to start on their tans before moving to the southern training base. Franz Rosenbaum motored by and asked them to put up a spinnaker. They explained to him that the spinnaker, their only spinnaker, was ripped.

Rosenbaum didn't believe them and became quite insistent. "Sorry, Franz," they replied. Nothing doing.

"Oh, you guys," he concluded and roared off. They would meet again, and with far stranger results.

Bob Whitehouse and Jeff Boyd arrived at Harbour Marine Services on December 5 to find that their day would be spent giving people rides on *Canada 1*. Alan Adelkind, a local yacht broker, had sold excursions on the 12-Metre for $100 at the Lake Ontario Racing Council's year-end banquet. Bobo and Boyd, who had not been informed of the scheme, were furious with Adelkind, but after some thought decided the rides might be useful. Whitehouse needed funds to carry on with some work on *Canada 1*, and he was continually having trouble requisitioning it. Adelkind's effort would produce some hands-on cash.

It was a cold, rainy day, with a strong easterly wind. Boyd warned the first load of paying passengers that the trip would be wet and uncomfortable, which deterred no one. Despite the weather, the passengers enjoyed themselves, and Boyd returned *Canada 1* to dock for another load.

It wasn't the most dignified beginning for a newly launched 12-Metre. *Canada 1* hadn't been in the water ten days and already the pressures of fund-raising had managed to reduce it to a tour boat. Twelve-Metres are supposed to be the elite of yachts, the Formula 1 breed; *Canada 1* was being treated like a new ride at Disney World. Robin Wynne-Edwards was insulted. "A hundred bucks!" he exclaimed. "You can't put a price on a ride. You have to *earn* it."

Leaving the dock with her third load of paying passengers, *Canada 1* snagged her keel on a concrete crib. Boyd decided not to go any further. The boat had been shipping a worrisome amount of water, the bilge pumps weren't functioning properly and, at the end of the first excursion that day, Sandy Andrews had been forced to bail out the bilges with a bucket, which Jeff Boyd, on deck, emptied overboard.

The third tour group was not pleased. Boyd stood his ground. The group went home without a ride, and the crew freed *Canada 1* from the harbour bottom and returned her to her slip.

With the boat squared away, the crew headed for the Port Credit Yacht Club. Its membership had shown boundless hospitality during *Canada 1*'s stay at Harbour Marine Services and had invited the crew to the clubhouse for a few beers.

There Jeff Boyd ran into Paul Phillips. Boyd and McLaughlin had already discussed his future with the program; they didn't think he could cut it as a crew but were interested in having him rejoin the program as a sailmaker.

Back on November 12, the day of the Mariners' Ball, a fund-raising dance in Toronto, Boyd and McLaughlin had interviewed as many of the other crew candidates as possible. Crew training was becoming their responsibility, and McLaughlin had begun a crew notebook. They had reviewed with the individual sailors their strong points, their weaknesses and what to do to improve themselves. They had stressed that no one should return to the program once training resumed unless he was prepared to work especially hard. (Unfortunately, as Boyd and McLaughlin would later discover, it took more than sheer hard work to win the America's Cup.)

Neither Boyd nor McLaughlin ever found it easy to tell a friend where he stood in the crew selection process, and Boyd found himself tackling the delicate matter with Paul Phillips without Terry's support. Boyd tactfully explained where they thought he might fit in. Phillips indicated that he had been thinking the same thing and that he was eager to do anything to help the challenge.

His attitude came as a great relief. That night Jeff Boyd drove back to Kingston. The next day *Canada 1* was hauled from the water, its future in limbo.

Paul Phelan took Eric Jespersen, Don Campbell, Daniel Palardy, Bob Whitehouse and Sandy Andrews to launch at the Victoria Hotel in downtown Toronto to thank them for their help in completing *Canada 1*. With the Lake Ontario trials finished and the boat hauled from the water, he explained, he was officially out of the program. His financial commitment, which in the end totalled $300,000, had been met, and he would no longer be involved. From behind his hand there was a wink and smile. "But don't you believe it," he assured them. "We'll see this thing through to the end."

With that, Paul Phelan moved to the topic of Marvin McDill. When the entire eastern establishment was bent on ousting McDill from leadership, he observed, McDill had taken them on singlehandedly – without an ace up his sleeve, without anything in his favour – and had managed to beat them to a standstill. Although he might not agree with everything Marvin McDill had said and done, Paul Phelan had to admit that he could only respect someone with such tenacious ability.

15

back on the campaign trail

Jeff Boyd had been back in Kingston for two days when the telephone rang in the basement of Sepp's Ski Shop on December 7. What tidings that innocuous basement telephone had borne over the years! This time it was Doug Keary. He wanted to sit down and talk with Jeff.

"When?"

"As soon as possible."

The next day, Boyd drove to Toronto to meet Keary at Bramaco Marketing Services, the business owned by Basil Rodomar that had taken over Warwick-Bradshaw's promotional and merchandising responsibilities. Keary wanted to absorb all he could about 12-Metres. Boyd told him – before lunch, during lunch and well after lunch.

"I'm not quite sure what I've gotten myself into," Doug Keary admitted, but he was committed, and pledged to see the challenge through come hell or high water. And he wanted Jeff to come to Toronto to give him a hand, full time, as an assistant director.

"Well, I've got my dad's car right now," Boyd explained. "My van isn't running. I've also got a job. . . ." He gave the situation a moment's thought. "Give me tomorrow in Kingston. I'll be back on Friday." He returned home and left his job at the ski shop for the umpteenth time. His van started. Jeff Boyd's management career with Canada's America's Cup Challenge Inc. was launched.

Doug Keary had been asked to establish an operations office in Toronto to handle the snowballing concerns of the challenge. He called a friend of his daughter, Jennifer Scott, on a Saturday night and asked her to come to work on Monday morning. He'd tell her what it was about when she got there. She appeared, no questions asked.

And then everything became very strange. For some reason, nobody would offer him any information. There were no records delivered to him, not a single piece of paper relating to the challenge. *Where are the files?* he demanded. They'd bought things – *where are the purchase orders?* They'd made deals – *where are the contracts?*

The challenge was still operating an office in Newport, manned by Kevin Singleton. He was alone down there, like the last member of the Lost Patrol, or some ambassador whose government back home has been toppled in a coup. Now he had somebody named Keary ringing him up all the time, asking what they owed whom, whether they had any inventory. Singleton was in a awkward position – he wasn't certain who was in charge and the status of his Newport office was a bit fuzzy. Keary finally decided to drop the kindly mediator schtick and told Singleton to get the goddamned files up to Toronto, right away.

Assembling the paperwork had been like pulling teeth, but for Keary it was well worth the effort. Reading the contracts, he found a surprise around every corner, the sort that brought out the whites in one's eyes. They were already, it turned out, in default on a contract calling for the challenge to use the exclusive services of one trucking firm. Another revealed that they would be in default to the tune of $15,000 on January 1. It was all a bit too much for Keary. The idea of lawsuits sent chills down his spine. There were a lot of conversations that went something like this:

> Keary: Marvin, we have this contract with so-and-so.
> McDill: We cancelled that contract.
> Keary: But he's suing us!
> McDill: Well, don't get too excited. . . .

Cedric Gyles concluded that it was McDill's tremendous legal experience that kept him calm in the face of so many near-disasters. Keary, on the other hand, would go through the roof. Gyles would have to calm Keary down, then get on the phone to McDill to make sure the matters were being settled. It was a potentially explosive situation – Marvin McDill turning himself inside-out to find new backers for the challenge, while Doug Keary kept popping up like the grim reaper with one horror from the past after another.

For Jeff Boyd, the period of teeth-pulling was a distressing one. He was immersed in the affairs of the challenge and was learning far more than he wanted to about the syndicate's problems. The circumstances looked hopeless.

On December 10 Jeff Boyd and Doug Keary met with Cedric Gyles. The issue was simple: how could the challenge regain six months of lost training time and in the process undertake a sail development program?

Several options were considered. They could establish a training camp in Florida with *Canada 1* in late January (the idea of Charleston, South Carolina, was all but discarded). They could take *Clipper* too, if the money was available. They could stay in Toronto, ship *Clipper* north and train on Lake Ontario all winter. Or they could ship *Canada 1* to Newport and begin training in early March.

It was decided that Jeff Boyd and Bob Whitehouse would leave for Florida on Monday, December 13, to investigate sites for a training base.

"Good idea," said Boyd. "We'll need some money."

Doug Keary made his first financial contribution to the challenge, handing Boyd and Whitehouse $2000. Had Keary not dug into his own pocket, the fact-finding mission would not have been possible. It was an apt illustration of the state of a challenge that had pledged not to go any further if $1.5 million was not raised by December 17. The deadline was in four days' time.

Jeff Boyd and Bob Whitehouse left Kingston in the only remaining CACC van on December 15. They dropped in at the Navtec facilities in Boston to have some rigging shortened and pick up a few miscellaneous parts, then headed southwest for Newport. There they met Kevin Singleton, still holding the fort, and helped him unload some property from the 54-foot Hatteras, *Slingshot* (alias *Slapshot*). The boat was being sold to help clear the syndicate's debts, and the sale would leave the challenge without a tender.

The following day they returned to Boston to catch a plane to Miami. The flight was delayed; Boyd and Bobo killed time by drawing up a plan of attack for their whirlwind tour of Florida's Atlantic coast. The criteria for an ideal site were many. There was the sailing area itself, and the general weather and sea conditions – they needed winds and seas close to those of Newport, a prerequisite that ruled out returning to Florida's west coast. And what about the local current, and access to the sea? And water depth? And tidal range?

As for the yard facilities: how much space? What's the dockage like? How about haul-out facilities? And trailer storage? Is there a machine shop? And plenty of parking? A spare parts supply? How about office space? And security?

Is there a tender available? A place to dock it? A local dealer for servicing? And a nearby fuel supply?

And housing: of serviceable quality? Where can the crew eat? How far are the housing facilities from the yard? And the town? Is there even a town? Where's the airport? Is there a shuttle available? Can you rent vehicles? Or tools? And is there a yacht club in the neighbourhood?

Is there a sail loft in the area? Or a place to establish a loft? How much room? Is there the necessary machinery? And electronics: is there a facility for servicing and parts?

They were met at Miami Airport by Tom Corness, who was living in a condominiun in Coconut Grove. In a rented car, they headed for South Shore Marina in Miami Beach, the base of the French challenge. Driving across the causeway connecting Miami with the south end of Miami Beach, surrounded by careering automobiles, they stared down on the narrow stretches of Government Cut. There, 100 yards away from the congested roadway, *France 3* was going through her paces.

Miami Beach was the pre-tour favourite for a Canadian training base. The French were already there and were ready to welcome the Canadians to South Shore Marina with open arms. At the conclusion of the Xerox regatta, Marvin McDill discussed with Yves Rousset-Rouard, chairman of the French syndicate, the possibility of the two campaigns cooperating in their winter training. From 1970 to 1980 France's four consecutive America's Cup challenges, each as ineffective as the last, had been bankrolled by Baron Bich of Bic pen, lighter, razor and sailboard fame. Having built three 12-Metres without making the finals against the Americans, the Baron called it a day. Rousset-Rouard, a French film producer best known for his soft-core triumph, *Emmanuelle* (and known to the Canadian 12-Metre sailors simply as Mr. Porn), stepped forward with about half the funds necessary for the low-budget 1983 effort. Bruno Troublé, who was an employee of Bic, agreed to stay on as skipper of *France 3*; Jacques Faroux was hired to redesign the yacht's keel and deck layout; the challenge designed and built a badly needed new mast; and a regular summer training camp was established in Newport. But *France 3* lacked the crucial trial horse for serious fine-tuning, and in September they had been prepared to arrange free accommodation for the Canadians to make sure *Clipper* and *Canada 1* appeared in Miami Beach.

The owners of South Shore Marina were also eager to have two more 12-Metres gracing their docks. Bob Whitehouse, Jeff Boyd and Tom Corness met with the proprietors, Merle Rubens and Charlie Seryader, who offered the Canadian challenge much-reduced slip fees for its yachts and tenders. Since the Xerox regatta, the challenge's financial crisis had produced costly delays in management decisions, and the free accommodations the French already enjoyed, arranged through the Muss Corporation, were no longer available to the Canadians. Merle Rubens made one well-placed telephone call and conjured up enough free suites at the Carillon Beach Hotel on Miami Beach's waterfront.

The location was tempting, and the presence of the French meant that, if one of the Canadian 12-Metres was put temporarily out of commission by a breakdown, they would still have another boat to train with. Although a strong tide coursed through the marina, making for resourceful docking techniques, the facility was a short distance from the open sea; and, as *France 3* had demonstrated that day, the protected shipping channels were roomy enough to accommodate the sailing manoeuvres of a 12-Metre, should the Atlantic on occasion prove too rough.

Dropping Tom Corness off in Coconut Grove, Jeff Boyd and Bob Whitehouse began a six-hour drive north to investigate the other options.

In St. Augustine, they all but broke out the marching bands for the Canadian
fact-finding mission. Boyd and Whitehouse met the proprietor of the
Comanche Cove Marina and members of the local yacht club; and when
they were through at the yacht club, they were escorted to the Ponce de
Leon Motor Inn for lunch with the mayor and the chairman of the chamber
of commerce. They were taken for a ride out the inlet to the Atlantic. It took
45 minutes to reach open water, and there was a bridge that would likely
impede the progress of a 12-Metre rig. The yard where the training base
would be located was heavily commercialized, and members of the camp
would be required to wear hard hats at all times. Mind you, the condomini-
ums offered were temptingly gorgeous. The verdict: wonderful people, but
abominable logistics.
   They visited Port Canaveral, and Fort Lauderdale, and North Palm Beach.
From a sailing standpoint, Port Canaveral was the best of all, Miami Beach
included. The Atlantic was easily accessible, and locks at the end of the
roomy harbour, regularly frequented by cruise ships and submarines, controlled the tide and waves. But the financial package, as well as the presence
of the French, made Miami Beach the best choice.
   Checking in with Toronto on December 17, Boyd and Whitehouse were
told that Cedric Gyles wanted them back in town for his regular Saturday
morning conference – in other words, the next day. On the plane to Boston,
they drafted their report and recommendations. Arriving in Boston at 8:00
p.m., they boarded their van and rolled down the Massachusetts Turnpike.
At 5:30 a.m. they arrived at Whitehouse's apartment, collapsing into sleep.
Three hours later, the two men were standing in Cedric Gyles's office
delivering their report.
   Boyd would learn later that, before he and Whitehouse had even completed their survey of Florida, the eastern operations committee had
decided to scrap the idea of a southern training base. It was all just a little bit
weird, Boyd and Whitehouse flogging to Gyles's committee the need to set
up in Miami, to recapture six months of lost training time, order new sails
right away, spend a minimum of $300,000 by Monday morning, with the
syndicate still flat broke. The ambition of their plans, when compared with
the challenge's utter poverty, was giving Boyd headaches. The deadline for
$1.5 million had passed, and the syndicate was far from reaching its target.
But Marvin McDill had succeeded in securing a personal commitment of
$200,000 from James Richardson, who, through his own connections,
would then bring almost one million dollars into the challenge coffers. On

the basis of the Richardson commitment, Gyles was prepared to go ahead.

But it had not been an easy decision. Gyles resolved to run the operation on the basis of cash flow, bolstered by the occasional gamble. If the money was in hand, or looked like it was about to be in hand, another phase of the challenge would be undertaken. So long as money kept materializing at the critical moments, *Canada 1* would continue to sail. Gyles was not insensitive to the risks of the undertaking – the process gave him the odd bout of butterflies. He wasn't happy with the idea of starting something he couldn't be sure of finishing. But he was determined. ("I'm still very competitive at my age," he notes. "Just come pheasant shooting with me sometime.")

The question of going to Florida was analyzed *ad nauseam*. Having to justify their decision to the many backers who had contributed their nickels, dimes and dollars, the committee didn't want to do anything rash. Gyles was all for going, but Gord Norton and Doug Keary tried to talk him out of it. Then Keary did an abrupt about-face, appearing before Gyles with a scheme for making the training base possible. The report by Jeff Boyd and Bob Whitehouse provided the final shove. *Canada 1* and *Clipper* were headed for Miami Beach.

While Jeff Boyd was in Cedric Gyles's office, Terry McLaughlin called from Australia for an update. He leaned heavily on Boyd, stressing that someone had to order some new sails soon. In his sail program notes of November 21, McLaughlin had argued that "the sail program must have top priority for funds available at the expense of other areas of expenditure if we are to do well." Boyd agreed that someone had to order sails, but he reminded Terry that someone had to pay their bills too. Another frustrating subject; another frustrating conversation.

The collapse of the Canadian challenge in August of 1982 was a serious setback to the sail development program, not only in its progress but also in the morale of the principal sailmaker. A dejected Hans Fogh wrote Paul Phelan on October 14, confessing that "it's a little discouraging after all of our work to build sails in our busiest time and my efforts to help down in Newport, that not only are we owed so much money but also that Terry is telling everyone he wants Sobstad Sails on the boat. . . . The total amount owing from what is invoiced is $21,831.52. The total of the sails started in my loft (1 mainsail and 3 spinnakers) is $33,820.00. Total $55,651.52 owing us. When these sails are finished, *Canada 1* will have one mainsail, 3 1980 *Freedom* design genoas, two 1980 design genoas and four spinnakers. This is short of even one complete inventory for *Canada 1*, let alone sails for *Clipper* needed to properly evaluate *Canada 1*."

On November 12 Jay Hansen of North-Fogh wrote Terry McLaughlin. He advised abandoning Phase 1 of the sail program (establishing a basic *Freedom* inventory on which to build) and moving straight to Phase 2 – developing a 1982 generation sail inventory. Hansen proposed the purchase of three mainsails, seven genoas and six spinnakers, one of which had already been completed.

The new cloth technology associated with 1982 generation sails would mean spider- or quilt-cut Mylar/Kevlar genoas. These were vertical-cut sails in which the panels were cut into smaller sections, with each section rotated so that the Kevlar threads aligned more accurately with the stress patterns in the sail. Such engineering would help produce Mylar/Kevlar sails that were stronger *and* lighter. Hansen also noted, "We have new ideas on building bigger spinnakers that budget and time permitting we want to test." He advised ordering a large staysail, which is sometimes set in the slot between the spinnaker and the mainsail for additional power, an extra-large triradial headsail and a star-cut reaching headsail.

"Terry, I must confess it is disappointing to me that seemingly you have less faith than the others in our ability to produce the fastest 12-Metre sails," Hansen concluded. "I only ask that you explore the possibility of working with North and Hans in the limited time available and not experimenting with other sailmakers and the inevitable conflicting personalities and opinions. I guarantee you will get much more out of us that way and achieve more in the long run."

Hans Fogh's loft and Terry McLaughlin could not have been more at odds. "Cutting back on Phase 1 is not possible," McLaughlin stated in his sail program update of November 21, and ignored Hansen's plea to return to a one-sailmaker program. He also disregarded the recommendation that a staysail and the two specialized headsails be ordered. Instead, McLaughlin recommended that, by December 15, in addition to the sails already on order from North-Fogh, the challenge should order two more mainsails, a #4 and #5 genoa and a half-ounce spinnaker. Sobstad Storer would be asked to build one medium and one heavy-air mainsail, five genoas and five spinnakers. These orders, when combined with the sails received and on order from North-Fogh, would give the challenge two basic 12-Metre inventories with which to equip *Canada 1* and *Clipper*. McLaughlin also recommended that the syndicate purchase the two dozen-odd sails Russell Long still had left over from the 1980 trials aboard *Clipper*, which he was offering to the Canadians for about $20,000. "If we use our good sails for practice starts, tacking duels and races," McLaughlin warned, "they will be trashed two weeks after we receive them." And to keep the entire sail inventory in working order, he advised that the syndicate hire Kent Luxton away from the North loft in the Virgin Islands. Luxton, a New Zealander, was one of four full-time sailmakers employed by the *Australia* effort in 1980. He had been part of the Canadian training camp less than a week when it folded in August.

Terry McLaughlin and the North-Fogh loft saw eye-to-eye on at least one issue: "I agree with Hans Fogh that you can't conduct proper sail testing with two different masts. *Canada 1* will need a spare mast, so perhaps if the Proctor mast looks good in the next few weeks we should order another. If not then order something else (ideally two). For February or March I'd probably put *Clipper*'s spare mast in *Canada 1* to conduct proper sail testing.

"I am prepared to continue with any scenario," Terry McLaughlin observed, "but I really would like to do well."

On December 15, Terry McLaughlin's stated deadline for placing sail orders, Jay Hansen was meeting with Cedric Gyles to revise yet again the sail program. Hansen was back to discussing a program with an intact Phase 1; after conferring with Gyles, he outlined a proposed new order, designed in part to provide duplicate testing between *Clipper* and *Canada 1*. He also warned that the syndicate might not be able to order exactly what sails it wanted during the final phase of the sail program. That November, the Offshore Racing Council, fearing Kevlar was too exotic and expensive, banned its use in IOR competition; Hansen predicted, correctly, that the output of cloth manufacturers would be drastically reduced. Even more difficult to obtain would be the special-warp Kevlar cloths produced by North Sails, in which the Kevlar thread in the Kevlar/Dacron weave runs vertically, thereby making it the ideal fabric for the construction of the new generation of vertical-cut sails.

The North-Fogh loft had at last come to terms with sharing sailmaking duties with Richard Storer's Sobstad Storer loft, although Hansen would never change his conviction that Terry McLaughlin was prejudiced toward the competition. "We understand that Terry and some members of the syndicate want a two-sailmaker sail program," Jay Hansen acknowledged in his December 16 proposal to Cedric Gyles. "While we don't think that the program can afford the time *and* money necessary, we understand the desire to test Sobstad against North. We welcome the challenge and look forward to proving that we build the fastest 12-Metre sails."

But the North loft could not bring itself to leave the future of the sail program entirely to fate. "To compliment your well organized efforts," Jay Hansen wrote, "we have decided to donate, free of cost the 1.5 oz. large 12-Metre spinnaker as mentioned in Phase 1, conditional on having the 12-Metre [sail] program as you and I discussed."

The ball was now with Jeff Boyd, who had been vested with the authority of Terry McLaughlin in the skipper's absence. Boyd rejected the Hansen proposal in a proposal of his own on December 20. "We are not set up for duplicate testing," he wrote. "Duplication implies hull or rig testing. *We don't have time to test*, let alone do major modifications on the hull. *We must simply sail with what we have.*"

Boyd thought they should take only one of the two light-medium main-sails Hansen suggested, order as proposed a half-ounce spinnaker, forget a three-quarter-ounce chute and pay for the spinnaker the North loft was offering for free. And instead of a second light-medium mainsail, they should order a medium-heavy Mylar/Kevlar mainsail. Then they should call up Richard Storer and order a #2 and #3 genoa, a medium-ply Mylar/Kevlar mainsail and two spinnakers.

"The proposed inventory allows us to sail with new sails in up to 24 knots of apparent wind," Boyd declared. "We can't test, but we can compare. This is more in line with the skipper's attitude and philosophy about the sail program. It also covers our commitments to semi-completed sails. With the addition of a few #4s and #5s from Russell Long's stash of sails, *Clipper's* inventory and the acceptance of my proposal, *we would be able to sail in all conditions*. This would fill the lag time between the resumption of our training and the reception of our next order of sails.

"Crew morale is quite low," Boyd took time to warn, hoping that decisions would be made that would allow the challenge to regain momentum. "Our first trials race is June 20, six months away."

In early January of 1983, *Canada 1* became the star attraction of the Toronto International Boat Show. It was a tremendous boost to the challenge; the operator of the show, the Canadian National Sportsmen's Shows, donated 50 cents to the challenge from every admission ticket. When the show was over, $75,000 had been turned over, and earnings from sales of T-shirts, posters, square-foot sections of sail and other paraphernalia (one could buy one of 100 limited-edition *Canada 1* ties for $10,000) boosted the challenge's total take to more than $100,000. *Canada 1* was christened with much fanfare by the wife of Canadian diplomat Ken Taylor, and an opportunity was provided for the crew (except Terry McLaughlin, who was still girdling the globe) to reunite. Not to be overlooked was the tremendous amount of publicity the show generated; it was a golden opportunity for potential corporate sponsors to become aware of the growing public interest in *Canada 1*.

When the show was over, the boat returned to Harbour Marine Services in Port Credit for a final going over. Of particular concern was a problem of continuity between the hull and the keel, which was creating an electrolysis problem that threatened to turn the 12-Metre into a giant storage battery. The entire keel had to be removed and refitted.

On January 13, it became official that *Canada 1* and *Clipper* would move to a training base at South Shore Marina in Miami Beach. Jeff Boyd travelled to Newport on January 18 with Doug Keary and Ben Colenbrander to smooth out the details for moving the Canadian training base back from Miami Beach in May.

Though the Canadian sailors might have left Newport in September of 1982 as darling underdogs, their syndicate was being treated like a leper by the town's business community. The challenge's relationship with the Newport Shipyard was shaky at best. It owed the Shipyard money, and the owners, who were in the process of negotiating the sale of the property, would just as soon not have had to deal with the challenge any more. The Shipyard stonewalled the Canadians, who were attempting to tidy up their debts, refusing to return their calls. Concerned that it might lose its operations site, the syndicate explored the possibility of moving to Newport Offshore with the rest of the syndicates, or to the Derektor yard a few miles up Narragansett Bay. They finally had to position a representative outside the office door of the company in possession of the shipyard and wait until someone in authority ventured out. The base was saved.

Doug Keary's main assignment in Newport was to clean up the loose ends surrounding the lease of Sherman House. The owner, Salve Regina College, was another enterprise that would have dearly loved not to see the Canadians back in 1983. If the Canadians would only buzz off, the college could spend the summer correcting all those defects under the fire regulations (the challenge was able to live in the building in its current state because it was considered a "family"; consequently the building was not under public use) and get on with converting the house into a dormitory.

Keary met with the college treasurer, a solemn old fellow parked behind an enormous mahogany desk. There to confirm that everything was copacetic, Keary danced around a bit, trying to be cheery and salesmanlike. The treasurer just glowered and Keary ran out of things to say. Finally the treasurer broke the silence.

"We haven't been paid," he grumbled.

Haven't been paid! How fortuitous! According to the lease, a payment had been due on January 1, with a period of grace of 15 days. It was now the 18th and the Canadians were in default. The college could fire up the cement saws and what have you, start altering the stairwells, screwing in the fire doors and making the kitchen safe for enquiring young minds.

Deep down inside, Doug Keary was doing a slow burn. He had left Toronto with the assurance that the cheque had gone out in plenty of time. He grabbed the nearest telephone and dialled David Yule at Clarkson Gordon, the challenge's financial heart.

David Yule wasn't there.

But, god bless him, David Thomas *was* there, who was a co-signer on the challenge's account. Keary instructed Thomas to tell the nice gentleman why the cheque wasn't there (Why *wasn't* the cheque there anyway?). And all the while Keary beefed up David Thomas's credentials: president of the Canadian Yachting Association, a senior partner of Clarkson Gordon... Keary wasn't entirely sure about the senior partnership, but time was of the essence and there were impressions to be made.

And, as a thread weaves through the fraternity of yachting, so too does a thread bind diverse members of the business community. In a coincidence no self-respecting fiction writer would dare concoct, it turned out that the sister company of Clarkson Gordon in the United States happened to be the auditor of none other than Salve Regina College. Instant respectability! The treasurer softened, the deal stayed. The Canadians could leave Newport knowing the door to the town wasn't going to be locked behind them.

16

miami beach

On January 25, Jay McKinnell was in Newport, hunting down a graveyard of 12-Metre sails. Russell Long had completed the sale of *Clipper* to the Canadian America's Cup challenge; a group of western businessmen had come up with the funds to close the deal. The final price was $475,000 Canadian, perhaps the most money ever paid for a used 12-Metre. Accompanied by Kim Roberts, the professor of 12-Metre sailing at the Palmetto camp, McKinnell was now searching out the 20 sails remaining from *Clipper*'s 1980 inventory, which Long had offered to the Canadians and Terry McLaughlin had advised they buy.

The sails were hidden in a third-floor loft belonging to the *Defender-Courageous* group. Russell Long had supplied a list of the sails; only 15 could be positively identified, and these were removed by McKinnell. The vast majority of the sails had come to *Clipper* from Ted Hood's 1977 *Independence* campaign, as had *Clipper*'s deck, keel and masts. The inventory included eight 1977 Hood genoas, one 1980 Ratsey genoa, four 1977 Hood spinnakers, one 1977 Hood mainsail and one 1980 North Mylar/Kevlar mainsail. From Ted Hood to Russell Long to Terry McLaughlin – a six-year-old inventory received still another lease on life. The most that was expected of them was that they keep *Canada 1* and *Clipper* moving through the water during their training exercises. All they had to do was stay in one piece. For a while, they would.

With Jeff Boyd's van as an escort, *Clipper* rolled out of Newport on January 24, arriving in Miami Beach on January 28. The United States was embroiled in a violence-prone truckers' strike. Luckily *Clipper*, *Canada 1* and their inventory of masts arrived at the training camp without incident. Only the driver hauling the newly leased tender, *Prowler* (promptly renamed *Slapshot II*), encountered difficulties on the road, spending a night in jail in Georgia for transporting a wide load during forbidden hours.

Until *Slapshot II* did arrive, tender duties would be hospitably provided by

Jeff Boyd and Bruce Kirby aboard Clipper

the French, with *Nanny. Canada 1* left dock for the first time in Miami Beach on February 17. There was plenty of wind for a trial run – a steady 25 knots, with gusts to 30. At first, they sailed "inside," on Government Cut, repeatedly beating up the channel and running back down under spinnaker, dodging freighters. The 45-minute routine was brought to a halt when Double Stuff, a two-ply, four-ounce Dacron Hood genoa from 1977, was torn when hoisting it in preparation for a spinnaker drop. Rather than reset a new genoa, they decided to carry on down the cut, into the open waters of the Gulf Stream.

Gear problems persisted. The mast ram bracket snapped in two, allowing the base of the mast to move freely fore and aft. Cannibalizing the tacking line, they jury-rigged a puller to keep the mast butt under control. Despite the breakdown, the new Proctor spar brought smiles to the faces of the crew.

Then, on the way in to dock, the mainsail refused to drop – the halyard car was jammed. Rob Webb was hoisted aloft and coaxed the sail down with a screwdriver. It was a foreboding start for *Canada 1,* and in the few days *Clipper* had been sailing, she had already collapsed a jumper strut and torn a

A wet ride for Rob Webb and Sandy Andrews (at bow) in a sail against Clipper

jib from leech to luff. The Miami training camp was threatening to become a repeat of the frustrating Newport summer of 1982.

Friday, February 18, *Canada 1* and her trail horse, *Clipper,* were at last about to sail together. The sky was clear, the wind eight to 12 knots from the northeast. Out on the Gulf Stream, the wind was slightly stronger, and there was a ground swell of six to eight feet running. A perfect day.

With all the sailors not yet in camp, *Clipper* and *Canada 1* were outfitted with rag-tag crews. Jeff Boyd, who would serve as *Clipper's* helmsman for most of the Miami camp, rounded up an afterguard consisting of Bruce Kirby and Franz Rosenbaum, the sailing photographer. The rest of his crew was composed of Tom Corness and Bob Whitehorse from maintenance, Eric Jespersen, John Millen, Robin Wynne-Edwards, Jay McKinnell, Ed Gyles and Rob Burton, a newly arrived crew candidate from Vancouver. Aboard *Canada 1,* Terry McLaughlin would sail with Peter Wilson, Jim Teague (a friend of Rob Muru who had once tried out with the camp), Rob Muru, Bob Vaughan-Jones, Daniel Palardy, Phil Gow, Don Campbell, Paul Phillips, Rob Webb and Sandy Andrews.

A relaxed moment aboard Clipper. *Jeff Boyd is at the wheel. Daniel Palardy, to the left, tails a spinnaker sheet. In the centre of the boat, face obscured, is Fred Schueddekopp. Tom Cummings is at the extreme right.*

Before leaving dock, McLaughlin warned his crew that the filmmaker, Dale Hartleben, had wired him for sound. Hence there would be no barking or other discouraging audible remarks should *Canada 1* prove slower than *Clipper* on their first outing together. Whatever they said had to be positive for the sake of fund-raising publicity.

It turned out that the crew required no such coaching. Boyd and McLaughlin began comparing the two boats by sailing for 25 minutes on port tack, with *Canada 1* to leeward. The two 12-Metres were quite even for some time, each taking turns moving out on the other. Then *Canada 1* began to climb to windward and squeeze out *Clipper*. Jeff Boyd was doing his best to steer *Clipper* competitively but didn't feel he was getting much help from the rest of the crew. It seemed they all had their eyes on *Canada 1* instead of their sails.

They regrouped, settling into a 20-minute sail on starboard tack, with *Canada 1* to windward. *Canada 1* pulled out initially. The two boats lined up again. *Clipper* began to move ahead, then took a terrible nose-dive. Again, *Canada 1* looked impressive. They moved on to tacking. After about 15 tacks, *Canada 1,* trailing, was able to sail past *Clipper.* (Franz Rosenbaum, unable to resist, continually reached for his camera. "Franz, if you don't put that thing away," Bruce Kirby warned, "one of these guys is going to throw you overboard.") Bruce Kirby then asked for the helm of *Clipper.* He did poorly: *Canada 1,* as a result, looked devastating.

It was a good day for *Canada 1* to appear devastating. Above the two 12-Metres had been a small airplane making low-level passes. In it were Dennis Conner and Tom Whidden. At the end of the day, the Americans dropped by to have a look at *Canada 1* and congratulate Bruce Kirby on what seemed to be a fast design. *It must make Conner wonder to see* CANADA I *walk all over* CLIPPER *the first time out,* Sandy Andrews wrote. *It makes me wonder too.*

The next day, *Canada 1* and *Clipper* put on a show for the Southern Ocean Racing Conference fleet departing Miami for the Ocean Triangle race. That *Canada 1* put on a show there was no doubt; her old North mainsail, Aggie, exploded, tearing from luff to leech in three places. If that extravagant display wasn't enough, Rob Webb was sent up in the bosun's chair again to coax down a stubborn halyard car. In the 20 minutes Omar was aloft, the Canadians came as close to killing a crew member as they ever would. It was one of the roughest rides they had ever experienced in a 12-Metre. On board *Clipper,* Jeff Boyd had completed his crew with two French sailors and Tom Corness, who had a nasty reputation for falling overboard. Although Corness succeeded in staying with the boat throughout the day, Boyd worried about him uninterruptedly.

They had brought the training program to the east coast of Florida for the opportunity to sail in waves. There was certainly no shortage of them. Some were enormous, tossing the 12-Metres about like dinghies. The first few windy days were frightening. The waves were steep, not the long rollers of Newport, and the battering caused numerous breakdowns, washed jibs off the deck, and generally made life hell for the foredeck crews. Twelve-Metres have no lifelines because of the problems they would cause with the foot of a genoa. It was only after persistent lobbying that Omar and Sandy Andrews were able to have toe rails installed on *Canada 1's* foredeck – Bruce Kirby had initially been afraid they would add extra weight and windage.

Staring up at the rig as *Clipper* pounded through the seas off Miami Beach placed undue strain on the heart. Jeff Boyd was convinced that they were destined to lose a mast.

On February 20, Terry McLaughlin announced the "A" and "B" teams, which would sail *Canada 1* and *Clipper* respectively. It was a far from firm division of the crew ranks, he explained, and, as time proved, there would be plenty of opportunity for promotion, and demotion – the dreaded outbasket.

There were several new faces in camp. Al Megarry had left Queen's University mid-way through his final year to join the campaign after sailing aboard *Canada 1* in Toronto in December. And, in addition to Rob Burton, the Miami camp had seen the debut of Tom Cummings and Paul Parsons. Tom "Cumboy" Cummings was a happy-go-lucky young Toronto sailor with a background in International 14 and IOR competition who would serve as *Clipper*'s navigator. Paul "Project" Parsons was a Laser and Finn sailor from Goderich, Ontario, who had IOR experience on Lake Huron. Although officially he would become the back-up tactician, Parsons, a highly organized individual, was always tending carefully to some assignment or another. He would videotape *Canada 1*'s races in Newport in 1983 and produce footage of crucial value in the protest room.

On February 21 several crew members were sent forth to various Canadian cities to participate in a series of important press conferences. Labatt's, the brewing company, had decided to come aboard as a major corporate sponsor of *Canada 1*. The brewery pledged a total of $250,000; $50,000 was a direct cash donation, $100,000 was set aside to underwrite fundraising promotions and $100,000 was earmarked for the production costs of Dale Hartleben's official documentary. No sooner had they announced the package than Labatt's decided to increase the cash donation to $100,000.

It was a day of ceremony. The mayor of Miami Beach gave a function at which the Canadians were made honorary citizens of the city and presented with its key. The Canadians, in turn, made the mayor and vice-mayor honorary crew members of *Canada 1*. During the numerous speeches, the Canadians made sure to mouth the name "Labatt's" until they were blue in the face.

That evening, it was on to more ceremonies. The Italian America's Cup syndicate, which had a booth at the Miami International Boat Show to display the wares of some of its 16 corporate sponsors, held a reception in honour of the French and Canadian syndicates, as well as a few important guests.

One of those guests was Tom Blackaller, the skipper of the American 12-Metre *Defender*. Blackaller had been instrumental in the mounting of an Italian America's Cup challenge. He was a close friend of Cino Ricci, a respected offshore racer who was managing the challenge and serving as the sailing master of *Azzurra,* named in honour of the traditional blue of the uniforms of Italy's national sport teams. Blackaller had persuaded Ricci to involve Italy in the 1983 America's Cup, and a formidably financed challenge gelled around the Costa Smeralda of Sardinia, the heart of a resort development under the control of His Highness Prince Aga Khan, a Moslem leader of staggering wealth. Costa Smeralda had only recently given birth to the Sardinia Cup, an international yacht racing series patterned on England's

Jay "Bondo" McKinnell, in sunglasses, works the grinder handles of Clipper *with Paul Hansen, who will graduate to* Canada 1. *Bob Vaughan-Jones stands in the tailer's cockpit.*

Admiral's Cup, and its almost overnight status as a first-class event was aided in no small part by the participation of high-profile American sailors like Blackaller.

At the Miami International Boat Show reception, the Canadians were shown one film about the good life at the Yacht Club Costa Smeralda and another about *Azzurra.* The popular view of the Italians as long shots in 1983, which was shared by the Canadians, was bolstered by the Italians themselves. Well financed and organized, they spoke of the upcoming America's Cup as a learning process – they were not coming to take the cup away from the New York Yacht Club. Still, their easygoing, if not winning, attitude concealed their sound preparation. The Italians had acquired as a trial horse *Enterprise,* Lowell North's defence contender of 1977, which Dennis Conner had used to fine-tune *Freedom* in 1980. *Enterprise* was considered by many to be the fastest straight-line 12-Metre in the world. Having this boat around undoubtedly did not hurt in the process of design-ing the Italian contender, but it should not cloud the fact that *Azzurra's* designer, Andrea Vallicelli of Rome, a former Sparkman & Stephens draughtsman, was a highly respected offshore designer in Europe.

But one of the Italians' greatest assets was Cino Ricci's friend, Tom Blackaller. Having persuaded them to challenge, he went further. According to Hans Fogh, Blackaller outlined the Italian crew-training program and even helped select their helmsman, who would steer *Azzurra* under Ricci's ever-watchful eye. And when it came time to make sails, the Italians took full advantage of the woolly nationality regulations. Their sail designer was designated as the North loft manager in Naples, but the sails were actually cut and sewn, as the rules allowed, in the North empire's San Francisco loft. And that loft was owned and the managed by Tom Blackaller.

For the first day in some time, Miami Beach was blessed with light winds. On February 23, *Canada 1* and *Clipper* made their way out of the marina to examine two newly arrived sails from Sobstad Storer, a half-ounce spinnaker and a #2 headsail. In the hours of side-by-side pacing that ensued, *Canada 1* no longer appeared so indomitable. She seemed to point higher, but in the concluding tacking duel *Clipper* opened up noticeably.

In the afternoon, *Canada 1*, *Clipper* and *France 3* engaged in a series of practice starts. After beating *Clipper* once and splitting a pair of starts with *Canada 1*, the French were eager to continue, but Terry McLaughlin indi-cated that the Canadians wanted to head in. With that, the French chal-lenged *Canada 1* and *Clipper* to a race back to the marina, offering a bottle of champagne to the winner. They were on.

With a combination of good boat-speed and superior navigation, *Can-ada 1* arrived at the outer channel marks comfortably ahead of *France 3* and *Clipper*. Reaching into his bag of team-racing tricks, Terry McLaughlin held *Canada 1* back long enough to cover *France 3* and allow *Clipper* to slip by into second place.

After docking, the Canadians ventured over to the French compound to collect their prize. Instead of receiving a bottle of champagne, the French broke open an entire case and threw in an additional magnum – all from Mumm's, one of their sponsors. *They were pouring it with joyous abandon,* noted Sandy Andrews. *They didn't seem to mind losing at all.*

It was difficult to know what to make of the French. Of all the challenges, theirs made least sense to Jeff Boyd. At the Xerox regatta, the Canadians had been well aware of how little money the *France 3* effort had for such necessities as sails. Yet, when invited over for dinner following the regatta, they had been astounded by the lavishness of the meal prepared by the two French chefs on staff.

Their priorities seemed to be in the wrong places. They had invested much time and effort designing and building their own mast and electronics, things which could have been purchased, with no compromise in quality, off-the-shelf. Bruno Troublé and his tactician, Patrick Haegeli, were seldom

Sandy Andrews tends to the cracked mast of Canada 1.

seen in Miami. Troublé, busy with his responsibilities at Bic, seemed only partially committed to the *France 3* effort.

The crew of *France 3,* young and inexperienced, were introduced to 12-Metre sailing in a conservative manner by Troublé. A few were in the military in France and were still being paid while sailing for the French challenge. All were very charming and easy to mix with. (One member of the French camp in Miami married an American girl and simply disappeared.) But they hardly ever sailed in Miami. The French, 13 years after their first America's Cup challenge, still failed to live up to their considerable potential.

Monday, February 28. With winds of 25 to 30 knots, *Canada 1* and *Clipper* ventured onto the Gulf Stream. The previous day three inches of rain had fallen: the French had taken advantage of the bad weather to model raingear for *Vogue.*

Clipper charged through the stream without a hitch; by now a seasoned performer, the boat ran like clockwork. Jeff Boyd felt spoiled by her. Terry McLaughlin was becoming increasingly frustrated by continuing break-downs on *Canada 1.* Before the Miami Beach camp was through, the list of malfunctions would include winches, the spinnaker pole, mast fittings, sheet jammers and the steering mechanism. Running downwind, *Canada 1* developed problems with the spinnaker pole end fitting. McLaughlin brought Canada 1 back on the wind and discovered another problem. The boat was sinking.

Low freeboard and the swells off Miami Beach had combined to produce an inflow of water that taxed the capacity of the bilge pumps. Water was being shipped everywhere – through the forward hatches, the spinnaker take-down hatch, the mast collar, the foxhole hatch, the running backstay and spinnaker sheet holes, and the tailers' cockpits. The crew was spending more time bailing than sailing. Paul Hansen, tactician for the day, sat in a cockpit as full as a bathtub, scooping up water with his boots. The rest of the crew bailed with spinnaker turtles, with duffle bags, with water jugs that had their bottoms hastily removed, with the spinnaker bucket, its open bottom taped over, and with their bare hands.

Realizing he was fighting a losing battle, Terry McLaughlin pointed Canada 1 back toward harbour, storming ahead on a tight reach at over 10 knots. They had come ashore to waterproof the 12-Metre but in the process found something requiring equally urgent attention. As Sandy Andrews performed his usual mast check, he noticed an inverted "V" crack, five inches long, which had opened about $1/32$ inch.

The mast was promptly hauled out of the boat. The crack was in the top of the weld securing the bottom splice of the spar, immediately below the track for the spinnaker pole butt hoist. A repair could be made with a reinforcing plate. It was a poor place for a weld; halfway between the first set of spreaders and the deck, it rested in an area of high compression. Because it would take a few days to fix the mast, it was decided to pull Canada 1 out of the water to cut a number of through-hulls for cockpit drains, rather than have the cockpit continue to empty through the joint between the trim tab and the keel.

For the next few days, the crew pored over the boat, sealing gaps, installing new chainplate covers, removing and permanently covering the spinnaker take-down hatch, replacing the forward hatches, installing experimental splash rails and increasing the gearing on the bilge pumps. On March 3, Canada 1 was launched again. Her spar was stepped and she was ready to sail by eleven o'clock. And then the winches began to misbehave.

They were true 12-Metre sounds, loud, gruesome bangs that rang out whenever the Barient primary winches were under load. On March 4 they became even worse, sending vibrations into the genoa sheets. If that wasn't sufficiently disturbing, the mast also began emitting jarring bangs that shook the leeward shrouds. Enough was enough. Terry McLaughlin returned to base to confront Bob Whitehouse with the boat's latest quirk.

It was a bit embarrassing. No one could figure out precisely what was causing the noises. The crew took Bobo for a sail to demonstrate, and the boat refused to make the damned sounds. Bobo was not impressed. A telltale *bang* at last reverberated through the hull. The crew cheered.

Back at dock, Don Campbell stripped down both primary winches and carted the pieces into the tool trailer for a thorough inspection. Sandy Andrews crawled all over the mast again, looking for broken welds, new cracks, loose screws and fittings, anything slightly out of whack. Nothing. The winches and the mast checked out.

It began to look as if all of March 5 would be spent going over *Canada 1* with a magnifying glass and a fine-tooth comb. But shortly after lunch, *Clipper* returned to dock with an old jib and spinnaker in shreds, bearing tales of how they had just clocked 13.2 knots. The report touched the essence of Terry McLaughlin. Within half an hour *Canada 1* was reassembled and heading onto the ocean.

Miraculously the boat had ceased to make its unamusing little noises. Eric Jespersen discovered that the bangs from the mast had been caused by some play in the pins holding the jacking plates at the mast step. The crew concluded that the winches had been misbehaving because of slippage in the belts, which must have been tightened when they were reinstalled. (A few days later, a visiting Barient representative would confirm that the belts were indeed slipping. The deck was buckling because frames had been cut away during construction to make room to mount the winches, and with the buckling deck the winches were improperly aligned.)

With 32 knots of wind across the deck and enormous waves, it proved to be a wild ride for the foredeck crew. While attempting to lower the tack on the jib, Sandy Andrews was lifted clear off the deck by a breaking wave and tossed astern in a back somersault. His hands firmly gripping the loose spinnaker sheet and guy, he landed on deck beneath Omar, who in turn found himself beneath the spinnaker pole.

On the ride home under spinnaker, *Canada 1* generated a huge wall of spray forward of the shrouds, clocking a record 13.63 knots in the process. The bow played hide-and-seek, at one moment riding high above the seas, the next buried under a foot of blue-green water. McLaughlin, grinning from ear to ear with the rest of the crew, steered the boat through a series of gybes. During one, the foreguy snagged the side of Sandy Andrews and spun him around the forestay while he remained attached to the boat by one hand. He walked back to the cockpit and put on a life jacket. At the end of the sail, the crew jokingly asked Bruce Kirby if *Canada 1* was the first submarine he had designed.

With the boats and gear put away, the sailors made their way to the Embassy, a handsome Spanish-style house the challenge had recently rented, for a barbecue with some of the French sailors. The house was where a number of the base management personnel lived, as well as Terry

Hans Fogh lectures at the Miami Beach camp as Terry McLaughlin's father, Paul, watches from the steps of the sail trailer.

McLaughlin and his girlfriend, Mickey, and was used to put up visiting VIPs. During the barbecue, Terry McLaughlin delivered a solemn eulogy for Aggie, the weathered and beaten North mainsail that had seen them through Palmetto and the Xerox regatta and so much more. The Canadians and Aggie had endured much together, and McLaughlin provided a tender farewell. Aggie's remains were bundled up and deposited in a quiet corner of the sail trailer, while the challenge processed a respectful insurance claim on her long-postponed demise—chronically short of funds, they were willing to try anything to fill the coffers. Rob Muru had bade farewell to The Brick, their seasoned heavy #4 genoa, only a few weeks previous. For the other sails of their generation in camp – Double Stuff, Short Foot, Skylab I, Skylab II, 4-IR, Quilt, CG5B, Slam Dunk, Headly and No Headly, collectively known as the Shabbies – the passage to the Great Dacron Beyond was tearfully inevitable. Goodbye, Aggie.

With so much training time to make up, the Miami Beach camp became a grind. Only one day off was taken during the entire stay in Florida. The average day began at 6:30; the crew was down at the yard by 8:00 and worked and sailed for 12 hours. Most were in bed before 10:00. With so little extra time, the base had no specific fitness program. Phil Gow, however,

Crewmen of Canada 1 *struggle to retrieve the shredded spinnaker after the blow-out on Government Cut.*

continued to amaze everyone by running the six miles back to the hotel every night. No one knew where he got his energy.

Despite the long hours, it seemed there was never enough time to sail. Press and public relations duties made heavy demands on their time. More than once Gord Smeaton, a Bramaco representative responsible for PR at the base, radioed *Canada 1* and *Clipper* that the two boats had to be sailing together at a certain time because somebody or other was coming out in a rented helicopter or airplane to shoot photographs. During the training camp, the sailors were visited by film crews from CBC's "The Journal" and "The Nature of Things," CTV's "W5" and Global's news department. Scheduling four film crews into six weeks of sailing, on top of the regular needs of Dale Hartleben's crew and the odd VIP, necessitated frequent interruptions in the training process. But, desperate for money and eager to increase their public exposure, the sailors cooperated as best they could. This myriad of demands, in addition to planning the move to Newport, took its toll on Keary, Whitehouse, McLaughlin and Boyd. There were spirited exchanges of words, caused more by the three-ring-circus atmosphere than by actual differences.

Nonetheless, Miami Beach was proving to be a tremendous learning experience. McLaughlin and Boyd organized seminars and talks, some

A view from Clipper *of a training session with* Canada 1. *Ed Gyles is at the mast of* Clipper; *Brent Foxall sports the cycling cap.*

given by crew members on their own roles, and racing rule tests, and the camp was visited by a stream of guest experts, among them Pat Healy, Canada's national sailing team coach and a number of team members; Hans Fogh, Dave Miller and Jim Allsopp of the North Sails organization; and American sailors Augie Diaz and Carl Buchan.

With *Clipper* relatively free of breakdowns, the B team improved steadily with regular practice and quite a few advanced to the A team. On board *Canada 1,* Terry McLaughlin was pursuing a private experiment in human endurance. By sailing the boat in heavy weather, he was discovering how it behaved in extreme conditions and was teaching himself and the crew how to handle her. He pushed the crew very hard. And, in the process, he discovered just how hard people were willing to be pushed.

Friday, March 11. The day was sunny, though cooled by a strong breeze. In the morning, the mast was dropped back in *Canada 1;* it had been removed to install an improved repair plate over the crack below the butt hoist track. Fred Schueddekopp and Rob Muru examined a newly arrived mainsail from Sobstad Storer. The headboard was all wrong, incompatible with the halyard cars on the two 12-Metres. The sail was worth about $14,000 and, until alterations were made, it was useless.

By noon the sky had greyed over; a breeze of 20 to 25 knots was darkening the waters of the marina. The French, having been sailing for two hours, returned to dock. Out on the Gulf Stream, *Clipper* reported a true wind reading of 28 knots. There was much discussion over whether *Canada 1* should sail. Terry McLaughlin cast the deciding vote. "Unless we have a problem with sails, I think we should go. We have to learn to sail in this stuff."

At two o'clock, *Slapshot II* towed *Canada 1* out of the marina. Sails were hoisted and the 12-Metre began tacking up the flat waters of the main shipping channel leading to Miami. *Clipper* appeared, under tow from *Mako*, the 23-foot, better known as "the Rocket." While reaching under spinnaker in heavy seas, *Clipper* had broached, breaking her spinnaker pole against the forestay.

Shortly thereafter, *Canada 1* ran aground in the channel, the churning silt changing the colour of the water like cream poured into coffee. With the wind a steady 30 knots, *Slapshot II* pulled her free and she continued sailing.

After progressing up the channel, *Canada 1* bore off and hoisted an old *Clipper* spinnaker. For a time she made a magnificent sight, powering through the water with a tremendous quarter wake. Then all hell broke loose. The hydraulic vang snapped, sending the boom canting skyward, and *Canada 1* began to roll crazily, side to side, as no one had ever seen a 12-Metre roll before. Struck by a 40-knot gust, the spinnaker burst in half. *Canada 1* made a sharp right-hand turn and raced across the channel, streaming the torn sail behind her. Before running aground a second time, Terry McLaughlin wrestled the boat to a halt and the remains of the spinnaker were collected. Sailing practice was through for the day.

Sunday, March 13, was grey and mild, with a light wind out of the north. While the rest of the sailors prepared the boats – marching mainsails on board conga-line fashion, trundling spinnakers about in wheelbarrows – Rob Webb strolled into camp with his left arm in a sling. Omar had been plagued by pain from elbow to wrist; a doctor had told him his arm was overworked, that there was damage to the nerves. Omar had been advised to consider an operation or stay inactive for a few weeks. He wasn't too big on the idea of an operation. Ironically, Dave Shaw was on his way down that day to try out for Omar's position as mast man on *Canada 1*.

Terry McLaughlin had been working on getting Shaw to join the campaign for months. "Shorty" Shaw stood six feet eight inches tall, making him by far the biggest sailor in camp. A spare crew on the 1976 Olympic team, Shaw, from Calgary, had been the Canadian Star crew when the Olympic boycott came down in 1980. He was also Tom Blackaller's crew when the Californian won the Star World Championship in 1980. He would assume almost uncontested the mast man role, establishing himself as a team leader from

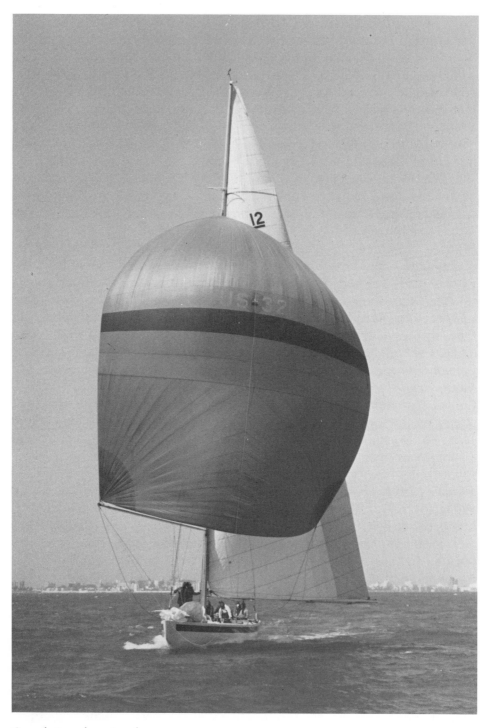

Canada 1 *under spinnaker*

his position in the centre of *Canada 1*. Everyone found him a likable fellow with a heart to match his size. He brought experience, ability and credibility to the program.

Another arrival was Bruno Troublé. He strolled through the Canadian ranks, keeping to himself as he stared at the two Canadian 12-Metres, then headed over to the French side of the marina for his first spell at the helm of *France 3* since the Xerox regatta the previous September.

With almost no wind, *Canada 1* and *Clipper* waited until noon before leaving dock. Both held their tows until out on the ocean before hoisting sails in the wandering breeze. *Clipper* had brought the new Sobstad Storer mainsail, equipped with a newly fashioned headboard from the tool trailer. Her crew slowly hoisted the sail. With more than a foot of the luff still to be fed into the mast slot, the halyard car, unbeknownst to the crew, had reached the top of the mast and had locked in position. They kept hoisting. There was a loud *ping* as the halyard snapped, and the mainsail fluttered down on the deck. Incredibly, the sail was about 18 inches too long in the hoist for both *Clipper* and *Canada 1*.

Before *Clipper* could head in to rig a new halyard and switch mainsails, Terry McLaughlin was on the radio to Jeff Boyd with more novel difficulties. Bruno Troublé, out on *France 3,* was badgering McLaughlin about some agreement. Did Jeff know anything about a deal to practise with the French three times a week in exchange for their having arranged accommodations for the Canadians?

"No and no," Boyd replied, now thoroughly annoyed with the turn the day had taken. There was no such agreement, and the French had *not* arranged their accommodations. Bruno Troublé had obviously arrived in Miami Beach with a dated impression of the situation.

While *Clipper* returned to dock for repairs, Terry McLaughlin consented to a spell of practice with the French. He did not take the exercise especially seriously. At one stage he instructed the entire crew of *Canada 1* to lie down in the cockpit so it appeared that no one was on board. Still in a playful mood, he instructed the crew to rotate one position to the right after every tack, until everyone had experienced every role on board. When McLaughlin was manning the grinder handles opposite Peter Wilson, Robin Wynne-Edwards at the adjoining set spun them so fast that Two Ton couldn't hang on and accidentally punched McLaughlin in the face. Terry only laughed.

McLaughlin had been mellowing somewhat. In his human-endurance experiment – a kind of marine corps process of pushing people to the point of breaking their spirit, to get a rise out of them, to see what they were made of and what they were capable of – he always seemed to know when he had gone too far, when to pull back and soften up. The sailors began to sense a relaxation of his usual grimness. He was trying to be more open, more approachable now; he seemed to have reached many of the conclusions he wanted. But the sailors weren't entirely sure of his motives. Some feared that if they let down their guard he might go on the offensive again. Terry McLaughlin was a foreign language that not everyone could read.

Up in the air, there was a stuttering drone. A single-engine plane flew overhead. Franz Rosenbaum had gotten himself airborne at some fantastic cost to fulfil his assignment to produce promotional photos of *Canada 1* under sail. As Rosenbaum made his pass, McLaughlin gave the order and everyone aboard dropped his pants. The words *you bastards* fell gently from the sky, like snow.

Monday, March 14. The wind was again light. The day began with a lecture by Hans Fogh on sail trim. He was followed by Pat Healy, the national sailing team coach, who gave a *tour de force* on racing rules, protests, what his grandfather always told him, and baby chickens who wanted to be eagles. He also threw in a few amusing vignettes about his days as coach of the championship U.S. Naval Academy sailing team.

Healy was a man who visibly enjoyed his job. His energetic approach seemed more appropriate to the coaching of basketball players or swimmers, and his good humour could only be broken by the bleeping of a digital watch – he despised the machines with a vengeance. Out on the Gulf Stream, while dolphins splashed nearby, Healy hustled *Canada 1, Clipper* and *France 3* through a series of practice starts and short windward-leeward courses. "This is the semi-finals of the America's Cup challenge series," he announced to *Clipper* as she cruised by before a start against *Canada 1.* "You're *Australia II.* Anybody can sail better than a bunch of sailors who spend their winters in igloos. Let's beat those crumbs!" The crew of *Clipper* gaped, amazed.

Friday, March 18. A best-of-seven series between the French and Canadian camps began, sponsored by Seacoast Towers, a local real estate developer. The series was to have been sailed between *Canada 1* and *France 3,* but Terry McLaughlin elected to use *Clipper.* There were problems with *Canada 1* – the fairing flaps on the trim tab were askew and the mast's upper spreaders had proved too long for ideal genoa trim – and McLaughlin did not want to risk losing the series with *Canada 1* and damaging fund-raising efforts.

The series began less than smoothly. After hoisting their mainsail on the way to the starting area, the Canadians noticed that one of the battens was broken. They dropped the sail, fashioned a makeshift batten and rehoisted, only to discover that another batten had torn its pocket. While *Clipper* ran away from the starting area, the crew hoisted aloft Omar, who had returned to sailing, to apply a patch.

The race committee waited until the Canadian repairs were completed before firing the ten-minute gun. They postponed the start again when the mark drifted. As they waited for the mark to be reset, a helicopter swooped close overhead and blew out *France 3*'s mainsail. The French decided to take *France 3* all the way back to the marina to change sails. On the way in, they decided they didn't have a mainsail they were willing to risk in the 25-knot breeze and proposed they forfeit the first race. Terry McLaughlin declined, offering the French one of his own mainsails. Bruno Troublé accepted. While the French fiddled, McLaughlin ran his crew through spinnaker hoists and drops. By the time the race started, at 3:30, they were exhausted. They won anyway, by over three minutes.

Only three races were completed in the series. Canada won two. The French protested the outcome of the second race, claiming the time limit had run out. The jury agreed and threw the race out. In the third race the Canadians and the French protested each other, and the agreeable jury threw out both boats. *Clipper* won the best-of-seven series, 1-0.

Saturday, March 26. After sailing for several days against Dave Miller, Terry McLaughlin called a crew meeting. He was unhappy with the way things were going, he informed everyone, and invited comments. No one knew quite what to say. McLaughlin continued, indicating that there was an attitude problem in the crew ranks – they weren't showing the killer instinct McLaughlin had. Their minds weren't fixed on 12-Metres.

In reply, some of the crew politely told him that they thought he was, how to put it, an overbearing, hypercritical, unforgiving, abusive, tyrannical perfectionist. People were getting burned out because of a lack of free time, they suggested, and claimed there was a lack of feedback from McLaughlin on short-term directions and goals. McLaughlin replied that, if they weren't tough enough to withstand the abuse and the pace of the program, they could be easily replaced. That brought on charges of poor people management.

It was strange, but some who had found themselves at odds with Terry McLaughlin on the water now found themselves agreeing with him – that there was an excess of destructive negativism in the camp. Still, there was a need for both sides – McLaughlin and the disgruntled crew – to bend a bit and communicate more. Although McLaughlin was unrelenting during the meeting, he seemed to give a touch the next day. After venturing out aboard the Rocket and finding 25 knots of wind on the ocean, he returned to give the camp the afternoon off. The A and B teams headed down to the beach for a relaxing game of football.

The A team, driven by Terry McLaughlin's usual determination and organization, won.

17

base camp

On April 4, Terry McLaughlin, Jeff Boyd, Sandy Andrews, John Millen and Eric Jespersen flew to England to compete in the Lymington Cup, an invitational round-robin match-race series hosted by the Royal Lymington Yacht Club. The series was sailed in Offshore One Design 34s. The Canadians drew *Red Coat*, supposedly the hottest boat in the fleet.

The races would be held on a short windward-leeward-windward course, with the start and finish half-way up the windward leg. The opening day of competition was held on the Solent in bitterly cold conditions stirred up by a strong sea breeze. For their first race, the Canadians were paired with Phil Crebbin, the British 470 skipper in Kingston in 1976 who was a helmsman candidate for *Victory 83*, Peter de Savary's latest 12-Metre. A strong ebb tide threatened to force the contestants over the starting line early. The tide proved to be the least of Terry McLaughlin's worries. Forty-five seconds before the start Jeff Boyd, who was lending a hand as a tailer in addition to his tactician's duties, was struck on the head by the boom. The blow dazed him; Boyd's hair became caked with blood. Although he continued to race, the cut would require four stitches to close that night.

McLaughlin reached the weather mark ahead of Crebbin. The race committee, which was employing code flags to instruct the competitors on which sails to fly or how much they were to reef, commanded them to hoist a 1.5-ounce spinnaker. The spinnaker the Canadians had been supplied with was a flat star-cut suitable for heavy-air reaching. Crebbin hoisted a full 1.5-ounce triradial and stormed into the lead.

After losing to Crebbin, Terry McLaughlin was matched with John Bertrand, who counted in his crew two other sailors from *Australia II* – bow man Scotty McAllister and hard-nosed tactician Hugh Treharne. Bertrand led narrowly at the windward mark. McLaughlin pestered him down the run, veering inside to establish an overlap. Bertrand, shouting, "No room!" cut him off and rounded the mark. The Canadians immediately displayed their protest flag.

Soon after rounding, Bertrand tacked onto starboard and into the path of McLaughlin, who bore away. "We're protesting you again," Bertrand was informed. "Tacking too close."

McLaughlin tacked on Bertrand's quarter. The Australian came about; unable to cross, Bertrand lee-bowed him. McLaughlin tacked away to avoid a collision. "Protest!" McLaughlin announced. "You tacked too close again!" Bertrand was first across the finish line.

Against Harold Cudmore, the second of three British 12-Metre helmsman candidates participating in the series, the Canadians circled in an attempt to get on his wind, but Cudmore consistently broke away and could not be pinned. Caught unaware by a now strongly flooding tide, McLaughlin was well below the starting line at the gun. They sailed a poor race to collect their third straight loss.

Following the defeat, the crew held a heartfelt discussion. What were they doing wrong? Had they come all this way to perform so miserably? They took out their frustration on their final opponent of the day, Peter Scholfield, a British army officer who had qualified for the regatta by winning the class's match-racing championship. The Canadians jumped on his wind early in the start sequence. Scholfield could not escape. If he tried to bail out by gybing away, McLaughlin would simply sail down and smother him again. Though the Canadians were 30 seconds late at the gun, Scholfield was at least one minute from reaching the line. McLaughlin sailed to a comfortable victory.

The satisfaction of the win was cooled by the evening's events. While Jeff Boyd went off to have his head sewn up, McLaughlin began a long night in the protest room against John Bertrand. Protests at Lymington were fed by video camera to a monitor in the yacht club bar. The patrons were treated to three separate protests filed by McLaughlin against Bertrand, two of which, for tacking too close, placed the onus of proof on Bertrand.

The protest committee dismissed all three. McLaughlin concluded that the committee was against him because they thought he had been inventing incidents to have Bertrand thrown out. McLaughlin sincerely believed that he had been fouled. "I didn't go into that room for five hours for nothing," he later complained.

But the victory over Peter Scholfield had been the beginning of a turn-around. Sailing the next day in light air to the west of the Solent on Christchurch Bay, the Canadians won three straight races. They first defeated Iain MacDonald-Smith, the British 12-Metre program's sail co-ordinator (a helmsman candidate, Rodney Pattisson, and Peter de Savary attended Lymington as spectators). Next they bested the Italian crew. On board their boat were two candidates for the helm of *Azzurra* – Mauro Pelaschier, Italy's Finn representative in Kingston in 1976, and Flavio Scala, who had finished fifth in the Star class at the 1972 Olympics. It was the first time the Canadians had sailed against the Italians, and the encounter produced an odd incident. While circling during the pre-start, the Italians bore away on starboard, claiming they were forced to avoid a collision. The

Terry McLaughlin at the Lymington Cup

two boats were never closer than three lengths, and the protest was later dismissed. The only explanation for the behaviour of the Italians seemed to be that they had wanted to find out what happened in the protest room in match racing.

Their last race of the day was against Chris Law, who had been the British Olympic team's back-up Finn sailor in Kingston. He had since switched to the three-man Soling and had won the Long Beach pre-Olympic regatta the previous year. Before the Canadians defeated him, Law had lost only one race. McLaughlin's start was his most impressive of the series. He locked on

Law's tail early in the sequence and Law was never able to shake him. McLaughlin started on port tack in a safe leeward position. In a close race, McLaughlin rounded the leeward mark with a narrow lead and pulled away on the final leg.

The win felt good; they were on a roll. But poor weather on the final day of competition cut the series short at seven races, denying the Canadians the opportunity to race against Bruno Troublé. At 6-1, John Bertrand was the series winner. Phil Crebbin, Chris Law and Bruno Troublé tied at 5-2. Terry McLaughlin tied with Harold Cudmore at 4-3.

Princess Anne, the club's royal patron, paid the regatta an afternoon visit. Only skippers were allowed to meet her; to control mingling, the clubhouse was segregated into areas for the privileged and the commoners.

During the regatta, the Canadians chatted with John Bertrand about his America's Cup program. Bertrand was congenial as always and was clearly excited about the Perth challenge. When asked about *Australia II*, though, Bertrand only smiled. The Australians were sitting on top of an enormous secret.

While Terry McLaughlin and his crew raced in England, Doug Keary prepared for the America's Cup summer. The Miami Beach training camp was disbanded in early April; the Canadians would be back in business in Newport within a month. In the meantime, there was much business to settle, not least the persistent interest of the government of Ontario in becoming involved in the challenge. More specifically, the government of Ontario was Bob Fleming, a member of the Royal Canadian Yacht Club who was also the government's director of administration. Fleming had been conducting his own fact-finding missions in Newport. He located a used-car dealership in the heart of town which the government could lease as a promotional site for the province. The rear portion of the property would be made available to the Canadian challenge for use as a sail loft. But the owner of the property decided to lease the property for use as a pizza parlour, and the deal fell through.

Fleming abandoned the idea of a promotional site for the province and instead concentrated on the needs of the challenge. He photographed an abandoned roller-skating rink just north of Newport in the town of Portsmouth. Its spacious floor, perfect for sailmaking, was capable of accommodating four or more 12-Metre mainsails at once. The building was available for about $1700 per month.

Doug Keary met with Fleming and two representatives of the Department of Industry and Trade at Queen's Park in Toronto on April 7. On April 13 Kent Luxton, the New Zealander hired to maintain the challenge's sails, called Keary to report that he had visited the roller rink and recommended

Canada 1 *in the Travelift*

they lease it. The only thing standing in the way of government support for the rink was Marvin McDill. At a fund-raising luncheon on March 31, McDill had made his customary comments about a true "people's challenge" and the shunning of government support. With McDill's words fresh in their memories, the Ontario representatives didn't want to do anything that could lead him to accuse them of meddling. Keary assured them there was nothing to worry about. McDill's thunderings about the evils of government involvement were, well, a touch rhetorical. What was important to McDill was that the *spirit* of the challenge not be undermined. Doug Keary and the rest of the operations committee, desperate for money to keep the challenge alive, did not want to see a potential donor scared away by the fund-raising oratory of Marvin McDill.

The bureaucrats came to understand. Before the summer was out, the government of Ontario would underwrite $51,500 of the people's campaign's Newport activities.

The roller rink was a mess. The roof leaked, the lights flickered, the hardwood floor was filthy and the surrounding property was full of junk. Kent Luxton recruited crew members to make repairs – clearing away debris, patching the roof, rewiring the lights, and cleaning and varnishing

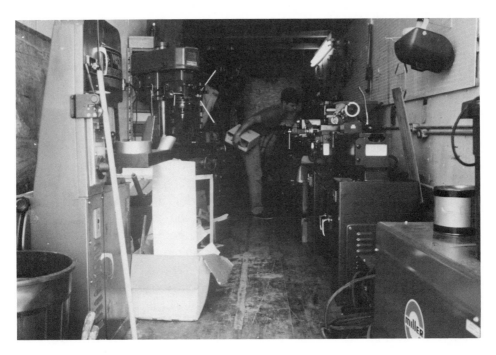

Canada 1's machine-shop trailer

the gorgeous floor. He moved his ultralight aircraft into the building, where it would remain all summer, casting shadows over *Canada 1*'s sails.

Luxton then commandeered one of the challenge's vans. He wired plastic red geraniums to the grill, painted his trademark, Dr. Dacron, on the side, and plastered the body with sail tell-tales which fluttered in the wind as the van tore back and forth through Newport.

When money in camp became especially tight, Luxton suggested the syndicate hire a band and hold a fund-raising dance at the roller rink. Management turned down the proposal for fear of contravening fire regulations. But the name the aborted fund-raising effort suggested – Dr. Dacron's Dance Hall – remained with the roller rink for the rest of the Newport summer.

Jeff Boyd arrived in Newport on Tuesday, May 3. With him in his van were Tom Cummings and Rob Kidd. Most of the sailors had been at the base more than a week. The only challenge already sailing was the British. *Clipper* and *Canada 1* were being prepared for launching. Kevin Singleton had somehow negotiated the use of a Travelift, which would give the camp access to the water around the clock. It felt good to be self-sufficient.

McLaughlin and Boyd held meeting after meeting with Doug Keary, who had been searching in vain for a "Mr. X" to manage the maintenance program. He had polled a variety of people: George Cuthbertson, who had left C&C Yachts and was operating his own design office; George Hinterhoeller, a co-founder of C&C who had departed in 1976 to establish his own boat-building firm in St. Catharines, Ontario; Henry Adriaanse, an engineer who had once worked for C&C and who had been hired by Bruce Kirby to design some of *Canada 1*'s structural components; and many others. But none of his candidates could make the required commitment. For some it was a matter of time; for others it was their ignorance of aluminum construction; for many it was no doubt the magnitude of the task of keeping two 12-Metres and their fleet of tenders in operating order. Keary decided that Bob Whitehouse could handle the increasingly demanding role, provided he had an assistant. Steve Fleck, a newly graduated engineer, from Toronto, was hired. Terry McLaughlin wasn't entirely sold on the idea of Whitehouse as Mr. X but had little choice – Whitehouse was the only person either brave or foolhardy enough to accept the assignment.

The family changed and grew. Jimmy Johnston became the camp's full-time photographer and Brook Hamilton moved over to maintenance. This created a need for more tender drivers. Rob Burton was moved from the crew to the driver ranks but left the program after two weeks in Newport. John Millen's brother Mark, a Toronto ferry captain, and his girlfriend, Fran Ford, would plug the gap in tender personnel. In June the camp would enlist John Begg, a local high school student, as a tender mate and pay him with a free lunch. The camp acquired a rigger, Brian Pearson, another Peter Wilson, on the maintenance squad (aptly named Three Ton by McLaughlin), and a welder known only as Julius. Rob Webb's New Zealand-born wife, Dale, became secretary/receptionist. Tom Corness's girlfriend, Denise Larue, handled *Canada 1* souvenir sales at the America's Cup gallery in Newport.

Doug Keary had invited Hugh Drake to handle public relations for the base in Newport, with Gord Smeaton remaining as his assistant. A semi-retired insurance salesman with London Life, Drake was an RCYC member who since 1981 had served as Terry McLaughlin's Flying Dutchman coach. Coaching McLaughlin had little to do with tactics and sail trim – Drake made sure that McLaughlin had a place to stay, that his boat got to wherever it was supposed to and that other logistical details were in order as the 1980 world champion attended one international regatta after another.

Hugh Drake had met Doug Keary for the first time at the Miami Beach training base in March. Visiting Miami because of the Flying Dutchman Can-Am series, he decided to poke his head into the 12-Metre camp.

He found Keary in the rear of the office trailer at his desk, holding his head in his hands.

"How are you doing?" Drake enquired.

"How much time do you have?" Keary replied.

Drake offered his services – whatever he could do to help. He soon took up residence with his wife at Roselawn, the Newport mansion maintained by the Canadian syndicate for members of management and visiting VIPs. Roselawn also became his responsibility. In the untended rose beds, he planted a vegetable garden, something he hadn't done since he was a boy. It had occurred to him that a garden might help him keep his grip on reality as the summer progressed.

The only thing the rose beds would grow was onions.

With the start of the 1983 summer, *Canada 1*'s electronics package was complete. The challenge had originally intended to have director John Morgan's son, Jamie Morgan, custom-design a system, but the plan disappeared with the managerial reorganization of the fall of 1982. Instead, all components were purchased off-the-shelf.

An Ockam instruments unit displayed boat, true wind and apparent wind speeds, and true wind and apparent wind angles. Connected with it were a Hewlett-Packard HP 75C hand-held computer, positioned at the navigator's station, and a Loran C navigation device. Peter Wilson would use the arsenal of data in association with a dead reckoning plotting board and the computer to guide *Canada 1* around the race course.

The system was capable of, among other things, determining the apparent wind angle of an upcoming leg as an aid to sail selection. And in its memory were the target speeds for various headings in various winds, developed by recording *Canada 1*'s performance in training and modifying it with computer performance predictions from Steve Killing. These target speeds were the infamous Numbers – the blueprint of the 12-Metre's capabilities which could be recalled during a race to determine if the yacht was sailing to its potential. With the assistance of electronics, the afterguard could decide how fast *Canada 1* was going, how fast she should be going, where she was and where she was going, and what sails should be used to get there faster.

Late on Wednesday, May 4, *Clipper* was launched and had her mast stepped; *Canada 1* joined her in the water at 7:00 a.m. the next day. While work on *Canada 1* continued, *Clipper* enjoyed a short sail.

With only six weeks left before their first race, the Canadians could begin to test, in a very restricted sense, their newly arrived sails. There was not enough time to do a proper job, but it was essential at least to determine what sails performed the best in given conditions.

Shortage of time was not the only problem. There had been serious difficulties with the sails received in Miami Beach from Sobstad Storer. Kent Luxton had written a scathing letter to the challenge management in April, primarily citing poor construction as the problem with the sails. Sobstab Storer's efforts, he charged, made a mockery of the two-sailmaker program. As Luxton explained to Doug Keary on April 24, the sailcloth from Wind-master (a company which had since gone out of business) had not been tested for wet strength. Sobstad Storer had been caught with a shipment of bad cloth.

Kent Luxton, Cedric Gyles and Terry McLaughlin had visited Richard Storer in Barrie soon after Luxton had explained the cloth problem to Keary. Gyles then reported back to Keary on the meeting. Storer had generally admitted to the cloth problem. He would reinforce and repair all four genoas he had built for the campaign and would make new #2 and #4 genoas at no charge. If the problems persisted, he conceded that he might have to make further replacements. Keary then warned Luxton about writing any more letters about sail construction. Should one of the New Zealander's letters fall into the wrong hands, it could be construed as sail design by a non-Canadian and so invalidate *Canada 1*'s inventory.

On May 6 Richard Storer joined Tom Whidden and two other employees from the Sobstad loft in Connecticut, Peter Conrad and Andy Halsey, for a day of sail inspection aboard *Clipper*. Of particular interest was the S2.1 medium mainsail, which had proved excessively long in the hoist in Miami Beach and, after repairs, had begun to disintegrate. The mainsail had since been completely rebuilt, its back half constructed of new material. Boyd still viewed the sail as something of a white elephant, as it actually had been built in Connecticut, not Barrie. Whidden, however, was reluctant to admit to that fact, which left everyone attempting to discuss the sail's state playing verbal hopscotch.

Having Whidden on board *Clipper* provided an opportunity to pick the brains of someone who had been a sail trimmer on *Freedom* in 1980 and was now serving as Dennis Conner's tactician. McLaughlin and Boyd overwhelmed him with questions. Whidden was a touch restrained. It was hard to blame him – he was probably in enough trouble as it was just sailing with the Canadians.

It proved to be a perfect day for testing the sail inventory. *Clipper* began by sailing up Narragansett Bay in a light northerly. They turned back to inspect three different half-ounce spinnakers. Nearing the Newport Bridge, the sea breeze filled in and they steered onto the Sound, evaluating their #3, #4 and #6 headsails.

While they had no boat to test against, the experts were happy with the shape of the S2.1 mainsail. "Fine," Terry McLaughlin impatiently replied, "but isn't the real problem with the cloth?"

Terry McLaughlin spins Clipper *during starting practice under the watchful eyes of Sandy Andrews, at the bow of* Canada 1.

Back on shore, the sailmakers met for a final discussion with McLaughlin, Keary and visiting guest expert Peter Hall. Keary felt sorry for Richard Storer. He might not be as smoothly professional as Hans Fogh (Fogh, as accomplished a businessman as sailor, ran one of the most profitable North lofts on the continent), but he was deeply, personally committed to the *Canada 1* program. While Fogh was always happy to accompany his latest sail shipment to Newport and lend what advice he could, his interest in the challenge had waned when it opted for a two-sailmaker program, and he lacked faith in Bruce Kirby's design. Fogh liked to work for someone who was loyal to him; it made him work harder. He couldn't imagine being in either Tom Whidden's or John Marshall's shoes, both sailing on the same boat and having Conner play them off against each other.

Richard Storer was taking a gamble committing himself to the *Canada 1* program, and he would rush to Newport at the drop of a hat if summoned. But the sailors in the camp did not respect him as a sailor the way they did Hans Fogh, and the need for Storer to rush to Newport became paramount when the sailcloth he employed proved defective. Doug Keary could not understand how Storer managed to absorb the cost of the sails he was forced to rebuild or replace and still stay in business.

Saturday, May 7. Sail testing, which progressed for much of the day, was brought to a halt when *Canada 1*'s outhaul car broke. Terry McLaughlin began to lobby for an adjustable boom ram on *Canada 1*, similar to *Clipper*'s. The day's excitement came from accidentally running over a fish trap; inspection revealed no damage to the hull.

After the previous day's sail, Tom Whidden had indicated that *Clipper* had excessive weather helm and that it should be rectified by moving her mast forward. Doug Keary raised the point with Bruce Kirby, who replied that *Clipper* was set up exactly as she was in 1980. She was a known quantity and would not be changed.

On Sunday more sail testing was conducted, and a few races were run in the afternoon. *Canada 1* and *Clipper* seemed quite even. Doug Keary met with Peter Hall and his Soling crew, Phil Kerrigan, to review their observations. They voiced a need for an expert for the sail program. They were also concerned about the maturity of some of the crew, their ability to handle the heat of competition and the psychological setback of losses. They stressed the need to bone up on rule knowledge and avoid protest situations.

Hall and Kerrigan were impressed by Dave Miller of the North Vancouver loft whenever their paths had crossed. As a sailmaker and Canada's only Olympic medallist in sailing since 1932, he would be an ideal sail expert. Hall felt that ideally Miller should be the mainsail trimmer, but the wiry Miller was not strong enough. To keep him on board, the challenge could make Jeff Boyd the mainsail trimmer and Miller the tactician. To McLaughlin and Boyd, this became known as the "Hall Plan." They were careful never to tell the existing mainsail trimmer, Rob Muru, of the proposal.

Monday, May 9. Doug Keary began the routine of a 7:15 a.m. management meeting of department heads (Terry McLaughlin and Jeff Boyd from sailing, Hugh Drake from public relations, Kevin Singleton from the office and Bob Whitehouse from maintenance), followed by a 7:30 crew meeting to review the day's plans.

It was a cold day with a strong breeze from the northwest. Terry McLaughlin and Jeff Boyd ventured out in *Clipper* first. When they at last met up with *Canada 1* to test spinnakers, the crew aboard *Clipper* attempted a "peel," changing spinnakers by hoisting a second one inside the first before dropping the first. The peel was a disaster. The fitting on the first chute's guy refused to trip, and they were unable to gather it in from the leeward clew. Instead they attempted a "belly cord drop," hauling in the sail by a retrieval line attached to its centre. *Clipper* was making 8 knots, and when the halyard was released the spinnaker hit the water and began to disappear astern: the fearsome "tea bag" manoeuvre. The drag from the sail brought *Clipper* to a virtual halt, and Ed Gyles cut the halyard before it could tow the rig out of the boat. In the midst of the mishap, both the spinnaker sheet and the guy wrapped around the rudder post. *Clipper* had to be hoisted out of the water to clear the lines.

In the afternoon, *Clipper* returned to Rhode Island Sound for practice starts against Peter Hall. The camp's one and only inflatable mark sank. Hall and Kerrigan didn't seem impressed.

Wednesday, May 11. Hans Fogh appeared in camp with a new mainsail and several spinnakers. Although there were mechanical problems with both boats, the Canadians managed to get in a few hours of sail testing.

The maintenance list had grown such that the crews were given Thursday off. That evening they attended the first social event of the season, a party hosted by Peter de Savary and the British syndicate at the Victory Bar. A few Australians appeared; true to form, the Canadians were out in full force.

With Sam Lazier in Newport to measure *Canada 1*, the holiday was extended through Friday. Omar, Don Campbell and Eric Jespersen drove to Warren, Rhode Island, to buy bicycles. On the way home, they stopped in at Cove Haven, where *Freedom* was being readied for the long summer. While two of the Canadians chatted with some of the *Freedom* personnel, the third poked his head into one of the boat's trimmer cockpits to see how the sheet jammers worked. It was the first certified espionage activity by Canadians that summer.

Espionage, or, more innocuously, information gathering, had become an important pastime for the Canadians. Although Jay "Bondo" McKinnell had been placed in charge of surveillance after tearing the cartilage in his knee late in the Miami Beach camp, the entire challenge was enlisted to go forth and learn whatever they could about 12-Metres. They were always to keep their ears open for loose talk and friendly advice. McKinnell crawled the bars of the waterfront to chat up other crews, and it was during one such outing that several *Freedom* crew members had proudly raved about the jammer system they used that allowed for flawless spinnaker gybes and peels.

Terry McLaughlin was fascinated by the idea of espionage. He regularly offered incentives: a free case of beer for photos and drawings of *Freedom*'s jammers; $50 to the first person to photograph *Australia II*'s keel before a week was out. With McLaughlin, it was difficult to know where to draw a line between spying incentives and one of his favourite activities – making wagers. He would risk money on just about anything, at the slightest impulse. Once, on the way out of harbour for a sail, he wagered with Fred Schueddekopp to identify a loose piece of material near the top of the mainsail. A thread or a piece of seam tape, Fred? McLaughlin, of course, guessed correctly.

Clipper *under spinnaker*

For Doug Keary, keeping the eyes and ears of the camp open was a necessity. They had so much to learn in so little time – he sometimes wondered if the management had really understood what they were asking the challenge to accomplish back in January, when they had an unproven boat, no racing mast, virtually no sail program and a lagging training schedule. In a matter of a few months, they were expected to shape an America's Cup winner. Part of making *Canada 1* competitive, Keary knew, was paying attention to what everyone else was doing. If purists couldn't understand that, they didn't understand the nature of the sport, or their circumstances.

Saturday, May 14. While *Clipper* was having her compasses swung by Dick Sadler, a grinder for Ted Turner aboard *Courageous* in 1977 and 1980, Terry McLaughlin staged his first grinder contest. It was, after much thought, the best way McLaughlin could come up with of assessing the skills of the grinder candidates. With the tailer lending only a minimum of assistance, one man would grind Tom Cummings up the mast in the bosun's chair. Eric Jespersen was like a machine; in first gear he propelled Cumboy clear to the first set of spreaders 20 seconds faster than anyone else.

The next day, Dick Sadler returned to swing *Canada 1*'s compasses. Sadler rarely arrived on time for such appointments and seemed to take forever to get the job done. But he always had some stories to share, and the crew, ears open, were willing to listen, even if it delayed their departure. They were initiates before a master of the Zen of 12-Metre sailing. Patience – the truth could be known to them, Pat Healy's baby chickens who dared to be eagles.

The sky was overcast, the wind sweeping onto Rhode Island Sound from the north, as *Canada 1* and *Clipper* left dock Monday morning to test half-ounce "C" sized spinnakers. In inventory terminology, "C" referred to maximum width, which in the case of a half-ounce spinnaker was about 43 feet; an "A" size measured 39 feet, a "B" 41 feet. Generally, the less wind there was, the more efficient the smaller spinnaker. The testing today produced the first conclusive results of May: the North spinnaker seemed much faster than the Sobstad.

Determining the difference carried the two 12-Metres out to the vicinity of Block Island. The wind now up to 20 knots, *Canada 1* wanted to change mainsails. With only one tender along, the switch was long and difficult. When they were ready to begin pacing upwind the 20 miles back to harbour, the wind suddenly increased to 30 knots.

Clipper's mainsail came apart. Shep Higley brought *Mako*, the tender, into position to attach a tow line. While attempting to secure the line, Don Campbell fell overboard under *Clipper*'s bow; he was retrieved, unhurt.

Higley towed *Clipper* for a short time, but the seas made the exercise slow and dangerous, and *Clipper* sailed home under genoa only. In biting cold weather, the crew sang songs to stay warm and keep spirits high.

Back on shore, Jeff Boyd ran into Glen Darden, a tailer on *Defender*. He was a young Texan who had won the Mallory Cup, the men's sailing championships of the United States, as well as the Lightning world championship in 1979. He told Boyd that whenever a northerly blew in Newport the American 12-Metres usually stayed on Narragansett Bay. Out on the Sound the wind was too unpredictable. Another hard-earned lesson.

Tuesday, May 17. A day of collisions. During a start on Narragansett Bay, Terry McLaughlin and *Canada 1* approached the line too soon. Jeff Boyd swept in astern with *Clipper* and established a leeward overlap. Before he had even attempted to luff *Canada 1*, McLaughlin eased his mainsail and Boyd drove into *Canada 1*'s boom. McLaughlin, deciding the best case was a loud case, left the wheel to holler at Boyd, even though he had been at fault.

"What did you do *that* for?" Boyd demanded.

Terry shrugged and smiled. The act was over. "I was doing a Bruno Troublé," he suggested.

The start began a race south to the Castle Hill bell buoy. *Clipper* started to leeward and ahead, solidified her lead on a beneficial wind shift. Her crew was psyched, tacking well and grinding hard, talking up the spinnaker hoist.

Nearing Castle Hill, Jeff Boyd brought *Clipper* over onto port and promptly noticed another boat, on starboard, running toward him. *Clipper* hadn't finished accelerating after the tack. Still racing, Boyd thought that he could steer below the approaching yacht and lose distance to windward in the process, or avoid her by holding his close-hauled course and not accelerating any further.

The skipper of the other yacht bore off sharply, saving Boyd from making the decision. He waved in appreciation and continued racing.

"*Go up,*" Tom Cummings, *Clipper*'s navigator, abruptly yelled as he grabbed for the wheel. There was a loud bang; a 51-foot yacht slid past their starboard side. The top of the other yacht's mast had clipped the jumper struts of the heeled *Clipper*, and a quick inspection revealed that they had collapsed.

Boyd felt terrible. It was one of the most embarrassing thing he had ever done in a sailboat.

After returning to dock, Jeff Boyd, Tom Cummings and Jay McKinnell searched out the yacht's owner. "That wasn't a very good show out there," the South African observed. His name was Bertie Reed. He had just placed second overall in the BOC singlehanded round-the-world race.

Boyd apologized for the accident and promised to replace the damaged electronics atop Reed's mast. Cumboy ascended the mast and found that his trilight was broken as well, and retrieved the smashed equipment. Reed was very sporting about the mishap. A friend had been at the helm, he explained, and there had been a film crew on board recreating his finish in the BOC race.

Eric Jespersen, who had been grinding aboard *Canada 1*, later told Boyd that the fellow at the helm had steered well clear of *Clipper*, only to veer in for a closer look. It made Boyd feel better, but not much.

Wednesday, May 18. *Clipper* and *Canada 1* sailed together for almost eight hours as they tested #3 headsails. The sail comparisons had gone well and the sailors were buoyed by the feeling they were actually learning something. After only two weeks of training together again since the Miami Beach camp, though, the sailors were becoming restless with familiar anxieties, and Jeff Boyd warned Terry McLaughlin of the fact before the day was out.

At the crew meeting the following morning, the frustrations exploded into a full-scale revolt, with Terry McLaughlin as the target. Eric Jespersen delivered the most cutting accusation. "Terry," he charged, "you said that when you were treated badly by the Admiral, you wanted to go home. Now I feel like *I'm* being treated badly by the Admiral, and *I* want to go home."

The oldest irony – the liberator had become the tyrant he had replaced; in the minds of a number of the crew, Terry had become the Admiral.

That evening the Canadians hosted a barbecue for the crew of *France 3*. Before dinner started, Terry McLaughlin dropped by Jeff Boyd's room. He had done what Boyd always liked to do, he reported, and written down what he felt. He handed Boyd the note.

McLaughlin had been unhappy with Boyd's performance at the crew meeting. When the crew had announced that they preferred to sail with Boyd, he had sat on the fence, failing to support McLaughlin. Dave Shaw had been more supportive. It was as if Boyd wanted to take over. He had tried to change, McLaughlin said. If he hadn't changed enough, maybe he should leave. "Today I went out and I didn't yell," he wrote. "I didn't complain. I just went through the motions. I didn't have fun."

McLaughlin's response to his accusers during the morning crew meeting had amazed Boyd. Terry had made a heartfelt and highly uncharacteristic effort to *explain himself*. At one point he had revealed how, as a boy, he had capsized during a dinghy race, and his father had sailed by, calling out to make sure that Terry's crew was all right. It went without saying that Terry was all right. He was a McLaughlin. He could take care of himself. He didn't run on slaps on the back. His entire competitive career had been based on focusing on the things that were wrong, not applauding the things that were

Azzurra, *one of the surprises of the Newport summer*

right. Handing out praise freely did not come naturally to him. But he was trying to change. Team spirit was important to Terry; understandably he couldn't live with the thought that everyone on board might despise him.

In charting the pressures Terry McLaughlin brought upon those around him, it was too easy to forget the enormous pressures under which McLaughlin himself was forced to function. The ultimate success of *Canada 1* weighed most heavily on Terry's shoulders, and at such a relatively young age he had accepted without question not only that responsibility but many others, and with no comparable experience to prepare him for it. He had been, and continued to be, one of the key people in keeping the challenge going. Whatever the merits of the complaints of his detractors, they had to remember that McLaughlin had helped make it possible for them even to be in Newport.

At the barbecue, Boyd assured McLaughlin that he wasn't leading any revolt. The stuff about the crew preferring to sail with him had been an embarrassment. "You're dealing with ordinary sailors who aren't accustomed to a campaign," he reminded McLaughlin. "They're Canadians. They *like* to complain."

The crisis between them passed. The next day the two friends went sailing together on *Clipper*.

Saturday, May 21. That morning, Doug Keary met with Terry McLaughlin about the mutinous crew. Keary invited Bob Whitehouse and Hugh Drake to join in, figuring they knew Terry as well as anybody, and that it was time to build up his self-confidence again.

Keary decided that McLaughlin had taken too much upon himself. He was running the sail program, skippering *Canada 1*, doing public relations duties for the fund-raisers, and above all attempting to operate a crew selection program while at the same time trying to remain chummy with the sailors. Forget *Clipper*, Keary told him. Just sail *Canada 1* and worry about your own boat. He'd absorb the heat from the crew ranks himself.

With that, McLaughlin broke one of Keary's rules by taking an outsider, Rob Muru's father, for a sail on *Canada 1*. McLaughlin's accommodating gesture backfired. Before dinner, he was summoned to meet with Doug Keary and Hugh Drake at Keary's apartment. No more free rides.

After dinner, Doug Keary held a complaints seminar with the crew at Sherman House, jotting their objections on a blackboard. They didn't like being intimidated by Terry, the yelling, the constant pressure. They were afraid Terry's aggressiveness would involve them in no-win protest hearings. They weren't using time efficiently on the water. They weren't happy with the "A" and "B" team labels, especially with how second-rate the "B" team label came across in the press. They didn't get enough time to work out at the Nautilus fitness centre. They didn't know what was happening from one day to the next. And they didn't like the morning management meeting delaying the start of the crew meetings.

It was quite a list. Keary promised to have some answers soon.

Sunday, May 22. With Hugh Drake on *Canada 1* and Doug Keary aboard *Clipper* to monitor the mood of the crews, the Canadians sailed into an impromptu team race against *France 3* and *Azzurra*. Jeff Boyd, helming *Clipper*, cockily assumed that the French and the Italians didn't stand a chance if they stuck to proper team-racing rules.

Bruno Troublé secured a fine start and *France 3* disappeared up the course. *Clipper* was second, *Azzurra* third, *Canada 1* last. There were only five knots of wind and the water was smooth. Boyd decided to sail down on *Azzurra*'s wind to allow McLaughlin to pass her. But Boyd couldn't get on *Azzurra*'s air. When he laid off, Mauro Pelaschier (who had been appointed the Italian challenge's helmsman after the Lymington Cup) would lay off further and sail even faster. Finally, to the amazement of Boyd, *Azzurra* sailed out from underneath *Clipper*. Boyd had succeeded in dragging *Azzurra* far enough back, though, that McLaughlin was able to spurt through and round the weather mark behind *France 3*. On the first reach, McLaughlin slowed to luff Pelaschier, allowing Boyd to slip into second place. The Canadians finished 2-3 to win the race.

But the victory was tempered by *Azzurra*'s obvious ability. It was the first time the Canadians had encountered the Italian dark horse and her performance in light air had been nothing short of frightening.

Monday, May 23. The rigs were pulled from *Canada 1* and *Clipper* in preparation for the installation of a newly arrived racing mast for *Canada 1*. Proctor of England had shipped a 12-Metre extrusion in three sections to Klacko of Oakville. Klacko had then assembled the mast, including a sail track designed by Bob Whitehouse, and shipped it to Newport.

The original Proctor mast from *Canada 1* was equipped with a new sail track similar to the one designed by Whitehouse so that it could serve as a back-up spar. *Clipper*'s mast was given a new, compatible Hood track. When the two-day task was completed, it was discovered that none of the luff tapes on the mainsails were compatible with the new track. Kent Luxton, alias Dr. Dacron, spent all of Wednesday at the roller rink installing new luff tapes. A dumb mistake, but the Canadians were consoled when they discovered a week later that the *Australia II* camp had made a similar error.

At the Wednesday morning crew meeting, Doug Keary replied to the complaints registered at his chalk-board seminar on May 21. He announced that Terry McLaughlin was not leaving the program. Some of the responsibilities McLaughlin had shouldered, however, would be delegated, particularly to Keary and other management members. And from now on, the A and B teams would be publicly referred to as "M & M." Keary, in turn, demanded from the crew ranks a more Olympic attitude to training. "New determination in camp," he recorded in his diary. "Mt. Everest to meet." Keary, McLaughlin and Boyd held individual meetings with crew members in the afternoon. A few, who were more enamoured with the Newport social whirl than with the idea of winning the America's Cup, were told to clean up their acts or go home. "*Canada 1* team OK in commitment and attitude," Keary recorded with some relief.

Keary then met with Hans Fogh and Bruce Kirby to discuss the sail program. Fogh was sorry to say that there was not enough time to test sails properly. (In his April 7, 1982, letter to Don Green, Jay Hansen of Fogh's loft had warned, "Actual figures from *Freedom*'s 1980 campaign are that 20 hours of concentrated sail testing time were necessary to choose between one sail and another. The differences we need to measure are .04 to .05 per cent, or 3 to 5 hundredths of a knot. Unless these differences can be determined, sail testing is impossible.") Fogh advised that they simply pick some sails by looking at them, then learn how to set them and stick with them. They would do what they could.

Thursday, May 26. When the Klacko spar was installed in *Canada 1* that morning, a rash of problems arose. The mainsail halyard car wouldn't work, the running backstays were all wrong and the rigging wasn't the proper length. Without a spare set of rigging, they had to make do with what they had.

They weren't able to sail *Canada 1* until five o'clock. Bruce Kirby and Hans Fogh were aboard, with Jeff Boyd at the helm. Terry McLaughlin rode in a tender, inspecting the rig and a new 1.5-ounce spinnaker Fogh had brought that looked for all the world like a Hudson's Bay blanket. That was no accident – the company had promised to pay for the sail, and so had arranged for its black, green, yellow and red stripes.

In a 15-knot easterly, *Canada 1* ran down Narragansett Bay toward Newport Bridge. When they hoisted a genoa to return home, one of the jumper struts on the new mast snapped. Boyd had the routine of dropping sails and picking up a tow down pat. It was the third jumper breakdown he had experienced in the last week, coming on the heels of the first breakdown in the collision with Bertie Reed and a second strut failure aboard *Clipper*. Boyd was becoming a touch paranoid about rig failures. He was convinced it was only a matter of time before they lost a mast while he was at the helm.

That evening the Canadians had the Italians over for dinner. At first they had not known what to make of them, but the Canadians soon came to respect and admire the Italians. *Azzurra*'s crew were by and large older than

Cockpit action aboard Clipper

the Canadians; they had experienced more in their sailing careers, and hence were more mature, better equipped to handle setbacks. Though they were very organized, they were also having a lot of fun. They had a healthy, see-how-it-goes attitude. "I wish we could have their attitude," Terry McLaughlin would remark to Jeff Boyd. "Look at those guys. They're doing stuff that *I* want to do." They replaced the Canadians as the darling underdogs of Newport. With low expectations, hard work, sound financing and a fast light-air boat, it would not be surprising at summer's end that they had done so well.

Canada 1 and *Clipper* were out together again on Friday, May 27. In strong winds and pouring rain, the halyard car of *Canada 1* broke, and Terry McLaughlin, with Hans Fogh on board, returned to base. *Clipper* soon followed. It was her first day out since her mast was reinstalled, and it was wobbling all over creation. In no hurry to meet his rendezvous with a broken mast, Jeff Boyd headed home.

The next day *Canada 1* remained sidelined with halyard car problems. Terry McLaughlin and *Clipper* joined *Azzurra* for a foggy tuning session. The two yachts were even on the flat waters of the harbour, but once out on the Sound, *Clipper* seemed superior.

On Sunday, May 29, *Canada 1* was ready to sail again. With the B team on board, Terry McLaughlin taped a fund-raising commercial financed by Labatt's, then joined Jeff Boyd and *Clipper* for an afternoon of racing. In 10 to 12 knots of wind, *Clipper* was going like hell. Boyd and McLaughlin split the first two races, although halfway up the second beat of the opening race, *Canada 1* had been having perplexing difficulty sheeting her mainsail. Omar had been sent aloft to clamp together an unruly halyard car with a pair of vise grips. Satisfied that the mainsail problem was corrected, *Canada 1* continued to race.

In the third race, the two yachts started even. *Clipper* moved into the lead and covered *Canada 1* loosely. Jeff Boyd shifted away from his position on the weather rail to see how Terry McLaughlin was doing.

"Holy shit," Boyd managed. "They've just lost their mast."

There was stunned silence. *Clipper* circled the crippled *Canada 1*, piecing the scene together, like a swan whose mate has just been gunned down by hunters. The mast rose eight feet above the deck; there was nothing but empty sky where *Canada 1*'s sails should have spread. Most of the mast was over the side, in the water with Omar, who had launched himself into tidying the disaster. Below deck, the mast had collapsed at the ram position used to induce pre-bend in the rig. No one could explain why a brand-new mast had snapped in about 10 knots of wind.

A post-mortem revealed that, when the crew had been raking the mast forward when sailing downwind to increase performance, the ram bracket had not been realigned. The reinforcement in the mast at the ram position was not sufficient to withstand the stresses of the rig without the support of the ram bracket. Badly weakened in downwind sailing, the mast had gone over the side in innocent circumstances. Later, the strength of the lower section of the mast was questioned. On June 22 Doug Keary learned from Bruce Kirby that the new lower extrusion prepared for the Klacko mast by Alcan Canada was tested at 45,000 pounds per square inch; the broken section of the mast tested at only 19,000 p.s.i.

The dismasting was a huge setback. Rigging was irreparably damaged and the mainsail they had been flying was in shreds. Although Kent Luxton painstakingly sewed it back together, the sail was never the same. The disaster added another seven to the mounting total of sailing days lost due to breakdowns. Training time was slipping away. *Canada 1* would not be back in the water, with her old Proctor mast, until June 6.

While *Canada 1* underwent repairs, the A team sailed as much as they could on *Clipper* against *France 3* and other foreign 12-Metres. On June 5 Terry McLaughlin, Jeff Boyd and Jay McKinnell boarded the Boston Whaler and ventured onto a foggy Rhode Island Sound to observe the other challenge candidates. They watched *Azzurra* and *France 3* pace together, then moved in closer to see if what they were seeing really was what they were seeing. It was. The Italians were tuning *Azzurra's* rig by trying to tighten the loaded weather shrouds, rather than the slacker leeward ones. A very strange sight.

Then the Italians spotted the Canadians and began making indecipherable gestures. The espionage party thought they were being shooed away. Far from it – the Italians wanted help. The Whaler pulled alongside *Azzurra* so that two crew members could transfer aboard for a better view of the rig. The rapport between the Italians and the Canadians was excellent from the start. It never waned.

Tuesday, June 7. More setbacks. Dave Shaw tore a ligament in his chest and would not be healed in time for the first race of the challengers' trials on June 18. Bob Whitehouse approached Doug Keary with the complaint that some of the crew, particularly from *Clipper*, were not cooperating with his maintenance efforts and were not sufficiently committed to the program. McLaughlin and Boyd, sailing *Canada 1*, demolished Dave Miller and *Clipper* in starting practice. Miller, who had arrived in camp on June 3, would stay until the middle of the first challengers' series.

On June 8 a new sailor was added: Terry McLaughlin had recruited his Flying Dutchman crew, Evert Bastet of Hudson, Quebec, who also happened to be a spar builder, to serve as *Canada 1's* port headsail trimmer. With Bastet on board, McLaughlin won four starts, yet lost four races to Dave Miller. The culprit was identified as a loose trim tab. With the problem fixed, *Canada 1* won four straight races the next day, flying the rebuilt S2.1 mainsail from Sobstad Storer.

While Terry McLaughlin ran up a winning streak, Kent Luxton became embroiled in an argument with Peter Conrad at the Sobstad loft in Connecticut over the quality of the company's product. Back at home in Canada, Doug Keary assessed a final contract with Stearn Sailing Systems of Wisconsin for a new racing mast for *Canada 1*. The price of the spar would be $43,000 if delivered by July 7, $40,000 by July 14, $35,000 by July 28 or $30,000 by August 1. A future order was planned for a back-up mast, with a tentative July 28 delivery cost of $35,000.

On Friday, June 10, *Canada 1* began her official measurement at Cove Haven. Another crack had appeared above the spinnaker pole butt hoist in the old Proctor mast. The state of the Canadian challenge verged on chaotic. Sam Lazier, at Cove Haven for the official measuring, exchanged brief words with one of the official measurers about the mysterious *Australia II*. "I just hope," the measurer allowed, "that she doesn't meet up with an amorous whale." The broad hint at fins did not register with Lazier. The Canadians had almost no idea of what they were up against. The first challengers' trials began in eight days.

18

trials and errors

On Saturday, June 11, the various challenging syndicates paraded from the Newport Armory on Thames Street to the baseball park for an official welcome from the city of Newport and the state of Rhode Island. Every challenging syndicate was represented (the Americans were out sailing) and their members were decked out in traditional blue blazers. The British, outnumbering everyone, sported straw hats.

At the ballpark the syndicates lined up on the infield, Olympic-opening-ceremonies style. The Canadians were positioned on the pitcher's mound, which gave them a clear view of the proceedings. The bleachers were packed with spectators. Each syndicate had a representative on the speakers' platform at home plate. The governor and the mayor welcomed one and all, and the syndicates took turns replying. Most syndicates were represented by management – Warren Jones of the *Australia II* effort wished everyone good luck and mediocre boat-speed. Daniel Palardy of the Canadian challenge, the only sailor on the platform, kept his speech short and precise.

Peter de Savary did the talking for the British. When he was through, 70 Englishmen doffed their straw hats. There was a "Three cheers for the other syndicates, boys," and a host of hip, hip, hoorays followed. Then an enormous inflatable version of Winston, the *Victory* syndicate's mascot bulldog logo, bedecked in naval garb appropriate for Trafalgar, rose from the ground between home plate and the backstop. The British were certainly flashy. Back at the pitcher's mound, Paul Hansen kicked himself for not bringing a bottle rocket.

Jeff Boyd and Jay "Bondo" McKinnell reflected on what a wonderful game the America's Cup must be for a rich man like Peter de Savary. There were the yachts – the large, expensive, custom-built 12-Metres, and the power boats that tended to them. There were the men working for you, and the women all around. And the press hanging on your every word. It was just like starting your own war and fielding your own army – and the casualties were never fatal, only outbaskets.

Canada 1 was still at Cove Haven being measured. With one week left until the first race of the Series A challengers' trials, the Canadians didn't feel well prepared. *Canada 1* had run into a few snags during measuring. Her jib hoist height proved to be greater than the maximum 75 per cent of rig height by a little more than an inch, which meant relocating the forestay terminus. In addition, the underbody of the hull aft of the rudder was concave when viewed from the side, which the rules did not allow, and additional fairing was required to flesh it out.

Following the parade and welcoming ceremonies, the crew was given the afternoon off. Jeff Boyd took a long bicycle ride to enjoy the sun and grab a few moments away from the boatyard and the rest of the Canadians. After dinner, he, Terry, Two Ton, Mickey and the meteorologist, Sharon Mooney, went to the movies to see *War Games*. They arrived back at Sherman House after 11:00 and had to turn down offers of beer before heading for bed.

The next day, Rhode Island Sound was hot and hazy, with a 12-knot breeze from the west. Terry McLaughlin and Jamie Kidd (an RCYC dinghy helmsman, newly arrived in camp to sail with Dave Miller) headed out aboard *Clipper*. Jeff Boyd, Jay Bondo, Dave Miller and Richard Storer followed in the Whaler for some productive sightseeing – all of the 12s in Newport were out, running through their paces.

Clipper and *Challenge 12* from Melbourne hooked up and began pacing upwind. *Challenge 12* was Ben Lexcen's conventional 12-Metre design for 1983. The boat's syndicate had foundered in January, and Alan Bond had stepped in to charter *Challenge 12* as a trial horse for *Australia II*, thereby holding off the creditors for a time. Richard Pratt, chairman of Visy Board, a giant cardboard box manufacturer, then came through with $250,000 to put the Royal Victoria Yacht Club challenge back on its feet; he had already contributed $100,000 to the challenge before the financial crisis. A novel lottery was created to raise public donations, with a first prize of $200,000 or *Challenge 12* itself. Sailed by John Savage, who had won the Etchells 22 world title in Toronto, *Challenge 12* was considered a frontrunner in the five-nation bid for the challenge nomination.

While *Clipper* and *Challenge 12* sailed side by side, the Whaler tagged along. McKinnell snapped photographs of the slot width between main and genoa and the sail leeches on both boats, then powered off to watch Rodney Pattisson and Chris Law, on *Australia*, beat Lawrie Smith and Phil Crebbin, aboard *Victory 83*, in a practice race. The Canadian sightseeing launch carefully noted that *Victory 83*, Peter de Savary's newest 12-Metre, gained substantially on *Australia* on the run. Then it was off to watch Dennis Conner and *Liberty* outperform *Freedom*. The Conner race featured far more action than did the British, particularly in the number of tacks. After the race, the Canadians watched *Freedom* and *Liberty* swap mainsails. The

Sydney's Advance, *with her peculiar anteater bow*

manoeuvre took 15 minutes; the crew work on the American boats was impressive.

Clipper, in the meantime, was proving to sail faster, though at a broader angle to the wind, than *Challenge 12*. Terry McLaughlin believed that the advantages cancelled each other out and that both boats probably produced the same VMG. The Whaler returned to watch *Victory 83* demolish *Australia*. Dave Miller clocked their spinnaker hoists – *eight seconds...ten seconds* – and Jeff Boyd observed crew positions.

Late in the afternoon, *Clipper* returned to dock. *Canada 1* was returning from Cove Haven that evening on the high tide. Though it had been a good day for casual espionage, Boyd would rather have been sailing than watching. Observation alone could be psychologically damaging.

While they were hoisting *Clipper's* mainsail on June 13, the halyard car broke, bringing her day's sail to a quick end. *Canada 1* had departed dock earlier to tune the mast; with *Clipper* sidelined, Terry McLaughlin decided to carry on alone. It had been some time since the two boats had sailed together. McLaughlin was uninspired without a sparring partner and opted to concentrate on crew work.

Unfortunately Dave Shaw, the mast man, was still injured, and it appeared that Omar would not be able to fill his shoes. (Omar also possessed the unfortunate ability to drive McLaughlin to distraction at precisely the wrong time.) Jeff Boyd decided to try to fill this key position with Eric Jespersen, who since the last crew shuffle had been tending to grinding duties.

When *Canada 1* returned to shore, the crew sought word on the progress on *Clipper*. "Should be ready by nine o'clock in the morning," Bob Whitehouse said. In a campaign fraught with repair headaches, the sailors had heard such promises before, but didn't say anything.

But the next morning *Clipper* was indeed ready. Dave Miller and Jamie Kidd would sail her against Terry McLaughlin and Jeff Boyd aboard *Canada 1*. *Canada 1* concluded the day at 2-1; Terry McLaughlin was buoyant.

On the second beat of the day's second race, with *Canada 1* to weather of *Clipper*, the Canadian 12-Metres had become entangled with *Australia II* and *Advance*. A spontaneous tuning session ensued, with the four boats settling into a long starboard tack.

Advance was the freak of the 1983 summer. She was designed by Alan Payne of *Gretel* and *Gretel II* fame for a Sydney syndicate. Her skipper was Iain Murray, a 24-year-old Australian 18 champion with virtually no keelboat racing experience. Her young crew was constantly at odds with Syd Fisher, the manager of the badly underfunded syndicate, and *Advance* was at odds with every known concept of 12-Metre design. She was extremely high-sided, with an anteater-nose bow, a tiny keel, a huge bustle and rudder, and a mast without jumpers. She was also very heavy. Alan Payne was held in great esteem by the design community, and there was much scratching of heads over exactly what he was up to. There was talk of low wetted surface, a low-rating waterline length, a maximizing of the lifting body effect. Alan Payne offered that she had been designed for narrow performance range – about 12 knots of wind and a short chop, typical of Newport. The boat was an utter mystery.

Shep Higley and Mark Millen on *Slapshot II* radioed *Canada 1*, wondering what had happened to the race with *Clipper*. McLaughlin explained the impromptu tuning session. After five minutes, *Australia II* squeezed out from below *Clipper*, which was in danger of being rolled by *Advance*. But *Clipper* began to work out on *Advance*, still losing ground to *Australia II*. *Canada 1* was well to windward, and in clear air appeared to be moving well.

Eventually Jeff Boyd informed Terry McLaughlin that *Australia II* had gained bearing on them. Terry laid *Canada 1* off; *Clipper* followed. Boyd radioed *Clipper* and asked for their observations.

"Well, after we got out of the Vegemite sandwich we thought we did okay," Tom Cummings replied, "but *Australia II* seemed quick."

"Just the way it should be," Terry optimistically observed. "The two challengers pulling out on their trial horses." So much for the status of

The rubber duck, laden with sails, Jay McKinnell, Fran Ford, and Rob Webb.

Advance. Jeff Boyd found it hard to draw conclusions about the other boats, but there was growing suspicion about *Canada 1*'s North 2.1 mainsail. For the past few days, it had been compiling a disturbing performance record.

But the mainsail problems did not end there. Richard Storer called Doug Keary about progress on still more repairs to the S2.1 mainsail, which were being performed at the Sobstad loft in Connecticut. The sail would be ready in a few days, and Tom Whidden was in Newport with some cloth samples for Keary to see. Whidden didn't want to come to the Canadian base. Would Keary meet him in a bar? Keary, who more than any other person was keeping the Canadian challenge on its feet, consented.

Wednesday, June 15. It had been planned all week to stage a dress rehearsal of *Canada 1*'s first trial race. Both 12-Metres were off the dock at 8:30. Once on Rhode Island Sound, Mark Millen in *Slapshot II* set a starting line and Shep Higley in the Rocket laid the racing buoys. Millen had been employing the same code flags lately that would be used by the race committee in the trials so that the crew would be accustomed to its signals. Two Ton had managed to memorize every code flag. Jeff Boyd was working on it.

Millen gave an 11-minute, then a 10-minute starting signal over the radio. The boats approached each other from their assigned ends of the starting line, dipping into the "cone" from the windward side of the line. McLaughlin and Boyd had been winning the majority of starts, for a number of reasons. Not the least, *Canada 1* was more manoeuvrable than most 12-Metres, *Clipper* included. But Dave Miller and Jamie Kidd were further handicapped by the fact that they still weren't as familiar with the breed of yacht as Boyd and McLaughlin.

Canada 1 usually achieved a quick advantage, and sometimes McLaughlin would throw a start to see if he could come back from a disadvantage. Today was such a day, but *Canada 1* was unable to recover. *Canada 1* then won the next two practice starts, but in the subsequent race *Clipper* sailed well to round the weather mark slightly ahead of *Canada 1*, then opened up a little on the reaches and a lot on the second beat. Whenever a boat was well ahead at the end of the run during practice, it was customary to stop the race and start another one. The race was scrubbed. *Canada 1* had been unable to pass *Clipper* all day.

Back on shore, Dave Miller, Jamie Kidd and Jeff Boyd gazed at *Canada 1's* mast. With full rig tension, it was dead straight.

"Most of the 12-Metre masts here in Newport are pre-bent under tension," Boyd observed.

Jamie Kidd agreed. "Maybe if we angled the spreaders back . . ."

McLaughlin joined the group. "No way," he said. "The mast is too soft already." Nothing was resolved.

Bruce Kirby approached Dave Miller and Jeff Boyd. "Why's *Canada 1* not going well?" he asked. Miller shrugged. Boyd looked away. Who knew? Boyd and Miller were worried. The first race was on Saturday, three days away. Now was not the best time for *Canada 1* to start going slow.

On Thursday *Canada 1* still was not going fast. New problems were coming to light which, in retrospect, were probably old problems – it had just taken till then to identify them. *Canada 1* was not pointing well, and Terry McLaughlin was unhappy with the mast; reinforcing placed along the front near the spinnaker pole butt hoist to repair the cracked wall had made the lower section excessively stiff.

The butt hoist itself was a problem. The boat was supposed to be equipped with a custom-designed system from Bob Whitehouse and Klacko. It had not materialized, so the inboard end of the spinnaker pole had to be hoisted up and down with a jury-rig cleated line. From time to time the rope would slip the cleat and the pole end would come slamming down. Fortunately no one had yet been hurt in the process. (Jeff Boyd had had the weighty pole glance off his back; Dave Shaw caught it with his shoulder once and nonchalantly stood up and pushed it back into place.)

By mid-afternoon, racing between *Canada 1* and *Clipper* was abandoned in favour of side-by-side tuning. Terry McLaughlin transferred to the Rocket to inspect the sails. *Clipper* still seemed to be moving better, and Rob Muru began to experiment with the rake of *Canada 1*'s mast. Rake had been a persistent problem, because every mainsail in their inventory had a different leech length (all were usually too short) and it seemed that they were never able to sheet the outboard end of the boom down to deck level. At six o'clock and at least an hour from home, *Canada 1* and *Clipper* headed in.

Terry McLaughlin and Dave Miller were ferried in aboard the Rocket to represent *Canada 1* at a party thrown by the Aga Khan. The Italians had been racing the French all week in a best-of-seven tune-up series. Each race *France 3* would win the start, only to have *Azzurra* grind her down. Today *Azzurra* had clinched the series, 4-1.

Back at Sherman House, Marvin McDill was hosting an 8:30 dinner for the entire Canadian squad. *Canada 1* was hauled and scrubbed down, and her crew made the McDill good-luck feast just in time. Terry McLaughlin, back from the Italian festivities, was pleased to report that he shook the hand of the Aga Khan.

Six months earlier, Jeff Boyd had told Terry McLaughlin that, no matter what, the crew should take the day off before the first race. Unsure of their speed, they reconsidered, and elected to sail for a few hours the following morning.

Friday, June 17, brought dense fog to Rhode Island Sound. *Clipper* and *Canada 1* headed out anyway, with only about six sailors on board each boat. Tom Corness had not wanted them to leave dock, with 12 hours of scheduled work still to be done on the boat before the first race the next day.

At one o'clock the two yachts picked up tows and returned home. The wind had been light and variable, which made it difficult to draw conclusions, but it had seemed that *Canada 1* and *Clipper* had been more equal. Still, there was the feeling aboard *Canada 1* that the crew of *Clipper*, wanting so badly for *Canada 1* to prove superior, might have been unconsciously sandbagging.

Back on shore, there was pandemonium, the entire base attacking last-minute jobs. Terry McLaughlin and Jeff Boyd read the race instructions one last time. Shortly before four o'clock, they headed over to the Ida Lewis Yacht Club, the summer station of the New York Yacht Club, for the skippers' meeting.

The Ida Lewis Yacht Club is a smallish building, resting on a rock at the south end of Newport Harbour. It is joined to land by a 150-yard-long causeway. From the shore end of the causeway, Boyd and McLaughlin could

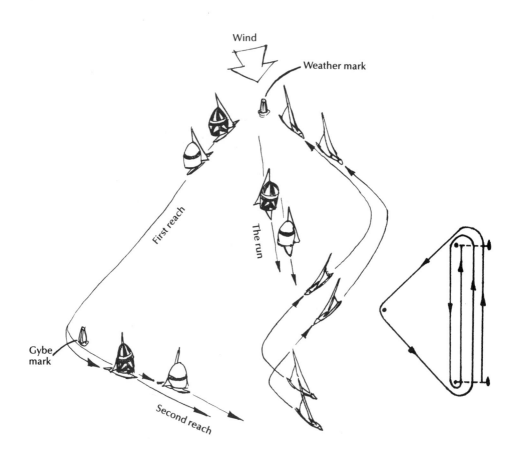

see an enormous crowd milling on the rock. Upon arriving at the clubhouse, they were surrounded by the press.

"What do you think about meeting *Australia II* in the first race?" asked one reporter. Microphones appeared out of thin air and were poked in front of McLaughlin. Boyd looked around for familiar faces.

"We just got here," Terry replied, surprised. "When was the draw?"

"Just a few minutes ago."

"Well, we're psyched," offered Terry. "Might as well meet the best first." For the next half hour, McLaughlin and Boyd were hounded by reporters and television cameras. They began to wonder what had happened to the skippers' meeting.

Jeff Boyd gains a spreader's-eye view of a start, while Challenge 12 *cruises by.*

At 4:45 the meeting began – without the press. What should have been a basic review of the racing procedures dragged on to well after six o'clock. The British, with their "sea lawyer" Brian Willis, nitpicked everything. They also announced that, contrary to the nationality rules, they would have an Australian in their crew for Series A, and wondered if anyone had any objections. There were none. And, for the past few weeks, the British had been trying to enter both *Victory* and *Victory 83* in the trials under the banner of the Royal Burnham Yacht Club. The Canadians thought it meant the British were still unsure which boat was faster. The British plan was disallowed, and they opted for *Victory 83*.

With the nitpicking continuing, Terry McLaughlin suggested to the group that they should stop the ridiculous questions so that they could get out of the yacht club sometime that night. Shortly thereafter, the meeting concluded. Boyd and McLaughlin returned to Sherman House and let the camp know who their first opponent would be. Following dinner, everyone in the house went to bed. Down at the yard, repairs continued on *Canada 1*.

The round-robin draw had pitted *Canada 1* against the two toughest foreign challengers for Saturday, June 18 – *Australia II*, and then *Challenge 12*. After

Australia II, *with her distinctive radial clew sails*

breakfast, Doug Keary explained who was slotted into what responsibility for the next few days and concluded with a pep talk. The team uniform for the day was announced as come-as-you-are, with no specific colour requirements.

Canada 1 left dock under tow at 8:30, right on schedule. Rhode Island Sound was socked in with dense fog. *Slapshot II* towed *Canada 1* to the rendezvous buoy "Alpha," where they waited for visibility to improve. In what would become a daily race habit, Mark Millen then slowly brought *Canada 1* past the "Alpha" buoy so that Two Ton could check his Loran readings.

The crew was anxious to begin racing. It had taken them more than a year of training to reach this point, and now they were forced to wait until they could see where they were going. To keep their minds at ease, Terry McLaughlin and Jeff Boyd played euchre against Phil Gow and Fran Ford.

There was a large spectator fleet in motion, always heard but never seen. Fog horns moaned everywhere in varying pitches. Occasionally a deep, extended blast would sound, marking the presence of Peter de Savary's *Kalizma*, a luxury power yacht once owned by Richard Burton and Elizabeth Taylor. Every now and then another 12-Metre would ghost into their field of vision, only to be enveloped once again by the fog. They could see about 100 yards. Being new at this sort of racing, the Canadians weren't sure how much visibility was needed to start a race. Logically it would have to be about 400 yards, the length of the starting line.

Shortly past noon, the fog lifted enough that *Canada 1* and *Clipper* hoisted sails and began pacing upwind. The air was light, a marginal #2 headsail breeze, the water blue-grey and glassy. A mile from the starting line, they decided to head back.

Course signals were displayed by the race committee at 12:30; *Canada 1* would start at one o'clock. The delay caused by the fog meant that there would be only one heat of races over the 14-mile short courses being used for Series A. The Canadians lazed on the sidelines, watching *Challenge 12* and *Victory 83* start, then turned their attention to their own start. They had been assigned the port end of the starting line for the ten-minute gun, and McLaughlin and Boyd decided that, after the start, they should sail to the right, where the fog seemed to be clearing and the wind was likely to freshen.

The gun sounded. With ten minutes to go, *Canada 1* slid by the mark and into the starting area. Boyd was nervous, and he knew he wasn't the only jumpy person on board. They sailed by *Australia II* to leeward, their eyes fixed on John Bertrand and his crew. Whatever Bertrand did next, they wanted to duplicate.

Australia II started to come about. *Canada 1* slammed into a tack, while the Australians broke off the tack and gybed. A classic fake. *Canada 1* laid off on starboard and gybed back onto port tack, only to discover that *Australia II*, incredibly, had completed her gybe, tacked, and was steaming at the Canadians on starboard, forcing them to gybe onto the same tack.

This didn't help the confidence of *Canada 1*'s crew. All the rumours, the hype, the speculation, were true. *Australia II* could spin on a dime, like no other 12-Metre. With eight and a half minutes to go in the start sequence and only half a circle completed, *Australia II* was locked on *Canada 1*'s tail.

Terry McLaughlin remained cool. He ran downwind for a time, then turned and parked head-to-wind. Intelligence from Bruce Kirby had it that, while *Australia II* could spin, her smaller underwater profile area meant that she was prone to going sideways when stalled. After a few minutes of luffing, *Canada 1* was on the verge of losing steerage, but *Australia II* was falling off to leeward.

Terry McLaughlin called for the genoa to be backed to push *Canada 1*'s bow over onto starboard tack. But the crew confused the order, backing the jib the wrong way, and *Canada 1* fell over onto port tack and into serious trouble. It was painful to watch *Australia II* slowly approach on starboard as they struggled to accelerate on port. All that preparation, and the Canadians were about to be disqualified from their first race for a port-starboard incident! Fortunately *Canada 1* moved enough to avoid *Australia II* and regained enough confidence (how could they do worse) to manage an even start.

But it was a far from perfect start. *Canada 1* crossed the line going to the left, contrary to the game plan. The sail trimmers were nervous, a condition that usually results in overtrimmed sails, and for some time the boat sailed below target speed; it was five minutes before the crew settled down.

After going right, *Australia II* came back at the Canadians on starboard tack. As Boyd and McLaughlin had predicted, the wind clocked and built, but to the Australian advantage. Boosted by the 25-degree wind shift, *Australia II* rounded the weather mark 1:45 ahead. On the first reaching leg, the Canadians changed spinnakers, "peeling" to a ¾-ounce, then watched the Australians execute a flawless gybe peel at the gybe mark. There was no confusing the seamanship of the two boats. The Australians were ready to win the America's Cup. The Canadians were ready to regroup. Though the wind built to 15 knots on the second beat, it was of no use to *Canada 1*, which eventually rolled in a distant 2:42 behind *Australia II*.

Back on shore, the crew debriefed with Doug Keary, Bruce Kirby and Dave Miller. All came to the conclusion that crew skills had not looked sharp and that they had lost the most ground on the major shift on the first leg. Keary informed them that Marvin McDill had been upset by the crew's rag-tag appearance. A dress code for *Canada 1* was duly enforced.

In other races that day, *Challenge 12* had bested *Victory 83* by 2:03; *France 3* had fallen to *Azzurra* by 1:34. *Advance* had enjoyed a bye for the first day. In the American trials, *Courageous* had defeated *Liberty*, which had flown a questionable sail inventory and was suspected, loudly, of sandbagging by Tom Blackaller (Dennis Conner had also been accused of sandbagging in losing the first trial race of 1980, supposedly to mask his yacht's true capabilities).

On the way home, Terry McLaughlin crossed paths with Blackaller, who was curious about how his race had gone.

"It wasn't much of a race," said McLaughlin," since we lost by 2:42."

Blackaller was shocked. "In 12s that's very far off the pace. Especially on a short course."

That night Jeff Boyd wrote in his diary, "We sailed slow and sloppy against the best."

Sunday, June 19, was foggy and damp. The only real change from the previous day was the red shirts and white pants being sported by the crew of

Canada 1 *leading* Advance

Canada 1. After reaching the "Alpha" buoy, *Slapshot II* anchored, and the crew of *Canada 1* sat, waiting. *Clipper* had not joined them; its mast needed repairs. The boredom of the long wait for the weather to improve was broken by playing cards. *Canada 1* and *Challenge 12* were scheduled for the first start; whenever the visibility improved slightly, Two Ton would suggest that they hoist sail. They didn't move.

Suddenly there was a gun. Course signals were displayed. The crew of *Canada 1* scrambled to hoist the mainsail and prepare to race. With visibility having improved to only 300 yards, it was difficult to make out both ends of the starting line. Regardless, they were soon into a starting sequence. *Challenge 12* was not aggressive, breaking off with *Canada 1* two minutes before the gun, and Terry McLaughlin was able to start ahead and to leeward.

After only a few minutes of sailing in the 15-knot breeze, however, it was evident that *Canada 1* was about to be rolled by *Challenge 12*. McLaughlin spun into a quick tack, narrowly missing *Challenge 12's* transom. The Australians waited 15 seconds, then tacked to cover and began working out to windward.

The two boats split tacks. When they crossed again, John Savage ham-

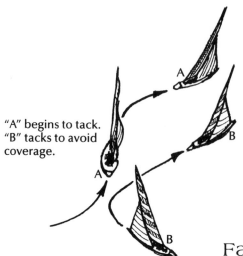

"A" begins to tack.
"B" tacks to avoid
coverage.

"A", instead of completing
tack, falls back onto
course, trapping "B" in
a windward cover.

Fake Tack

mered *Canada 1*, tacking directly on her air. The Canadians tacked away.
Challenge 12 followed and seemed to gain on every subsequent tack.

Despite trying an assortment of jibs and initiating a flurry of tacks on the
final beat, *Canada 1* was demolished by *Challenge 12*. Back on shore there
was another debriefing, attended by Doug Keary, Bruce Kirby, Terry
McLaughlin, Jeff Boyd, Dave Miller, a visiting Peter Hall and Marvin McDill.
Despite the 2:01 loss, McDill found pleasure in the improved crew attire. It
was concluded that their sails might be too full, hence the problem pointing.
They would also try to get the Klacko mast, now repaired with a new lower
section from Alcan Canada, back in the boat.

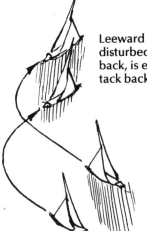

A boat protects one
side of the course
by covering loosely
on one tack and
closely on the other
to encourage the
trailing opposition
to sail away from
the favoured side.

Leeward boat, delivered
disturbed air on port
back, is encouraged to
tack back, onto port.

Leeward boat has clear
air, is encouraged to
stay on starboard tack.

Back at the base, a disgruntled Terry McLaughlin informed Gord Smeaton that he was not interested in talking with anyone. Nonetheless a Canadian Press reporter caught up with Terry while he was inspecting the trim tab of *Canada 1* as the boat hung in the Travelift. McLaughlin told him he had nothing to say. "I'll talk to you when we win," he managed.

Monday, June 20. *Canada 1* would race against *Advance* and then *France 3*, both of which were also winless. The previous day, gear failure had forced *France 3* to forfeit its race against *Victory 83*; *Advance* had lost by a colossal 3:57 to *Australia II* and was fast establishing her reputation as the dog of the challenge fleet.

Although there was no fog on Monday, there wasn't any wind either. Again the prescribed starting time of 11 o'clock passed without activity. Finally, after one o'clock, racing began. The wind had filled in from the southeast, with a tremendous sheer: it clocked 20 knots at the masthead, but there seemed to be half as much on the water. After some deliberation, the Canadians selected their N32 headsail, a vertical-cut Mylar genoa.

With the word out that *Advance* was a sitting duck, and with *Canada 1* badly in need of a win for fund-raising and morale purposes, the pressure was on the Canadians. They decided to jump all over *Advance* at the start, to show it no mercy. It was the one and only time the Australian boat attempted to manoeuvre with *Canada 1* during a pre-start. Jeff Boyd found it difficult to believe how awkward the boat was. After forcing *Advance* to be late at the committee boat end, *Canada 1* crossed the starting line safely ahead and to leeward.

The Canadians had heard tales of *Advance* being so tender that whenever it blew 15 knots the Alan Payne design would lie over and fill up with water. Here we are, considered Boyd, with 15 knots of wind, and *Advance* isn't filling up. She wasn't going all that slowly either, but gradually *Canada 1* began to pull away.

So arose Jeff Boyd's first crucial decision of the Newport summer. "Can we tack and cross them?" Terry McLaughlin asked.

Boyd studied the bearing. "Yes."

McLaughlin sailed on some more. "Are you *sure?*"

"Yeah, I'm sure."

McLaughlin still sailed on. "Are you sure we can tack and cross?" he persisted.

"Terry, *tack*. We'll cross."

Terry tacked. The crew of *Advance* immediately began shouting, "Starboard!" Was it a bluff or were they serious? The sailors aboard *Advance* seemed to believe there would be a collision. Boyd was sure Murray had thought he had *Canada 1* pinned. Unlike the Canadians, the *Advance* crew didn't seem to have a grasp of what one could and could not do with a 12-Metre. Twelve-Metres tack through 70 to 80 degrees. Was Murray's mind still back in his Australian 18, which tacks through 90 degrees like most other boats? *Canada 1* cleared *Advance*'s bow with one and a half lengths to spare.

When *Canada 1* tacked to cover, *Advance* promptly tacked away, to stay out of phase. They continued to split tacks for several more crossings. Then McLaughlin had had enough and executed a fake tack. *Advance* fell for it, tacking into phase with *Canada 1*. Positioned directly on *Advance*'s wind, *Canada 1* had the race in the bag and went on to win by 1:56.

The French were next. With *France 3* crossing the line early, *Canada 1* began the race with a lead of well over a minute. However, in light air and flat water, the French staged a frightening comeback, trailing by only three lengths at the weather mark. On the second beat, the Canadians built a comfortable lead by consistently protecting the right side of the course, tacking directly on *France 3*'s wind whenever she tried to sail on port tack, covering her loosely on starboard. With the wind dying, *Canada 1* began to race more against the clock than against *France 3*. Beginning the final leg, Two Ton predicted it would be close. The clock won, by about one minute. With the time limit up, the race was abandoned. It would be resailed the next day.

The victory over *Advance* and the near win over *France 3* gave the Canadians a touch more confidence, but neither Terry McLaughlin nor Jeff Boyd was happy with their boat-speed. They did not return to dock until 7:30; by then most of the shore staff had left for Sherman House. Back on land, they learned that all hell had broken loose in the newspapers back home over Terry McLaughlin's offhand comment to the CP reporter. Terry had come across like a spoiled child. Doug Keary and Marvin McDill were not pleased, and the fund-raisers were livid. With Terry.

Tuesday, June 21, was pleasantly sunny, and there was another lengthy wait for racing to begin before the breeze filled in from the west at six to eight knots. For the rematch with *France 3*, Terry McLaughlin had shuffled almost the entire crew of *Canada 1* with the exception of the afterguard. McLaughlin was brilliant on the starting line, protecting his access to the right side of the course. At the gun, *Canada 1* was heading right on port tack. *France 3* followed for a time, then tacked away. *Canada 1* sailed into an accommodating shift and tacked just shy of the lay-line.

With an enormous lead at the weather mark, *Canada 1* executed a gybe set with the spinnaker to begin the second leg of the windward-leeward-windward course. *France 3* closed on the run, and on the final beat the Canadians threw themselves a scare by tinkering with headsails. *France 3*

Doug Keary

closed substantially, and *Canada 1* switched from their full Mylar cross-cut S12 to a flatter N32 better suited to the equally flat water. The Canadians won by 1:27.

Terry McLaughlin and Jeff Boyd were becoming increasingly confident about their starting skills and were determined that, in the race against *Azzurra* the next day, they would fix on the Italian yacht's tail as soon as possible. In conditions that were *Azzurra's* forte, light air and flat water, it took *Canada 1* half a circle to do so. The Canadians controlled *Azzurra* for the entire start sequence, forcing her to start late at the committee boat end of the line, as they had with *Advance*.

As soon as they cleared the starting line, the Italians changed genoas and initiated an intense tacking duel. Realizing that *Azzurra* was gaining substantially, *Canada 1* broke off the duel, altering the nature of the game so that they simply protected the right side of the course. The strategy worked and *Canada 1* led at the weather mark by over a minute. Plagued by poor crew work and mechanical problems that included a spinnaker which refused to come down, the Italians faded. *Canada 1* collected a convincing 2:34 victory.

After five days of racing, *Australia II* and *Challenge 12* topped the standings at 5-0 and 5-1 respectively, *Canada 1* and *Victory 83* were tied at 3-2, *Azzurra* and *France 3* had 1-4 records, and *Advance* was winless at 0-5.

At the debriefing following the win over *Azzurra*, the Canadians decided to change masts, pulling out the old Proctor spar in favour of the newly repaired Klacko. It was not an entirely popular decision. Peter Wilson, for one, was furious. He was certain it would cost them a race and was concerned about getting the masthead sensors on the new rig to work properly. They were on a winning streak. Why risk spoiling it? Although a loss in Series A would make little difference in the overall process to determine the four semi-finalists (only 20 per cent of accumulated points would be carried forward into Series B), it could be damaging from the ever-present fund-raising point of view. But *Canada 1's* three victories had come against the weaker contenders. If the Canadians were to start winning against *Australia II*, *Victory 83* and *Challenge 12*, something would have to change. And the easiest problem to rectify was the mast.

While *Canada 1* had been racing, Doug Keary had been meeting with Russell Long. Convinced that *Clipper* was the fastest 12-Metre in Newport, Long wanted to lease her back and enter her in the American defence trials. As he explained, he could find sailors by raiding Dennis Conner's camp for disgruntled crew members, particularly of *Liberty's* trial horse, *Freedom*. The Canadians would continue to maintain *Clipper*, and Long's people would share the sail loft facilities out at the roller rink.

Long wasn't offering much in the way of money. What he was offering was sail technology. He could get great sails for himself, he assured Keary, from the North lofts in California. And while these sails were lying around the roller rink, the Canadians could learn volumes about the latest thinking in design and construction. The payoff in allowing Long to use *Clipper* would not be in money but in sail technology.

It was, Keary had to admit, tempting. Tempting but *crazy*. Long's plan was a perfect illustration of the kind of goofy thinking that the America's Cup encouraged in otherwise competent individuals. The scheme never would have been approved by the New York Yacht Club, which abhorred any relationship between challenge and defence candidates.

When Doug Keary turned down Russell Long without consulting with Marvin McDill, the Calgary lawyer made his displeasure known.

Thursday, June 23. The Canadian maintenance team had been up all night making the mast switch. The installation of the Klacko spar was completed at seven o'clock in the morning; and an hour and a half later, with no time to tune the rig properly, *Canada 1* left dock to race *Victory 83* and *Australia II*.

With 15 to 18 knots of wind, a short, steep sea was running on the Sound. The day was sunny, and hot. On the way out of Newport Harbor, *Canada 1*, under tow, was passed by an inbound *Bluenose II*. The schooner, on a goodwill tour for the province of Nova Scotia, fired a one-gun salute. For most of the trip out to the race course, Sandy Andrews was aloft in the bosun's chair, making frantic, last-minute adjustments to the new rig. The British tender, *Revenge*, gleaming blue and gold, followed astern, towing both *Victory 83* and *Australia*. *Australia II* passed close by under tow and hoisted one of Tom Schnackenberg's flawless vertical-cut mainsails.

In no time tow lines were dropped and the contenders began to limber up. *Australia* and *Victory 83* sliced through the chop, with *Victory 83* flying a full Mylar/Kevlar mainsail that was, for all intents and purposes, inside-out with the backwind from the genoa. The next time she passed by the Canadians, *Victory 83* had dropped her vertical-cut headsail and Mylar/Kevlar mainsail for an all-Kevlar inventory. The British yacht looked exquisitely tuned, the seas sending shock waves through the ripples in the luff of her mainsail.

A few minutes after 11 o'clock, the first race of the day began. *Advance* and *Azzurra* approached the line, side by side on starboard tack. Both were a minute early. *Advance*, furthest to the left, bore away and gybed; *Azzurra* tacked. The two yachts then headed for the line on port. *Azzurra* would lead by 23 seconds at the weather mark and go on to win by 1:28.

Canada 1 was struggling. In the tune-up for her race, half of the mainsail was backwinding, and Jeff Boyd reported that the jumper struts, which controlled the bend of the top of the mast, should be angled forward another 15 degrees.

At 11:25, *France 3* and *Australia II* started. The Australian contender nosed across the starting line at full speed on port tack, near the race committee. *France 3*, attempting to stay clear of *Australia II*, had tacked shortly before the gun onto starboard near the starting mark, six seconds behind.

Victory 83 was nearly a minute late entering the starting area against *Canada 1*, and its performance over the next nine minutes bordered on inept. It was almost as though the British thought the start didn't matter, being supremely confident of their speed. *Canada 1* drove *Victory 83* over to the left side of the starting area, outside the cone, then tacked onto port for the starting mark. *Victory 83* paraded in her wake, nine seconds behind.

As soon as they were over the starting line, the British threw a false tack, which the Canadians bought, leaving themselves foolishly sailing off on starboard tack while *Victory 83* stormed away into clear air on port.

When *Canada 1* tacked back to cover, its afterguard quickly realized how slowly the boat was moving. The leeward shrouds were loose, and *Canada 1* fell into *Victory 83*'s wake. When the British tacked back, they were able to cross the Canadians. Further up the course *Australia II* was rounding the weather mark a full minute ahead of *France 3*.

At the weather mark, it was *Victory 83* by 33 seconds; by 34 seconds at the gybe; and by 41 seconds at the leeward mark. On the second windward leg, *Canada 1* initiated a tacking duel, and *Victory 83* added another minute to her lead. *Australia II* defeated *France 3* by 1:35. *Canada 1* trailed *Victory 83* across the finish line by 2:30.

At the end of the race, Dave Miller radioed *Canada 1* to discuss their problems. Rig tension was too loose, and Miller noted that the mast had been too straight, hence the excessive fullness in the mainsail. Terry McLaughlin transferred aboard *Slapshot II* to radio the race committee that *Canada 1* would need a delay in the start of her next race. Back on board, the mast was lowered and turns were taken on the shrouds. New mast step plates were ordered from Bob Whitehouse, and a heavier North mainsail was brought aboard.

Canada 1 was rolling side to side, running through the short, steep seas, dodging the lobster pots that dotted the race course. While the crew raised the new mainsail, the halyard car tore away the top two feet of track on the mast. Sandy Andrews was despatched over 80 feet aloft with a hacksaw to make repairs. A small runabout from the *Australia II* camp hovered nearby. The task was hopeless. *Canada 1* forfeited the race; *Australia II* sailed the course alone and added another win to her collection. *Victory 83* defeated *Challenge 12* to improve her record to 5-2. *Canada 1*, tied with the British at the beginning of the day, fell to 3-4.

Canada 1 was towed back to dock for repairs. Terry McLaughlin and Jeff

Boyd hopped aboard the Rocket to watch *Liberty* and *Defender* race. Competition was much closer than over on the challengers' course. They weren't sure what to make of that. Back at the shipyard, the maintenance crew prepared for another unbroken night of repairs to *Canada 1*.

Friday, June 24. *Canada 1* was lowered back into the water shortly before eight o'clock and was under tow by nine. The Rocket raced out of Newport Harbor with Jay McKinnell aboard for a day of videotaping on the American race course. The Rocket's crew, Jimmy Johnston and Shep Higley, had equipped themselves with Trivial Pursuit cards to help pass the time while Jay Bondo carried on with his espionage duties.

In a little more than an hour, *Canada 1* was out on the race course. The wind had built to 15 knots, the seas were lumpy. The rig seemed better tuned, but Jeff Boyd had to report that the foot of the mast was twisting five degrees with every tack or gybe; Bob Whitehouse would be ferried out between races to take measurements in order to modify the mast step.

The start, as was becoming a habit, went to *Canada 1* in her first race of the day. The Canadians held *Challenge 12* off to leeward, below the race committee, then tacked onto port to cross the line with a nine-second lead. The opening leg of the windward-leeward-windward course was a pitched battle, with *Canada 1* resorting to every possible tactic to keep a slippery *Challenge 12* under wraps.

The Canadians rounded the weather mark with a narrow lead. *Canada 1* then gybed before hoisting the spinnaker, assuming that *Challenge 12* would do the same, but the Australians simply bore off and hoisted, sailing away from the Canadians. *Challenge 12* proceeded to sail slightly faster and smarter down the leeward leg, and succeeded in securing an inside overlap at the mark. On the final beat, *Challenge 12* opened up a greater lead in the ensuing tacking duel and won by 47 seconds. At the finish *Canada 1* was flying a protest over an incident during the pre-start manoeuvres.

The second race of the day was against *Advance*, which had begun to modify its starting strategy. Unable to manoeuvre with the other 12-Metres, its crew opted to run away from the line in a classic "Vanderbilt" strategy, turning back only when there was just enough time to return to the line. In a starting area crowded with spectator craft, *Canada 1* followed *Advance* away from the line, then parked on her wind to take the start by one second.

Although a weak performer off the wind, *Advance* was capable of showing a creditable turn of speed upwind, and it was only a matter of time before she caught a competitor unawares and collected her first win. It was not to come today, however. Apart from a strong windshift to the left, atypical of Newport, the race was uneventful. *Canada 1* led by 33 seconds at the windward mark, and steadily opened up to win by 1:33.

It had been a long day. Terry McLaughlin and Jeff Boyd were whisked ashore to fill out their protest against *Challenge 12*, which they then decided to drop. It was dinner time when *Canada 1* slipped past Castle Hill under tow by *Slapshot II*. There was barely a breath of wind; *Bluenose II*, with a full spread of canvas, was motoring through the harbour, packed to the rails with sightseers.

Back at the shipyard were Bill Cox and several busloads of Labatt's employees. It had been decided by the *Toronto Star*, Labatt's and the challenge's management that *Canada 1* and *Bluenose II* sailing together would make a terrific publicity shot. A *Star* photographer was placed in the rubber duck and shipped out, and the operations base contacted the skipper of *Bluenose II* to explain what they had in mind.

But the crew of *Canada 1* didn't want any part of it. They were exhausted and had just finished packing away the sails and tidying the deck. Jeff Boyd was put on the radio by Doug Keary to tell the crew to rehoist the sails.

The crew attempted to evade the duty by explaining that Sandy Andrews was still aloft, repairing the spinnaker halyard exit. There was also no wind, they pointed out. It didn't matter. They still had to do it.

"Is that an order?" asked Al Megarry.

Boyd had not enjoyed being forced into this confrontation. "Yeah," he replied, "it is."

Slapshot II towed *Canada 1* around to the windward side of *Bluenose II*, while an annoyed group of sailors unpacked the sails and raised them for the photographer. "I understand the picture is going on the new dime," Doug Keary joked over the radio, "and if it's really good they'll use it on the new quarter." It did little to reduce the tension aboard *Canada 1*.

The shooting completed, Mark Millen moved *Slapshot II* alongside *Canada 1* to reattach the tow rope. "You didn't smile!" he shouted to the crew.

Eric Jespersen spoke for many aboard *Canada 1*. "I should have done *this*." He jabbed a middle finger into the air.

Back on shore, Bill Cox delivered Jeff Boyd a stiff lecture about how poorly Terry McLaughlin was coming across in the press. He offered a few corrective suggestions. Fund-raising, he stressed, depended on good public relations.

When *Canada 1* finally reached the base, the docks were lined with Labatt's personnel, who broke into applause. Jeff Boyd appeared to help carry the sails back into the sail trailer. The Labatt's people boarded their Bluebird buses and headed out for dinner.

The photo of *Canada 1* and *Bluenose II* ran in colour on the front page of the Sunday edition of the *Star*, Canada's largest newspaper.

Saturday, June 25. In winds of 25 knots out of the northwest, *Canada 1* was towed out for her only race of the day, against *France 3*. Opting for a heavy-

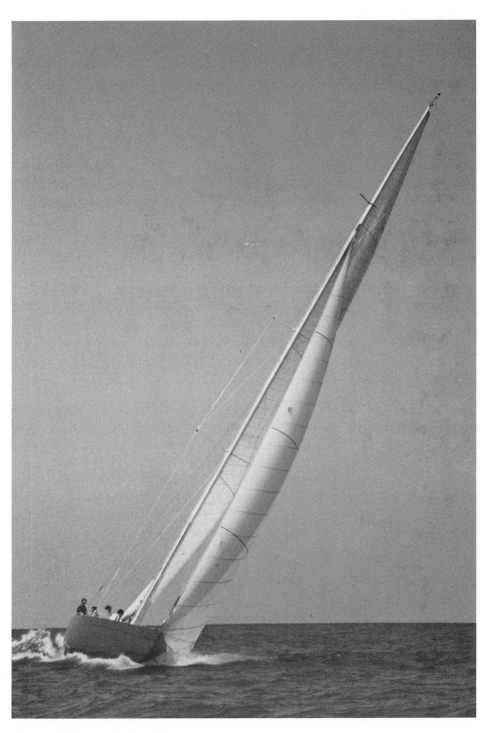

Clipper *driving to windward*

air Sobstad mainsail, *Canada 1* attempted to hook up with *Clipper* for some upwind pacing, but with gusts in excess of 30 knots, they elected to drop their sails, pick up a tow from *Slapshot II* and wait for conditions to improve.

When the wind slowed to 18 knots, the race committee set the challengers off on a windward-leeward-windward course. On board the committee boat was Robin Wynne-Edwards, *Canada 1*'s newly appointed race committee representative. Decked out in jacket and tie, he cut a fine figure among the veterans aboard the launch.

Canada 1 managed an even start against *France 3*, but the French were moving well in the breeze and rounded the weather mark with a four-length lead. After a terrific gybe set, the Canadians steadily gained on the run but fell shy of establishing an overlap. On the beat to the finish, *Canada 1* tacked 51 times in a futile effort to break through. *France 3* won by 52 seconds.

The final duel had only served to emphasize *Canada 1*'s increasingly evident problems tacking. The jib didn't pass through the foretriangle well, its leech impeded by halyards, spreaders, the pole butt hoist and just about everything else on the mast. Once through the foretriangle, the jib did not sheet in smoothly; and once sheeted, the boat accelerated poorly. During the end-of-day debriefing, the problems were discussed in detail. Dave Miller stuck to a longstanding theory of his, pointing to the mainsail inventory as the culprit.

Sunday, June 26. In light air and flat water, *Canada 1* lost her last two races of Series A. *Azzurra* took advantage of a mistake by *Canada 1* on the starting line and never looked back, winning by 1:42. The Canadians won the start against *Victory 83* and rounded only two lengths behind at the weather mark, but the British steamed away on the run to amass a winning margin of 1:15. The losses dropped *Canada 1* to 4-8 and a dismal tie for fifth place with *France 3*, behind *Australia II* (11-1), *Challenge 12* (10-2), *Victory 83* (8-4) and *Azzurra* (5-7). Only sorry *Advance*, at 0-12, had fared worse.

A plan of attack was drawn up for the five precious days separating Series A from Series B. They would order some new mainsails and recut the existing ones to a flatter shape. The mast would be moved forward, in the hope of improving tacking by simultaneously moving the centre of effort forward and relieving pressure on the helm coming out of the tack (Terry McLaughlin received the suggestion from *Freedom*'s mainsail trimmer over a few beers at the Raw Bar).

It had been a productive meeting. Though he realized they still had a long way to go, Jeff Boyd had been encouraged by the resolutions. Later in the summer, looking back on that meeting, he considered that it was always easier to *talk* about doing well than actually going out and doing well.

That night, an enormous seafood feast was held by the *Defender/Coura-*

geous effort at the Oceancliff mansion near Castle Hill, featuring a Dixieland band and upwards of 700 guests. Conspicuously absent was any member of Dennis Conner's *Liberty* syndicate. At the party, John Bertrand, 11-1, bumped into Terry McLaughlin, 4-8. "I guess you guys are getting some sails soon," the Australian skipper managed. McLaughlin guessed so.

Monday, June 27. While *Canada 1*'s mast was moved, Terry McLaughlin and Jeff Boyd met with Bruce Kirby and Doug Keary. The session degenerated into finger-pointing. Kirby blamed the sails and the sail trimmers for the boat's poor performance. Boyd and McLaughlin hinted that they weren't especially happy that *Canada 1* was so different from conventional 12-Metres like *Azzurra*, *Clipper* and *Victory 83* below the waterline. The steep leading edge on the keel was of extreme annoyance to Terry.

The next day there was ceaseless rain. *Canada 1* ventured out to perform hundreds of tacks with *Clipper*. No conclusions were reached. At the end of the day, Peter Wilson and Jeff Boyd contacted Steve Killing, who was in Annapolis establishing a computer software service for yacht designers with his partner, George Hazen. The two sailors wanted his opinion on the use of the trim tab during a tack.

As Killing explained, the trim tab was a high-lift, high-drag device – it generated extra lift in the keel, while at the same time slowing the boat down a bit. A classic trade-off. There were a lot of theories on what to do with the trim tab in a tack, partly because its use did vary from one 12-Metre to another. (*Courageous* used sensors on her trim tab to monitor its performance.) The trick, Killing thought, was putting the trim tab on at precisely the right time when coming out of the tack. He advised keeping it neutral when falling onto the new tack, and not putting it back on until the boat had regained its target speed. The only problem with that strategy, Killing admitted, was that without the trim tab you were forced to use more rudder, which only served to create drag.

And then Peter Wilson had a brainstorm. The boat-speed display reading on *Canada 1*'s Ockam instruments was based on a 10-second averaging of data. Thus, the indicated speed when falling onto a new tack was not the speed at that exact moment, but an averaging that took into account the speed of the yacht throughout the entire tack. Therein lay a critical danger in steering by the Numbers. If the instruments were telling the skipper that his speed was lower than usual falling onto the new tack, his normal reaction would be to lay the boat off further, building speed while losing precious distance to windward. But what if the boat was actually accelerating as it should and the instruments, relying on a 10-second averaging, were telling the skipper that it wasn't? The skipper would be needlessly laying the boat off.

Peter Wilson changed the averaging from ten seconds to two. Although the display readings were now more erratic, they gave a better indication of what the boat was up to at the precise moment one looked at the instruments. It was an improvement, but unfortunately it far from solved *Canada 1*'s tacking problem.

For June 29 and 30 Jeff Boyd and *Clipper* stayed on shore, Boyd because of back pains, *Clipper* because her halyard car was unserviceable. Terry McLaughlin spent the day out on *Canada 1*, practising and inspecting recut sails. On June 30 he took *Canada 1* out again to look at a new mainsail from Sobstad Storer.

That day, Terry McLaughlin, Jeff Boyd and Doug Keary met individually with every sailor in the camp to discuss the role of each with the challenge. The final crew for *Canada 1* had been picked. In addition to the afterguard of McLaughlin, Wilson and Boyd, there were Sandy Andrews, bow man; Dave Shaw, mast man; Bob Vaughan-Jones, foxhole; Phil Gow and Paul Hansen, grinders; Rob Muru, mainsail trimmer; Al Megarry, starboard headsail trimmer; and, as port headsail trimmer, Evert Bastet. The basic alternate crew, sailing *Clipper* under the command of Fred Schueddekopp, would be composed of Brent Foxall, Don Campbell, John Millen, Eric Jespersen, Daniel Palardy and Robin Wynne-Edwards. Ed Gyles, Tom Cummings, Rob Kidd and Rob Webb (alias Omar) were moved to the maintenance squad. At last, after 16 months of training and racing, everyone knew where he stood and what was expected of him. It was a great relief for Terry McLaughlin.

Friday, July 1. Canada Day. Terry McLaughlin was interviewed on American television by Jane Pauley. Noting Canada's long absence from America's Cup competition, Pauley wanted to know what the Canadians had been up to for the last 100 years.

Terry shrugged. "Playing hockey, I guess."

To celebrate Canada Day, the Canadians organized a road hockey tournament, and invited the other camps over for a pancake and maple syrup breakfast. About 200 Stetsons and Canada pins and hockey sticks were distributed. Only the *Defender/Courageous* effort failed to show. The street behind Roselawn was blocked off by the police and four authentic goal nets were set in place so that two games could be run simultaneously in deciding the winner of the Dudley Do-Right Trophy.

Fearing injuries, the *Australia II* crew attended but did not field a team. Similarly, Doug Keary forbade the *Canada 1* crew from participating; teams representing *Canada 1* and *Clipper* were assembled from other members of the camp. The British team was composed mostly of women – the men were out sailing – who drew upon their considerable field hockey skills. The referees, who were issued uniforms, were Paul Gaines, the mayor of Newport; Tom Ehman, executive director of the United States Yacht Racing Union (who happened to have refereed collegiate hockey); Bill Fesq, chairman of the challengers' trials series; Dr. Robin Wallace, vice-chairman of the challengers' race committee; Ted King, one of the challengers' series' jury members; and Dyer Jones, chairman of the New York Yacht Club's defence selection committee.

In the first set of games, Sandy Andrews wrote in his diary, *the French defeated the Brits. The* Canada 1 *team, at the same time, was beating the Italians in a very spirited game. The Italians didn't really know what they were doing but they did pick up their sticks a few days early for practice. The game was the best of the series and they certainly added a new element to the game of hockey. They used all their soccer skills to move the ball down the rink. They kicked and headed it and took chest passes with great flair and accuracy. I think they got the biggest kick out of the tournament.*

In the next set of games the Freedom *team beat the* Challenge 12 *team and the* Clipper *team beat the French. Then the* Canada 1 *team played against* Advance. *It seemed the* Advance *team had a lot of winning pent up inside them because they sure played with a lot of energy. They charged up and down the street, carrying their sticks around but not knowing what to do with them. Their sheer energy put them in a 2-0 lead before* Canada 1's *finesse got five unanswered goals.*

The *Canada 1* and *Clipper* teams emerged as the finalists, but instead they joined forces to play *Advance* to decide who would meet the *Freedom* team in the finals. The Canadians dealt matter-of-factly with the Australians. Then, in an America's Cup match contested with hockey sticks, Dennis Conner's impeccable defence machine broke down, losing 4-1. The Canadians had found something in Newport at which they were undisputed champions.

July 1 was also the day of the obituary, as the infamous *Globe and Mail* article became known. Its proper title was "Canadian dream fades for America's Cup raid." Wrote Robert Martin: "The dream that a cocky young crew could descend from the Great White North to lift the America's Cup is fading as the second round-robin series starts tomorrow. For *Canada 1* – 4-8 after the first series – a realistic goal is simply to survive the Aug. 6 elimination of the bottom three yachts. It would be a legitimate accomplishment – and a genuine encouragement for the 1986 challenge – just to make the semi-finals."

The article was charitable, but firm, and went on to list the challenge's many problems – sails, financing, time, the boat – with fairness. Then Martin turned to the crew: "Terry McLaughlin has taken on much more than anyone can be expected to handle in an immensely complex 12-Metre campaign. . . . As a result of the strain, McLaughlin has fallen back on old friends, with unfortunate results for morale in camp. Several crew members have privately expressed resentment at the recent 'parachuting' in of Evert Bastet of Hudson, Que., to be the port-side genoa trimmer. Bastet is McLaughlin's Flying Dutchman crewman, a world champion and acknowledged as a superb dinghy sailor. However, some crew members question whether he can make the jump to a keelboat this late in the game."

And that was not all: "Another source of resentment was the demotion of several crew members such as Ed Gyles, Eric Jespersen, Don Campbell and Daniel Palardy to the B team, not because they lack ability but because of criticisms they expressed during team meetings. . . . the feeling is that the time has come for McLaughlin to forget about who is mouthy, go with his best sailors and get on with the job of making the Aug. 6 cut."

The reasons for the demotions had been oversimplified. It was true that Eric Jespersen had ceased to function and communicate with McLaughlin, and that was regrettable, because Jespersen was a strong, capable individual. But Jespersen's incompatibility with McLaughlin, whatever the justice of the situation, made it impossible for the two to sail together. It was simply unthinkable to assemble a crew in which one member exhibited a worrisome lack of confidence in the skipper. No other helmsman in Newport would have put up with the situation. Jespersen was still young and had enormous potential, thought Boyd. With two more years added to his age, he might have had the experience and maturity to cope with McLaughlin's ceaselessly driving personality. Other skippers might not have asked as much mentally of their crew, but McLaughlin had, and Eric Jespersen was a casualty.

As for Gyles, Campbell and Palardy? Good sailors, but others in the camp had proven better. All three had been doubtful as *Canada 1* crew members since the Miami camp. But lumping Jespersen, Gyles, Campbell and Palardy together as victims of the outbasket through sheer mouthiness was not what disturbed Jeff Boyd the most; it was not the fact that it was in the newspaper as much as how it got there. After the interviews on June 30, with everyone's role in the challenge mapped out, Boyd had felt satisfied that they would all now work together as a team. Instead, a number of disgruntled crew members had taken it upon themselves to *go behind the team's back* and air their grievances in the press about demotions, about the arrival of Evert Bastet to bolster the ranks of the sail trimmers – an area that had been seen in need of improvement not only by Terry McLaughlin, but by Jeff Boyd and Bruce Kirby as well. Boyd found this complaining to the press disillusioning.

The article created such an uproar in the Canadian challenge that Robert

Martin was compelled to file a follow-up story the next day. "I would say that morale is extremely high," Terry McLaughlin told Martin. "You're always going to have some guy complaining, because everyone wants to sail on *Canada 1*."

Basil Rodomar, the syndicate director in charge of marketing, accused Martin's article of having cost the challenge $100,000 "from a major foundation." That raised an interesting question. Was a Canadian newspaper reporter capable of singlehandedly undermining the fund-raising efforts of an America's Cup challenge? Perhaps, but should that possibility prevent him from covering the challenge as he saw fit? Robert Martin was a *Globe and Mail* travel writer who had been given responsibility for the newspaper's sailing column. Although he was a member of the Royal Canadian Yacht Club and owned an Albacore dinghy, he didn't consider himself a sailing expert. And, although privately he demonstrated great enthusiasm for the Canadian challenge, he remained grimly determined to treat *Canada 1* impartially, as a straight news story. If he thought or was told things were amiss, he would write about it. And he did.

"I don't really care what's said in the press about us," Terry McLaughlin informed Martin, "except that it does upset the fund-raisers. What really matters is for us to go out and win some races." The day those words were printed, Series B began.

19

renaissance

For Series B, each yacht would race its counterparts twice, first in a round of short-course races, then over full America's Cup courses. Forty per cent of the points at the end of the series would be carried forward into Series C. *Canada 1* began the series with the mast about eight inches further forward, a final crew line-up, reprogrammed electronics, a recut inventory of sails, and the promise of new sails arriving before the series was out. Her crew began the series with their prowess on the starting line recognized, having been awarded a Louis Vuitton trophy for the most successful starting record in Series A.

Before their first start against *Australia II,* Richard Storer was on board to inspect the new Sobstad Storer 2.2 mainsail, the replacement for the repeatedly repaired S2.1 mainsail which had debuted in Miami Beach with its excessive hoist length. Unfortunately, as Kent Luxton informed Jeff Boyd, the replacement mainsail's Mylar/Kevlar construction was already delaminating. And, although its shape appeared satisfactory, the sail suffered slightly from "batten poke," a distortion indicated by a hard line running from head to clew just in front of the battens. But with the race being against *Australia II,* the crew decided there was plenty of room for experimenting and opted to race with the S2.2.

After an active series of pre-start manoeuvres, *Australia II* accelerated into the medium breeze narrowly ahead and to windward of *Canada 1.* Boyd noticed that John Bertrand wasn't on board the Lexcen design. His tactician, Hugh Treharne, was steering. Treharne's place was taken by Sir James ("Gentleman Jim") Hardy, a member of *Australia II*'s support staff whose efforts to win the America's Cup as the skipper of previous Australian challengers had earned him a knighthood.

After two rapid tacks, it was clear that *Canada 1* would only lose by pressing the duel and the Canadians sailed for the starboard lay-line. *Canada 1*'s speed through the water was encouraging, but the boat could not point with *Australia II.* The Canadians finished the race 59 seconds behind, which was an improvement over the last time the boats had completed a race course together – the Australians had won by nearly three minutes. The Canadian crew work was also much smoother. A loss, but a heartening one.

In the other opening races, *Azzurra* had bested *France 3* by 52 seconds. *Challenge 12*, trailing *Victory 83* by but a few boat-lengths, had broken its boom and been forced to retire. The Australians, however, were able to make repairs in time to race *Canada 1*.

There was little friendship between the crews of *Challenge 12* and *Australia II*. As John Bertrand and others related to the Canadians, after training with *Australia II* in Perth, the *Challenge 12* sailors had become boastful about their chances, crowing that they were going to win the America's Cup. That had not sat well with the folks on *Australia II*, some of whom were making their second, third, or, in the case of Bertrand, fourth trip to Newport. No one assumes that he's going to win the cup first time out, the Perth sailors maintained.

Series B was not starting well for the *Challenge 12* crew. Having lost to *Victory 83* in the opening race on a breakdown, they then sailed into a port-starboard altercation shortly after the beginning of their race against *Canada 1*. The Canadians were attempting to cross the Australians on port tack; it was close, but they were confident they could make it. Before the crew of *Canada 1* could find out, *Challenge 12* tacked below them onto port, and the air turned blue with the clamouring of outraged Australians.

"Get off the race course!"

"Go home!"

"What the hell do you think you're doing?"

A perplexed Terry McLaughlin turned to Jeff Boyd. "How close *were* we?" They couldn't tell, because the Australians had tacked away, but the two boats had never been closer than 20 feet. Despite the suggestions otherwise from *Challenge 12*, they remained on the race course.

Canada 1 rounded the weather mark narrowly ahead of *Challenge 12* in fog and heavy wind. When the wind was light, they would delay their hoist momentarily to burn off their apparent wind, shedding the excess speed they could not carry on the reach before attempting to fly a spinnaker. Today they hoisted immediately, in a fashion they had learned while watching *Challenge 12* and *Australia II* practise earlier in the summer. It was important to get the first eight feet of the genoa down to let the spinnaker breathe. While Eric Jespersen, filling in for an injured Dave Shaw, "bumped" the spinnaker halyard at the mast, helping the halyard's tailer, Bob Vaughan-Jones in the foxhole, raise the sail, Sandy Andrews fed the three-quarter-ounce spinnaker out of the hatch. Andrews then ran forward to the bow, where he was joined by Jeff Boyd in collecting the descending genoa; its halyard had been released by the port grinder, Paul Hansen, who had temporarily moved into the foxhole with Vaughan-Jones. Vaughan-Jones

Victory 83 *leading* Challenge 12

continued to keep himself busy, adjusting the pole height and releasing the mainsail inhaul and cunningham. It was important to limit the number of people on the bow to Andrews and Boyd to maintain fore-and-aft trim; Carl Buchan had told them that, aboard *Intrepid* in 1974, whenever a man went to the bow another was sent to the stern to compensate.

The entire spinnaker hoist took eight seconds. The Canadians were rewarded for their efforts by the sight of the sail ripping apart. Eric Jespersen hooked up the 1.5-ounce spinnaker on the alternate halyard while the genoa was rehoisted. With the new spinnaker raised, the geneoa came down for the second time.

It was tough to fold the "bullet-proof" genoa with *Canada 1* heeled as she raced down the first reach. They always made a point of bagging a headsail after it was dropped. It made the foredeck neater and left options open for selecting a genoa for the next windward leg. Everyone else's genoas appeared to drop easier, though, and seemed more manageable. Many of the Canadian headsails, built with basic Mylar/Kevlar technology, were over-engineered when compared to the lighter and more sophisticatedly constructed sails developed for yachts like *Australia II.* Whereas the first

Mylar/Kevlar sails of 1980 were constructed out of the sailcloth industry's version of boiler plate, the latest sails were surprisingly soft and easy to handle.

While the rest of the boat settled into their respective duties, Jeff Boyd made the rounds, cleaning up loose lines, making sure everyone got a drink of water and cleaning their sunglasses. On a breezy day like this, his principal mechanical duty over the two reaching legs was bailing, which he did almost nonstop. The mainsail winch was disconnected from its grinder pedestal and operated by a handle; the pedestal was then engaged with the bilge pumps. Down below, Eric Jespersen and Sandy Andrews did their best to keep a cluttered "downstairs" orderly. One genoa hastily stored could choke the below-decks area and cause chaos later in the race.

Back on deck Boyd, at the grinder pedestal, consulted Two Ton on bearing and wind strength and direction, planning for the upcoming reach and beat. He conferred with Terry McLaughlin on the tactical situation, which was not good. During the spinnaker blow-out, *Challenge 12* had succeeded in gaining an inside overlap, which they might well hold to the gybe mark and use to take the lead. But then, out of the fog appeared the gybe mark – ten degrees higher than both boats were sailing. McLaughlin swung *Canada 1* up onto the proper course and so doing broke the Australian overlap.

After the gybe, Sandy Andrews went aloft in the bosun's chair to clear away the remnants of the demolished spinnaker. Now completely squared away, *Canada 1* surged into a greater lead. At the leeward mark, they faced a genoa hoist complicated by the heavy winds. If the sail fell in the water

Advance's "Vanderbilt" Starting Technique

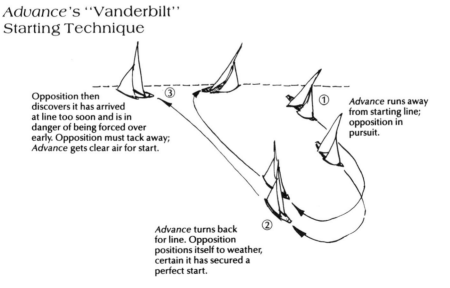

Opposition then discovers it has arrived at line too soon and is in danger of being forced over early. Opposition must tack away; *Advance* gets clear air for start.

Advance runs away from starting line; opposition in pursuit.

Advance turns back for line. Opposition positions itself to weather, certain it has secured a perfect start.

during the hoist or began to draw as it snaked skyward, it could easily tear the luff out of the headstay groove. The hoist went flawlessly. Al Megarry, the starboard headsail trimmer, overtrimmed the spinnaker in preparation for the rounding, then jammed off the spinnaker sheet with a foot pedal in his cockpit. Before the spinnaker was doused, he cleared the spinnaker sheet from the primary winch drum, then loaded up the genoa sheet for the rounding.

"We're better at handling disasters than in Palmetto," an ecstatic Terry McLaughlin shouted as *Canada 1* moved onto the second windward leg with a sound lead. "Keep it up, boys."

The lead held over the next two legs. On the final beat, *Canada 1* lost track of *Challenge 12* in a thickening fog. At one point Paul Hansen thought he saw the Australians sail across *Canada 1*'s stern, and they tacked to cover. It was like chasing a ghost. They didn't positively identify *Challenge 12* until late in the leg, and by that time the Melbourne yacht had closed considerable ground. On the final tack for the finish, the grinder handles for *Canada 1*'s primary winches fell apart. The crew hung in to win by 26 seconds.

Two yachts are converging, and it is too close for the port tack yacht to cross. It tacks early, ahead and to leeward on the other yacht's bow, delivering it disturbed air.

A "lee-bow" must be perfectly timed. Otherwise, the approaching yacht will "roll" the tacking yacht.

In other races, *Victory 83* sailed the course to chalk up a decision over *France 3*, which had failed to start because of a gear failure, and *Australia II* humiliated *Advance* by nearly four minutes.

The Canadian victory, their first against a serious contender, was far from secure. *Challenge 12* protested *Canada 1* for the port-starboard incident, and the nature of the altercation placed the onus of proof on the Canadians. But the jury agreed with the Canadian version, disallowing the protest. The victory stayed.

Jeff Boyd felt that *Challenge 12*'s skipper, John Savage, had botched a strong case. Savage had actually intended to protest the Canadians for an additional two incidents involving tacking too close, but had only filed the port-starboard altercation, presumably thinking that it would be a cut-and-dried affair. He had undermined his case by not having had the bow man on station to relay him information as the two yachts converged. Judging distances from the cockpit of a 12-Metre is not a simple task, and it is easy to make a mistake. Not having a bow man stationed robbed him of a key witness in the protest room. Their first time in a protest hearing, the Canadians had been very lucky indeed.

Sunday, July 3. In light winds, *Advance* revealed her refined Vanderbilt-type starting technique. With ten minutes to go, the Sydney yacht met *Canada 1* on port tack...and kept right on going, sailing away below the line toward the *Viking Queen,* a large spectator launch. With six minutes remaining, *Advance* turned back, beginning a stop-and-go race back to the starting line. *Canada 1* had no option but to park to windward and try to slow *Advance* down. The Australian starting strategy worked well. With one minute remaining, *Advance* was squeezing *Canada 1* closer and closer to the line, and the Canadians were forced to bail out, leaving *Advance* with clear air at the committee boat end.

Both boats started on port tack, with *Canada 1* at the favoured pin end. After sailing together for 15 minutes in winds of only five knots, it was clear that *Advance* was moving faster; *Canada 1,* though still ahead, was steadily falling into her lee. It became important for the Canadians to know just how close the two boats were. Because they had progressed so far to the right side of the course, *Canada 1*, if trailing, might be left in the position of being blanketed by *Advance* all the way to the weather mark on starboard tack.

But were they far enough ahead that, when *Advance* tacked back toward them, *Canada 1* could tack on her lee bow and force the Australians still further to the right? Jeff Boyd felt they and *Advance* were close and that trying a lee-bow would be risky – in light air a 12-Metre took some time to accelerate after a tack, and that produced the very real danger of being rolled.

Advance tacked onto starboard, and the two yachts began to converge. Terry elected to try a lee-bow. Aware that the ensuing meeting might well produce plenty of ammunition on both sides for protests, Boyd began collecting evidence. He punched on the on-board tape recorder as *Canada 1* tacked.

There is nothing more helpless in yacht racing than watching your opponent steadily grind over top of you after an unsuccessful lee-bow. Once settled onto starboard tack, it was evident the Canadians had miscalculated. Hindsight would indicate that they should have begun the tack sooner, but it was dangerous to second-guess Terry McLaughlin. His greatest asset was his utter unpredictability, which provided him with a grab-bag of surprises to spring on the unwary opposition. He was not through yet.

With *Advance* slowly overtaking *Canada 1*, McLaughlin bore off to build up speed. *Advance* did the same, and soon the two boats were close-reaching, bow to bow, with *Advance* still inching forward. Boyd watched *Advance* slipping by, her crew grim and determined, hiding their excitement. They were about to roll their first victim. Iain Murray had tunnel vision, his eye locked on his genoa. All was quiet; only the sloshing of the bow waves broke the silence.

"They're going to roll us," warned Boyd.

"How about a luff?" McLaughlin suggested.

"Sure," Boyd replied, "we've got to do something," and thought to himself, *Great idea, why couldn't I have come up with that?*

A leeward yacht can luff a windward yacht head-to-wind, providing the mast of the leeward yacht is not abeam, or aft, of the helmsman of the windward yacht. While luffing is common enough in fleet racing while reaching or running, it is only rarely seen while sailing upwind. In a two-boat match, however, luffing an opposing yacht while beating can be a critical tactical tool.

"Sandy, go to the mast," Terry McLaughlin commanded in a subdued shout. Andrews complied. "Here we go . . ." McLaughlin said as he spun both the rudder and the trim tab and *Canada 1* nosed into the wind.

The first contact was made by *Canada 1*'s spreaders, which jabbed into *Advance*'s mainsail. Then their topsides slammed together. Iain Murray, taken completely by surprise, began hollering, "Mast abeam!"

"You didn't have it, but I laid off anyway," McLaughlin countered. "Protest."

Sandy Andrews then confirmed that Murray had been at least 15 feet shy of being aligned with *Canada 1*'s mast. Jeff Boyd hopped onto the transom and attached the red protest flag to the backstay. *Canada 1* settled down and pulled away from a confused and still-luffing *Advance*. Boyd shut off the tape recorder.

The Canadians led by 10 lengths at the weather mark. *Advance* closed on the first reach as *Canada 1* sailed through a series of windless holes. At the gybe mark, the Canadians made a serious mistake, sailing far past the lay-line to the gybe mark before gybing in an attempt to peel to a different spinnaker. *Advance* gybed simultaneously onto *Canada 1*'s wind and coasted back into the lead.

Then things began to go weird. Looking ahead, the Canadians noticed that the other pairings for the morning race – *Australia II* and *Victory 83*, *Challenge 12* and *Azzurra* – had stopped moving in an enormous hole near the leeward mark. Boyd had never truly understood holes. With wind on one side of an imaginary line and none on the other, where did the wind go? Up, no doubt, but theoretical explanations were of little comfort for a sailor trapped in one, watching his lead dissipate.

Advance hit the hole first. *Canada I* closed until they were drifting in unison, with *Canada 1* trailing by a length. Judging by the other yachts, the quickest way to regain the favour of the wind was to go left after rounding the leeward mark. *Advance* did just that, forcing *Canada 1* to sail to the right for a few precious minutes to clear her air, although in truth there wasn't much air around to clear. The manoeuvre kept *Canada 1* trapped in the hole longer, while *Advance* nosed into the new breeze and rounded the weather mark in 10 knots of wind with an astonishing lead of more than seven minutes.

With *Advance*'s transom at least a half-mile ahead on the run, *Canada 1*'s afterguard concluded that, apart from having a fairly sound protest in their pockets, their major tactical considerations were the hole still at the leeward mark and the time limit. They decided to approach the mark from the favoured side and peel to a smaller spinnaker as the wind dropped at the hole. Although the Canadians succeeded in closing to within 2:50 of *Advance,* the Australians crossed the finish line with five minutes remaining on the time limit. (The hole did not make the race as interesting for *Canada 1* and *Advance* as it did for *Australia II* and *Victory 83*. The British, trailing by almost four minutes at the end of the second windward leg, ran a wide end sweep around both *Australia II* and the hole to record a 3:56 winning margin.)

While waiting for the race committee to decide whether to start the second heat of races, Terry McLaughlin began making plans for his protest over the luffing incident. Approaching a protest hearing, the Canadians always put themselves in their opponent's position. How would they defend themselves? What would they try to disprove? In this case, the Australians might try to deny that there was contact. Jay McKinnell took a wonderful photograph of Two Ton smiling and pointing to the dent in *Canada 1*'s starboard side. McLaughlin then instructed McKinnell to motor over to

Advance and discreetly snap a few frames of their battered port side. While McKinnell rushed the film back to shore to Jimmy Johnston for developing in his lab at Sherman House, Terry transferred to *Vendy, Canada 1*'s 46-foot tender, to examine the videotape footage collected by Paul Parsons, which definitely proved contact.

At 4:30 the race committee sent *Canada 1* and *France 3* off on a windward-leeward-windward course. The Canadians controlled most of the prestart manoeuvring, but *France 3* split away with two minutes remaining. *Canada 1* was where she wanted to be, at the race committee end of the line, but her crew decided to head back into the cone earlier than planned on starboard tack to finish off the French. *France 3* crossed *Canada 1* and tacked to windward to cover.

Canada 1, carrying much more momentum, was able to establish a leeward overlap. The Canadians began to slowly luff *France 3*, and carried through her lee until they were forward of the mast abeam position and thus able to luff the French head-to-wind. Having cut off her access to the starting line, the Canadians ran *France 3* into the committee boat.

The starting gun sounded, followed by a horn – *France 3* was across the line early. Sandwiched between the race committee and *Canada 1*, *France 3* caromed off her opponent three times. Jeff Boyd broke out the protest flag and suggested to Bruno Troublé that he retire. Instead, Troublé dipped *France 3* below the line to clear himself of the premature start and continued racing.

Sailing from one patch of ripples to another, *Canada 1* covered *France 3* conservatively in the light wind to lead by one and a half minutes at the weather mark. Although *France 3* then closed ground, *Canada 1* still sailed to a 54-second victory. *Azzurra*, which had been trounced by *Challenge 12* in the morning race, came back to top *Victory 83* by two minutes. In her second race of the day, *Advance* led *Challenge 12* down the run but couldn't hang on and lost by 56 seconds. *Advance* was getting closer all the time; the Canadians weren't the only team that was improving.

Terry McLaughlin and Jeff Boyd transferred to *Vendy* for a quick ride back to shore. After filling out protest forms against *Advance* and *France 3*, they headed to Sherman House for a fast bite to eat and a shower. Joining Project Parsons and his television screen and video machine, they made their way to the challengers' race committee office, on the second floor of Island Windsurfing on Thames Street.

It would be a long night. Bruno Troublé's protest form, as the Canadians had expected, contained opinions rather contradictory to their own. According to Troublé's diagram, *Canada 1* had luffed *France 3* past head-to-wind and onto port tack. The protest was quickly decided in favour of the Canadians, who nonetheless remained on friendly terms with the French.

The *Advance* protest took considerably more time. During the prehearing banter, Iain Murray described the *Australia II* keel. "Like a manta ray," he said, "painted anti-submarine blue-green to disguise the reverse leading edge."

Sitting in the hallway outside the closed door of the protest room, Sandy Andrews, Al Megarry and Jeff Boyd waited to be called as witnesses by Terry McLaughlin. The Canadian case was sound and Boyd was never called. Back at their crew house, the Sydney sailors had champagne on ice waiting to celebrate their first victory. It would have to wait. *Advance* was disqualified.

After the first four races of Series B, *Canada 1* had compiled a 3-1 record. The Canadians had been in the protest room for every win.

Monday, July 4. With a bye for the morning race, the Canadians spent their time tuning up *Canada 1* with *Clipper*. Heavy fog then cancelled the afternoon races, giving them the entire day off.

Terry McLaughlin stayed ashore for the morning, having his photo taken with a pair of binoculars hanging around his neck as he succumbed to publicity duties. He then met with Doug Keary to discuss Dave Miller. Keary, who seemed to be under pressure from above to get Miller onto the boat, wanted to know how the Vancouver sailmaker could further aid the campaign and whether Terry would want him as part of the crew. Miller, when he arrived for another visit, would remain ashore where he could serve most effectively as a coach.

During the day's racing, there were no surprises. *Victory 83*, *Challenge 12* and *Australia II* all won easily. Boyd steered *Canada 1* against Fred Schueddekopp and *Clipper* for a few hours, and *Clipper* seemed to have an edge. McLaughlin joined them at three o'clock and the two boats did not return to dock until eight-thirty. Boyd wasn't entirely sure why they sailed for so long; it appeared that, whenever Terry got the feeling the crew wanted to head in, he would stay out even longer. And with night approaching, *Clipper* continued to demonstrate an advantage.

Tuesday, July 5. More fog, and no racing. The series had just begun, and already it was starting to drag. On the way back to dock under tow, *Challenge 12* radioed *Canada 1* to see if the Canadians were interested in pacing. McLaughlin, not feeling confident about *Canada 1*'s speed and no doubt remembering the previous day's late sail, declined the offer.

McLaughlin and Boyd ventured over to Newport Shipyard to look at keels. They took photographs of the leading edge profiles of *France 3*, *Azzurra* and *Challenge 12*, which were conveniently lined up in their hoists. The Italians, always more than cooperative, invited Boyd and McLaughlin into their compound so that they could stand on their floating docks for a better view of *Azzurra*'s keel and rudder. The location also gave them a better view of *Challenge 12* and *Australia II*. While McLaughlin snapped a picture of *Australia II's* rudder, protruding from the well-known green security skirt that concealed the keel, a peeved Aussie appeared.

"Bugger off with that camera, mate," McLaughlin was told. Their mission was over.

The problems with the medium-air mainsail from Sobstad Storer would not go away. Doug Keary headed for the roller rink to see for himself the S2.1's replacement, the S2.2. A representative of the cloth manufacturer, Howe & Bainbridge, had beaten him there.

There was no question. The new sail, as Kent Luxton had pointed out, was definitely delaminating.

Keary was furious. Only two days earlier, he had paid Storer $8500 for the new sail – little more than half the normal price of a 12-Metre mainsail. The next day, he spoke with both Cedric Gyles and Richard Storer. The sailmaker advised using the S2.2 for light to medium winds only and offered to build still another replacement.

"Have not said anything about money," Doug Keary jotted to himself, "but I will not pay anything until totally satisfied quality is OK and then only labour, no material cost." Richard Storer would defend his product by asserting that sail failures were common to many 12-Metre syndicates, and were part of the risk of building sails at the cutting edge of industry technology.

The S2.3 was on its way.

Wednesday, July 6. Another light-air day. *Azzurra* provided the Canadians with a surprise by jumping into the lead at the start and rounding the weather mark one and a half minutes ahead. Because of a wind shift, the second reach became a slow run, delivering the Canadians a terrific chance to get back in the race. *Canada 1* faked a gybe, thereby managing to split tacks on the impromptu run and close ground. At the leeward mark, the Canadians trailed by only three boat-lengths.

Then, in the fading breeze, *Azzurra* simply steamed away. If *Canada 1* tacked with the Italians, she lost ground; if *Canada 1* sailed in a straight line, she still fell behind. *Azzurra* looked every inch a winner. The time limit was the last hope for the Canadians. They began tacking at the end of the second beat to see if *Azzurra* would cover and consequently slow down.

Beginning the third and final beat, it was *Azzurra* against the clock: *Canada 1* was completely out of the running. The Italians were showing such a turn of speed that they managed to pass *France 3*, which had started 15 minutes ahead and was in the process of losing to *Advance*. The Italians crossed the finish line one second within the time limit. *One second!* The Canadians decided to protest the race committee, questioning the accuracy of their timing. A cheap protest, but the management aboard *Vendy* felt it was a

Canada 1 *starting against* Victory 83

legitimate one. It would be disallowed. Neither of the other pairings made the time limit, and they were forced to hold a resail, thus giving the Canadians the afternoon off to sail *Canada 1* against *Clipper*. *Canada 1* did poorly. Terry McLaughlin was becoming vocally sceptical of the boat's abilities.

In the resail, *Advance*, which had been denied the morning win by the time limit, led *France 3* around the course – until the run, when her bow man fell overboard. The unscheduled swim cost *Advance* that elusive first victory. The champagne was still waiting.

Thursday, July 7. The final short-course race of Series B would be sailed. The 24-mile America's Cup course would be used for the final round-robin of the series. In the start against *Victory 83*, the wind backed considerably, favouring port tack on the opening leg. Terry McLaughlin played the start perfectly, working the British down to the leeward end of the line, leaving *Victory 83*'s starting helmsman, Phil Crebbin, lacking in speed, time and room to manoeuvre. Moving slightly faster, *Canada 1* rolled over *Victory 83* as Crebbin squeezed his yacht around the pin end of the line at the gun.

The British tacked onto port; the Canadians covered, and continued to cover when *Victory 83* flipped onto starboard and then back onto port again. When the British came about onto starboard for the second time, the Canadians let them go. With two and a half miles standing between the windward mark and *Canada 1*, Terry McLaughlin played it by the book. If *Canada 1* was lifted, he'd lay the mark; if she was headed, he'd gain on the trailing British. There was no point in covering.

Jeff Boyd kept an eye on *Victory 83* through the hand-bearing compass, and the British seemed slightly faster. A lift late on the beat helped the British close ground, but *Canada 1* rounded the weather mark with a 30-second lead. *Victory 83* crept forward on the reaches, rounding only two lengths behind at the leeward mark. On the second weather leg, *Victory 83*'s upwind helmsman, Lawrie Smith, seemed content to sit in *Canada 1*'s disturbed air, and the Canadians increased their lead in 12 knots of wind.

The run proved to be their undoing. *Victory 83* simply overran *Canada 1*, stealing her wind just before the leeward mark to round ahead. Terry McLaughlin felt that the British had sailed down on *Canada 1* when passing her. Out came the protest flag as *Canada 1* rounded the mark on *Victory 83*'s transom. The British performed slightly better in the 16 tacks up the final leg, delivering *Canada 1* just enough disturbed air to win by 34 seconds. That night, the Canadian protest was disallowed.

Jeff Boyd was extremely frustrated. It had been Dave Shaw's first race since his chest injury, and crew work had been sloppy, but the sloppiness made it appear that the Canadians had choked. Boyd tried to separate emotion from facts. Did they steer the wrong downwind angles? Did they not fly the proper spinnaker? Was the boat that slow? What more could he have done to help Terry? Whatever the causes, the camp was depressed.

For their regular Thursday night barbecue, the Canadians played host to the crew of *Australia II*. The fact that they would be racing each other the next day prompted the usual dumb jokes about drugged food and booze. Boyd found the Australians confident but approachable, and learned that John Bertrand was not sailing because he had "a crick in 'is neck, mate."

During the barbecue, Bruce Kirby told Al Megarry, then Terry McLaughlin, then Jeff Boyd, that their sail trim on the run had not been good. In fact, Kirby had seen better sail trim from junior club sailors. Fortunately, no one lost his head; tempers cooled and they reviewed the loss. Kirby was clearly pointing his finger at the crew as the root of the problems.

"Let's get out of here," Kirby finally said to his wife. "I feel sick." The despondent designer left the party.

Friday, July 8. A sunny day with a strong sea breeze. The Canadians were about to sail their first full-length America's Cup course since the Xerox regatta. Against an *Australia II* afterguard of helmsman Hugh Treharne and tactician Ben Lexcen (the designer had served the same role aboard *Australia* in 1980), Terry McLaughlin spun *Canada 1* as never before during the pre-start manoeuvres. He managed to rattle Treharne once, preventing *Australia II* from gybing by beating them onto the new tack. It was a fun start sequence, but the fun was over when *Canada 1* split off with *Australia II* with 40 seconds remaining and executed a tight turn – laying off, gybing, then heading up hard onto the wind. *Australia II* was able to follow *Canada 1* and spin inside her radius. How she did it is still a mystery – any other 12-Metre would have cut *Canada 1* in two.

   Canada 1's bow poked ahead at the gun. A horn sounded; she was over the line early. The Canadians returned to start the race one minute behind the Australians. It was a nice day for a sail. *Canada 1* cruised out to the starboard lay-line and proceeded to chase *Australia II* around the course. Two jib sheets were successively blown out on the opening leg. The crew performed a number of headsail changes on the second and third windward legs. They lost anyway, by 1:34.

   During the pre-start manoeuvres, the Canadians had followed Bruno Troublé's example by forcing an incident, catching *Australia II* tacking too close. Back on shore, they watched the video footage. It looked inconclusive and they decided not to file their protest. This was one race they could not win through legal cunning.

Saturday, July 9. *Canada 1*'s race with *Challenge 12* began in eight to ten knots of wind, but disturbed weather to the northwest soon strengthened the breeze. The boats started evenly on port tack, with *Canada 1* to leeward. Flying the vertical-cut Mylar N32 genoa, *Canada 1* was showing an encouraging turn of speed. Jeff Boyd deduced that they were gaining bearing on the Australians, and after sailing for about seven minutes on port tack, the Canadians flipped onto starboard. At the same time they brought their #3 headsail, the N23, on deck. The port luff groove was clear and they wanted to change genoas when they tacked back onto port.

   The Canadians were doing even better than they thought. *Challenge 12* was forced to lee-bow them, and in the increasing wind *Canada 1* began to roll the Australian boat. Then the N32 exploded. Two minutes later, the Canadians had replaced the tattered sail with the #3 and were trailing *Challenge 12* by 200 yards. The moment the Canadian sail had disintegrated, the Australians had opted to change headsails, replacing a #1 Kevlar genoa suitable for only one to 14 knots of wind.

At the weather mark *Canada 1* trailed by two minutes and they remained even with *Challenge 12* during the reaches. On the second beat *Canada 1's* main halyard slipped, and the crew was forced to rag the mainsail while repairs were made. Then the clew patch on the Sobstad 2.2 mainsail began to tear. It was time to retire. *Canada 1* dropped to 3-5 for Series B.

Back on shore, they discussed their sail problems at the debriefing. The Canadians badly needed a replacement for the North 32 headsail, and the Sobstad 2.2 mainsail, which had only arrived in camp about a week earlier to replace the hopeless S2.1, was not worth saving. The crew also received the disheartening news that the new Stearn spar, which had arrived the previous day to take the place of the spliced Klacko, had not measured in. As with the Proctor, the forestay was one inch too high.

But there was one positive note. Dave Miller was back in camp.

Sunday, July 10. *Today we reached new depths*, Jeff Boyd wrote in his diary at the end of the day. He had just finished sailing against *Advance*, and the Australians, who had painted a black nose on the bow of their boat and had begun to call her a "good dog," at last had found a reason to uncork the champagne.

The start waited until two o'clock, when the wind filled in to a wandering six to ten knots. The sky was sunny, the water flat as slate. *Advance* secured a perfect start at the pin end, forcing *Canada 1* to tack over onto port. The opening beat was slow, driven along by erratic puffs and shifts. Taking advantage of the favoured left side, Iain Murray brought *Advance* to the weather mark with a two-minute lead.

The Canadians had begun the race with a new medium North Mylar/Kevler mainsail, designated N22, and the Sobstad Storer S22 genoa, which was supposed to be a high-range #2. After seeing it in action, Fred Schueddekopp had thought it was more like a #4.

That morning Dave Miller had begun his tradition of coming aboard *Canada 1* for her pre-race tuning session, helping Rob Muru set up the mainsail. He was sorely needed; as an unofficial coach, he was a welcome change that brought a fresh attitude to the challenge. But the crew couldn't reward Miller with a victory on his first day in camp. On the first reach *Canada 1* parked in a hole and was nearly 12 minutes behind at the gybe. They began to pray for the time limit to expire. *Canada 1* steadily closed ground throughout the rest of the race but lost by four minutes. *Australia II* and *Challenge 12* also won their races, thus creating the only Australian sweep of the challengers' trials over the summer of 1983.

On the way back to base, the crew of *Canada 1* radioed their congratulations to *Advance* and arranged for Gord Smeaton to deliver a bottle of rum to their crew house. The *Advance* crew were young and inexperienced, with hearts that would not give out. They deserved to win a race. Coming as it did against the Canadians, it dropped *Canada 1* to 3-6. It was her fifth straight loss, and something had to be done.

After the race, Terry McLaughlin and Jeff Boyd transferred to *Vendy* for a debriefing with Dave Miller, a visiting Cedric Gyles, Doug Keary and Gord Norton, who would take Keary's place for a week while Keary tended to business back home. Miller thought that the mainsail looked fine, except that the leech was short; the end of the boom had been two feet off the deck when sailing upwind. He only questioned their choice of headsails on the opening leg. A meeting was set for 8:30 at Roselawn. They would discuss modifying *Canada 1*.

Boyd and McLaughlin appeared, armed with photographs of other 12-Metres, determined to push for changes. The meeting lasted three hours. The two sailors argued strongly for some sort of alteration, perhaps a more gradual slope in the leading edge of the keel...like the kind in the photos they were waving around.

Canada 1 *and* France 3 *engage in pre-start manoeuvres.*

But Kirby held his ground. "Well, from what I gather from the boys," he concluded, "they aren't happy with the boat. And if they don't *think* it's fast, it won't be."

Boyd thought to himself that they hadn't been doing much winning lately and that any kind of change would help their state of mind rather than having to head out each day with the same losing setup.

Cedric Gyles indicated that they had to leave the modifications to Kirby; no one else was qualified to make judgements. And under Kirby's contract, no change could be made without his consent. Gyles also wanted to inform Marvin McDill of any decision. "It's Marvin's boat," he stressed. "We can't just start cutting it up."

Dave Miller sided with McLaughlin and Boyd, not so much on specific changes but on the fact that *something* should be changed, if only for the psychological benefit. And they would start with the keel.

Monday, July 11. With no wind, there would be no races, but the challengers waited on Rhode Island Sound until three o'clock before the race committee decided to call it a day.

The night before, Kent Luxton and his crew had done a superb job at the roller rink, increasing the leech length of the N2.2 mainsail by 14 inches. That evening, the maintenance crew prepared themselves for a similar all-nighter, rounding off the toe of the keel. In short, they returned the keel closer to its test tank shape, doing away with the hard edges Kirby had added, partly for psychological effect, during construction. But the edges had backfired – to the crew the keel represented everything that was different and therefore slow about *Canada 1*. Not sure what was holding the boat back – crew work, sails, the design? – the sailors now preferred that the boat blend in with the crowd. No more strange corners and angles. If *Canada 1* looked more like a conventional 12-Metre, maybe she would start going as fast as one. Or maybe the crew would *believe* she could go as fast as one.

Dave Miller was a confidence builder. After he came aboard for the pre-start tune-up on July 12 and fiddled with the mainsail, *Canada 1* actually appeared faster than *Clipper*.

Just before the start, Miller slipped into the rubber duck and gave the crew the thumbs up. "Looks fast, guys."

Terry McLaughlin, smiling, turned to *Clipper*. "Thanks for sandbagging, Fred." Schueddekopp just waved.

"Let's play heads-up hockey out there," John Millen, aboard *Clipper*, replied. The crew of *Canada 1* enjoyed the loose laughter, then fell into the serious, tense feeling that always overcame them in the final moments before the course signals were displayed.

The start against the French was a marvel. McLaughlin did a tremendous job of covering from in front, running *France 3* down the line toward the pin. Like *Victory 83* a few days earlier, *France 3* found herself boxed in at the port end of the line with no momentum at the gun. While *France 3* luffed above the pin, *Canada 1* charged across the line on port tack.

A few minutes later, *Canada 1* tacked onto starboard and headed left. *France 3* came about onto port. It would be close. The two boats were now far to the left side of the course, and the Canadians wondered whether they should tack in front of the French or try to continue to the left. *France 3* took care of the decision for them, executing a sloppy lee-bow. *Canada 1* rolled right over her. The French had just hit a routine ground stroke into the net. Advantage Canada.

The French then began an intense tacking duel and succeeded in getting the Canadians out of phase. But *Canada 1* was eventually able to force the opposition over to the port lay-line and sat on them all the way to the weather mark. At the rounding, *France 3* trailed by over a minute. The Canadians went on to win by 2:17. Jeff Boyd could feel the confidence in the crew returning; it never seemed to take much to change their attitude.

In other races *Victory 83* annihilated *Azzurra* by 4:39 – a surprise win, as light air was *Azzurra*'s forte. In the race between *Advance* and *Challenge 12*, *Advance* had led the Melbourne yacht all the way to the gybe mark, then lost her lead and a tremendous amount of ground on the broad second reach. *Challenge 12* beat *Advance* to the finish line by over three minutes, snuffing out her winning streak at one race.

There was a joke circulating in Newport which went that, if *Australia II* and *Challenge 12* were glass slippers from Down Under, then *Advance* must be the box they came in. Only the Canadians, it seemed, had figured out how to lose to the Shoebox. But, despite the misfire against *Challenge 12*, the Shoebox was on the verge of claiming its second victim.

Wednesday, July 13. With *Canada 1* enjoying a bye, the camp decided to unstep the spliced Klacko mast and insert the new spar from Stearn, a company that had recently been sold to another American rig manufacturer, Sparcraft of California, by its owner, Don Green, who had briefly overseen the sail program of the Canadian challenge. It had been agreed by Cedric Gyles, Gord Norton and Doug Keary that the new mast was to be installed only for inspection; the Klacko rig would be restepped in time for racing the next day. Testing of the Stearn mast would wait until the lay-days between Series B and C.

While the Canadians juggled masts, upsets were in the making on Rhode Island Sound. The big losers of the previous day, *Azzurra* and *Advance*, struck back with astonishing performances. *Azzurra*, sailed by her B crew (as there seemed nothing to lose), took advantage of a breakdown to one of

Australia II's running backstays – to save weight, the Australians used Kevlar line instead of wire for sheets, halyards and running rigging. The Italians didn't even attempt to cover the swift-tacking *Australia II* once they were ahead. The strategy worked and *Azzurra* won by 32 seconds.

Advance provided the other shocker of the day, passing *Victory 83* on the run, one of the British yacht's strongest points of sail. *Advance* survived a 30-tack duel on the final beat to win by a comfortable 1:15.

But the strangest race of all was saved for *Challenge 12* and *France 3*. The Australians won the race but were then disqualified for a pre-start infraction. *Challenge 12* countered by having *France 3* tossed out because the French tender had been trailing the contestants closer than the prescribed 400 yards. Both boats thus lost the race.

It was often said that, in 12-Metre racing, *anything* could happen on a given day. July 13 was more than ample proof of that. In the evening, the Canadians hosted a volleyball tournament attended by the crews of *Advance* and *Azzurra*. The clear night air resounded with the voices of joyful sailors.

At 11 o'clock that night, Gord Norton checked in with Bob Whitehouse to make sure the temporary mast switch was going as planned. Everything was understood and in order.

The next morning, Norton arrived at seven o'clock to find *Canada 1* still sporting the new Stearn rig. Whitehouse was unable to provide a reasonable explanation. Norton soon learned that Terry McLaughlin had appeared at the base at one o'clock that morning, insisting that the new spar stay in the boat. The skipper had rallied the staff of Dr. Dacron to put in an all-nighter at the roller rink to change the luff tapes on all the mainsails so that they would be compatible with the groove in the new mast. Revolting against the camp's conservative planning, McLaughlin had got his way, and there was no turning back. He and his crew were due to meet the Italians on the Sound in a few hours.

Thursday, July 14. It was not always easy to explain the swings in the collective mood of *Canada 1*'s crew, but they awoke with zeal and determination, stoked perhaps by the satisfying win over *France 3*, the new mast or the altered keel. Or perhaps it was *Azzurra*'s victory over *Australia II* which drove the Canadians to prove themselves by beating the Italians. Whatever the cause, they were psyched. They craved a victory, today more than any other, and they knew it could be theirs.

Canada 1's afterguard, as always with the Italians, was determined to lock on the tail of *Azzurra* during the very first circle. In six knots of wind and flat water, Terry McLaughlin cranked *Canada 1* hither and thither; Mauro Pelaschier, at the wheel of *Azzurra*, could not shake him. *Canada 1* drove *Azzurra* deep into the cone and suffocated her. Both yachts crossed the line a minute after the gun, but with *Canada 1* positioned on *Azzurra*'s air.

After a few tacks, *Azzurra* cleared her air and sailed off on port, with *Canada 1* covering parallel, to windward. The Italians were slicing across the Sound with a familiar, silent magnificence; Boyd became concerned that they might sail out from under *Canada 1* and into a beneficial clocking shift. The Canadians decided to lay off and sail down on *Azzurra*'s wind. The decision to sacrifice so much distance to windward betrayed their lack of confidence in *Canada 1*'s speed and pointing ability. After five nail-biting minutes, *Canada 1* was able to blanket the Italians. The graceful blue machine stuttered and was forced to tack. From then on, the Canadians covered closely, feeding *Azzurra* a steady stream of disturbed air, fouling her fuel line and pressing her back.

Canada 1 rounded the weather mark with a 41-second lead. On a reach too tight for spinnakers, *Azzurra* did the impossible, closing ground as she sailed in *Canada 1*'s quarter wake. At the gybe, the Canadians held a 30-second lead; at the leeward mark, the Italians were only 17 seconds behind. For the second beat, *Canada 1* tried a Sobstad Storer S12 genoa, a fuller cross-cut Mylar sail, in the light chop, and it seemed to work. *Canada 1* moved out and held the lead on the run.

The final beat was nightmarish, fraught with wild windshifts and scattered holes. The Canadians sailed conservatively and won by 2:17. During the leg, however, Boyd had noticed a protest flag on *Azzurra*'s backstay. The crew speculated on the reason for the flag but couldn't come up with a logical explanation. After both yachts had finished, they learned over the radio that the Italians were protesting one of the Canadian navy launches, which were serving as race patrol vessels while carrying spectators, for following too closely. It was a disappointing move by the Italians, a feeble copycat of the protest successfully pursued by *Challenge 12* against *France 3*. The protest was dismissed and the Canadian victory stood, raising their record to 5-6 for the series.

Terry McLaughlin and Jeff Boyd were exuberant. They felt they had sailed a tremendous race, always staying one step ahead of what had proved to be a faster opponent. *Canada 1*, for whatever reason, seemed to be improving. The sails, for one, had looked very good. With one race left in Series B, *Canada 1* had already improved on her record in Series A. If they won their final race, the Canadians would wrap up the series with an even won-lost record. It would be nice to conclude on a positive note.

Friday, July 15. The weather was unstable, the wind veering considerably, and the Canadians could not decide which mainsail to use in their race against *Victory 83*. Twenty minutes before the course signals were raised,

Canada 1 was registering 25 knots of wind; the Sobstad Storer 3.1 mainsail was slotted on the boom. With six minutes to go to the course signals, the wind had dropped to 15 knots, and the crew elected to switch to the North 2.2 mainsail.

The gun sounded and the course signals were displayed. The Canadians, who had just removed Dave Miller from *Canada 1*, withdrew their support craft outside the 400-yard limit. At the ten-minute gun, neither *Canada 1* nor *Victory 83* had selected a headsail; they bore down on each other under mainsails only. With the wind again piping 25 knots, *Canada 1* raised her Dacron N15, and began an aggressive pursuit, in the process creating two beneficial incidents – one in which the British tacked too close, another in which they, as windward yacht, failed to keep clear.

At the starting gun *Canada 1* was ahead and to leeward, and the boats sailed together on starboard tack for 15 minutes. Their relative speeds remained even until the wind dropped and *Canada 1*'s N15 became a liability. Wanting to change headsails during a tack, *Canada 1* came about and prepared the N23. The British covered. *Canada 1* tacked away and hoisted the N23, then tacked back and dropped the N15.

It was a fine manoeuvre, but in the process *Canada 1* had badly overstood the port tack lay-line. The weather mark was still two miles away. Terry McLaughlin was angry with himself for allowing such a mistake to occur; Peter Wilson was quiet. *Canada 1* rounded the mark a minute behind *Victory 83*.

The wind was beginning to meander. On the second reach *Canada 1* sailed as high as possible, and in the dying breeze quickly gained on the British. For a time the breeze almost died completely and *Canada 1* doused the spinnaker in favour of a headsail. When the wind returned, it brought rain. McLaughlin called for a spinnaker again. *Victory 83* tried in vain to work up to a parallel course, but *Canada 1* sailed over her and into the lead.

The British steered across *Canada 1*'s transom and continued on a higher course. "They've got a rip in their chute, near the head," Al Megarry told McLaughlin. The crew looked back. They were sure the British were flying a half-ounce spinnaker. It couldn't last in the building breeze.

Seconds later, *Victory 83*'s spinnaker collapsed in shreds. She bore off for the leeward mark while her crew scurried to set a new sail.

Back on *Canada 1*, the foredeck was in a shambles. With the wind having increased to 20 knots, McLaughlin had called for the N15 headsail for the next leg. The sail, however, wasn't one of the two already on deck. After a mad scramble downstairs, the N15 was hoisted in time for *Canada 1* to round the leeward mark with a three-length lead.

For the first half of the beat, *Canada 1* clung to *Victory 83*. The wind was now dying, and McLaughlin ran through a series of genoas in his search for

Canada 1*'s revised keel, the hard angles eliminated*

the right sail combination. Two miles from the weather mark in the centre of the course, it was evident that the British were gaining. The Canadians gambled, splitting tacks with *Victory 83*. It paid off: *Canada 1* sailed into a favourable shift and padded her lead.

The two yachts headed down the run, the leg which had been *Canada 1*'s undoing in their last encounter. Soon after rounding the weather mark, the British sailed off on their own, throwing whatever chance they had overboard. In 12 knots of breeze, *Canada 1*'s lead ballooned to almost two minutes at the leeward mark. On the final windward leg *Victory 83* closed by nearly 40 seconds. It was far from enough to turn the race around, though. *Canada 1* won by 1:03. It was their first defeat of the British, a victory made all the sweeter by the fact that Queen Elizabeth's second son, Prince Andrew, who was in Newport for Peter de Savary's Victory Ball, had witnessed the entire race.

After making sure that *Victory 83* had not hallucinated a protest incident, the Canadians informed the race committee that they would not file their own protests, and returned to base.

With Series B over, *Canada 1* headed directly to Cove Haven for further modifications. The leading edge of the keel would be faired more gradually into the hull and the tip further rounded. The trim tab was also extended four inches to help reduce pressure on the helm. The five-day layover between Series B and Series C had been reduced by one day because of delays in completing the series. All Canadian support personnel were placed on rotating 12-hour shifts so that the modifications could be made in time for the next race.

On the way home from the base after the win over *Victory 83*, the Canadian crew made a point of stopping in for a beer at the Raw Bar, a favourite watering hole of the British. For the next four days they simply relaxed. They had hoped to inspect sails with *Clipper*, but a new luff track had not yet been installed on her spar to make it compatible with the Stearn rig in *Canada 1*. McLaughlin and Boyd spent a day watching *Defender* and *Courageous* in practice and witnessed another display of American 12-Metre mastery – a record five-minute mainsail switch.

For McLaughlin and Boyd, the break lapsed into still more sightseeing. They took in the latest *Star Wars* film, watched a women's professional tennis tournament at the Casino, and lazed on the sidelines as Omar, Bob Whitehouse and Peter Wilson (not to be confused with *Canada 1*'s navigator) of the maintenance squad and an assortment of other colonials played cricket against the British. Prince Andrew, who was surrounded by swarthy men with bulging clothes concealing all manner of anti-personnel devices, played on the English side. His first bowl scattered the wicket and the confidence of the opposition.

More than anything else, *Canada 1*'s crew caught up on sleep in preparation for the long and decisive Series C. In the last four days of Series B, *Canada 1* (with 6.8 points) had left *Advance* (2.0) and *France 3* (2.8) behind to join *Challenge 12* (9.0), *Victory 83* (8.6) and *Azzurra* (8.0) in pursuit of *Australia II* (12.2). In a triple-round-robin series – two short-course rounds separated by a round over full America's Cup courses – each win would be worth one point. By the end of the series, the summer would be over for three boats. All along, Terry McLaughlin had prepared *Canada 1* specifically for this series. With *Canada 1* resting one position shy of qualifying for the semi-finals, it was time to start winning races.

20

i spy

What makes the America's Cup so appealing is that it's got all kinds of things to write about. People spending millions and getting drunk and diving in the water to look at keels. People have a need to feel they understand the apparent simplicity of the race.

– Doug Keary

Wednesday, July 20. Under clear skies and driven along by a 12-knot sea breeze, *Canada 1* powered into the starting area for her first race of Series C, against *Australia II*. John Bertrand was back at the helm of the Perth contender; with two minutes remaining, he broke off circling, content to allow *Canada 1* to have the race committee end of the line to herself.

The start was even. The two boats split tacks, with *Canada 1* heading right. After five minutes of solitary sailing, the Canadians tacked back; *Australia II* crossed and slammed through a tack directly to windward. Jeff Boyd was amazed to see how quickly the Australians matched their speed after completing their tack. That singular manoeuvre convinced them to sail conservatively – in short, leave *Australia II* to her own devices and steer straight for the port lay-line.

At the weather mark *Canada 1* trailed by 30 seconds. The Australians stretched their lead on the second beat and began the final leg with a 58-second margin. The Canadians were quite satisfied with their speed, but *Australia II* was still sailing to her own unmatchable standards. At the beginning of the last beat, one of the two wires sharing the load at the base of the forestay parted, and *Canada 1*'s crew decided to retire from a lost cause in the hope that repairs could be made in time for the next race.

A few quick calls to the shore base confirmed that they had been wise to drop out – one wire would not have been able to hold up the rig. They were ferried out a jury-rigged replacement and a new genoa, an all-Kevlar horizontal-cut #3 from North dubbed the N33. The new sail, with its fanned or "rockered" panels, so aligned to better handle the high-load directions in

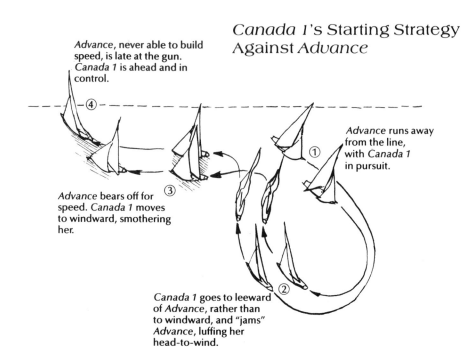

Canada 1's Starting Strategy Against *Advance*

Advance, never able to build speed, is late at the gun. *Canada 1* is ahead and in control.

Advance runs away from the line, with *Canada 1* in pursuit.

Advance bears off for speed. *Canada 1* moves to windward, smothering her.

Canada 1 goes to leeward of *Advance*, rather than to windward, and "jams" *Advance*, luffing her head-to-wind.

the sail and thus make for lighter and more durable construction, was quite similar to sails in the inventory of the British and the Italians. That was no accident. As the summer progressed, the Canadians had turned to other 12-Metre camps for inspiration. Mimicking the Australians was out of the question, but the sails of the British and the Italians looked fast and comparatively uncomplicated. Just as the sails on *Azzurra* always seemed to match the developments in American 12-Metre sail design, what was eventually hoisted aboard *Canada 1* sometimes depended on what the other camps had come up with. (Hans Fogh would freely admit that he often called the other North lofts to "check his numbers.")

With 15 to 18 knots of wind and an increasingly lumpy sea, *Canada 1* hoisted the new North genoa. It was an instant hit with the crew, and they ventured into an uneventful pre-start with John Savage and *Challenge 12*. Savage bailed out of the circling with two minutes remaining; it occurred to Boyd that other challengers were beginning to avoid *Canada 1* on the starting line.

After several close crossings after the start, *Canada 1* sailed into a beneficial shift and tacked back to compare notes. It became apparent that they had made ground, but not enough to risk crossing the starboard-tack *Challenge 12*. Instead Terry McLaughlin executed a well-placed lee-bow, forcing the Australians to clear their air by tacking onto port. When Savage came back at McLaughlin, the Canadian skipper lee-bowed him a second time, and at the next encounter *Canada 1* crossed *Challenge 12* by two boat-lengths.

McLaughlin had taken advantage of another shift, and the boat was moving well. He shouldered the Australians over to the port-tack lay-line, then forced them to make two extra tacks to round the weather mark. *Canada 1* bore off onto the reach with a four-length lead. The wind had swung to the left, making the first reach a tight one. The Canadians delayed their spinnaker hoist until they were sure *Challenge 12* would deploy hers. *Canada 1*'s hoist was terrible but the lead held.

On the second beat McLaughlin made further gains as he again muscled the Australians over to the left side. The spinnaker hoist for the run was not impressive; *Canada 1* went on to win all the same, by 1:06. For the first time all summer, they had been able to use boat-speed to outdistance the competition. *Canada 1*'s straight-line speed was slightly lower, but she was achieving impressive height when sailing upwind. Terry McLaughlin was beginning to take large bites to windward whenever he felt he had sufficient speed. Even their tacks had improved – they weren't easing the genoa as much and laying off as far once through the wind. Whether it was the modifications to the hull, the sails, the rest between series or the wind strength they were sailing in, *Canada 1* had come into her own. The boat felt good.

Thursday, July 21. *Advance*, which had won for the first time during their last encounter, resorted to their Vanderbilt technique during the pre-start with *Canada 1*. But this time the Canadians had an answer. Terry McLaughlin and Jeff Boyd hoped to drastically slow down *Advance*'s stop-and-go return to the starting line by forcing the Australians into a windward overlap and then "jamming" them, luffing them head-to-wind.

After performing her customary run away from the starting line, *Advance* turned back, expecting *Canada 1* to park to windward. Instead, McLaughlin stayed low and drove *Advance* head-to-wind for about 45 seconds. *Advance*, as hoped, then bore away below *Canada 1*. McLaughlin moved into a windward cover, smothering *Advance*. Without clear air, the Australian boat could not accelerate. Her crew panicked after a fruitless minute of attempting to shake the cover, realizing that they would be late. When the gun sounded, *Canada 1* was on port tack, with *Advance* dead to leeward.

McLaughlin drove *Canada 1* dramatically to windward. Flying a North N32 genoa and N2.2 mainsail, the Canadians showed a considerable speed advantage and went on to win with perfect spinnaker sets by 4:04. In the third heat of the morning race, *Azzurra* defeated *Challenge 12* for the first time; the Melbourne yacht, a heavy favourite at the beginning of the summer, was slumping as funding began to dwindle.

The second race of the day was sailed in the same conditions as *Canada 1*'s race against *Challenge 12*. The Canadians consequently opted for the same sails that had proved so successful on Wednesday. *Canada 1* and *France 3* (whose skipper, Bruno Troublé, and back-up tactician, Michel Teweles, had switched positions) remained even for much of the opening leg. Taking advantage of a shift, *Canada 1* tacked and narrowly cleared *France 3* to begin a loose cover.

McLaughlin, wanting to fall into phase with the French, decided to perform a fake tack. A scary move – a 12-Metre loses almost all of its momentum in the process – but if it works it can be a race-winning move. The only defence against a fake tack, once you have fallen for it, is to complete your own tack and then tack some more. You maintain your momentum and, so doing, may be able to achieve a safe leeward position. The French did just that, and were almost, but not quite, able to sail out from under *Canada 1*. The cover held fast, and *Canada 1* pushed *France 3* back. Terry McLaughlin had just transformed a close race into a healthy lead at the weather mark. After another perfect spinnaker set, *Canada 1* barrelled down the reaches. She rounded the leeward mark with a lead of over a minute. *France 3* retired with a broken spreader, handing *Canada 1* her first sailover.

The win improved *Canada 1*'s record to 3-1 and vaulted her to second place in the standings. The shipyard was bursting with spectators, and a more-at-ease Terry McLaughlin found generous time for an intrigued press. Jeff Boyd persisted in conducting himself at odds with the festive mood, trying to warn the other sailors that they still had 14 scheduled races ahead of them.

"Come on Boyd, relax. Enjoy our success."

"I'll relax when we're in the semis," he replied.

There was still *Canada 1* to tidy up. For Series C, the Canadians had been carrying the maximum number of sails permitted aboard during each race. Normally, shortly before the course signals, the crew would dump on the rubber duck the lunch coolers (grinders would always hoard food anyway, so they were never as upset to see the coolers leave as one might expect) and any unnecessary sails. For example, with five to ten knots of wind, they would offload the N15 and S16 headsails and the S1.5B spinnaker. All this loading and offloading meant that, at the end of the day, not only the boat but her tenders were swamped with sails. Jeff Boyd found it amusing to note how many people actually volunteered to manhandle the heavy sails back into their trailer at the end of a winning day.

Mind you, he never complained.

Friday, July 22. The Canadian challenge's momentum was temporarily broken by the weather. A gale tore through from the north; the electronics aboard *Canada 1*, which was now hoisted nightly from the water with the Travelift, recorded gusts of over 50 knots. The race committee, on the other hand, was reporting winds of 35 knots. Jeff Boyd thought that the committee was on the verge of sending them out to race, but they evidently recovered their sanity and cancelled for the day.

For the past few days, Bob Whitehouse had been giving Boyd an earful about how the crew never worked on the boat, how they didn't take care of her or show any pride in her. Boyd didn't have much in the way of a rebuttal, saying only that the crew were putting in long days on the water and that if they were going to get through the series they would need their sleep.

Nonetheless, it was a point well taken. Boyd, Al Megarry, Eric Jespersen, Dave Shaw, Sandy Andrews, Bob Vaughan-Jones, Evert Bastet, Phil Gow and Paul Hansen spent three hours wet-sanding *Canada 1*'s hull. When they were through, Bob Whitehouse informed them that the job had not been necessary. Boyd decided that, in the eyes of the maintenance crew, the sailors would be wrong no matter what they did.

Saturday, July 23. They – Terry McLaughlin, Jeff Boyd, Hugh Drake, Doug Keary, Bruce Kirby, Kevin Singleton and Bob Whitehouse – were seated at their standard 7:00 a.m. pre-breakfast meeting at Sherman House when McLaughlin was summoned to take a telephone call from Jay McKinnell. Terry returned to his seat, barely suppressing a giggle. Brook Hamilton soon appeared in the house looking a bit, well, *damp*. He told the people milling about the residence what had happened. It sounded hilarious.

Australia II's winged keel provided a focal point for the 1983 America's Cup summer. As interesting a configuration as it was, its fascination stemmed far more from the fact that it could not be seen. When *Australia II* was not in the water, she was up in the air in her Travelift, her famous appendage concealed by a lime-green security skirt that reached down to the water. The idea of hiding the keel until the contest was over has been attributed to her tactician, Hugh Treharne, the head of Sobstad Sails in Australia. As tactical decisions go, it was one of the best in the history of organized sport. While a desire by the Perth challenge to preserve its monopoly on the secret of winged keel design should be seen as the main reason for the security skirt, the skirt also paid huge dividends in publicity and one-upmanship. No casual observer could resist speculating on the exact shape of the keel, and publications kept the debate raging by producing one interpretation after another. Down at the America's Cup Gallery on Thames Street, sightseers could spend five dollars on a poster that was essentially a copy of *Sail* magazine's version of what *Australia II* looked like.

Exactly how well-kept a secret the keel was is a matter of speculation. It would be foolish, though, to believe that the lack of knowledge on the part of the press and the public was shared by the other 12-Metre syndicates. The only way to find out what the keel looked like was to take a swim under the security skirt, which was reputedly impervious to X-rays. The Italians were thought to have paid the keel a visit within days of *Australia II*'s arrival in Newport, and it is generally believed that they weren't the only 12-Metre sailors who got away with an examination.

Bruce Kirby was constantly pressing Doug Keary about the need to learn everything they could about the technology of other 12-Metre camps. Keary was all for watching, listening and learning, but he drew the line at anyone in camp spying on *Australia II*'s keel. "If somebody will *show* us what it looks like, fine," Keary conceded, "but we're not going and looking at it."

Soon thereafter, Tom Corness dropped by the room of a fellow maintenance staff member, Brook Hamilton. He wanted to borrow Hamilton's diving equipment. Brook had used the equipment in Miami to scrub the bottoms of *Clipper* and *Canada 1*, and had brought the gear to Newport – one never knew when a 12-Metre might require an impromptu rub-down, or a tender need its prop cleared of a fouled line. Corness would not reveal why he needed the equipment. It was all very hush-hush. Brook Hamilton, without question, handed over his tank, regulator, mask, fins and wetsuit.

Someone outside the camp ranks had been found to undertake the spying mission on *Australia II*'s keel. "Binky" had joined the support staff in Palmetto in April 1982. More accurately, Binky had simply appeared in camp, a friend to all, an enthusiastic participant in the social side of 12-Metre sailing. He very much wanted to become part of the crew, but he could get no closer than the support staff, running errands for Roger Sweeny. It was enough. He was part of the team. When the training camp moved to Newport for the summer of 1982, Binky moved with it.

His undoing came in a bedroom check. Caught with several girls in his room, he was banished from camp as a disciplinary example. It broke his heart. He stayed on in Newport, finding work maintaining Bruce Kirby's *Runaway* for a time, hovering on the periphery of the challenge.

Binky never quite went away. He flitted in and out of camp life, and when he rolled into Newport in the summer of 1983, he seemed to some a natural for the spying mission – a familiar face, but sufficiently arm's-length from the heart of the challenge to protect it from the fallout should something go wrong.

It was never clear why the Canadians should even risk such an espionage mission and the headaches it would create were it detected. What would they do with the photographs? Equipping *Canada 1* with a proper winged keel was impossible at this stage. There was, it appeared, nothing more than a deep interest in what was hiding behind all that green cloth – about what was making *Australia II* such an unearthly 12-Metre. They needed to know for the sake of knowing.

Doug Keary was aware of the mission. It was all so prankish to him – they would get the photos, everyone would sate his curiosity and they could get on with the business of racing *Canada 1*. It was an indulgence he was reluctantly willing to tolerate, provided that it was kept secret. Not even Keary knew it was Binky who was supplied with Brook Hamilton's diving gear and Tom Corness's compact underwater Minolta.

But the mission couldn't seem to get off the ground. Keary didn't know if the pictures hadn't turned out, if the mysterious diver had not actually been beneath *Australia II*, or if he was even capable of carrying out the assignment.

Then Terry McLaughlin shredded the veil of secrecy. "I hear Binky's getting us pictures of the keel," he casually allowed to Keary.

"Where'd you hear *that*?" demanded a shocked Keary.

All over the place, revealed McLaughlin. The Newport waterfront was abuzz with news of the impending mission. Binky had obviously been unable to contain his excitement. Shaken by the monster he had allowed to flourish, Keary put a stop to the exercise.

But curiosity about the keel would not go away. More than anyone else, Jay "Bondo" McKinnell was aware of that interest. As he was responsible for espionage activities, a spying mission would naturally have fallen under his jurisdiction. But Bondo's activities were far more innocuous than the "espionage" label suggested. He was an information gatherer, an eye and ear and video camera trained on the other 12-Metres. It was his duty to determine what the other camps knew – how they trimmed their sails, what sort of gear they used – and he had counterparts in every other syndicate.

Peeking at *Australia II*'s keel went beyond what he felt comfortable pursuing. Despite Terry McLaughlin's half-joking suggestions that they find out what it looked like, McKinnell shied away from doing so. Early in the summer, he went so far as to ask Bruce Kirby if an inspection was in order. Kirby thought not, and McKinnell continued to avoid the question of the keel's nature, and played no part in the aborted Binky mission.

By July Bruce Kirby had changed his mind. With *Australia II* going like mad, he was becoming understandably interested in her keel. Kirby admits to being in favour of a photography mission – he wanted to know what the keel looked like, not for this challenge but for the next one, just in case the Australians left Newport without ever unwrapping the thing. But Kirby asserts that he was not happy with the idea of looking at *Australia II* while she was up in her hoist. There were plenty of days when the foreign 12s were floating idle on Rhode Island Sound, waiting for the wind to fill in so that a race could start, when a diver (he knew of a member of Dale

Hartleben's film crew who was game) could slip into the water, swim over to *Australia II* and have a look without breaking a single law.

Be that as it may, Kirby's change in attitude also changed the attitude of the camp. There was now a plausible reason for undertaking a mission: the designer of *Canada 1* felt the need to fully understand the opposition. Two Canadian navy launches were soon due in Newport, to carry spectators and serve as patrol vessels on the challengers' race course. Why not get the navy divers to carry out the assignment when they arrived, it was suggested. The naval commander was aghast at the idea. Could one imagine the uproar if the Canadian government was implicated in such an undertaking?

That didn't put a stop to the navy mission, however. Jay McKinnell approached the divers as private citizens and explained the keel – how it was supposed to be this winged bomb, how nobody knew exactly how it was put together, and how nice it would be if someone with the necessary skills could perform the reconnaissance assignment.

The divers got the hint. One enquired whether McKinnell would like him to saw off the wings and bring them back for closer inspection. No, Jay said, that was not necessary. Just get pictures. He supplied them with Bruce Kirby's waterproof Nikonos camera.

They went early in the morning, McKinnell driving the runabout across an almost unlit Newport Harbor, the divers suited up in jet-black wetsuits, the shiny areas of their equipment taped over. Very professional. Silently penetrating the security surrounding *Australia II*, they viewed the keel undetected.

Jimmy Johnston, the team photographer, developed the film. Jay McKinnell arrived at the base with the prints, and a crowd, which included a few outsiders, closed around him.

The mission was a dud. Though exquisite frogmen, the navy personnel were not photographers, and a whirlwind lecture on camera manipulation had not helped. Almost all the frames were badly underexposed; it was said that the diver with the camera had tried to take some of the pictures while still under water. The two keepers were close-ups that told little about the keel. An Australian might have been able to confirm that they were of *Australia II*, but no one in the Canadian camp knew what they were supposed to be looking at. They would have to try again.

Brook isn't sure of who first thought of doing it. Probably Jimmy.

Brook Hamilton, a stocky, bilingual young Montrealer, had spotted a newspaper article in early 1982 about the Canadian challenge. Rear Admiral Brock was inviting all able-bodied Canadians to try out for the crew. What the hell, Hamilton thought. He wrote the Admiral a letter.

Brook Hamilton

Hamilton had been in Newport during the summer of 1980 and had been impressed by the spectacle of the America's Cup. He was an active sailor, but did not have the competitive background of those who would become crew candidates. He didn't even belong to a yacht club. At the time, he was running his own business as a licensed general contractor, keeping himself occupied with house renovations. When he wrote the Admiral, he told only his partner, Kevin Curran. It was a one-in-a-million opportunity, he explained. He wouldn't be able to resist if the challenge invited him aboard.

It didn't. Hamilton received a kindly rejection letter from Bill Stuart in Palmetto. Undaunted, Hamilton wrote a second letter, emphasizing his interest and elaborating on his background – his sailing and maintenance skills, and the maturity being out on one's own in the business world developed.

He got a call from Roger Sweeny, who offered him a job on the support staff. Sweeny was all right, a straight shooter. He explained the chores of the Hatteras and the Mako runabout, emphasizing that there was a lot of hard work, but that the other guys in camp did have their fun.

The other guys. Sweeny told Hamilton about the two fellows he would be working with, Shep Higley and Jimmy Johnston. They were in their late thirties, single, and had seen their share of life and women. Good men, dependable, but well schooled in the ways of the world. That didn't seem to bother Hamilton. He left the business in Curran's hands for the summer and joined the camp. Curran would later join him on the maintenance staff.

Jeff Boyd would ask Brook why he had enlisted in the challenge. "I want to be there when Canada makes sports history," was his reply. He certainly would be. Front row centre.

Brook became close to Jimmy and Shep, but mostly to Jimmy. Johnston had a wide and varied background. A native of Courtenay, British Columbia, he had spent much of the 1960s in the Canadian army; he had served in the Coast Guard, on the weather ships with Higley far out on the Pacific Ocean; he had run a photography store in Banff; and he had served with Shep and Sweeny aboard the *Prince George*, a west-coast cruise ship.

Jimmy had also been an amateur boxer, and he told a story of leaving Banff after the collapse of his camera store with all his worldly possessions strapped to his car, heading to Vancouver for his final bout. He left his car parked in front of a Vancouver gym while he went inside to pay his fee so that he could begin training. When he returned to the street, his car – his everything – was gone. With the insurance money from the theft, he was able to support himself as he prepared for the fight in one month's time.

Jimmy was knocked out in the match. As on so many other occasions, he picked himself up off the mat and carried on with his life.

For the mission to be a success, it would require people with both swimming and photography skills. They knew they had what it took – Brook even owned his own Nikonos camera. "Well, shit, let's *us* do it," Jimmy decided not long after the failure of the navy divers. That was about as far as their planning went. A little later they thought they should do it at high tide so the keel wouldn't be ten feet above their heads.

Hamilton never bothered to look at a tide table or set a date. Johnston did. "The tide's going to be right in a couple of days," he revealed during the third week in July. "Let's go."

"Okay. Sure." Hamilton didn't give the suggestion much thought. He had never mentioned the mission to anyone. He was too busy spending his waking hours keeping the 12-Metres operational.

Jimmy had been discussing the mission with Jay McKinnell. "It's on tomorrow," Bondo informed Hamilton the night of July 22. *Fine*, Brook thought. *Where's the getaway plan, the contingency plan?* But the lack of preparation didn't seem to bother him for long. He was hardly in awe of the

Brook Hamilton's sea-level view of Australia II, *moments before he and Jimmy Johnston swam beneath the security skirt*

task. The navy divers had shown that it could be done, and Hamilton was convinced that still others had succeeded.

On the morning of July 23, Brook Hamilton, Jimmy Johnston and Jay McKinnell headed down to the base in complete darkness. The security guard the Canadian camp employed was on duty. He came from the same firm that served Newport Offshore, where *Australia II* was docked. He saw the espionage team and the espionage team saw him. Nothing was said. It was understood that he would keep what he witnessed to himself.

They prepared the runabout, and Jimmy and Brook went into Hugh Drake's office trailer to don their wetsuits. There would be no tanks or masks, just flippers. Jimmy's camera wasn't waterproof; he sealed it in a plastic bag. Over their wetsuits they put on street clothes. Johnston would later assert that they did so just in case they had to make a getaway by land. Hamilton never thought about things going awry and having to walk home. He simply didn't want to look too conspicuous motoring toward *Australia II* in an open boat at the crack of dawn.

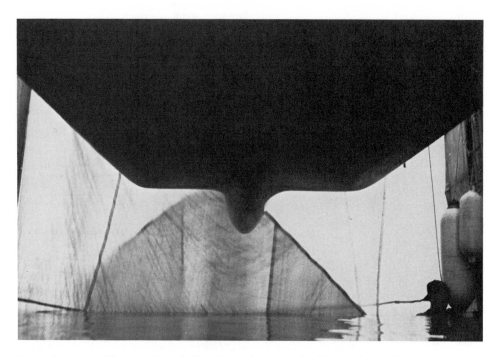

Incriminating evidence: a Brook Hamilton photograph of Australia II*'s keel, seen from below and astern, with its wings spreading overhead. In the lower right corner, sporting a backwards baseball cap, is Jimmy Johnston, struggling with his camera.*

On the way across Newport Harbor, Jimmy Johnston snapped a group portrait of the spy team. It was the only picture he would take that day, and they would never know if it turned out.

They came in from the north. It was 5:30 a.m.; the sky was beginning to lighten. They stopped about four docks away from *Australia II*. The 12-Metre with the magical one per cent margin of superiority hung in the air alongside *Challenge 12*, *Azzurra* and *France 3* like some atomic-age dirigible.

"See you in a little while," Jimmy and Brook said to Jay. They slipped into the water.

To reach *Australia II* they had to swim beneath a series of boats and floating docks. The adrenalin was roaring in their ears, and they were soon half winded from holding their breath. Jimmy was lagging behind. Brook was negotiating the final stretch of open water before *Australia II* when one of Newport Offshore's security guards strolled down the dock along the 12-

Metre's starboard side. Hamilton scooted under the dock, but Johnston was still in open water when the guard passed by.

The guard failed to notice Johnston and walked back down the dock.

Jimmy joined Brook beneath the dock, all *whew* and *phew* and whispering excitedly. The sight of the security guard had given him a start. He hadn't counted on there being a guard pacing the dock like something out of *Stalag 17*. It made him consider that there was a lot more to this excursion than he had anticipated.

Australia II was enclosed on either side by long plywood fences which reached far enough down to conceal the keel at low tide. Raised from the water, she was swaddled from ahead of the keel to just forward of the rudder in the enormous green security skirt, which also descended into the water below the fences. The Australians had asserted that there was an electrified net inside the skirt. There wasn't. Hamilton grabbed the skirt, which was weighted with chain, and began to haul it up to see how deep it went. Reluctant to pull it all the way up because of the noise, he estimated that it reached five feet below the surface. Then he swam beneath it.

As soon as he was under, Brook began taking pictures. Jimmy, exhausted, struggling with a camera in a bag full of air, thrashed madly as he fought his way beneath the tarp. The noise made Brook's heart leap; through the fold where the skirt wrapped about *Australia II*'s stern, he could see the security guard at his chair. Brook was apprehensive, certain that the guard would have heard all the splashing. But he stayed at his chair. It went through Hamilton's mind that the guard knew what was going on but wasn't inclined to do anything – yet.

The first thing Jimmy said when he saw the keel was a loud "Holy *fuck*."

There was this *thing* attached to the bottom of *Australia II* that looked to Johnston like a jet fighter. The bottom of the keel, it was true, was longer than the top, and the reverse leading edge, as Iain Murray had described, was camouflaged from aerial photographers by a blue-green paint. But the bottom of the keel was not, as had been touted, at all full and bomb-like. *And the wings*. They were huge, spanning six feet from tip to tip. Jimmy Johnston could not believe his eyes.

Brook Hamilton could not believe his ears. Hamilton was busy shooting away at the stern, figuring that Johnston would cover the bow, and was beginning to wonder what his partner was up to. He looked over to see Johnston cursing and swearing and messing with his camera. The plastic bag had fogged up, and Jimmy had taken the camera out in an attempt to clean the lens. He was half sinking, treading water and splashing some more, and at one point nearly dropped the camera in the harbour.

Three docks away, Jay McKinnell could hear the splashing. He watched in horror as the guard raced down the dock. The peep show was over.

Hamilton and Johnston were doomed. The runabout roared to life and McKinnell tore out of the harbour.

Refusing to return to the base for fear that the police would be waiting for him, Bondo steered up Narragansett Bay. Terrible, terrible. He continued his flight from the mission he had long avoided until he found a sheltered cove to his liking and put ashore. He tried to relax and collect his thoughts as he watched the sun rise over the bay, regretting that he had not taken firmer control of the venture.

McKinnell found a pay phone. For the longest time he couldn't get through to anybody. At last, shortly after 7:00 a.m., he connected with Sherman House and asked to speak with Terry McLaughlin.

Brook Hamilton was on the far side of the keel, away from the escape route, when the security guard's feet pounded down the dock. Johnston paled. "Look," he said to Hamilton, "the fucking caper's over. We're out of here."

Hamilton kept thinking that there was a door in the plywood and that the guard was going to swing it open and catch them enshrouded, *in situ*, with the famed keel. Instead, he continued down the dock and awakened the Australians sleeping on their tender, *Black Swan* – the black swan being a symbol of Western Australia, the Swan River being the home waters of the Royal Perth Yacht Club, and Swan Lager being a product of a brewery owned by Alan Bond.

Hamilton ducked under the skirt where they had entered. Again Johnston had difficulty clearing the barrier. When Brook reached the first dock to the north, he waited for Jimmy.

Whenever they reached another dock, the guard and the Australians would run up it and order them to stop. Of course they didn't. The guards at Newport Offshore were regular budding Wyatt Earps – young and cocky, in official-looking blue uniforms with badges and shoulder patches and walkie-talkies and handcuffs and night sticks . . . and *guns*. At one point Brook swore the guard had his revolver drawn as he screamed at them to hold it right there. Johnston thought he might start shooting. They didn't stop to find out.

Under more docks and boats they scrambled until they reached the rendezvous point with Jay McKinnell. But Bondo was gone. They were under the final dock. It was a long swim, though, to the nearest refuge, Christie's Landing.

Helpless, cornered and frustrated, Jimmy declared, "I'm going for it."

"We can't go that way," Brook pleaded. "Let's be sneaky here. We'll hide behind the boats. They're not going to jump in the water and look around everywhere for us. If you go, they'll see you."

At his wits' end, Jimmy went anyway. Remaining hidden, Brook removed his Nikonos from around his neck and stuffed it in his baggy trousers.

By now a second guard had been called in. As Jimmy made his way to

Christie's in plain view, an Australian charged down the dock, bounced off the boat Brook was hiding behind and dived into the water.

Johnston was struggling more than swimming. He was trying to make headway while carrying his camera and a swim fin whose heel had torn. The Australian was soon upon him and repeatedly shoved him under water to slow him down. "You can't take pictures of our boat," he said matter-of-factly.

"Okay, okay. Here's my camera," Jimmy offered. Satisfied, the Australian took the camera and returned to the dock.

Johnston was free. He could have kept swimming. But he suddenly thought, *I just gave that guy my whole camera when all he wanted was the film*. He followed the Australian, who seemed tame enough, back to the dock.

Hamilton had worked his way 40 yards up the dock, further into the harbour. He watched as the beady-eyed Wyatt Earps arrived, steaming from the lack of respect the Canadians had shown them.

"Is this one of the guys that was under your boat?" the Australian was asked.

"That's right."

Things got ugly. The guards began to manhandle Johnston. "What the hell do you think you're doing?" they exploded. At the moment, Jimmy was busy showing the Australian how to remove the film from the camera. He was soon face-down on the dock with a pair of handcuffs jammed tightly on his wrists. In a matter of minutes he was bundled in the rear seat of a police car. *This*, he thought, *is getting way out of hand*.

When he reached the end of the dock, Brook Hamilton didn't know where to go. He considered swimming to a moored boat in the harbour and getting a water taxi back to shore, but the closest yacht looked pretty far away. He decided, as Johnston had, to head for Christie's. There were some power-boats the size of bungalows tied up there, with their generators snarling away. There was a chance he could fade into all the fuss and noise.

The security guard Hamilton earlier thought had been waving a gun spotted him. He pointed at him, this time with his finger. "Get back here!" he ordered.

Hamilton turned to face him. "If you want me," he taunted, "come and get me. I don't have anything anyway." He held up both hands to emphasize the point – the camera was still in his pants. Then he continued on to Christie's.

The head of the security service had taken to the water in a Boston Whaler to search him out. The waterfront was crawling with cops. Brook continued north through the docks toward Bannister's Wharf and came to rest at the Commercial Wharf, concealed among the fishing boats.

He stayed there for over an hour, afraid to come out of the darkness, his imagination running wild. *A goddamned fugitive!* He was freezing his butt off in the water and he had to go to the can. Around him Newport was stirring awake. The morning routine was about to start.

Hamilton spotted an old Portuguese man fishing off one of the steel trawlers. "Do you mind if I get up on your boat?" he enquired.

The fellow just stared. What the hell was *this*? "No speeka da Englesh," he muttered. *Do what you want*, his eyes said.

Hamilton hoisted himself hand-over-hand up eight feet of chain, still wearing his fins. Concealed behind the trawler's bulwarks, he stripped on the deck, removing his wetsuit and putting back on his sodden clothes. He stashed his wetsuit, fins and camera in a trash bin on the dock and proceeded to wander in circles.

He encountered a change-room used by the fishermen. It had a pay phone. Brook had no money. One of the fishermen explained that he could make a collect local call.

He rang Sherman House. Steve Fleck, Bob Whitehouse's assistant, answered.

"I heard you guys were doing it," Fleck said eagerly. "What's happening?" Hamilton didn't know that the mission was such common knowledge.

"Aw, Jesus, the whole thing's botched," Brook replied disgustedly. "Jimmy's in jail for all I know."

Fleck began yelling to the rest of the house that Johnston was behind bars.

"Fleck, forget about Johnston," Hamilton said wearily. "Just get me Corness."

Corness came on the line. "Tom, it's a fuck-up," Hamilton said. "I got pictures of the boat, but Johnston's caught. There's cops everywhere." He couldn't possibly walk home in his state and asked Corness to come pick him up.

Corness collected Brook Hamilton and his gear and ferried him back to Sherman House. Hamilton hid the film in his room, showered, changed and rejoined the normal routine of the camp, as if nothing had ever happened.

No one at the pre-breakfast meeting had known anything about the mission, and the repercussions landed in Doug Keary's lap. Keary had been bicycling through Newport when Kevin Singleton pulled up beside him in the challenge's white station wagon to inform him that Jimmy Johnston was in jail. He soon heard from Robin Wallace, chairman of the race committee, who told him that the Australians wished to keep the handling of the incident between syndicates as much as possible. That was cheery news, but Johnston was facing a court appearance that very morning. Keary contacted the challenge's local lawyer, Arthur Murphy, who met with Johnston in jail and advised him to plead not guilty; he assured him that the trespassing charge, which carried a $50 fine, would not stick.

Johnston was led out of jail to be transported to the court house with a half-dozen other detainees. He was still a bit soggy, wearing his wetsuit and a Lee Action Wear sweatshirt. Murphy noted that he might want to put on his hat – an Atlanta Braves baseball cap – before stepping outside. Not entirely sure why, Johnston complied.

When he ventured into the sun, he was greeted by snapping shutters and the whirr of motor drives, sounds he knew so well.

That morning there was a meeting in the yard of the base led by Doug Keary and attended by just about everyone in camp. Keary explained how Jimmy Johnston had been arrested, how the trespassing charge was a serious one, and how the challenge's official position was that they knew nothing about a second swimmer.

Fifty people turned and looked at Brook.

Hugh Drake was at his office trailer when the police car swung onto the travel grounds of the Canadian base. Jimmy Johnston got out, still dressed in his wetsuit and damp clothes, shivering from the cold and from the trauma of his arrest and court appearance. He wanted to use Drake's trailer to change. Drake burst out laughing.

Canada 1 had a bye in the morning and was paired with *Azzurra* in the afternoon. Raising the N33 genoa and N2.2 mainsail, the Canadians sailed an aggressive start and carried good speed off the line to lead by a boat-length. In the ensuing tacking duel, *Canada 1* succeeded in opening ground but the Italians were able to break cover. The Canadians led by a few lengths after one lap of the triangular course.

On the second beat *Canada 1* added another 30 seconds to her lead as the breeze increased. Unsure after the opening leg whether he could tack with *Azzurra*, Terry McLaughlin nonetheless wanted to deliver the Italians as much disturbed air as possible. After being delivered several generous doses of "dirt," *Azzurra* made two quick tacks to get out of phase. The Canadians let them go and didn't tack to cover until they had regained speed. They then began a slow process of covering tightly on port tack and loosely on starboard to force the Italians over to the port lay-line to keep them under wraps.

On the final beat, with 25 knots of wind, *Azzurra* ripped her genoa; the Canadians immediately changed to their Dacron N15. The Italians took a disastrous amount of time to change headsails and *Canada 1* went on to win by 1:43.

As always, the slow cruise back was more enjoyable after a satisfying victory. The Aga Khan powered by in a speedboat over 50 feet long; he slowed as everyone on board broke into applause. The Italians were terrific to race against. The crew of *Canada 1* waved their appreciation of the gesture.

Back on shore, *Canada 1* was greeted by another large crowd. Not many people were interested in the boat's fourth straight win, however. Jimmy Johnston was fast becoming an international celebrity. Bill Cox, Gord Smeaton and Doug Keary had just concocted and issued a press release on what would soon be known as "Keelgate." It treated the incident as a joke that had backfired and said that, because the case was now before the court, the syndicate was not in a position to elaborate. *Australia II*'s winged bomb, it seemed, had blown up in the face of the Canadian challenge.

That evening, the cook for the Canadian navy launches delivered a cake to Sherman House for Jimmy Johnston. There was a file in it.

Sunday, July 24. In her final short-course race of the first third of Series C, *Canada 1* met *Victory 83*. In 15 knots of wind, *Canada 1* enjoyed another successful pre-start. With three minutes remaining, the British starting helmsman, Phil Crebbin, lost steerage, and *Victory 83* drifted helplessly over onto port tack. The boom of *Canada 1*, on starboard, clipped *Victory 83*'s forestay. Jeff Boyd promptly unfurled the protest flag.

The two yachts drove across the line on port tack, with *Canada 1* only a boat-length to windward. They were bow to bow; Terry McLaughlin bore off slightly to try to roll the British. Warning McLaughlin that Lawrie Smith, *Victory 83*'s upwind helmsman, might attempt a luff, Jeff Boyd fixed his eyes on Smith's hands.

He had guessed correctly. When it became apparent that *Canada 1* was about to roll *Victory 83*, Smith put over the wheel. But McLaughlin had expected it and luffed hard with both rudder and trim tab, keeping *Canada 1* well clear. The two yachts then fell back onto starboard tack, with *Canada 1* even further ahead.

"You luffed me past head-to-wind, you bastards!" McLaughlin screamed. "You cheating Pommies!"

Lawrie Smith straightened visibly. "Shut up, McLaughlin, you stupid bugger!" he snarled. Boyd thought that the normally cool Smith was about to leave the wheel and launch himself at the cockpit of *Canada 1* in an attempt to get his fingers on Terry McLaughlin's throat.

Instead Smith initiated a tacking duel, tearing a genoa in the process. The British crew made a superb headsail change and lost little ground because of the mishap. *Canada 1*'s own jib then began to tear. The Canadians decided to hang in with the sail until the weather mark. The wind was now piping 25 knots and an overcast sky promised much more.

Canada 1 rounded the weather mark first, setting a 1.5-ounce spinnaker and racing down the first reach. On the second reach her crew rigged the Dacron genoa and under Terry's orders doused the spinnaker early to allow for a good rounding. The manoeuvre went perfectly, with sails being trimmed as the boat turned onto the second beat. *Victory 83* followed, her sails ragging.

The breeze had swung well to the right; the Canadians tacked, assuming that they were nearing the lay-line to the weather mark. The wind had increased to 30 knots, turning their mainsail inside-out with backwind from the genoa. Still, their lead appeared to be increasing.

Crash. The boom collapsed on the stern deck and the mainsail descended into the cockpit. The halyard car had evaporated. The crew folded up the mainsail and continued sailing under genoa only – they had to finish the race to be able to collect a point should their protest be upheld.

There were people watching the race who later told the crew that *Canada 1* actually went *faster* without her mainsail in the stiff breeze. The boat settled more upright and carved ahead nicely. Whatever the change in performance, the breakdown left Rob Muru twiddling his thumbs for the rest of the race.

The race became an interesting exercise in how long a mainsail-less *Canada 1* could hold off the British. Under genoa and spinnaker, she maintained her lead down the run, and *Victory 83* was only able to take the lead early in the final beat to win by 1:18.

The protest was a long-drawn-out affair. Having been in the protest room with the Canadians in Series B with one video camera position as evidence, the British showed up with two separate video angles. The Canadians used video footage offered to them by *Challenge 12*; the Australians were eager to see the British record another loss. Terry McLaughlin arranged for Graeme Hayward, the current Canadian race committee representative, to argue *Canada 1*'s case and call McLaughlin as a witness. It was an interesting approach and Hayward did an outstanding job, winning the protest.

The evening was full of oddities. Derek Clark, *Victory 83*'s navigator and the least popular Pommie with the Canadian crew, poked fun at the inept espionage efforts. He hinted broadly at their own photographs of the keel. "Don't you know there is a special film you can use in the dark?" he needled.

Lawrie Smith took time to deliver Terry McLaughlin a lesson in shipboard manners. "Terence," he lectured, "you must learn not to yell obscenities." Henceforth, when drawing Smith's attention to a possible rule infraction, McLaughlin was to exercise graceful Etonian respect. For example, Smith illustrated, rather than yapping, "Mast abeam, you (insert favourite expletive)," he must call, "I say, old bean, I do believe I have mast abeam." Terry McLaughlin readily agreed to this truce.

The protest decided in *Canada 1*'s favour, the attending crew members took McLaughlin to the Ark to buy him a beer. It was his 27th birthday and the night's events had interrupted a celebratory meal with his parents. An ebullient Paul Parsons, enamoured with the consistently demonstrated strength of his videotape footage and the cleverly presented cases of McLaughlin, suddenly fixed on the possibility of the Canadians protesting their way right into the America's Cup finals. They could ride a wave of victories based on protest incidents to a final glorious triumph over the Americans. The rest of the sailors weren't so sure.

At Sherman House that night, the crew enjoyed their 5-1 record in the opening round of Series C by flopping in the video room and watching television. Jimmy Johnston, a free man until his next court appearance on Wednesday, was sprawled on the floor. There was a rough growth of beard on his face and neck. Propped up on his elbows, he looked exhausted.

Al Megarry walked into the room. He stood near the television and studied Johnston.

"You're on the news in England," he finally announced.

At two o'clock on the afternoon of the 24th, Doug Keary met with Arthur Murphy and Bill Cox to review strategy over the "Johnston affair." They agreed to maintain the position that they would make no further comments to anyone pending the court hearing on Wednesday.

Keary was due at a reception hosted by the governor of Rhode Island at six o'clock, but he had received a surprise invitation to dine aboard *Fox Hunter*, the NYYC's official launch for the America's Cup. Arranging for Hugh Drake to take his place at the reception, Keary joined Bruce Kirby aboard the launch, where they met with Robert (Bob) McCullough, the chairman of the NYYC America's Cup committee, and his wife and daughter; Briggs Cunningham, a former 12-Metre helmsman who was a member of the club's committee; and Richard (Dick) Latham, another committee member.

It was an enjoyable, relaxed occasion. After the dinner, Doug Keary wrote in his diary, "Lots of encouragement re Johnston incident. They maintain that we are fully within our rights if we did look at keel."

The encouragement was rather calculated. Bruce Kirby (a member of the New York Yacht Club) was slipped some papers at the end of the evening. They contained a copy of a letter, dated that very day, from McCullough to Mark Vinbury, the chief measurer of the United States Yacht Racing Union, who had been one of three measurers – in addition to Tony Watts, the chief measurer of the International Yacht Racing Union, and Jack Savage, the chief measurer of the Australian Yachting Federation – to assess and approve the ratings of all 12-Metres competing for the challenge nomination. The NYYC, the letter revealed, believed that the keel of *Australia II* was illegal. A note attached to the copy of the letter passed to Kirby suggested that the Canadians consider filing a protest.

The concept of keel wings had been borrowed from the aircraft industry, where fins called end plates are sometimes used at the wing-tips; and because the design of aircraft wings and yacht keels is based on the same principles, it is not surprising that there would be efforts to adapt end plates to the needs of naval architecture. Gas or liquid flowing across a foil section tends to migrate toward the tip. At the tip, the flow on the high-pressure side curls around to the low-pressure side, thereby producing tip loss, or drag-inducing turbulence. Such turbulence is lost energy, and the greater the tip length relative to the length of the foil, the more problematic the loss of energy. Where they are practical, end plates close off the flow from the high- to low-pressure side, and in the process create a more efficient foil.

Until *Australia II*, tip loss in keels was minimized by tapering the keel profile and thus minimizing the tip length. Relatively lenient restrictions on draught and girth measurement under the International Offshore Rule allowed for the development of efficient, high-aspect ratio (i.e. deep and narrow) keels, and there was no great crying need to introduce end plates to IOR design. But there was a greater need under the International Rule, which governs the shape and nature of 12-Metres. With America's Cup yachts, the problem of tip loss was directly related to the problem of efficient placement of ballast, something aircraft engineers didn't have to worry about. With stringent limitations on draught, 12-Metre designers were unable to develop high-aspect IOR-type keels. To control tip loss in the low-aspect foils they were stuck with, the designers resorted to dramatically tapering the keel profile, thereby creating the tremendous sweep of the leading edge. This tapering meant very short keel tips, and consequently very little room for ballast at the foil's extremity.

We can safely assume that Ben Lexcen was led to solving tip loss with end plates or wings by the problem of the effective placement of ballast in a 12-Metre. Lexcen wanted to create a relatively light boat without sacrificing stiffness, the ability to stand up to stronger breezes. Lexcen could compensate for reducing displacement, say, 4000 pounds by making best use of what ballast he had left at his disposal. (Any reduction in weight had to come at the expense of ballast – the scantlings governing 12-Metre construction are too rigid to allow significant savings in the weight of the hull and deck.)

The best way to make use of that ballast was to get it as low as possible in the boat. As we discussed earlier, Bruce Kirby was able to create a stiff *Canada 1* by resorting to a keel configuration with a long tip. But Kirby did not attempt to reduce overall displacement, which in the case of *Canada 1*

What all the fuss was about: Australia II*'s winged keel*

rested at about 55,000 pounds. To make a boat that was as light as 51,000 pounds as stiff as a boat 4000 pounds heavier, Lexcen would have to do a lot better than Kirby at packing down the lead.

Lexcen tackled the problem from two directions. With *Challenge 12*, he fattened up a fairly conventional keel. With *Australia II*, he arrived at an "upside-down" keel which was much longer at the tip than at the junction with the hull. This provided a tremendous tip length in which to house ballast, but it also meant a prohibitive amount of tip loss. To control that tip loss, Lexcen needed end plates – hence the wings.

The idea of a winged keel is not new. Johan Valentijn has indicated that he and Lexcen toyed with the idea of a winged keel when they designed *Australia* for the 1977 challenge. How many other yacht designers have allowed the idea of keel wings to flit through their minds is anyone's guess. During the summer of 1983, Ben Lexcen was approached by a still-anonymous Canadian from British Columbia who showed him drawings of a winged keel which the Canadian claimed to have copyrighted long before *Australia II* had come along. Lexcen knew all about the fruitlessness of trying to claim exclusivity to the configuration. His application for a patent with the British Patent Office was turned down after records revealed that at least eight other claims had been made on the same invention over the years. Bruce Kirby's assistant, Steve Killing, recalls discussing the idea of putting a bulbous tip and end plates on an IOR keel while he was a member of C&C's design office.

Despite widespread knowledge of the concept, Lexcen was the first to produce a successful version. Lengthy, expensive analysis was essential, for the keel would have to be an exquisitely balanced compromise. With an estimated budget of $1 million, Lexcen committed himself to an exhaustive test tank and computer analysis program for the winged keel of *Australia II*, as well as the fat keel of *Challenge 12*.

The end plates on a low-aspect keel would have to be quite large, and they would, as a result, increase the wetted surface of the hull, perhaps to a detrimental degree when sailing downwind. And the wings would have to function in conditions aircraft did not encounter – waves. What if, when *Australia II* began heaving about in a sea (and she *would* hobbyhorse – the pendulum effect of all that deeply located ballast would see to that), the horizontally mounted fins began churning up horrendous amounts of turbulence?

When Lexcen had finished, *Australia II*'s keel had a tip 11 feet long; her wings, cast in lead, spanned six feet. The reverse leading edge of the keel eliminated the enormous profile area normally found in the forebody of conventional "lifting body" 12-Metres. When Lexcen also decided to do away with the bustle, having no need for all that volume in his lighter-displacement design, he created a yacht that was devastatingly manoeuvrable. Eliminating the bustle, though, may have been a mistake. Because of provisions under the International Rule which force designers to link displacement to waterline length, Lexcen had already been compelled to give up about a foot of rated waterline length when he left the 4000-odd pounds on shore. By doing away with the bustle, which artificially increases the yacht's effective sailing length, Lexcen made *Australia II* especially vulnerable when reaching.

But no matter. It was upwind where the gains were to be made. With manoeuvrability that made her dangerous on the starting line, *Australia II* could then swing into the wind, beating to the weather mark like no other 12-Metre. While her straight-line speed was a touch slower than much of the competition, the efficiency of her keel made her sail closer to the wind than any 12-Metre in the world. If she found herself behind at the start, she could use her manoeuvrability to out-tack anyone. If she was ahead, she could sit back and smile. In light air, she used her reduced weight to advantage. In heavy air, her well-placed ballast took over. *Australia II* was a work of genius, the first 12-Metre in 16 years to defy successfully the hallowed *Intrepid* lineage. And the defiance drove the New York Yacht Club to desperation.

Apart from the fact that she was extremely fast, there were two things the NYYC didn't like about *Australia II*. One was that she was rated as a 12-Metre; the other was that she was supposed to be an Australian design.

The research on *Australia II*'s radical hull configuration was conducted in Holland. Tank testing of one-third scale models took place at the Netherlands Ship Model Basin under the direction of Dr. Peter van Oossanen, who had spent many years working in Australia. Computer analysis was farmed out to the National Aerospace Laboratory in Amsterdam.

The Americans suspected foul play. Had Ben Lexcen really produced the keel, or had the contribution of van Oossanen gone far beyond that of a research assistant? Was *Australia II*'s keel Australian, or Dutch?

On July 21, Dennis Conner's defence syndicate decided to find out. The premise of the telex it sent to van Oossanen was that the Americans wanted to buy a winged keel of their own, but the message contained the words, UNDERSTAND THAT YOU AND YOUR TEAM ARE RESPONSIBLE FOR THE DEVELOPMENT AND DESIGN OF SPECIAL KEEL FOR AUSTRALIA II. That loaded phrase was obviously crafted to wring an inadvertent confession out of the good doctor which would invalidate *Australia II* as a product of her country of origin. But van Oossanen refused to play along; the next day he informed the syndicate that the design was Lexcen's.

Temporarily stymied on the nationality question, the NYYC moved to have *Australia II* declared illegal on the grounds of improper measurement.

Robert McCullough drafted his letter to the American measurer, Mark Vinbury, who, as chief measurer of the United States Yacht Racing Union, could carry the case to the International Yacht Racing Union, which oversees the International Rule.

But first McCullough had to convince Vinbury that he was wrong in agreeing that *Australia II* was legal in the first place. McCullough pointed out that the measurement instructions called for the measurer to keep an eye peeled for any "peculiarity" that might allow a yacht to receive an unfair rating. If wings sticking out of an upside-down keel weren't peculiar, then the NYYC didn't know what was. Furthermore, the measurers had failed to take into account that the boat's draught increased when heeled because of the wings. The Americans seemed quite familiar with the dimensions of the Lexcen keel, noting that if heeling were taken into account, *Australia II* would actually rate 12.476 metres.

As much as the NYYC wished to see *Australia II* declared illegal, it did not relish the idea of launching legal action against the Perth challenge. The club, as the defender of the America's Cup and the overseer of its rules and regulations, had long suffered from a conflict of interest. Any move on its part to question the legality of *Australia II* was sure to be met by outraged charges from the Australians and the press of tinkering with the rules to preserve its grip on the trophy. But then the universe had thrown one of its curve balls: out of the clear blue sky had fallen Jimmy Johnston. Now that the Canadians knew for certain what the keel looked like, why not lay the facts on them and let them do the deed? A protest filed by a challenge candidate would be far less messy; the NYYC could stand back and ultimately reap all the benefits of a Canadian protest, should it be successful. Aboard *Fox Hunter*, Robert McCullough and the other members of his committee had planted the seeds of revolt within the ranks of the challenge contenders.

In Newport in 1983, the nationality regulations regarding equipment and technology were inadequate, the efforts to police them fitful. The New York Yacht Club made much noise about who designed the keel of *Australia II*, but there were other, more likely infractions by the various campaigns that went largely unaddressed, not because they were less serious, but because the transgressions were difficult to prove, or because it was not politically expedient to pursue them.

To its credit, the NYYC has gradually eased the nationality regulations over the years to make for fairer competition. In the process, though, loopholes have opened up. As we have seen, a foreign challenger can have its sails (and spars) built in the United States, provided the designs come from its own country. But how is one to determine who had a hand in designing them? How much help did an official sailmaker receive on the cutting room

The rear of a Canada 1 *van after keelgate*

floor from the American loft building the sails? And what of the computer programs on sail cloth and construction, which John Marshall of North Sails understood to be tools of the entire company and thus immune from nationality rulings, and which were crucial to sail shape in the 1983 America's Cup?

Presumably the NYYC recognized the futility of attempting to control the use of information routinely circulated within a large multinational sailmaking company like North or Sobstad. The America's Cup is a yacht-racing anomaly. For any other sailing event, boat owners shop the world for designers, builders, sails and technology. With *Evergreen II*, for example, Don Green, a Canadian, turned to German Frers, an Argentinian, for a design that was built by Carl Eichenlaub, an American. In the America's Cup this would be blasphemy.

Monday, July 25. Out on Rhode Island Sound, aboard *Vendy*, Doug Keary, Bruce Kirby and Cedric Gyles discussed the information passed to Kirby the previous night and the possibility of carrying through with a protest. A protest was far from out of the question. There was, in Gyles's mind, that ever-present responsibility to the people and corporations back home who had contributed money to the campaign. What if *Australia II was*, as the

Jimmy Johnston and Sandy Andrews

NYYC alleged, illegal? At the moment *Canada 1* stood in second place in the trials standings. The removal of the Australian boat would make *Canada 1* the leading contender to advance to the final match against the Americans in September. How would it look if the Canadians declined to protest, and the NYYC later did and won? Canada might have thrown away its opportunity to contest the trophy, thereby fumbling Marvin McDill's dream.

The three men decided not to do anything until they spoke with McDill. The Australians had been busy making representations to the syndicate through Arthur Murphy and Graeme Hayward. They wanted to make a deal: the charges against Johnston would be dropped if the Canadians handed over the alleged films – having spotted Brook Hamilton in the water, the Australians suspected that more film existed than was removed from Jimmy Johnston's camera.

At this point Arthur Murphy decided to withdraw from the case – because of his association with the American 12-Metre camps, he was risking a conflict of interest – and recommended that another lawyer, Anthony Quentin, take his place. The camp's management met with Quentin at seven o'clock that evening and decided to keep him on hold until Marvin McDill had been consulted. Keary telephoned McDill that night and laid bare the whole sorry story, including the NYYC's concern over *Australia II*'s keel and the extremely negative and highly aroused press swarming about the challenge.

The next day, Tuesday, July 26, Doug Keary met with Graeme Hayward and Cedric Gyles shortly before 9:00 a.m. at Roselawn. Having consulted with McDill, they decided not to file a protest, but to clear up the Johnston affair before the Americans decided to file one. All three men then spoke with McDill and advised him to get in touch with Tony Watts, one of the three measurers who had approved *Australia II*, to seek his advice on the legal position in which the Canadian challenge stood regarding the Perth yacht.

At 5:30 p.m., Keary, Gyles and Kirby met in Keary's office trailer with the lawyers appointed by McDill to deal with the Keelgate affair, Mark Mandell and Mike Schwartz of Providence. Mandell had met with *Australia II's* lawyers earlier in the day. It had been an emotional, stormy meeting, with the Australians concerned about the security of the keel design and the possibility of the Canadians using illegally obtained information in any manner. Mandell now revealed that for the charges against Johnston to be dropped, the challenge would have to sign a restraining order preventing it from making use of any photographs obtained on the reconnaissance mission. The challenge's management agreed to do so.

As to whether there *were* any photographs, the management admitted it had heard through the grapevine that Brook Hamilton had been present during the mission and that he had pictures. Keary asked Hamilton to step into the office and, while Keary, Gyles and Kirby waited outside, tell the lawyers what had happened. Keary and Gyles had never discussed the incident with Hamilton and preferred to keep it that way.

The two lawyers had already questioned Johnston when Hamilton entered the trailer. Johnston had been testy; with the charges about to be dropped, he couldn't see why the lawyers now had to start leaning on him about photographs. He denied that there were any photos and left in a sullen mood.

While not as rebellious as Johnston, Hamilton also had no patience for the lawyers. He did not want to be dragged publicly through the mud as Johnston had been; he was hoping to secure a job some day and didn't need an unsavoury reputation preceding him into interviews. Hamilton had also come to feel that management had handled the affair poorly – issuing a press release, for example, which identified Johnston simply as a "boat driver" when he was officially listed as the challenge's photographer.

"Are there pictures of the boat?" Mandell enquired.

"There are pictures of the boat," Brook said carefully as he constructed his lie. "They were taken a couple of weeks previous when nobody got caught, but there are no pictures from the day Jimmy got caught." Hamilton thought that would stop the agonizing in management. Whether or not there were pictures seemed irrelevant to him at that point.

"That's what Jimmy said," Mandell replied, pleased that their stories jibed. Brook had not known that Johnston had also denied the existence of the photographs. Hamilton was free to go.

When Keary, Gyles and Kirby returned to the office, Mandell informed them that there were no photographs from that day, and that *Australia II*'s lawyers would be duly informed. Keary's jaw dropped. Bruce Kirby must have been the most surprised – he had been shown the photographs.

The next morning, Jimmy Johnston made his final court appearance, this time in shirt and tie. The deal had been struck: the restraining order had been signed, and the trespassing charge was dropped. Amid a crowd of cheering spectators, Johnston hopped on his bicycle and pedalled away, pleased with his liberty.

21

making the grade

The second round of Series C began poorly for *Canada 1* as she lost to *Australia II* on July 25 and *Challenge 12* on July 26 in light air. The North N2.2 mainsail evidently was no longer effective. The crew had been successful with the sail and were saddened to see it shelved. In the race against *Australia II*, sailed in a dying northerly, the Canadians had resorted to a Sobstad Storer S2.3 mainsail (the replacement for the S2.2, which had been a replacement for the S2.1) and the Australians had simply sailed away from them.

The flu had begun to infiltrate the crew ranks. Phil Gow missed the race against *Australia II*. On Wednesday, July 27, Al Megarry stayed ashore while *Canada 1* raced *Advance*.

Against *Advance* they again resorted to the S2.3 mainsail. This time it looked quite good, but in light air *Advance* actually crossed *Canada 1* three-quarters of the way up the opening leg. As *Canada 1* approached the mark on starboard, *Advance* tacked into what should have been a safe leeward position, but Terry McLaughlin drove over Iain Murray. McLaughlin crossed himself and said thank-you as he gazed skyward. Once *Canada 1* was on *Advance*'s wind, the race was decided. She won by 2:11.

After the race, Jeff Boyd headed for Sherman House with the chills and a fever. The dreaded bug had struck. On Thursday morning he couldn't get out of bed and was forced to miss his first race of the summer. Dave Miller took his place. *Canada 1* fell behind against *France 3* on the first leg after being caught on the outside of a 25-degree windshift, but just before the weather mark McLaughlin was able to pin *France 3* and run Bruno Troublé past the port lay-line. *Canada 1* won by 2:19. Fifteen minutes behind her, *Azzurra* beat *Victory 83* by 11 seconds in the closest challengers' race of the summer.

Early that morning, Doug Keary had met with Warren Jones, the executive director of the *Australia II* challenge, and Ben Lexcen. It was a friendly encounter and relations between the two camps were fully mended. The spying, said the Canadians at the subsequent press conference, was neither authorized nor condoned. They regretted the incident and were happy that it had been settled in an amicable way. The Canadians very much wanted to return to the main issue – competing for the America's Cup.

Brook Hamilton lay low, keeping his name out of the newspapers. When he finally did speak about the mission in print, in an interview with Robert Martin of the *Globe and Mail*, he was identified, somewhat tongue-in-cheek, only as Deep Draft. He continued to walk the streets of Newport, unafraid of being identified as the unapprehended second swimmer – after the escapade, Jay McKinnell and Jimmy Johnston grew beards, and McKinnell took to wearing a hat and sunglasses. Hamilton was plainly embarrassed by the incident, by the stupidity of Johnston's having been apprehended.

Johnston, on the other hand, fell into the role of international celebrity. His face undoubtedly carried a higher recognition factor than that of Terry McLaughlin. While he shouldered the blame for the entire affair, he found amusement in the burden. In newspapers worldwide, he became the infamous "Canadian frogman," and clippings began to cover the walls of his basement room in Sherman House. Although he did not allow himself to be dragged into the media circus – no appearances on "Good Morning, America," no camera or swimsuit endorsements – he watched with a certain pride his spreading fame. He had not even taken the pictures. He had only been caught.

As soon as Jimmy was out of jail after his arrest, he had tackled the task of developing Brook's film. They had pushed the film somewhat, and Jimmy didn't want to botch the developing, so he called a friend at a local camera store. "The guy's airtight," Jimmy assured Brook, but the call made Hamilton uneasy – someone outside the camp now knew that photographs had been taken.

Only one set of prints of the 15 exposures was made, and Jimmy was keeping them in the same place as the negatives. Brook wanted to put the pictures on ice for a while. He was heading home that weekend for several weddings; he could take them to Montreal and stash them there, away from the heat of Newport. But getting them back from Jimmy might be awkward. As the lone Canadian publicly linked with the Keelgate mission, Johnston was beginning to treat the photos as his own.

On Thursday, July 28, the camp held its regular weekly barbecue. Jimmy, celebrating his release from the jaws of the law, got terribly hammered – he had not had a drink since the January boat show. Out came the keel photos. Before the barbecue, Johnston and Hamilton had shown the pictures only to a select few. Practically everybody at the party had a good look at them.

The next morning, Brook came to Jimmy's room to collect the photos. Jimmy couldn't find them. At first Brook thought that Johnston had hidden them in his drunken state and couldn't remember where, but it soon became obvious that the photos – and the negatives – had been stolen.

Johnston had spent much of the night in the company of two of the local racer chasers, and Binky. Hamilton immediately suspected Binky. So did Johnston. Jimmy caught up with him that morning. Binky denied stealing the photos, and Jimmy decided to believe him. That left the racer chasers.

Jimmy found one of the girls in a waterfront bar, but she wasn't the thief either. The other girl could not be found.

The theft had serious implications. Only that morning, the Canadians had held their press conference and seemingly written the final chapter in the Keelgate affair. Relations were back to normal with the Australians, who had been told that no film other than the blank one in Jimmy Johnston's camera existed. Now Brook Hamilton's negatives and the only set of prints were loose in the world. For all they knew, the photos could appear on the front page of the *Newport Daily News* the next day, as Johnston's own photo had following his arrest. The loss of face the publication of the photos would cause was incalculable. It would humiliate the Canadian challenge and perhaps even lead to its being disqualified for unsportsmanlike conduct.

The theft ruined Brook Hamilton's Montreal weekend. It was dumb to have gotten caught looking at the keel in the first place; it was even dumber that the photos had been stolen. "The only one I had to blame was Jimmy," Brook recalled. "I was pissed off at him. I let it get to me more than it should have."

The girl who had actually taken the photos had gone away for five days and left them in her apartment. When she returned home, she didn't know what to do with them and had a change of heart. A late-night waterfront rendezvous was arranged with Johnston.

It was dark and foggy. Jimmy had the awful feeling that he might be walking into a set-up, that at any moment the lights would switch on and the cameras start rolling. But nothing of the sort occurred. The girl handed back the photos.

Another set of prints was made which Brook kept, along with the negatives. Johnston showed his prints to enquiring representatives of *Sports Illustrated*, and on August 29 the magazine published the summer's most accurate speculative illustration of the keel. At the end of the Canadian campaign, Brook Hamilton gave his set of prints to a friend he knew would keep them to himself, and took the negatives home with him. Before leaving Newport, though, Hamilton was asked for some souvenir prints by Binky. Hamilton refused and Binky went to Johnston, who gave him two autographed photos.

During the final series between *Australia II* and *Liberty*, Hamilton gave his negatives to his brother to make a new set of prints. Brook's brother was driving down a Toronto street on the day of the final race when he spotted a *Globe and Mail* in a street-corner box. The front page had a photo of *Australia II*'s keel, and the photo looked suspiciously familiar. In fact, it was one of Brook's. He knew it couldn't have come from Brook – he had just returned the negatives and the fresh set of prints to him.

Binky had sold his two photos to Robert Martin of the *Globe and Mail*.

While the camp prepared for the barbecue at which the photos were stolen and while Boyd recovered from the flu, Doug Keary, Bob Whitehouse, Dave Miller, Terry McLaughlin and Bruce Kirby met to discuss changes to *Canada 1*. It was decided to remove some ballast to improve her light-air perform-ance. With Friday, July 29, a day off for *Canada 1*, the task was taken care of that morning. Mark Vinbury arrived to perform an in-water measurement at eight o'clock. The ballast was removed by nine, and at four-thirty that afternoon Kirby was pleased to report that the boat measured in at a satisfactory 11.992 metres.

During the day, Bruce Kirby, Doug Keary and John Morgan conferred by telephone with Marvin McDill on the subject of *Australia II*'s keel. Though the Keelgate incident had been settled, the keel's legal status had not. McDill had turned over the responsibility of raising the issue with Tony Watts to Paul Henderson. McDill now informed management in Newport that Henderson would speak with Watts at an IYRU meeting in Los Angeles on Tuesday, August 2.

Out on Rhode Island Sound, racing for the day was producing a glut of repairs for the maintenance crews. The race between *Challenge 12* and *France 3* was abandoned when *Challenge 12* suffered a breakdown before the start. *Azzurra* dropped out of her race with *Australia II* when her crew couldn't bail fast enough to keep her from sinking in the rough seas and 18-knot winds. And *Victory 83* earned a sailover from *Advance* when the Sydney yacht was dismasted. For *Advance* and *France 3*, their summers were all but over; both faced elimination unless they won their next race. Nonetheless, the *Advance* camp earned tremendous respect by staying up all night to install a new mast so that they could sail the race that would eliminate them.

Saturday, July 30. *Canada 1*'s tailspin continued. Using the Sobstad Storer S3.1 mainsail in 20 knots of wind, *Canada 1* started well against *Azzurra*. The first beat was exhilarating, as her crew executed about 30 tacks in an attempt to stay in phase with Mauro Pelaschier. The Canadians were never able to force the Italians over to a lay-line, where they could park on their wind and collect an almost-standard weather mark advantage of one minute. Instead, *Azzurra* refused to be covered and hung in to round the mark only two boat-lengths behind.

At the gybe *Canada 1*'s spinnaker pole end fitting jammed. *Azzurra* made a better rounding and rolled over the Canadians on the second reach. Upwind, a depleted sail inventory forced the *Canada 1* crew to select the weary Dacron N15 genoa. *Azzurra* pulled away and went on to win by 1:23.

At the post-race debriefing, problems were rehashed. McLaughlin and Boyd were not happy with their performance, and no one needed to remind them. Boyd was convinced that the N15 genoa had been the problem. It seemed that *Canada 1* moved well only in winds above 15 knots and below 20, or simply whenever the opportunity arose to use the N33 fan-cut genoa.

Sunday, July 31. With *Canada 1* limping with a 2-3 record for the second round of Series C, the pressure was on to score another win. Before the start against *Victory 83*, Peter de Savary motored by in *Lisanola*. Phil Crebbin, the British starting helmsman, was on the bow. When the Canadians asked what was wrong, Crebbin said that he was just taking the day off. It was, however, the beginning of Crebbin's bitter trip into de Savary's outbasket.

Crebbin announced that they had a surprise for the Canadians – Harold Cudmore, a former helmsman candidate, was back. At the last protest hearing between the two challenges, the Canadians had made a point of asking the British where Cudmore was, hinting that without him *Victory 83* had become an easy kill on the starting line.

An interesting announcement by Crebbin, but completely untrue. Lawrie Smith and Rodney Pattisson were sharing the helm. *Canada 1* chalked up yet another start against the British, pinning them away from the line at the port end to begin the race with a 30-second lead. In the light, veering easterly, though, *Victory 83* took the lead only halfway up the beat as *Canada 1* tested out a new vertical-cut Mylar genoa with a horizontal-cut Kevlar leech, dubbed the N24. On the second beat, a deflated Terry McLaughlin told Jeff Boyd to take the wheel. Boyd wasn't happy seeing McLaughlin give up and was careful to hand back the helm before they crossed the finish line, 3:08 behind.

The second round of Series C was over. *Canada 1*'s 2-4 record for the round left her 7-5 for the series. *Australia II* had defeated *Challenge 12* by 3:50, assuring herself a position in the semi-finals. The final race of the day, between *France 3* and *Advance*, was abandoned because of fog, further postponing the inevitable. The race for the final three semi-final positions was still among four boats – *Victory 83*, *Challenge 12*, *Azzurra* and *Canada 1*.

Monday, August 1. The resailed race between *Challenge 12* and *France 3*, abandoned on July 29, was the only one held. The race committee's decision to allow for a resail rather than grant *France 3* a sailover on the basis of *Challenge 12*'s breakdown had not sat well with some of the other challenge camps, not to mention the French. Regardless, the resail took place, with *Challenge 12* winning by 53 seconds in heavy fog.

While the Canadians enjoyed their day off, Jeff Boyd learned that the challenge was all but flat broke. It was not the kind of information he needed turning over in his mind. Should the crew strive to make the semi-finals and then not have enough money to continue, or should they just lose now and bring the summer to a merciful halt?

Whatever happened, they wouldn't be going to the finals against the Americans on the basis of a protest. That morning the race committee had met with the representatives of the challenge syndicates to discuss the implications of the letter Robert McCullough sent to Mark Vinbury. Copies of the letter were distributed.

The Australians had fought an effective battle against the allegations in McCullough's letter. Under the guidance of Warren Jones, they publicly ridiculed the position of the New York Yacht Club. The club could not appeal *Australia II*'s rating certificate at the IYRU through the United States Yacht Racing Union because the USYRU was the improper national authority – *Australia II*'s measurement certificate had been granted under the authority of the Australian Yachting Federation. And, as many observers agreed, whether *Australia II*'s draught increased when heeled was irrelevant. The measurement instructions called for draught to be assessed with the hull in an upright position. By questioning the fairness of the measurement process (and the fact that the draught did increase probably had little to do with the keel's purpose or effectiveness), the club was trying to change the rules at the last minute to suit its own convenience.

The syndicate's success in its running battle of words and letters and press releases with the NYYC had a significant effect on its fellow challenge aspirants. Recognizing that the measurement committee had declared *Australia II*'s keel legal, the challengers voted to stick together. No challenger would protest *Australia II* during the selection process. In ensuing discussions, the four semi-finalists would agree that, should *Australia II* later prove irreparably illegal, the runner-up in the challengers' trials would advance to the finals against the Americans. The challengers were determined to rally behind *Australia II*. The New York Yacht Club's effort to have the Canadians conduct its battles had failed.

Tuesday, August 2. Back to racing on the 14-mile short course, *Canada 1* began the day with a bye and ended with a gift. In the morning, while the Canadians passed the time, *Australia II* had defeated *Azzurra* by two minutes; *Victory 83* had nipped across the finish line 27 seconds ahead of

Challenge 12. *Advance* and *France 3* had attempted to resail their race left over from the second round when *Advance* lost her rig, but both boats broke down before the starting gun and were rewarded with losses.

In the afternoon *Victory 83* won over *Azzurra* by 1:12. Before her start against *Canada 1*, *Australia II* sent her bow man, Scotty McAllister, aloft to tend to a breakdown. The mast crane, which juts aft from the top of the mast and supports the backstay and mainsail halyard pulley, collapsed while McAllister was making repairs, breaking his arm and bringing his career aboard *Australia II* to an untimely end. *Canada 1* cruised around the course to earn a badly needed point, but the win was an unsatisfying one. The mutual losses by *Advance* and *France 3* in the morning meant that neither boat was statistically capable of qualifying for the semi-finals. Both were excused from further competition. The French fruitlessly resisted the out-basket, arguing that *France 3* should remain in competition at least until the end of the series so that there would be an even number of boats in the round-robin. *Advance* withdrew quietly.

Wednesday, August 3. To stay comfortably in the race for the last semi-final berth, *Canada 1* had to win at least one of her two races. She would win both starts but could not follow through to the finish line.

On the tow out to the race course, Rob Muru would not shut up about keel wings – they *had* to get some. He went on about two guys, Juan and Yvon, who worked in his dad's machine shop. In fact, Muru was always going on about Juan and Yvon. With those two in camp, why, they'd have a set of wings whipped up in ten minutes. Muru was wearing his usual cockeyed smile – the very smile he wore when the stereo system in his van was grinding out Stompin' Tom Connors tapes that immortalized the Ontario Provincial Police and truckers hauling P.E.I. spuds down the 401 – and it was hard to know whether to take him seriously.

Against *Victory 83*, the Canadians forced Phil Crebbin (back on board for a spell) to start early, which gave *Canada 1* a comfortable 45-second lead. In six knots of wind, the British closed quickly. Attempting to cover, *Canada 1* threw the race away in one manoeuvre. *Victory 83* was approaching on starboard, with *Canada 1* crossing on port. Terry McLaughlin wanted to tack on the opposition; Jeff Boyd told him to leave the British alone – they'd sail right through *Canada 1* if she tried to cover in this little wind. McLaughlin decided to tack, but left it too late. *Victory 83* spurted through *Canada 1*'s lee, and the race was decided. McLaughlin was furious with himself.

In the afternoon race, *Canada 1* sailed a tight opening leg against *Challenge 12*, but the Australians squeezed into the lead at the weather mark and slowly pulled away on the reaches. The Canadians suffered forestay damage and unofficially dropped out at the end of the run. They didn't want to officially withdraw, because if *Challenge 12* happened to lose her rig or sink before the end of the race, *Canada 1* could always turn around and limp to the finish to collect a point. The behaviour of *Canada 1* caused some confusion between the race committee and the Canadian tender. Only when *Challenge 12* crossed the line did *Canada 1* inform the race committee of the problem.

At the post-race debriefing, Terry McLaughlin pondered Rob Muru's morning performance. "Maybe Muru's right," he mused. "Maybe we do need wings. Pull out all stops."

There were only two races left in Series C, between *Canada 1* and *Azzurra*, and *Australia II* and *Challenge 12*. *Australia II*, with 19.8 points, had comfortably qualified for the semi-finals. *Victory 83*, at 13.4, had also advanced to the next round. *Azzurra*, at 12.2, could lose to *Canada 1* and still make the cut. That left *Canada 1*, at 10.7, and *Challenge 12*, at 10.6. Although *Challenge 12* had compiled a 2-1 record against *Canada 1* in Series C, the Melbourne yacht had lost all three races to *Azzurra* and could only beat *Victory 83* once. *Challenge 12* faced a near-impossible race against *Australia II*, a boat she had yet to beat in Series C. But should *Challenge 12* win her race, whether at the finish line or in the protest room, and should *Canada 1* lose to *Azzurra*, *Challenge 12* would advance to the semi-finals.

The Canadians were facing what Terry McLaughlin had always talked about, the ultimate outbasket. Earlier in the summer, while *Canada 1* was being towed out to the starting line and the routine of the long Newport day was setting in, Terry McLaughlin had turned to Jeff Boyd.

"Someday we'll be going out to race just like this," he said, "and we'll know that, if we lose, we won't ever get to do it again."

Thursday, August 4. It was another must-win race, another they resolved to win for Marvin McDill. They could lose and still advance to the semi-finals if *Australia II* defeated *Challenge 12*, but they wanted to control their own destiny, not rely on someone else's misfortune. And qualifying for the semi-finals by only one-tenth of a point over *Challenge 12* would only arouse the memory of the sailover they had enjoyed against *Australia II* – a fluke win that would make it seem they had backed into the next series. Despite having had dismal races the preceding day, the Canadians had to come up with a good race, and that was something they had usually managed against the Italians.

Storms and large windshifts caused the abandonment of the first start between *Azzurra* and *Canada 1*, as well as the race between *Australia II* and *Challenge 12*, with *Australia II* 100 yards ahead on the first reach. The race area was crowded with large spectator craft, including an Italian naval frigate and the 85-foot *Shazu*, chartered by the syndicate with funding from Labatt's as *Canada 1*'s official tender.

That morning Doug Keary had discovered that *Canada 1* had requested a half-hour delay in the start of her race against *Challenge 12* the previous day to tend to her forestay. The race committee had denied the Canadians the delay and they had, of course, gone on to suffer forestay damage and withdraw from the race. Keary thought that the denial was incorrect and highly suspicious considering the resail *Challenge 12* had been granted against *France 3* when the Australian yacht broke down. Keary had requested that the Canadians file a protest, and his decision was supported by John Morgan. The protest was dropped, however, when the race committee suggested that it would be unwise politically, possibly encouraging *Australia II* to throw her race against *Challenge 12*.

At three o'clock, the race between *Australia II* and *Challenge 12* was restarted. At the weather mark, *Australia II* led by only 12 seconds. *Challenge 12* was already flying a protest flag.

Under clearer skies and with 12- to 15-knot winds, Terry McLaughlin was his usual aggressive self on the starting line, keeping Mauro Pelaschier under control for most of the pre-start sequence. *Canada 1* protected the right, luffing to windward as she held *Azzurra* to the pin end of the line. With 30 seconds remaining, *Canada 1* tacked away onto port and drove for the line. *Azzurra* tacked with her and at the gun was up on *Canada 1*'s weather hip, trailing by about one boat-length.

A windshift had made the first beat virtually a long starboard fetch. Terry McLaughlin wanted to tack and position himself on the inside, between *Azzurra* and the weather mark. *Canada 1* came about, crossed the Italian 12-Metre ("Azzulu," as Al Megarry called her), then tacked back to apply a loose cover. That brought on a predictable tack from Pelaschier to stay out of phase. *Canada 1* followed through, coming about directly to windward to slam *Azzurra* with a right-on-the-face tack designed to force the Italians to the right, where they would eventually run out of room. The exchanges continued, with *Canada 1* covering tight on starboard and loose on port, until McLaughlin faked a tack to fall into phase with *Azzurra*, dumping dirty air on the Italians as they both headed to the right, on port.

Peter Wilson thought that they were close to the starboard lay-line and suggested they tack, which they did, leaving *Azzurra* to herself. *Azzurra* carried on for a few minutes, then joined *Canada 1* on starboard tack. It was now clear that, not only was *Canada 1* not on the lay-line, but *Azzurra* was moving well off on her own. The aft cockpit of *Canada 1* was tense, with Terry McLaughlin repeatedly asking Jeff Boyd how they were doing. Boyd was trying to be honest but at the same time keep McLaughlin psyched up.

They were soon almost upon the weather mark and the port tack lay-line. *Canada 1* came about.

"Can we cross?" McLaughlin demanded.

"I don't think so," Boyd said. "Close, though."

"What do we do?" McLaughlin pressed.

Boyd didn't have much time to think. Reactions were down to instinct. "Tack as close to him as possible," he said at last. It was a dangerous move – if the lee-bow didn't affect *Azzurra* immediately, she could run *Canada 1* right past the port tack lay-line, now only a minute or two away, then tack back for the mark at her leisure.

Right after the tack, *Canada 1* looked doomed. *Azzurra* had obviously been laying off slightly, building speed as she approached; when *Canada 1* tacked, *Azzurra* came back up onto course and began to roll the Canadians. Boyd's call wasn't looking too inspired.

"Sandy!" shouted Terry, and *Canada 1* suddenly veered into a luff. Her spreaders poked into one of *Azzurra*'s San Francisco mainsails.

"Protest, protest!" Terry McLaughlin cried. "You're not mast abeam. *You're not!*" Out came the red flag. The Italians were furious, stunned and confused all at once.

"...five-five, five-six, five-seven..." Al Megarry called out their velocity as they settled into the new tack.

"Go for speed. We need speed," Boyd coaxed McLaughlin.

"Trim the main. Get the traveller out," McLaughlin instructed Rob Muru. "Don't let anything out," he told everyone else.

"...five-eight, five-nine..." Overhead, airplanes droned.

"He's tacking, he's tacking," announced Boyd as Pelaschier, for some reason, swung *Azzurra* over onto port.

"Laying off for speed," announced McLaughlin. "Ease. *Ease*. Coming about," he then said, and *Canada 1* fell onto port tack, with the weather mark five or six lengths away. "Main in. Hold it, hold it. How far off the mark?"

"About a boat-length," said Peter Wilson.

"Trim, trim," McLaughlin ordered. Winches clattered. Wire leads strained in their blocks. "Hold it."

"...six-six, six-seven..."

Boyd dived to the leeward side to find *Azzurra*, fearing that the Italians would be coming back on starboard, but they were still holding on port. "A little below the mark right now," Boyd reported, returning to the weather side for a look.

"Hold it!" McLaughlin reminded the tailers. "Don't *fucking* trim."

"...seven-four, seven-six..."

"Don't do anything," McLaughlin commanded the tailers. He looked to Sandy Andrews, his second pair of eyes. "Sandy, get up there."

"I think he's overlaid by a mile," Boyd told his skipper, watching *Azzurra* tack onto starboard for the mark. "I think you can go now. Just go head to wind, and go for it."

"Tacking!"

McLaughlin spun *Canada 1* around the orange inflatable mark just in front of a stampeding *Azzurra*. The Italians broke out their own protest flag, claiming *Canada 1* had tacked too close. It was not unlike pulling out onto a highway from a feeder lane. If the oncoming driver has to brake to avoid tail-ending you, you've fouled him.

"Stay up, stay up!" the crew of *Canada 1* yelled at *Azzurra* as McLaughlin drove up *Canada 1* to avoid being rolled. But Rob Muru, expecting to round the mark, had completely eased the mainsail.

"Trim the main!" McLaughlin screamed. "Trim the fucking main! Trim the sails! *Trim the fucking sails!*" McLaughlin was verging on hysterical. All he had fought for at the end of the leg was in danger of slipping away. Boyd was on the foredeck awaiting the spinnaker hoist. Two Ton calmed Terry down, and he prepared to bear *Canada 1* off to begin the reach, with *Azzurra* still trailing. "Main out a little bit," he said evenly. "Laying off now... *Hoist.*"

The first reach was quite broad, almost a run, which made protecting against an inside overlap difficult. McLaughlin, continually steering low to shut out *Azzurra*, was wondering what to do at the gybe. Boyd suggested they gybe early to protect the inside. They could always gybe back again to lay the mark. There was no way *Azzurra* could sail all the way around them.

Ten boat-lengths from the mark, they made their gybe. Sailing very broad, *Canada 1* was able to lay the mark without gybing back. After rounding, they put on the reaching strut, which kept the weather spinnaker sheet clear of the shrouds. They increased their lead a few more lengths on the tight second reach, and added on still more when *Azzurra* blew out a spinnaker.

On the second beat, the wind was becoming quite shifty, and the course was pocked with holes. The Canadian strategy was to cover *Azzurra* closely on port and affect their air as much as possible for the few tacks before Pelaschier would get out of phase. At that point, they would cover loosely to keep them in check. They were able to work *Azzurra* to the left; after playing a number of shifts well, the Canadians began the run with a lead of well over one minute.

Azzurra powered down the run on her own breeze, closing some 45 seconds and rounding the leeward mark only a few lengths behind. *Canada 1* covered closely, avoided the usual disasters, and won by 39 seconds.

Australia II had beaten *Challenge 12* by 1:05, though *Challenge 12* was still flying her protest flag at the finish. The Canadians informed the race committee of their own protest and headed home. The race had been nerve-wracking, but it had also been fun.

Ed Gyles pulled alongside in the rubber duck to tell Terry McLaughlin and Jeff Boyd that they were wanted aboard *Shazu*. A sailor in a white suit helped them aboard the magnificent yacht, where they wandered into a floating cocktail party. Marvin McDill was there, as well as Hugh Drake, and Bruce Kirby, and Doug Keary, and John Morgan, and Basil Rodomar, and their wives and companions, and friends of McDill from Calgary and Rodomar from Toronto. McLaughlin and Boyd stood in their foul-weather gear, watching a video replay of the race and drinking Budweisers. They would win their protest against *Azzurra* and have the Italian protest for tacking too close dismissed. *Challenge 12* decided not to file their protest against *Australia II* and made a most unexpected exit from the challenge trials.

Back on shore, the Canadian sailors bumped into John Bertrand. "You should see the *Challenge 12* compound right now," Bertrand told them. "Those guys are *devastated*." The Melbourne crew were going home. Their boat was staying in Newport, chartered by the *Australia II* syndicate as a trial horse. She would be sailed by the crew of *Advance*. For the losingest sailors of the 1983 America's Cup, helping fine-tune the yacht that would make sporting history would be a sweet and deserving conclusion to a trying summer.

outbasket

Friday, August 5, was the start of a six-day layover between Series C and the semi-finals. It was decided to pull out the mast and move *Canada 1* to Newport Offshore, where further modifications would be performed. While management met in the morning to discuss sails, the rest of the camp concerned itself with the transport of *Canada 1* and the impending arrival of Bill Davis, the premier of Ontario.

At 12:30, the 85-foot *Shazu* docked alongside the yard to begin the Davis review. Davis, provincial cabinet minister Tom Wells and Allan Gotlieb, the Canadian ambassador to the United States, stepped ashore with their wives for a guided tour of the yard and an introduction to the crew of *Canada 1* and the camp's management. With *Clipper* out sailing, the politicians departed seaward for the opportunity to sail a 12-Metre. Bill Davis proved to be a very take-charge fellow. He steered *Shazu* on the way to the rendezvous on Rhode Island Sound and, while being transferred by the rubber duck to *Clipper*, bumped Ed Gyles off the helm. On board *Clipper* the crew wagered among themselves how long it would take the premier to out-basket the skipper and assume the wheel.

While the guests of honour took turns cavorting on *Clipper* and relaxing aboard the monstrous *Shazu*, Marvin McDill met with Doug Keary, Bruce Kirby, Bob Whitehouse, Dave Miller, Terry McLaughlin and Jeff Boyd to review the challenge's sorry finances. There was, McDill revealed, no immediate relief for the money shortage. They agreed that expenses during the layover period should be funded through subscription separate from the overall budget. Twenty-five thousand dollars was required for the back-up Stearn rig on the way; another $25,000 would be needed to fill the proposed sail orders. The sails and the mast would have to wait. A go-ahead was given for modifications to *Canada 1*'s hull at Newport Offshore, which would cost about $10,000.

Following the meeting, the camp's members made their way to Hammersmith Farm, once the "summer White House" of John F. Kennedy, for a clambake hosted by Louis Vuitton, the French luggage manufacturer which was sponsoring the challengers' trials. The clambake turned out to be a sit-down dinner for over 500 people and featured a 20-piece orchestra. At the

Removing a "window" of lead from Canada 1*'s keel*

end of the evening, the cash-poor Canadians returned to Sherman House loaded with catalogues, posters and booklets distributed by the munificent sponsor.

Saturday, August 6. Terry McLaughlin and Jeff Boyd wandered by Newport Offshore in the morning to see exactly what was being done to *Canada 1*. The work was being performed not in a shed, but in the open yard. Whenever a 12-Metre was visible on dry land it usually attracted a crowd, and *Canada 1* was no exception. Onlookers were further attracted by the dust and noise emanating from its area in the yard. At the same time, shut up in a shed and guarded by far tighter security, the American *Defender* was undergoing alterations to the aft 20 per cent of her underbody in a last-ditch effort to overcome Dennis Conner's *Liberty*. Earlier in the summer, *Defender* had undergone more radical surgery, with deep pie-shaped slivers cut into her amidship to raise her sagging ends, which had given her an excessive waterline length and cost her a considerable amount of sail area.

After Series C, the Canadians had considered moving *Canada 1*'s mast still further forward. In doing so, however, they would run out of bow in attempting to maintain a satisfactory distance between the mast and the forestay at deck level. Kirby toyed with the idea of a short bowsprit, but the mast move was ultimately shelved. Alterations to *Canada 1* focused on familiar territory – the keel.

McLaughlin and Boyd watched as workers used blow torches to melt lead away from the keel. To improve light-air performance, Kirby had elected to go beyond the removal of interior ballast undertaken late in Series C and put a "window" in the keel, removing some 800 pounds of lead. The leading edge of the keel was also further sloped, with the toe being rounded more and a "fillet" being installed to make for an even smoother junction between hull and keel at the leading edge. (Cino Ricci of *Azzurra* was enraged that the Canadians would undertake such major changes on the eve of the semi-finals – it just wasn't sporting – and he made his displeasure known to Rob Muru.) McLaughlin didn't think there had been much of a change to the leading edge, and he and Boyd returned to the base to speak with Doug Keary. The three men then visited Bruce Kirby at the house he rented in Newport.

The meeting lasted only 15 minutes. Kirby assured them that the changes were significant, and that he couldn't go any further in modifying the leading edge without radically altering the keel's cross-sectional foil shape. Boyd got the feeling that McLaughlin wasn't completely satisfied with the explanation.

Later that afternoon, Kirby telephoned Boyd at the base and asked him to come over to Newport Shipyard. "We've just cut *Liberty*'s toe off our boat," he reported. The implication was strong: Kirby wasn't thrilled with McLaughlin and Boyd having input on his design. Boyd felt Kirby's attitude was understandable – he and McLaughlin weren't exactly experts on naval architecture – but he also felt they had all agreed a change was needed.

Boyd joined Kirby in an examination of Dennis Conner's defence candidate, which was out of the water. Sure enough, *Liberty*'s keel had a fairly square-looking toe, and Kirby did his best to make Boyd feel some responsibility for the alterations to *Canada 1*. Still, Boyd thought *Liberty*'s leading edge was quite different.

When the 1983 America's Cup was over, Bruce Kirby would defend his design by emphasizing what he viewed as the ordinariness of her keel; it was no longer an exotic appendage that scored psyche points. Kirby would point out how similar its angular profile was to the keels in Pelle Petterson's 6-Metre and 8-Metre designs. Moreover, he would insist on the similarities between the angle of the leading edge of *Canada 1*'s keel and those of *Freedom*, *Liberty* and *Courageous*. But the question of the angular toe, which did indeed appear in Petterson's work, was complicated by the recollections of Steve Killing, Kirby's assistant. Killing had been under the impression that they intended to get rid of the toe sooner or later; in his mind the toe added significant drag to the keel.

In the aftermath of the challenge, Kirby would only concede that *Canada*

1 might have been a little too stiff, and that the removal of some 1000 pounds of ballast over the summer probably helped her performance, as it would *Liberty*'s for the final race of her match with *Australia II*. Kirby's attitude was plainly that *Canada 1* had not been given a fair shake. "As you know," he would say, "I thought her problems were from the deck up."

Sunday, August 7. An open 10-kilometre road race was held at Brenton Reef State Park, with a $1000 prize for the 12-Metre syndicate that fielded the fastest representative. Phil Gow and Paul Hansen, *Canada 1*'s grinders, entered the race. It was a scorching midsummer day; Gow overheated and was forced to rest for a few minutes, but Hansen placed 30th overall to collect the prize money for the challenge. With funds so short, the prize could well have allowed the crew to eat for the next week.

Monday, August 8. In fog that drastically reduced visibility, a crew of 7 sailed *Clipper* back and forth between Fort Adams and Goat Island, inspecting and taking photographs of four genoas. Terry McLaughlin had learned from Tom Whidden that *Canada 1*'s #1 and #2 headsails might be too flat at the upper speed stripe, with 8 per cent of draught instead of 12-13 per cent. With that, Kent Luxton had recut all of their lighter genoas.

While *Clipper* inspected sails, Terry McLaughlin raced in the America's Tea Cup, a regatta organized by Leeds Mitchell Jr. for 12-Metre representatives every cup summer. The regatta was sailed in Illusions – a class of 12-foot miniature 12-Metres – and 10-foot prams. Bill Campbell, the navigator of *Courageous*, won. McLaughlin finished third.

The following day was again devoted to examining sails as *Clipper* frolicked on Narragansett Bay. That evening, the French hosted a cocktail party at their crew house. Although the French had been eliminated and Bruno Troublé and Patrick Haegeli had headed home, the rest of the squad was still having its customary good time. *France 3* was staying on in Newport as a trial horse for *Azzurra*. *Ciao*.

Wednesday, August 10. With the semi-finals starting the next day, the Canadian effort was beginning to coalesce. On August 7 Marvin McDill had reported a promise of a $50,000 private donation, and so gave approval for placing an order for new sails. At the end of the first day of racing, the challenge would receive $115,000 from Harold Siebens, a friend of James Richardson who had made regular gifts to *Canada 1* on the basis of a performance incentive scheme.

After dinner on August 8 Bruce Kirby had telephoned Doug Keary with the idea of a "penalty pole," an overlong spinnaker pole used by the Americans which carried a rating penalty, but which, according to Kirby, could add one-tenth of a knot to the speed of the boat for every six inches of extra length. Although Sandy Andrews was not enthralled with the potential problems the pole represented for him, especially during gybes, the camp management decided on the morning of August 9 to try out one such pole.

On August 10, *Canada 1* was remeasured. White marks on the hull indicated the old, heavier-displacement measuring points; red marks indicated the measuring points for the new, lighter-displacement *Canada 1*. The Canadians would have the option of converting *Canada 1* back to her old displacement, providing the authorities were duly notified. Dennis Conner had set off a howl of protest from the *Defender-Courageous* camp earlier in the summer when it was revealed that *Liberty* had been racing in the selection trials with as many as three different rating certificates according to the amount of ballast she was carrying. The certificates were all legal, but Conner made the ballast changes without informing the opposition, who felt the practice undermined their efforts to sail to the best of their abilities against a known opposition.

At the end of remeasuring, *Canada 1* was allowed an extra six inches on the end of the standard spinnaker pole. Over ten inches would have been allowed, were it not for a draught penalty on the trim tab due to the boat's new fore-and-aft trim. Doug Keary concluded the day by ordering a new genoa from Hans Fogh. Known as the N4.5, it would never be used.

The semi-finals represented a clean slate for the four boats involved, as they all began the series with no points. The tried and tested Newport motto of anything being possible on a given day sprang to the mind of some who hoped for upsets, but the selection process had changed significantly. All races would be over 24-mile America's Cup courses. No more would *Canada 1* be able to pin the opposition coming off the line, sail for five minutes, then have Peter Wilson announce how far they had to go to the lay-line. The emphasis now would be on boat speed over the long legs.

And there was no longer a *France 3* or an *Advance* to steamroll for an easy win to rebuild the crew's confidence. The opposition would be tough, well prepared, and in the possession of terrific sail inventories. And then, of course, there was *Australia II*.

It would take a miracle or a breakdown for *Canada 1* to beat the Australians. Boyd was confident that they could defeat *Azzurra*, but the British had improved considerably. *Victory 83* had been fifth at one point in Series C and had come on strongly to finish second overall. Their vast resources and funding had begun to pay off. Stealing the second spot in the challengers' finals from the British was a Herculean assignment.

Thursday, August 11. The skies were overcast and threatening rain as *Canada 1* began circling with *Australia II*. With, as always, nothing to lose, Terry McLaughlin was at his most aggressive. He made the start an enjoyable experience for the rest of the crew, reacting to John Bertrand's moves completely on instinct. *Canada 1* weaved and pirouetted, dashing about in fitful stops and starts and sudden releases of pent-up energy. McLaughlin was like a freestyle skier thrown onto the same stage as a ballroom dancer.

The fast-pace manoeuvring did not let up until the starting gun, when *Canada 1* crossed the line ahead and to leeward of *Australia II*. The wind, an unsteady 15 knots, had built a steep, short chop. *Canada 1* was flying her N33 genoa and her new N2.3 mainsail, a copy of the successful N2.2 which had been equipped with a two-ply Kevlar leech.

The two boats sailed a long starboard tack together. *Australia II* climbed to weather while *Canada 1* footed ahead. After 15 minutes *Canada 1*'s position looked promising and she came about. The crossing was close. *Canada 1* dipped below *Australia II*'s transom, and Bertrand immediately came about. McLaughlin tacked back, the bow of *Canada 1* clearing *Australia II*'s transom by ten feet. *Australia II* tacked again to stay in phase. Normally such an intense series of tacks would rob a 12-Metre of its momentum, but *Australia II*, as usual, was matching *Canada 1*'s speed in no time.

The Canadians decided to carry on to the port lay-line. All the way out on starboard tack, McLaughlin pinched *Canada 1* into the wind to maintain the same fore-and-aft position with *Australia II* so that when *Australia II* tacked for the mark *Canada 1* could follow immediately and not have to overstand to clear her air.

The port tack to the mark was a rougher ride through the steepening chop. The wind had increased to over 20 knots, and *Canada 1* began to take aboard waves over the leeward side, a situation reminiscent of Miami Beach. *Australia II* was having little effect on *Canada 1*, and Jeff Boyd noticed that the Perth yacht was hobbyhorsing considerably. *Canada 1* was able to round the weather mark only six lengths behind, and maintained the gap over the two reaching legs.

Canada 1 rounded onto the second beat in over 22 knots of breeze with a #4 headsail. Soon after clearing the mark, Terry McLaughlin called for a heavier sail. Dave Shaw heaved the Sobstad Storer S16 up on deck. Sandy Andrews, Paul Hansen and Jeff Boyd manhandled the sail all the way forward. Andrews went to the bow with the tack, and Shaw handed the new halyard to Boyd, who was holding onto the sailbag about ten feet aft of the bow. Boyd in turn passed the halyard forward. When Andrews turned to accept the halyard, disaster struck.

The boat dropped into a huge trough. The following wave broke over the bow, tearing the N24 from tack to head, leaving only the luff tape in place while the rest of the sail flapped like a banner from the halyard terminus and the sheet block on deck. The wave continued on its destructive path, washing overboard Sandy Andrews and the S16. Chaos.

Al Megarry, in his tailer's cockpit, was able to grab Andrews as he swept along the side of the boat. He was wearing a drysuit, which gave him some buoyancy. Shaw and Hansen were able to hang on to the end of the S16 sausage bag at the aft side of the shrouds, leaving three-quarters of the bundled sail dragging in the water like a sea anchor.

Seven minutes later *Canada 1* was sailing again, with the S16 genoa up and the shreds of the N24 stuffed below. It had been a prickly situation, exhausting work that had required almost every available hand on the foredeck.

Australia II, in the meantime, had been cruising into an even greater lead. *Canada 1* began the final beat far behind. Another wave swallowed the bow, and the S16 blew out. They still had the Dacron N15 as a last resort, but Rob Muru noticed that the upper leech of the mainsail was tearing, and they elected to withdraw to make repairs.

In the other pairing *Azzurra* had dropped out on the opening beat with rigging problems. The British, having damaged their rudder, limped around the course, steering with the trim tab, to collect a win. By all accounts, it had been an interesting day.

Friday, August 12. Jeff Boyd awoke feeling as though he had been in a bar brawl. He was sore and slow from the previous day's foredeck struggle and felt little compulsion to get out of bed. The storm had blown all night; the wind in the morning was from the north in excess of 30 knots, and visibility was poor.

The race committee postponed racing until 1:30, about as late as they could wait to send the 12-Metres out and still get in a race, and told the semi-finalists to rendezvous at the "ACT" buoy. Now blowing 25 knots or more, a driving rain and fog limited visibility to 100 yards or less.

Rob Muru became seasick during the tow. Terry McLaughlin radioed the yard, better known as the Forum, and instructed them to get Fred Schueddekopp out to the "ACT" buoy to replace Muru. Jimmy Johnston and Schueddekopp piled into the Whaler, which had neither chart nor compass, to meet *Canada 1*.

The race committee changed their mind and redirected the 12-Metres to the "Alpha" buoy, which was even further from land. Once they reached the buoy, the committee changed their mind about racing entirely and sent everyone home. The day having been wasted, Mark Millen turned *Canada 1* around to begin the long journey home. *Canada 1*'s was the slowest tow and soon she was alone in the fog.

While *Canada 1* was returning to dock, Doug Keary was busy issuing an All Points Bulletin on one 16-foot Canadian runabout, two passengers.

Johnston and Schueddekopp had not known about the rendezvous change. No one knew where they were.

When the tow reached the base, there was still no word on the whereabouts of the most famous member of the challenge's support personnel and the pinch-hitting mainsail trimmer. Eventually a small cruiser towed the Whaler in. Johnston and Schueddekopp, unable to find any 12-Metres at the "ACT" buoy, had steered back to land in disgust. When their engine packed in at Castle Hill, they threw out a hook and waited for a hitch. The crew of Canada 1 found it difficult to tell them that, while they were out in the Whaler narrowly avoiding their death cruise, Rob Muru had recovered enough to sail anyway.

Sunday, August 14. Saturday had been another cancelled day of racing, with the wind howling out of the northeast and the waves reaching life-threatening dimensions. The sun was out on Sunday, and so were the spectators, in record numbers. With winds of 18 knots or more, Canada 1 attempted to engage with the British during the pre-start sequence, but Victory 83, on direct orders from Peter de Savary, ran off to hide in the spectator fleet. Their retreat strategy worked; Victory 83 popped back out of the fleet, taking Canada 1 by surprise and locking on her tail. Deep in the cone, Canada 1 luffed to shake the British, and Victory 83 coasted through her lee.

At the gun, Victory 83 nearly caught them with a lee-bow, but the Canadians, carrying greater momentum, climbed over her into clear air. A shifting wind had made the beat a long starboard tack. Canada 1 was moving well. After 20 minutes Victory 83 came about. The Canadians were clearly ahead, and McLaughlin tacked directly in front of her. The disturbed air should have had a prompt effect on the British, but Canada 1 somehow managed to lose considerable distance to windward after the tack, and they were then forced to pinch well above closehauled to avoid a fishing launch. It took five minutes of sailing to force the British to tack away.

When the boats next crossed, Victory 83 ducked Canada 1's transom; at the subsequent encounter, Canada 1 executed a lee-bow. It was obvious that on each tack the Canadians were losing perplexing distance to windward, so much so that when they again crossed, Victory 83 was able to tack on top of them.

Canada 1 began the first reach 18 seconds behind. The leg was quite broad; when Jeff Boyd returned to the aft cockpit after a routine hoist, he learned that there was trouble with the rudder. McLaughlin could feel through the wheel the blade wobbling back and forth. An inspection revealed that the top of the rudder quadrant was indeed moving, which explained Canada 1's poor performance to windward. A broken bearing meant that the rudder post was not being held in place. With the post wandering about under the usual stresses on the helm, there was a danger of causing damage to the through-hull shaft. They retired from the race soon after rounding the gybe mark. The crew were lucky not to have done serious harm to the boat. With *Australia II* on her way to demolishing *Azzurra* by 3:20, *Canada 1* returned to base to make repairs. After two races in the semi-finals, she had yet to reach the finish line.

Monday, August 15. The sunny day was the fourth that brought northerlies, although for once the wind was light. As had been the case all summer, *Canada 1* fixed on *Azzurra's* tail early in the pre-start manoeuvres. They pinned the Italians outside the cone at the port end. Both boats started late, with *Azzurra* trailing.

As soon as they cleared the line, the Italians tacked onto starboard; *Canada 1* covered. *Azzurra* was slightly faster in the light air, and *Canada 1* sacrificed distance to windward to sail down on her air and force her to tack. *Canada 1* went with her. When *Azzurra* tacked back again, *Canada 1* followed, but, unable to stay on her wind, was forced to let her go.

When they met again, the Canadians lee-bowed the Italians to protect the right side. They split and converged four times. *Canada 1* then sailed into a beneficial shift on the right side, and about a mile from the weather mark Terry McLaughlin resorted to a fake tack to fall into phase with the Italians.

McLaughlin hoped to push *Azzurra* back just before the weather mark so that he would have some breathing room at the rounding. On one of the final tacks of the leg, the permanent backstay parted at the masthead; suddenly *Canada 1* was dragging 100 feet of rod rigging in her wake. The backstay helped keep the mast aloft during heavy-air gybes, and was used in pre-bending the mast for upwind mainsail trim. They would have to live without it. Between tacks, Jeff Boyd was able to haul the backstay back aboard. Despite the breakdown, McLaughlin's strategy worked and *Canada 1* rounded the weather mark with a six-length lead.

On the first reach, while Boyd coiled the unmanageable rod rigging and stored it below, *Azzurra* closed until she was almost on their transom, but the Canadian lead held at the gybe mark and they were able to forge a four-length lead on the tighter second reach.

As soon as *Azzurra* rounded the leeward mark, heading left, *Canada 1* covered. In a dying breeze, tacking angles became broader as each 12-Metre cracked off to build up apparent wind. These were conditions in which *Azzurra* shone, and *Canada 1* found it impossible to stay on her air. The Canadians tacked away, hoping to find better wind to the right.

Instead they found a hole. *Canada 1* stopped and spun 360 degrees in her search for wind. Finally the sea breeze filled in from the opposite direction, turning the beat into a run. *Australia II* and *Victory* sailed through both *Canada 1* and *Azzurra*. *Canada 1*'s angle to the weather mark in the new wind was poor. *Azzurra*, finding herself on a perfect close-reaching angle, hoisted the spinnaker and arrived at the mark with a six-minute lead.

The last two legs were one long 9-mile beat as the race committee moved the finish line to accommodate the new wind. Deflated, the Canadians missed a few shifts and lost by a colossal 8:54. *Australia II* had used the sea breeze to turn a close race against *Victory 83* into a comfortable 1:54 win.

After three starts *Canada 1* was winless. There was encouragement to be found in the fact that they had been in every race. But, with the frustration of repeated breakdowns, Jeff Boyd could sense the confidence of the crew waning. The pre-start on-board chatter ("Talk it up, guys, talk it up. Let's win this one.") in the races that followed was half-hearted. The disappointment was beginning to show even in Terry McLaughlin.

The races of August 16 and 17 were sailed in similar conditions. They were bright days, with sea breezes of 10 knots that built to 16 to 18 knots by the end of the race. Against *Australia II* they wanted to split tacks off the line. They got what they wanted: *Canada 1* went right and *Australia II* left. The wind swung to the left, and John Bertrand reached the windward mark with a lead of well over a minute. While he nonchalantly tested sails on the second beat, his lead continued to grow. *Canada 1* closed enough ground on the run to suspect sandbagging on the part of the Australians. *Australia II* won by 1:19. In the most exciting race of the summer, *Azzurra* passed *Victory 83* on the final beat, only to lose by 28 seconds at the finish.

Unless *Canada 1* defeated *Victory 83* the next day, the Canadians would be mathematically eliminated from contention for the challengers' finals. Doug Keary began to make plans with Bob Whitehouse, Kevin Singleton and, in Toronto, Cedric Gyles to close down the camp the following week.

Against *Victory 83*, *Canada 1* forced an incident during the pre-start and raised the protest flag. The British then stayed out of their way to start ahead and to leeward. *Victory 83* hit a nice shift on the left. When they crossed for the first time, Paul Hansen looked up from his grinding position (the grinders never knew what was going on during most of a race) to see the blue and gold 12-Metre from the Royal Burnham Yacht Club surging across their path with enough clearance to accommodate the entire British flotilla. Jeff Boyd looked at a studious McLaughlin, who looked at Hansen, who looked at *Victory 83* and then looked at McLaughlin. Terry understood. The exhaustion and hopelessness on Paul Hansen's face mirrored perfectly the emotions of the entire crew.

They lost by 2:26. That night in the office above Island Windsurfing on Thames Street, the British resorted to the videotape evidence from three angles, including one from a helicopter, to have the Canadian protest disallowed. The dream was over.

At breakfast on Thursday, August 18, Jeff Boyd got the outbasket. With *Canada 1* out of the running, Terry McLaughlin felt that there should be a shake-up in the crew ranks, another change for change's sake. There were no heavy implications in Boyd's being left on shore; they shared some laughter over the switch – Dave Miller would take his place for the day. In addition, a number of *Clipper* sailors – Don Campbell, Daniel Palardy, Brent Foxall, Omar, John Millen and Fred Schueddekopp – were rotated aboard. McLaughlin, also feeling the need for a change, drove the tender on the way out while Boyd handled the tow line and the tender driver, Mark Millen, steered *Canada 1*.

The sky was overcast; the wind was light and a slight fog blanketed Rhode Island Sound. Terry McLaughlin did a fine job against *Azzurra* at the start, protecting the right side of the course. *Canada 1* led most of the way up the opening leg. Over the radio aboard the tender, Jeff Boyd learned that *Azzurra* led by 15 seconds at the weather mark. At the leeward mark, the margin was 55 seconds.

Azzurra continued to pull away, winning by 3:56. *Australia II* lost to *Victory 83* by 2:50; the British celebrated with a joyous abandon normally reserved for a coronation. The Americans weren't so sure about the result – Dennis Conner accused the Australians of throwing the race to take the heat off of the still-festering keel controversy.

Canada 1 was now officially out of the running, although she still had three races to sail. The end of all hope fell hard on Boyd. He badly wanted to leave, now that the challenge was only going through the motions. That night, while Sherman House played host to an especially animated Thursday-night barbecue – the crew demonstrating an odd mixture of regret and relief – he fixed on the idea of sailing his Laser again, of competing in a one-design fleet in which, even if he had a poor race, he could still cross the finish ahead of 20 boats.

He hadn't done a selfish thing, he felt, in over a year. In the summer of 1982 he had wanted to sail in the U.S. Laser Nationals. Terry McLaughlin thought that he should stay in camp and devote himself exclusively to 12-Metres. Boyd made a deal with McLaughlin – if he didn't finish in the top two, he would never again leave camp for a regatta. Boyd finished third. Until now, he had kept his word.

"I'm going home to sail in CORK," he told McLaughlin. It was time for another deal. McLaughlin would let him leave if he stayed tomorrow so that

Terry could get off the boat for a day. Boyd agreed. Dave Miller would be skipper, Paul Parsons tactician and Boyd navigator and starting helmsman.

The race never happened. Heavy fog choked the Sound. *Canada 1* returned to base late in the afternoon. Jeff Boyd and Dave Shaw, who was leaving camp with him, tied the spare tire onto the back of Boyd's van and drove to Sherman House to collect their luggage.

Boyd had cleared his departure with Doug Keary, but not everyone, Marvin McDill included, was happy with crew members leaving before the series was actually over. Boyd knew that he would probably lose face with some members of management, who championed *Advance* as a supreme example of dignified perseverance against hopeless odds. But it was easier for the *Advance* crew to stay in Newport – their homes were on the other side of the world, and they had the opportunity ahead of them to participate in *Australia II*'s drive for the cup. For Boyd, home was a day's drive away, and the challenge had entered a cul de sac. It was time for him to go.

His desire to leave bordered on compulsion – he *had* to get out of Newport. Boyd and Shaw drove all night to reach Kingston. They never stopped talking, their hopes, regrets and fond memories of the challenge pouring forth. They purged themselves of the daily routine of 12-Metre racing; by speaking of the challenge as a past event, an experience already subject to removed analysis, they put as much distance between themselves and Newport with words as they did with Boyd's van.

After nine hours of driving, they collapsed at the home of Boyd's parents. The next day, they shared a few drinks and Boyd saw Shaw off at the train station.

Boyd wasn't sure how the people of Kingston would react to his return. He felt conspicuous appearing in his home town while *Canada 1* continued to race in Newport – an officer whose army was still in the field. *I have a feeling we can go all the way*, he had written in his diary in Palmetto. The challenge had taken him this far: a refugee of the Newport summer, one more casualty of the America's Cup's demand for excellence. Almost two years of his life had been consumed by *Canada 1*. Although the outcome was not as disastrous as that of his Pan American Games campaign, he looked beyond all that he had learned about sailing and about people and found himself far from satisfied with the outcome of the challenge.

The rating of a 12-Metre takes into account only the measurable quantities of hull, sails and rig; it has not found a way to calculate the effects of fate and circumstance. There had been so many pitfalls awaiting the campaign – inexperience, financing, sails, management, crew, design – and before the two years were out *Canada 1* had fallen into one or all of them. Jeff Boyd had stepped back onto the solid ground of Kingston just as the challenge slipped beyond the reach of salvation.

He had returned to an old and close-knit fraternity. When he was a teenager, he and a group of other junior club sailors had pushed a wheelbarrow of ice and beer into the junior room of the Kingston Yacht Club, where they drank and caroused and pondered the larger questions of life. Someone offered the sobering observation that, statistically, one of them was destined to die within the next few years, and someone else took the initiative to make a list of everyone in the room. In the aftermath of *Canada 1*, Boyd would come to consider that the list probably still existed, and, despite the odds, so did everyone whose name had been inscribed on it.

A sailor home from the sea. *Welcome back*, said the fraternity, said Kingston.

On Saturday, August 20, Dave Miller skippered *Canada 1* against *Australia II*. Though he started poorly, Miller lost the race by a respectable 1:11.

After another loss to *Victory 83*, Terry McLaughlin was allowed one last race, against *Azzurra*, which had also been mathematically eliminated, leaving *Australia II* and *Victory 83* to contest the right to meet the Americans in the September finals.

The Canadian challenge was beyond all hope now. Not even Terry McLaughlin's arsenal of orneriness, inspiration and determination could make any difference. But he reached inside one last time. With a crew largely drawn from the ranks of *Clipper*, he sailed a navigator's nightmare which included thick fog and a misplaced weather mark. He led at every mark except the finish, where the Italians slipped through to win by 19 seconds and deliver *Canada 1* a winless record for the nine races of the semi-finals.

McLaughlin's prophecy had been borne out. He had left the base under tow, past Goat Island, and Fort Adams; past Newport Harbor, cluttered with moorings, the shoreline crowded with snapping flags and clapboard buildings painted ivory and ochre and cobalt blue; past Castle Hill and the magnificent estates; and past Brenton Reef Tower, until he was out of sight of land on Rhode Island Sound, one 12-Metre skipper among a select few; and the final defeat had come, and he would not be able to experience all that he had with these people, in this place, in this yacht, ever again.

23

infamy

Sailing against Australia II *is a little like racing at Belmont. The other horse has a blanket around her legs, and you don't know if she has three legs or five.*

– Dennis Conner, September 14, 1983.

Terry McLaughlin was summoned back to 12-Metre racing far sooner than expected. When he answered the telephone at home in Toronto in early September, John Bertrand was on the line. Bertrand wanted a sparring partner to help him prepare for the final match against Dennis Conner and *Liberty*. Would Terry mind coming back to Newport?

The series was scheduled to begin Tuesday, September 13. On Sunday McLaughlin spent a day at the helm of *Challenge 12*, squaring off against Bertrand and *Australia II*. They spent much of their time practising the close-quarters covering tacks known as "slam dunks." Bertrand was coolly familiar with the handling characteristics of his yacht. When Bertrand spun away from one such covering tack, Terry McLaughlin turned to see the bow of *Australia II* clip the radio aerial and then lift clear of the backstay of *Challenge 12* on a wave.

The day before the first race, McLaughlin, Bertrand and *Australia II*'s tactician, Hugh Treharne, spent three hours reviewing videotapes and discussing strategy. Bertrand had always struck McLaughlin as a very pensive person; he seemed constantly concerned about everything. Like someone studying before the day of the big exam, Bertrand wanted to make sure he had everything down pat and appeared deeply interested in McLaughlin's opinions. Although the Australian skipper was fairly confident about his boat speed, he was concerned about starting strategy. Bertrand thought that Conner would try to start near the race committee launch. McLaughlin agreed – in the American trial races he had witnessed over the summer, Conner would often begin circling below the middle of the line and work the circles over to the right, where he would then fight for the starboard lay-line of the cone below the race committee. Bertrand didn't want Conner to

315

succeed, and he didn't want *Liberty* starting anywhere to weather of him. *Liberty*, as he rightly guessed, footed faster than *Australia II*, and would be able to bear off and roll the Australians.

The three men reviewed a number of rule interpretations regarding woolly protest situations, and addressed the problem of covering Dennis Conner upwind. Bertrand wasn't sure how well *Liberty* could tack, although Conner had a formidable reputation for tacking his way out of trouble. Maybe when we get ahead, Bertrand wondered aloud, we shouldn't cover that closely. McLaughlin was taken aback and joined Treharne in convincing Bertrand that he should, whenever practical, keep Conner bound and gagged in a windward blanket.

"I know how fast you can tack, and I know how fast a traditional 12 can tack. If you let him get out of phase," McLaughlin warned Bertrand, "you're crazy."

There was a certain magnificence to John Bertrand; next to him, Dennis Conner looked very ordinary, very *American*, as different from Bertrand as *Liberty* was from *Australia II*, although at 41 Conner was only four years older than his nemesis – a bit paunchy, nervous, hair bleached by an endless summer of 12-Metre racing, a red nylon jacket on his back. Bertrand, when he mounted the podium and made his way to his seat at the opposite end of the long banquet table to the applause of the international press, appeared much larger in life than he did in photographs. Long and lean, broad-shouldered: a swimmer's body, a Finn sailor's body. Fresh from the cockpit of *Australia II* and an opening race loss to *Liberty* after a steering gear failure at the end of the run, he sported a long-sleeved green sweatshirt and yellow vest lined with white fuzz. The outfit made him stand apart, and his facial features only reinforced his alien-ness. Eyes almost oriental, cheekbones high and broad, a wide jaw, a toothy smile, and that Fu Manchu moustache. John Bertrand was almost elfin, an amiable Klingon.

He was a great *technical* sailor, Bruce Kirby would later reflect. Not a McLaughlin – no bursts of smoke and fire or sudden inspiration. Nothing that made you consider him outstandingly instinctive. He had studied hard and learned from his successes and failures over the years. A conservative sailor, not as conservative as Dennis Conner, and not as accomplished either. But a masterful technician. Boats were engines run by the wind, and he tinkered with them and made them go. Theory was his strength, whether in tactics or in science. When he moved to answer a question during press conferences in the Newport Armory, he leaned his long body forward on his elbows, considered the microphone before him on the table, adjusted it like part of *Australia II*'s rigging, and spoke politely in a version of "Strine" (alleged Australian speech) rounded by his years in the United States. He

Workmen attaching experimental wings to the keel of Liberty*'s trial horse,* Freedom

stared into the firing squad of television cameras only ten years away. Before he spoke, he would pause for the longest time, as though he were on a quiz show and there was a proper, perfect answer to be offered. He built his sentences piece by piece until, with a satisfied smile, he offered up the thought he had constructed.

Bertrand's smile was always trying to force itself to the surface – unlike Conner's, which always seemed tight and desperate to hide back inside him. Conner had won today, but it had been under fortuitous circumstances. The Australians had been the first 12-Metre challenger to reach the weather mark in the opening race ahead of the defender. *Liberty* had then slipped by on the second reaching leg, powering over a careless Australian crew. But *Australia II* had charged back on the run, pulling abreast near the end of the leg after trailing by 28 seconds at the windward mark. The run was supposed to be *Australia II*'s weakest point of sail. Despite assurances from the Australians that they had lately been experimenting with different spinnakers and sailing angles, many suspected that their sudden improvement was due to the fact that they had been sandbagging all summer, thereby concealing a formidable secret weapon. During the summer, Jay "Bondo"

McKinnell had dismissed the Lexcen design's chances in a final match, having concluded from his observations that no 12-Metre could regularly lose a minute on the fifth leg and expect to win the series. Terry McLaughlin, though, had begun to suspect sandbagging as early as Series C.

Australia II had shown herself to be vulnerable to *Liberty* on the reaches, but her superiority upwind and on the run (not to mention manoeuvring on the starting line) gave her an advantage on four of six legs. Dennis Conner was facing two hellish weeks of striving to save the America's Cup, and his own skin, which was vulnerable to the worst wishes of his detractors. Conner was talented, exquisitely prepared, and a tad driven to excel whatever the cost. In 1980 he had invited wrath from all sides when he attempted to protest *Australia* for racing without running lights. He was spoilsport to some, having drubbed Tom Blackaller's *Defender*, a self-promoted "people's" campaign which had continually baited Conner, and the sentimental favourite, John Kolius's *Courageous*, on his way to securing the defence nomination for *Liberty*. Conner had spent seven of his last 10 summers and a handful of California winters sailing 12-Metres. He had, since 1974, held the wheel of *Valiant*, and *Mariner,* and *Courageous*, and *Enterprise*, and *Freedom*, and *Magic*, and *Spirit*, and *Liberty*. No one else in the world was more familiar with the feel of a 12-Metre. No one else, despite his detractors, was better suited to defend the cup.

Such qualifications were irrelevant in some circles, both domestic and overseas. They could not make him the people's favourite. *Australia II* was probably the most popular contestant – not even the tainted circumstances surrounding the legality of the keel could detract from her place in the hearts of observers. The NYYC had finally abandoned almost all hope of having the Australian yacht declared illegal by late August, and experimental wings had appeared on the keels of *Freedom, Liberty*'s trial horse, and on *Defender*; in the challengers' finals, which *Australia II* won 4-1, *Victory 83* also tried wings.

Staring into the crowd packing the Newport Armory after the opening race of the 1983 America's Cup, Dennis Conner must have suspected that, polite as the reporters were, their hearts were with John Bertrand. Out on the official press boat, betting was running in favour of *Australia II* at 3 to 1 or more. There was a strong sentiment among professional observers who wanted to see the America's Cup and/or Dennis Conner fall that *Australia II* *had* to win match. If this yacht couldn't carry the series, no challenger ever would. She was the one great hope of the Everest climbers of the yachting fraternity.

There were over 20 aircraft aloft for the second race, including the Goodyear Blimp. With helicopters circling clockwise at 500 feet and airplanes circling counterclockwise at 1000 feet, the sky was filled with the sound of gas-powered lawn mowers; Rhode Island Sound had acquired an oddly suburban resonance. The aircraft had swept into view in a coordinated media strike shortly before the course signals were raised, roaring in above a spectator fleet too large and congested to estimate its size. One could imagine the power winders of the airborne photographers chattering away. Some of the cameras in Newport were mounted on rifle butts. At any moment, the plastic film canisters would surely rain down on the spectator fleet like spent ammunition.

Eric Sharp, a reporter for the *Miami Herald*, studied the sky. He had served in the air force in Vietnam. "Boy, this takes me back," he sighed.

The silver-haired man seated amongst the rest of the press grasped the microphone passed to him and identified himself. "Bob Ross, *Australian Sailing Magazine*. Alan, just a way of understanding what happened to the headboard car, can we ask you to go into a little bit more detail? How things passed up there, what actually gave way..."

Alan Bond's gravelly voice barked over the loudspeakers. "A two-part problem. As we went into a gybe manoeuvre at the start, a pin which holds the headboard into the clip first failed, causing the headboard to come down about 12 inches, where it caught and tore the head of the mainsail from the headboard. It was only fixed by a one-inch piece of Kevlar."

John Bertrand, in what was one of the finest moments in his sailing career, spent the first five minutes of the second race retuning the entire rig of *Australia II* so that he could achieve a serviceable amount of leech tension with the damaged mainsail. With the mast straighter and the boom sheeted down to the deck, Bertrand had actually been able to reach the weather mark with a three-length lead. *Australia II*'s lead held over the two reaching legs, during which crew member Colin Beashel made a half-successful attempt to repair the torn sail while suspended at the masthead in the bosun's chair. In a dying breeze, *Liberty* had been able to tack through the stricken *Australia II* on the second beat and go on to win by 1:33, but not before inviting a protest for tacking too close on the crossing that gave the Americans the lead.

An Australian radio reporter took the microphone. "You've said repeatedly, Alan, that this is the best boat to represent Australia in the America's Cup, the best crew, the most experienced crew.... We've had two races and in both of them there have been significant problems on board the boat, and it prompts the question, what the hell is going on?"

While Dennis Conner had been present, Alan Bond had been loath to discuss the circumstances surrounding the protest, not even the rule under which it was being filed. Now, with the credibility of his challenge questioned, and Conner having left the Armory, Bond could not resist the opportunity to play the wronged underdog.

"Well, I don't know if you'd call it Lady Luck or whatever it is," he replied with a laugh, "but it hasn't been with us." His face then set into a patented stern expression. "We should, if there's any justice in racing, win the protest quite clearly. The incident, at 2:15 . . . they tacked in our water, and we would have had a collision, and we should win the protest. So, maybe we'll be one-all by the end of this evening. Hopefully."

Bond was asked if he regretted not having called a lay-day for today after the steering gear breakdown in the first race.

"It's a very awkward decision," he confessed. "I think the decision we made for, that is, the explanation for. . ." The sentence unravelled and died. Bond couldn't tear his mind away from the more recent breakdown. "We went for a lighter main," he suddenly announced. "The weather forecast was for heavy winds with some gusts 18 to 20 with a gust of up to 24 and lightening off dramatically as the race proceeded. That forecast was very accurate, to us. So we went for a lighter mainsail. A gust of wind hit the boat at 24.6 knots just as we gybed. It was an unusual situation just to be gybing as a gust of wind hit us." He paused, and emphasized, "It's just one of those freak things that just happens in yachting sometimes. The correct decision was made. I think we would have seen a very fine performance from the yacht because we had the right mainsail up for the second and third weather legs particularly. I think we would have won the race today, quite frankly."

"If the committee should reach a decision on the protest tonight," a reporter asked, "how would we find out about it? Is there an unlisted phone number we can have?"

Bill Ficker, the 1970 America's Cup winner who was smoothly moderating the press conferences, waited for the laughter to die before delivering his own punch line. "I'll tell you, if you see a whole lot of Australians out celebrating tonight, I think it will be obvious."

That evening, John Marshall was sitting in the northernmost ground-floor room of the magnificent Seaview Terrace, a classic Newport mansion renamed Freedom House in honour of its occupant, Dennis Conner's defence camp. Marshall, the president of North Sails and *Liberty*'s mainsail trimmer, was nursing a cold. "If the blimp had been straight overhead," he said with congested vowels, "there would be no question of what happened. That's what's so annoying."

"From where we were," said one of two sailing writers with him, "you couldn't tell distance, but it looked like you were fairly far ahead." Behind the group, several sailors were watching a television show full of gunfire and hurtling vehicles.

"Were you tacking to leeward or to windward of him?" the other writer enquired.

"To windward. That's the whole issue, because I'm sure their claim – I haven't seen it yet – is going to be they would have hit our transom. And our view of reality is that, if they had kept going, they would have shot underneath us and been pinned. And to avoid that, they initiated a tack, and swung…they didn't come *close* to hitting us. They swung right across our transom and off on the other tack, no problem. Probably, you know, six feet of water."

"Where were the judges at that point?"

"Unlikely to be able to really see. Probably they didn't even perceive a problem. Slam dunks are so common a part of 12-Metre racing." As John Bertrand, who had spent a day practising both executing and avoiding them with Terry McLaughlin, knew so well.

Protests are rare occurrences in America's Cup matches. A jury's findings can never be certain beyond a shadow of doubt; its members depend on largely subjective testimony from parties and their witnesses and draw the fairest conclusion they can. In earlier America's Cups, fairness was not taken for granted, as the jury was composed of members of the New York Yacht Club. The club was particularly haunted by its jury's decision over a luffing incident on the starting line in 1970 between *Intrepid* and *Gretel II*. The Australian challenger won the race but was disqualified on the basis of a protest from *Intrepid* over the altercation. Although most knowledgeable observers have agreed that the jury decision was the proper one, the club elected to avoid any further conflicts of interest in the protest room by appointing an international jury in future. In 1983 the five-man jury was chaired by Livius Sherwood, a retired provincial court justice from Ottawa.

But the yachtsmen could be as lacking in fairness as any jury. On December 30, 1982, Robert MacArthur of Boston, who would serve as chairman of the jury for the challengers' selection series, had written Sherwood arguing that a jury boat be present on the water each day of racing during the trials. "I might explain here why I want a judge on the water at all. In 1980, that was not planned after the first [challengers'] series had begun. We had a protest on the first day. During testimony by the two yachts' representatives, the jury suspected that one of them was deliberately lying. After a crewman of one of the yachts gave witness testimony, we were sure that was so. After having received testimony from two independent witnesses, we knew which one of the two representatives was deliberately and grossly lying to us. In ordinary circumstances, up to and including a world class championship, we would have dismissed that yacht from the series and sent her home. Obviously, we could not do that in

America's Cup competition without causing a worldwide political firestorm; the head of that country's government would have been on the phone to President Carter the next morning. So that night I asked Bruno Bich [head of the French challenge] for a judge's boat. We had no further problem."

Livius Sherwood and his jury were in no hurry to produce a ruling on the *Australia II* protest. It was of paramount importance to appear and act fair and thorough. The protest hearing was scheduled for the morning of the lay-day following the disputed race, rather than the evening following the race, to allow plenty of time to hear the arguments. The hearing was held at the United States Yacht Racing Union's headquarters on Goat Island, away from Newport's traditional waterfront carnival.

At three-thirty in the afternoon, a decision was finally announced. It was accompanied by an explanatory diagram, borrowed from Conner's presentation, that would put a police accident report to shame. In the words of the jury:

> On the second windward leg of the second race for the 1983 America's Cup, AUSTRALIA II on port tack and LIBERTY on starboard tack converged. AUSTRALIA II was moving marginally slower than LIBERTY as a result of having just tacked onto port tack, and she was sailing about 15 degrees below close hauled. When AUSTRALIA II was about one boat length from LIBERTY, her course was pointing at the helmsman of LIBERTY. AUSTRALIA II would have passed astern of LIBERTY had AUSTRALIA II maintained this course.
>
> LIBERTY luffed to commence a covering tack ahead and slightly to windward of AUSTRALIA II. Until LIBERTY reached head to wind, the course sailed by AUSTRALIA II was clearing LIBERTY'S stern. As LIBERTY was luffing toward head to wind, AUSTRALIA II put her helm hard over to port in the locked position, luffed and tacked very rapidly onto starboard tack, clearing the stern of LIBERTY as LIBERTY was completing her tack onto port tack. When AUSTRALIA II's bow and LIBERTY's stern swung toward each other, they cleared by about four feet at their closest point.
>
> Protest is disallowed. AUSTRALIA II could have kept clear of LIBERTY either by maintaining her course or by tacking as she did to avoid LIBERTY's covering tack. LIBERTY has satisfied the jury that she completed her tack in accordance with rule 41.

Despite the apparent soundness of the decision, the Australians continued to suffer the subtle disadvantages of a challenger. The Goodyear Blimp, which had hovered above the yachts throughout the race, had provided key evidence in the American case in the form of film footage stills and a creditable eyewitness. That creditable eyewitness, Bob Bavier of the NYYC America's Cup committee, had been called to testify by *Liberty*. The Australians were unable to call such a witness; they had not been allowed, as the Americans had, an observer in the blimp.

The third race, sailed in light air, was abandoned with *Australia II* halfway up the final leg. She had been leading by almost six staggering minutes at the leeward mark, and when the 5 hour, 15 minute time limit ran out, was ahead of *Liberty* by at least half a mile.

"How come you were 11 seconds late at the start?" Bob Ross of *Australian Sailing* bluntly demanded of Dennis Conner at the post-race press conference.

Conner was clearly rattled by the experience of faring so abysmally against *Australia II* in light winds. There was a catch in his voice as his reply meandered and doubled back on itself. "Well, it was pretty light air, and we were still in the process of building speed, and the idea is to get up the course the fastest, not necessarily be on the starting line at the gun, because we could have been closer at the gun, when the gun went off, but that was not the ultimate goal . . . is to get up the course the fastest, and we were still in the process of building speed after a tack."

A representative of the Australian Broadcasting Corporation delicately balanced the microphone in his hand. He looked and sounded more like a theatre critic than a radio reporter. "The start seemed to me to be a fairly passive affair today," he observed for Conner. "John Bertrand got where he wanted to go. I want to hear what you have to say about your ability relative to *Australia II*'s ability to manoeuvre in light air."

"I don't think manoeuvrability was really a factor today," replied Conner, showing little enthusiasm for the question. "We only did one circle. Manoeuvrability wasn't really a big factor. If that answers your question."

"I just wondered whether it was a factor," the Australian persisted, "*Australia II*'s apparent superiority in manoeuvrability that led to just one circle, letting them get their own way fairly easily."

There was a long silence. "I don't choose to get into that right now," Conner managed.

John Stacks from *Time* identified himself. "When exactly did you begin to play the time limit as a last card?" he asked Conner. "What did you do?"

"I think I've covered that enough," Conner announced. He had already discussed the time limit for Dave Phillips of the *Providence Journal*. "I don't want to dwell on that because I don't want to take anything away from *Australia II*'s fine performance today. I think it's something I don't want to discuss." He added, intriguingly, "It might happen again."

The questions continued. Is it more fun when you have stiffer competition? "No, I like to be ten minutes ahead." Would the reaching headsail be used on the tight second reach stay in his inventory? "Depends." How far behind was he when the race was abandoned? "About a half a mile, I'd say. It was five minutes at the leeward mark and I don't think we were any closer when the time limit went off."

"Yesterday you said, or the day before yesterday you said, that God smiled on you," ventured a representative of the West Australia Newspapers. "Do you know what nationality God is?"

Dennis Conner rose to the occasion. "He's an American!"

John Bertrand and Warren Jones took the place of a departing Dennis Conner to the customary round of applause from the press. Bertrand was asked if he knew how far ahead he had been when the race was called.

"It was a *long* way," he deduced, to a burst of laughter from the press; the crowd was very much with him. "About three minutes to go before we ran out of time, we figured we had to do 30 knots to windward. No, we figured we couldn't do that."

"Were there any equipment problems on board the boat today?" a radio reporter enquired. "You did have a man up the mast at one stage. What was all that about?"

"He was looking for wind," Bertrand deadpanned.

The gentle questions flowed. "What goes through your mind out there as you see the line and you're running out of time?" wondered the man from the *Los Angeles Times*. "The last three days pulleys have snapped, mainsails have ripped, strange things have happened. . . . Do you feel star-crossed?"

"All we can do," asserted Bertrand, "is go out there and do the best job we can. It seemed to be unfortunate for us today that the breeze died away as it did in certain stages of the race. Our whole ambition is just to go out each day and do the best job we can, and if we're good enough – which I think we are – we can go on to win. There's no other philosophy that we can pursue."

The microphone was passed to John Powers of the *Boston Globe*. "Is there a point that you can remember in the race where you began to be gravely concerned that you would not finish within the time limit? When you had to think that you had to alter strategy, if that were in fact possible?"

"Well, the point about three minutes before the time limit expired, when all of the crew was sitting on the boom, I was concerned."

When the laughter died down, more questions about tactics and starting techniques arose. Then a woman from the *Sydney Morning Herald* stood up. "Alan Bond indicated yesterday after the failure of the protest that the Australians would be seeking some recourse. He also said the evidence was biased. What recourse is there? Do you agree that the evidence was biased, and should or could the Australians have presented a better case?"

Warren Jones, who had masterminded the Australian counter-propa-

ganda program against the NYYC during the controversy over the legality of
Australia II's keel, fielded the question. "Well, I don't think Alan Bond
indicated that the evidence was biased at all. What we are doing, because a
win is a win, of course, is completely analyzing the facts that were found. It
wouldn't come as a surprise to everybody that we don't agree with the facts
found, obviously, but that's another thing, trying to prove that the facts
weren't right. So what we are doing is completely analyzing the result of the
protest, and just having a look at what may or may not be done. There has
been no decision made firmly as to what we will do, but we will make the
decision by tomorrow night. The conditions of racing specify that there shall
be no appeal. There are certain grounds within yacht racing with regards to
new evidence, et cetera, and all we are doing really is looking at the
complete boundaries of where we may move with regard to that protest,
because obviously if the protest isn't a win we don't necessarily agree with
the decision."

The *Sydney Morning Herald* reporter would not let the issue of the protest
drop. "You said something about the rules of new evidence," she said to
Warren Jones near the end of the press conference. "Do you believe that
you have got evidence that was not considered yesterday? And are you
considering calling any other witnesses? Or would you like to do that?"

Jones stiffened. "Really, I don't think there's anything to be gained by
expanding on that. The jury has handed down a decision at this stage and
we are not seeking at this stage to pursue that any further, other than to say
that we are re-evaluating all of the evidence submitted to the protest just to
make sure that the facts found were correct, because we just don't agree
with the facts found."

"If you're saying that you don't agree with them," countered the exasper-
ated Sydney reporter, "I mean . . . What are you trying to do with it? Are you
confident or at all hopeful that you will be able to get something more out of
this decision?"

"I really believe we should discuss this maybe further tomorrow," Jones
concluded sharply. "At this particular juncture we're not really saying
anything."

The Australians would do nothing further about the dismissed protest.

Australia II's victory in the resailed third race was devastating to the American defender. In seven knots of wind the Perth challenger completed the
course in slightly less than four hours, defeating *Liberty* by 3:14, the largest
losing margin ever recorded by a defender. On the opening leg, Gary
Jobson, who had hopped aboard the press boat for the day, began to discuss
how the Americans should hold their challenge trials in Newport and send
one 12-Metre to Perth in 1987 should Dennis Conner lose the match.

The Associated Press wanted to know why Conner had asked for a lay-day. "We thought there might be more wind on Tuesday," he replied simply.

"For two days now in light air," observed Eric Sharp of the *Miami Herald*, "*Australia II* has been absolutely apparently superior in everything except power reaching. In the event that the series continues in light air, is the only thing that you can do now is hope for heavier weather, or are there still tactical moves you think you can make?"

Conner had no excuses. "We tried most everything we could think of today, and she looked like she was awfully good. We're hoping to have a little different weather and see how we go in that."

The would-be theatre critic from the Australian Broadcasting Corporation identified himself. "Those of us who have watched *Australia II*'s performance all summer have been surprised to see the way she has dramatically improved, downwind particularly. Do you think that *Australia II* has been sandbagging all summer?"

"I found out a month ago that sandbagging is something you do at the beach," Conner replied to a round of laughter. "I've never discussed that again about a sailboat race."

"Let me rephrase the question. Are you surprised at *Australia II*'s performance off the breeze?"

"She looks awfully good downwind," said Conner. "Maybe they're using some spinnakers they didn't use earlier and they've sped up, or else all the foreign boats were faster than the American boats. One or the other."

"What was that piece of yellow material that seemed to emanate from the top of the mast, I think on the third reaching leg?" asked another Australian reporter.

"It was on the second leg, and it was our staysail turtle, which normally comes down on deck, but..." Conner's mind seemed to dwell for a moment on the embarrassment of the staysail bag having gone aloft. "It came down in the water instead," he murmured.

"What happened at the start?" a third Australian abruptly, almost rudely, demanded.

The question jolted Conner away from the staysail turtle. "At the where?"

"The start!" *Staht*.

Bill Ficker was not happy with the decorum with which the question was delivered. The reporter didn't appear to care. "Your question," Ficker translated. " 'Would you explain the start, Dennis?' "

"Well, as we were coming up to the starting line," Conner rapidly explained in a breaking voice, "we were on the right; *Australia II* was on the left. We felt the breeze would go right during that leg, so we fought hard for the right-hand end and succeeded. Even though we were a few seconds ahead crossing the line – it looked like five or six seconds to me – there was a long anchor rode out on the committee boat, which may have looked a little funny, like we were doing something crazy, but we had to luff around the committee boat, which had an extra-long anchor line, and that may have been what you saw. Other than that, I can't think of anything unusual."

"I believe yesterday you claimed God was an American," said yet another Australian. "Does he have Sundays off?"

Conner was able to smile. "No, but even He couldn't cope with *Australia II* today."

John Stacks of *Time* addressed Conner. "Is it your feeling that, barring much different weather and sea conditions, this cause is hopeless?"

"All I can say to that is that, after four races last time, we had the same score, with a 2-1 lead and a bad race that ended in a time limit. So I'd say with a 2-1 lead things don't look too bleak. I'd rather have a 2-1 than a 1-2."

"Even though you have a 2-1 lead," suggested a Melbourne reporter, "*Australia II* has proven herself to be a very formidable opponent. Are you at all worried about losing the America's Cup?"

"I'm certainly aware that it's a possibility," Conner conceded, "but I don't believe in dwelling on the negative, and we're just going to do everything we can to work on the positive things that we have control over, and hope things go better. We're really no worse off than we were yesterday. We only have to win two races to win this cup."

"John, it's not a very original question, but I'd like to know, how do you feel right now after that win?"

"I think I can answer on behalf of all the crew on the boat," said a pleased John Bertrand. "We're all very happy and content tonight. We've finally seen the frustrations of the last couple of days come to an end. We've finally won a race for ourselves, at last. The crew certainly feel very good about it, and they feel very strong about the future."

"Can you go on and win the cup now? Do you really think that?"

Bertrand smiled. The win had proved without a doubt the strength of the Perth challenge; the psychological momentum had swung over to the Australians. "I've always maintained that we can win the America's Cup," he lectured. "We've got the people, we've got the expertise, we've got the boat, the equipment, the sails. It's just up to us. I think we're good enough to do it, and I think we *will* do it."

The monopoly had been broken. Dennis Conner had managed to win a letter-perfect race in *Australia II*'s conditions to take a 3-1 lead, but *Australia II* had stormed back, taking advantage of a broken jumper strut on *Liberty* in the fifth race to pull within one win and then tying the series at 3-3 with another stunning 3:25 victory. At the end of the deciding race, which *Liberty* had sailed 900 pounds lighter and with a television on board in hope of reading windshifts through the news cameras aboard the blimp, Dennis

Conner transferred aboard *Australia II*'s tender, *Black Swan*. He confronted his old rival, Sir James Hardy. "I can't sail any better than that," he said tearfully.

Conner was not interested in answering questions. He took his seat at the long banquet table in the Newport Armory to deliver a final statement.

"The race today, of course, was very exciting for the crew of *Liberty*. We felt first of all exhilarated to be part of it. It was very exciting. The start, as you probably noticed, wasn't all that dramatic because neither yacht wanted to make a mistake and end up in the protest room here.

"The boats finally came together, *Liberty* on the right-hand side. *Australia II* was halfway to the left, so *Liberty* started on port and *Australia II* on starboard. The two boats went up the first leg on port tack, in a port tack lift. About halfway up *Australia II* was in the lead, but *Liberty*, three to four boat-lengths behind, continued to tack on the shifts, in phase. Up near the weather mark we got a nice shift on port tack and *Australia II* had to tack underneath, so *Liberty* rounded with a nice lead of 30 to 40 seconds.

"The first reach was a fairly standard wind. *Liberty* seemed to gain a bit, a couple boat-lengths, and came around the reach mark with a comfortable lead. But on the second reach, the third leg of the course, the wind lightened, and *Australia II* showed her power to cut the lead. They had a nice spinnaker change and closed in on *Liberty* and rounded the leeward mark with a very small deficit.

"At which time the people on *Liberty* felt they were glad to be ahead! We certainly felt threatened in view of *Australia II*'s proven upwind speed, and just hung in there and tried to stay in phase with the windshifts. As you probably know, there was no close covering on the second windward leg. We just tried to ride the lifts and the headers the best we could. We felt we did a nice job on the second windward leg in as much as physically we doubled the lead. I can't say for the time. You all have the time. I don't think it is too important.

"On the run, which was critical, *Australia II* seemed to be gaining, so we tried to gybe on the shifts. About halfway down the run *Australia II* had cut our lead from about one minute to 15 seconds. So we just tried to hang in there, be patient, and hope that we could keep them from passing us. We gybed over to a situation where if they did pass us they'd have to pass us by sailing through our wind shadow. But unfortunately for *Liberty* they were able to just sail lower and faster and sail through us to leeward on the lower part of the run. Very frustrating for us, of course, but not much we could do at that point. That was the turning point in the race, half to three-quarters of the way down the run. So I'd like to congratulate John and *Australia II* for passing us on that leg.

"On the last windward leg they just covered us pretty much in phase and we just did the best we could to try to gain on them. In reality, they were in control most of the last windward leg. Nowhere on the last windward leg did we think we were in the lead or their victory in jeopardy.

"Today *Australia II* was just a better boat, and they beat us. We have no excuses. I'd like to at this point congratulate Alan Bond and *Australia II* on their superb effort over the summer. They proved they were an outstanding boat, and today was their day."

Conner's voice began to quaver. "I'd like to point out that our guys did a great job hanging in there in conditions that in the past have proved to be awfully good for *Australia II*. I'm very proud of them. I'd like to thank all of you for your support over the summer, and I don't think that there is any reason for America to feel that in any way they're in..." Words failed him. The sentence sputtered to a conclusion. "...any other position. Thank you."

Dennis Conner left the Armory.

Appendix

the formula

A 12-Metre is designed according to the International Rule, a rating formula created in 1907 to allow racing without handicap between heavy-displacement keelboats. Although many calculations are required by the Rule, the final components are entered into a simple, restrictive formula which, for America's Cup yachts, must produce "12 metres", a figure without any actual representation in the dimensions of the boat.

The formula is:

$$\frac{L + 2d + \sqrt{SA} - F}{2.37} = 12 \text{ metres}$$

"L" represents the length of the boat along a plane 180 millimetres above the waterline.

"d" is the difference between two girth measurements taken from the hull at a point 55 per cent aft of the forward end of the waterline. "Skin girth" is a straight-line measurement from a point on the keel 1500 millimetres below the waterline along a tangent with the cross-sectional curve of the hull. "Chain girth" represents the measurement between the same two points following the surface of the hull. The differences in these two girths are assessed on both sides of the hull and added together to form "d", which is then doubled in the formula.

"SA" is the yacht's rated sail area.

"F" is an average of three freeboard measurements, freeboard being the distance from the waterline to the deck.

"2.37" is a controlling number.